# LOCKED OUT

Jeff Manza and Christopher Uggen

# LOCKED OUT
Felon Disenfranchisement and American Democracy

OXFORD
UNIVERSITY PRESS

2006

# OXFORD
UNIVERSITY PRESS

Oxford University Press, Inc., publishes works that further
Oxford University's objective of excellence
in research, scholarship, and education.

Oxford   New York
Auckland   Cape Town   Dar es Salaam   Hong Kong   Karachi
Kuala Lumpur   Madrid   Melbourne   Mexico City   Nairobi
New Delhi   Shanghai   Taipei   Toronto

With offices in
Argentina   Austria   Brazil   Chile   Czech Republic   France   Greece
Guatemala   Hungary   Italy   Japan   Poland   Portugal   Singapore
South Korea   Switzerland   Thailand   Turkey   Ukraine   Vietnam

Published by Oxford University Press, Inc.
198 Madison Avenue, New York, New York 10016

www.oup.com

Oxford is a registered trademark of Oxford University Press

Library of Congress Cataloging-in-Publication Data
Manza, Jeff.
Locked out : felon disenfranchisement and American democracy /
Jeff Manza and Christopher Uggen.
p. cm.—(Studies in crime and public policy)
Includes bibliographical references and index.
ISBN-13 978-0-19-514932-6
ISBN 0-19-514932-7
1. Ex-convicts—Suffrage—United States.   2. Political rights, Loss of—
United States.   3. Punishment—United States.   I. Uggen, Christopher.
II. Title.   III. Series.
JK1846.M26 2006
324.6'2'0869270973—dc22   2005022723

9  8  7  6  5  4  3  2  1

Printed in the United States of America
on acid-free paper

# Preface

The 2000 presidential election, with the result hinging on an unprecedented struggle over a few votes in a single state, reminded all of us very
forcefully of the importance of the right to vote (and of having one's voting
intention accurately registered). On any national election day, millions of
Americans will make their way to local precincts to cast a ballot, while
many others will choose not to participate. Yet there are also more than
five million citizens who will neither vote nor voluntarily choose not to
participate. These ineligible citizens are current and former criminal offenders. Only one-quarter of them are confined in prisons or jails. While
some have committed violent offenses, most have been convicted only of
nonviolent crimes. But whatever the offense, having a felony conviction
imposes a harsh penalty on political rights that often does not end even
after a term of imprisonment. In many countries around the world, criminal offenders retain the right to vote even while in prison. In all other
democratic countries, virtually all offenders not currently in prison are
entitled to vote for the government officials who make the laws they are

expected to live by. The United States stands out for disqualifying people who are not in prison. This fact is all the more remarkable in view of the history of the right to vote, in which all other restrictions (whether based on race, ethnicity or gender, property ownership, length of residence, literacy, payment of taxes and debts, and other criteria) are no longer legitimate bases for exclusion. The right to vote is now a fundamental right of democratic citizenship. Except for criminal offenders.

In this book, we examine issues surrounding the voting rights of American citizens who have received a felony conviction. The underlying questions motivating our investigation are "big" ones: the state of democracy in America, the citizenship status of criminal offenders, and the persisting influence of race and racial inequality in American politics and in the criminal justice system. We do so with a series of empirically grounded investigations that seek to establish the "facts," analyze the factors that have brought us to where we are today, and finally explore some of the impacts of felon disenfranchisement for democracy and criminal justice.

To interrogate all of these questions, we have needed to draw upon the full sociological tool kit. Lacking suitable data to explore felon disenfranchisement, we generated a considerable amount of original qualitative and quantitative data, as well as piecing together and reanalyzing several sources of existing information. Our research for the book has included event-history analyses of historical-institutional data, quantitative analyses of longitudinal and voting data, in-depth interviews with offenders subject to felon disenfranchisement, content analyses of court cases and historical documents, and collection of new experimental survey data probing Americans attitudes toward disenfranchisement. We have also been forced, by the complex and interdisciplinary nature of the question, to push beyond our starting theoretical groundings in political sociology and criminology to consider the legal and philosophical literatures surrounding democracy, citizenship, and social justice, and their implications for individual lives and democratic institutions. Putting all of this together into a single volume has certainly pushed us in new and unanticipated directions, and we hope the final product reflects the effort that has gone into it.

This is surely a venture in public sociology, and we are grateful to work in a discipline where such projects are welcomed. We offer this book at a time when a national campaign to reconsider felon disenfranchisement laws is underway. A number of states have changed their laws in recent years, almost all in the direction of greater inclusion of nonincarcerated felons. There have also been a number of legal challenges to felon disenfranchisement in recent years. Finally, with very large numbers of felons being sent back into their communities each year from America's prisons and jails, there is growing bipartisan concern about how to help ex-inmates reintegrate successfully. President George W. Bush explicitly acknowledged and highlighted concern for ex-offender reintegration in his 2004 State of the Union address. We hope that the research we present might help inform these policy, political, and legal debates. While our concluding chapter will offer suggestions for possible changes in disenfranchisement policies that flow from our research, we understand that the issues raised are complicated and a broader national discussion is in order. We would be pleased if some of the information presented in this book helps participants in that dialogue reach a reasoned consensus.

## Some Notes on Terminology

Throughout this book, we use the phrase "disenfranchisement" to describe the loss of voting rights. This usage is predominant in the contemporary scholarly and journalistic literature. However, in the extensive nineteenth-century debates over the extension or contraction of the franchise, "disfranchisement" was the sole word used to describe the loss of voting rights, and most historians still employ that word today. Most dictionaries consider the two words identical. To avoid confusion, we follow the dominant contemporary usage and stick with the former term, even though our interest in historical questions might have pushed us to prefer the latter.

We also use three phrases throughout the book to describe individuals convicted of felonies that are not straightforward, and have potentially misleading connotations. First, we use the term "ex-felon" throughout the book as a shorthand way of describing convicted felons who have completed their entire sentence (including any term of prison, probation, or parole). In fact, however, as a growing body of literature has pointed out (and to which this book constitutes a further contribution), a felony conviction constitutes a permanent stain that will influence many aspects of individuals' lives, *even after* they have "paid their debt to society." In this sense, it is not so clear that anyone who has received a felony conviction is ever fully free of the implications of that conviction.

Second, we use the terms "felon" and "offender" interchangeably to describe individuals currently serving a felony conviction (including those released on probation or parole). These are loaded terms, with menacing connotations. Others prefer more neutral, if clunkier, descriptors, such as "persons convicted of felony-level crimes." The felons with whom we spoke often preferred the term "convict," signaling that they were convicted but not their guilt or innocence. In the end, in view of their legal significance we opted for the terms "felon" and "ex-felon." In using these words, we do not mean to imply that all "felons" are necessarily guilty of such significant crimes as to warrant the punishments they receive. Surely many of the people convicted of felonies in recent years would not have received that designation 25 or 30 years ago. The skyrocketing conviction and incarceration rates in the United States over this period have yielded a bumper crop of legally convicted criminals—far more than virtually any other place on earth—even though for most types of crimes actual rates of offending are not much higher in this country than in other similar countries.

Finally, we use a term common to criminologists that will likely be unfamiliar to other readers. The word "desistance" refers to the process by which individual criminals stop committing crimes. As interest in prisoner reentry and the study of crime over the life course has risen, studies of the desistance process have taken center stage in criminology. Eventually the phrase will work its way into public consciousness, although it now reads as a somewhat awkward term for noncriminologists.

# Acknowledgments

We are grateful to many people, organizations, and institutions for sup-
porting our work on this project. We began our collaboration shortly after
Marc Mauer and the Sentencing Project had released their stunning and
widely reported study in the spring of 1998 estimating that about 4 million
American citizens had lost the right to vote due to a felony conviction.
Around that time, Manza was visiting Uggen's sociology department at the
University of Minnesota to give a routine talk. In the course of that visit,
each of us was surprised to learn from the other that there had been virtually no academic social science research on disenfranchisement in either
of our principal fields of study (political sociology and criminology, respectively). This set us on a course that ultimately led to the production
of this work. We thank Marc and his entire Sentencing Project team (including Patricia Allard, Paul Hirshfield, and Ryan King) for their work on
felon disenfranchisement and other help throughout the course of this
project. They have provided a steady monitoring of journalistic and foreign

attention to the issue, and have enriched and assisted our work on numerous occasions along the way.

We received financial support early on from the Sociology Program of the National Science Foundation. That support was crucial in allowing us to hire a talented group of research assistants who carried out the detailed, time-consuming state-by-state investigations of the history and current practice of felon disenfranchisement that provide the basis for the entire study, as well as supporting the original survey data we conducted. We thank all of those research assistants who have worked with such care and dedication on one or another aspect of the project: Melissa Thompson, Sara Wakefield, Janna Cheney, Rebecca Colwell, Mike Vuolo, and Kim Gardner at the University of Minnesota; Kendra Schiffman, Marcus Brittan, Jinha Kim, Kate Lazarus, Gabi Abend, John Anderson, and Sarah Shumate at Northwestern; and Sarah Lowe at the Russell Sage Foundation. We have coauthored work related to this project with Angela Behrens and Melissa Thompson. We would especially like to recognize Angie's vital role. She has worked with us on numerous aspects of the project and made important intellectual and other contributions; indeed, she has been so central that we have listed her as our coauthor of three chapters. We also received support from the extraordinary but now regrettably defunct Individual Projects Fellowship Program of the Open Society Institute. This support permitted us to develop the qualitative component of the study, providing crucial release time from teaching to expand our research. In particular, we thank Gara LaMarche, the director of American Programs at the Open Society Institute for his support of this project, as well as former Individual Projects program coordinator Joanna Cohen.

The two original surveys we conducted for this study could not have been completed without the support and help of several individuals and organizations. When we started the project, there was no survey data in existence that would have allowed us to compare the political attitudes and voting behavior of criminals and noncriminals. We were fortunate to be able to add a series of relevant questions to the 2000 wave of the Youth Development Study. We thank Jeylan Mortimer, director of the Youth Development Study, for generously encouraging us to collect this important information. The National Institute of Mental Health and the National

Institute of Child Health and Human Development funded that survey. We also were interested in public attitudes about felon disenfranchisement, but again were confronted by the absence of existing data. We were fortunate to be able to place a number of complicated experimental survey items on the July 2002 monthly national telephone survey conducted by Harris Interactive, on a shoestring budget. We thank especially David Krane of Harris Interactive for his extensive help and insightful advice about our items, on a tight schedule; and Humphrey Taylor, the president of Harris Interactive, for helping us get that started. Clem Brooks collaborated with us on the design of that survey, coauthored a paper based on the results, and generally provided important advice at various points in the development of the entire project.

We have had the opportunity to present parts of this work at numerous academic and nonacademic conferences, and in invited lectures in various venues. These include: several annual meetings of the American Sociological Association and the American Society of Criminology, the Brooklyn Prisoner Reentry Conference, the Demos election reform spotlight on voting rights, the National Symposium on Felon Disenfranchisement organized by the Sentencing Project in October 2002, and a national conference sponsored by a a variety of organizations on "Rebuilding Lives" in Detroit, Michigan, in November 2004. We have presented talks based on the book to academic audiences at many universities. These include: the Center for Advanced Study in the Behavioral Sciences, the University of California–Berkeley (to both the Survey Research Center and to the Department of Sociology), the University of California–Davis, the University of California–Irvine, the University of California–Los Angeles, the University of California–Santa Barbara, Columbia University, Cornell University, Duke University, the University of Iowa, Northwestern University, the University of Minnesota, the University of North Carolina, North Carolina State University, Ohio State University, Stanford University, Temple University, the University of Washington, the University of Wisconsin–Madison, and Yale University. We thank participants (too numerous to name individually) in these various seminars, conferences, or events for their probing questions and valuable suggestions. We have also had numerous opportunities to discuss our work with journalists from a wide range of different media; these opportunities have not only publicized some of our key findings but also helped us think about our larger message and how to present it to a broader audience.

Many individuals have read or commented on parts of this work, or supplied us with valuable materials or advice. At the risk of inadvertently leaving someone out or unintentionally understating the important contributions of many of the people on this list, to keep things simple we would like to say a heartfelt thank you to many friends, colleagues, and in some cases strangers who have helped us in one way or another at various points along the way: Jesse Allen, Ron Aminzade, Nicki Beisel, Henry Brady, William Brustein, Jack Chin, Dalton Conley, Bruce Carruthers, Fay Lomax Cook, Mitch Duneier, Jack Goldstone, Eric Grodsky, Amy Hafter, John Hagan, Joseph "Jazz" Hayden, Doug Hartmann, Karen Heimer, Michael Hout, Pamela Karlan, Alex Keyssar, Eric Klinenberg, John Laub, Margy Love, John Markoff, Ross Matsueda, Phil Morgan, Robert Nelson, Nancy Northrup, Susan Olzak, Per-Olof Wikstrom, Benjamin Page, Devah Pager, Mary Pattillo, Miles Rappaport, Patricia Reese, Robert Sampson, Joachim Savelsberg, Kate Shaw, Art Stinchcombe, Robin Stryker, Bruce Western, and Howard Winant. We received enormously valuable and detailed comments on the penultimate version of the manuscript from Jack Chin, Alec Ewald, Alex Keyssar, and Michael Tonry. Alec went above and beyond the call of duty, thoroughly reviewing the manuscript line by line and offering numerous suggestions that significantly improved the final version. We also thank anonymous academic journal reviewers of several earlier papers from the project.

We thank the Minnesota Department of Corrections and the Hennepin County Department of Community Corrections for their cooperation and assistance with data collection. These departments have neither endorsed nor approved this book, so we assume sole responsibility for any errors. The staffs of these organizations (whom we cannot name for reasons of confidentiality) were generous in helping us arrange the in-depth interviews we report in chapter 6. We also owe a special debt to each of the felons and ex-felons who patiently answered our questions and thereby provided us with insights about the larger context of disenfranchisement. For reasons of confidentiality, we cannot thank them individually. Nevertheless, we learned much from them that would have been impossible to glean from other sources, and our work is undoubtedly much richer as a consequence.

We also thank our publishers—Oxford University Press, its Academic division publisher, Niko Pfund, series editor Michael Tonry, and especially our editor, Dedi Felman—for their encouragement and patience as this project proved more difficult to complete than we had anticipated. Dedi has been a delight to work with throughout the project, and provided incisive editorial advice as we neared completion. She also proved to us that in this age of editorial speed-up and commercialization, there is still room for a good editor to teach authors how to write. Lauren Osborne provided brilliant editorial suggestions for the final revisions to the manuscript.

Finally, we each have individual and institutional debts to acknowledge. Manza thanks his colleagues in the Department of Sociology, the Weinberg College of Arts and Sciences, and the Institute for Policy Research (IPR) at Northwestern for providing a wide range of intellectual and research support over the past five years. I would like to say a special thanks to IPR director Fay Lomax Cook for providing continual support for this and related work from the very beginning. I also had the good fortune to spend many of the hard months working on the book in residence at the Center for Advanced Study in the Behavioral Sciences at Stanford, a place where quotation marks must be placed around "hard." I thank the former director of the Center, Doug McAdam, and the Center staff for all of their help and assistance with tasks related to the project. I do not have the right words to express my gratitude and love for my two wonderful daughters, Dana and Zoë. Finally, while I'm grateful to many people for their patience with a project that has dragged on far longer we had anticipated, I'm especially thankful to Devah Pager for cracking the whip to get the final version of the book down on paper, and making it more than worthwhile to finally finish it.

Uggen thanks his faculty colleagues and Hilda Daniels, Mary Drew, Karl Krohn, and Carol Rachac for their outstanding support in the University of Minnesota sociology department. Dean Steven Rosenstone in the College of Liberal Arts has been a visionary leader and a wonderful champion for this research. Minnesota provides a remarkable environment for chasing down ideas. As fortunate as I am at the office, I am far luckier in love. My wife, Rhonda, has offered loving support at every turn. My children, Tor and Hope, have been wonderfully encouraging, taking special interest in this project. On separate occasions, I have overheard both my son and my daughter cogently sum up the findings of this book to friends. While these are heartwarming moments, they also suggest that perhaps I could work some other topics into our dinner-table conversation.

Finally, while all of the chapters in this book are either new or substantially reworked from earlier published research, parts of some chapters have appeared in earlier versions. The introduction, and chapters 1, 3, 4, and 10 appear here for the first time. Part of chapter 2 appeared in the *American Journal of Sociology* 109 (2003); pieces of some of the material in chapters 5 and 6 appeared in Mary Pattillo, Bruce Western, and David Weiman, eds., *Incarceration and Families* (New York: Russell Sage, 2003) and Shadd Maruna and Russ Immarigeon, ed., *After Crime and Punishment* (Portland: Willan, 2004); parts of chapters 7 and 8 draw upon findings first presented in an article published in the *American Sociological Review* 67 (2002); and parts of chapter 9 appeared in *Public Opinion Quarterly* 68 (2004). We are grateful to the publishers of these books and journals for allowing us to draw upon those earlier works.

# Contents

# LOCKED OUT

# Introduction

The right to vote matters. No clearer expression of the importance of the franchise can be found than in the words and writings of those to whom it has been denied. On trial for illegally attempting to vote in 1872, women's suffrage leader Susan B. Anthony declared to the court: "Your denial of my citizen's right to vote is the denial of my right of consent as one of the governed, the denial of my right of representation as one of the taxed . . . therefore, the denial of my sacred right to life, liberty, property."[1] In his famous essay "What the Black Man Wants," penned right at the end of the Civil War, Frederick Douglass described the importance of the right to vote for African Americans in the following terms.

> We want [the vote] because it is our right, first of all. No class of men can, without insulting their own nature, be content with any deprivation of their rights. We want it again, as a means for educating our race. Men are so constituted that they derive their conviction of their own possibilities largely from the estimate

formed of them by others. If nothing is expected of a people, that people will find it difficult to contradict that expectation. By depriving us of suffrage, you affirm our incapacity to form intelligent judgments respecting public measures . . . to rule us out is to make us an exception, to brand us with the stigma of inferiority.[2]

In the United States today, by far the largest group of citizens who are denied the right to vote are those who have received a felony conviction. Pamela Smith is one of those disenfranchised felons. A current prison inmate, she is in her midforties. Like many other Americans, she has had difficulty overcoming a dependency on prescription drugs. She is currently serving a felony sentence for falsifying a drug prescription. We met and interviewed Pamela in the course of doing research for this book. She explained to us how it felt to be subject to those penalties, including the loss of the right to vote.

It's just like a little salt in the wound. You've already got that wound and it's trying to heal and it's trying to heal, and you're trying to be a good taxpayer and be a homeowner. . . . Just one little vote, right? But that means a lot to me. . . . It's just loss after loss after loss. And this is just another one. Another to add to the pile. . . . When I said salt in the wound, the wound's already there. Me being able to vote isn't going to just whip up and heal that wound. . . . But it's like it's still open enough so that you telling me that I'm still really bad because I can't [vote] is like making it sting again. It's like haven't I paid enough yet? . . . You can't really feel like a part of your government because they're still going like this, "Oh, you're bad. Remember what you did way back then? Nope, you can't vote."

Even when the right to vote is regained, the memory of its loss is still painful. The owner of the New York Yankees baseball team, George Steinbrenner, is exceptionally privileged and has led an exciting life. He inherited a successful shipping business from his family and is a millionaire many times over. Heading a team of investors in the early 1970s, he acquired the storied Yankees baseball franchise at a low point in the history of the team. He willingly invested money to purchase top players, and quickly returned the Yankees to their former glory, winning two world championships in the late 1970s and four more in the late 1990s during one remarkable six-year stretch. Despite these accomplishments, Steinbrenner vividly describes one particular setback when looking back on his life. In 1974 he was convicted for making an illegal campaign contribution to Richard Nixon's 1972 reelection campaign. His was only one of many such illegal contributions from individuals and businesses intended to curry favor with the president, but he had the misfortune to be caught and convicted. The court-imposed penalty was modest for someone of his means: one felony count and a $15,000 fine. But his conviction made him ineligible to vote.

What difference could the right to vote make to such an individual? At first glance, a reasonable assumption would be not much. Yet nearly 30 years later, Steinbrenner is very clear about the pain it caused him: "Maybe people say, 'Oh, it means nothing. It was a petty felony.' Not me. I missed the right to vote until President Reagan, bless his soul, gave me a pardon. It was very tough for me. I am very patriotic. I believe in this country."[3]

Steinbrenner was fortunate enough to have his voting rights restored relatively quickly. Pamela Smith is not going to be so lucky. Her crimes are relatively minor. Yet even after she is released from prison, Pamela will still have to wait before her voting rights are restored. Unlike citizens in virtually all other democratic countries, she will remain disenfranchised until she has finished serving her time on supervised release or parole. She will be expected to obey all laws, yet have no say in the election of the officials who make those laws.

George Steinbrenner and Pamela Smith do not share much, but they both have been deprived of one of the basic rights of citizenship, one that most of us take for granted. Their description of the pain it caused them highlights how the loss of the right to vote feels to them as individuals, and for their sense of their standing in the community. But what about the impact of large-scale disenfranchisement on the political system? Paul Ferguson is a prisoner in his thirties, serving a long sentence for criminal sexual conduct. Because of the severity of his crime, he will remain disenfranchised far longer than Pamela. Absent some change in disenfranchisement laws for parolees, he will not have another opportunity to vote until he is in his seventies. Like other violent offenders, he presents a less sympathetic picture than Pamela. But Paul also has political views, and indeed was active in local politics before being incarcerated. To keep up with politics, he subscribes to a weekly newsletter that reports on developments in his state government. In telling us about his own disenfranchisement, Paul mentions some potentially important political consequences for the nation as a whole:

> I think it would have a huge effect . . . we're governed more
> than anyone and yet we have no voice in that government body
> . . . I think that's one reason the government does not want us
> to have the right to vote . . . as close as some of the elections
> have been lately, that could be the deciding factor. . . . You know
> two million people in prisons in the United States could have
> decided the presidency this year. No question.

Similarly, James Dwight, a third felon we met, is living in his community while on probation for a property crime committed during a bout of unemployment. James is in his midtwenties and has never been incarcerated—yet he had only been eligible to vote in one election. Like a number of other African Americans we talked to, James pointed specifically to the possibility that these restrictions may be racially motivated:

> Man, taking a person's rights away to vote . . . I don't know why
> they do it. I mean it don't make no sense to me. To be honest,
> I think that they, I think that they just want less blacks to vote,
> you know what I'm saying? 'Cause ninety percent of people's
> that's in jail, they's black anyway, or on probation or whatever. I
> feel, I feel that's what it is though. Less black people to vote,
> you know? . . . When less of us vote, that's more for the other
> races to vote. . . . I mean I feel like it's a racial issue . . . look at
> any jail across the world, we the most people that's in there. We
> the most people that's overcrowding the jails so that's why I
> think it's a racial thing towards us, you know.

For James, felon disenfranchisement not only implies consequences for individuals but also impacts the political power of all African Americans.

These three themes identified by Paul, James, and Pamela—democracy, race, and citizenship—frame our analysis and interpretation of felon disenfranchisement laws in the United States in this book. We examine whether and how large-scale disenfranchisement impacts democratic processes, as Paul suggests; how racial factors might help to explain the origins and impacts of these laws, as James suggests; and finally the importance of the right to vote in weaving former offenders such as Pamela back into the social fabric.

## Punishment and Democracy in America

When we begin to think about the disenfranchisement of convicted felons and ex-felons, we are reminded that democracy and punishment are inextricably, and perhaps inevitably, linked in important ways. Governments choose how and whom to punish, and with what severity. Public passions, and the mobilization of such passions by political elites, have provided a critical source of support for the development of unusually harsh criminal justice policies in the United States over the past 30 years. As public fear of crime has grown, stoked and stirred on by opportunistic political entrepreneurs, a slew of policies have been adopted that have dramatically increased the numbers of people convicted of crimes, the size of the incarcerated population, and the length of sentences. Phrases such as "tough on crime" and "war on drugs" have been remarkably successful politically. No politician or elected judge of whom we are aware has ever lost their seat because they were *too tough* on criminals.

While the path from democratic institutions to criminal justice policies is reasonably clear, the reverse path—from punishment to democracy—has received far less attention. Yet there are important ways in which the kinds of criminal justice policies adopted in the United States in recent decades are having an impact on the institutions of democracy. As we will show in this book, over 5 million adult citizens are currently denied the right to participate in democratic elections because of a past or current felony conviction, and the vast majority of these individuals are not currently in prison. This group makes up about 2.5 percent of the voting-eligible population.

The disenfranchisement of such a large group of felons, and former felons, from participation in democratic elections threatens the health of American democracy in a number of ways. First, it represents a failure to make good on the promise of universal suffrage. As democratic theorists have made clear, and the Supreme Court has repeatedly declared, the right to vote is "the essence of a democratic society," one that "makes all other political rights significant."[4] Second, it has influenced election outcomes, and thereby shaped public policy. For example, the disenfranchisement of hundreds of thousands of *former* offenders in the state of Florida—individuals who have completed their entire sentence—was a critical factor enabling George W. Bush to carry that state and win the 2000 presidential election.

Laws regulating voting rights of criminal offenders are far more extensive and punitive here than in other countries. One of the most startling aspects of current felon disenfranchisement laws is the extent to which they apply to relatively minor offenses. While the term "criminal" or "felon" often conjures up images of violence and brutality, people convicted of such offenses make up only a small fraction of the total felon population. Most disenfranchised felons have not been convicted of violent crime. Murderers and rapists make up about 4 percent of the felons convicted in recent years. Since the onset of the "war on drugs" in the mid-1980s, a rising proportion of felons have been convicted of possessing or selling illegal drugs—sometimes in very small amounts. Drug offenders today represent about one-third of the convicted felon population. Others are convicted of property crimes (such as burglary), various white–collar offenses (such as fraud or forgery), and even driving-related offenses (such as multiple drunk driving incidents).[5]

From the standpoint of the right to vote, the diversity of the felon population immediately suggests a number of anomalies. Once reserved for those convicted of "high crimes," disenfranchisement laws, since the Civil War, have generally barred *all* those convicted of felonies, irrespective of the nature of the conviction. This is all the more striking because the concept of what constitutes a "felony" has grown over time to encompass a greater range and number of offenses, including many minor offenses.[6]

At least six states also disenfranchise misdemeanants.[7] In addition, there are staggering disparities across the states. For example, possession of an ounce of marijuana can result in lifetime disenfranchisement in Florida, whereas commission of first-degree murder has no effect on voting rights in Maine.

The practice of felon disenfranchisement in the United States raises other, related issues as well. America's felon population has skyrocketed in recent years. We have estimated in other work that more than 16 million Americans now have a felony conviction on their records.[8] The country's felon population now exceeds the entire population of countries such as Cuba and Sweden, or medium-sized states like Illinois or Pennsylvania. Last year alone, more than 600,000 Americans were released from prison. This remarkable number of prisoners has led to growing (even bipartisan) concerns about how to help former offenders successfully reintegrate into their communities.[9]

Yet while the barriers faced by former inmates and, more generally, all convicted felons are substantial, they are usually ignored in public debate. Ex-offenders face legal restrictions on employment, they lack access to public social benefits and public housing, they are ineligible for many educational benefits, and they may lose parental rights. In many states, their criminal history is a matter of public record, readily searchable for anyone who wants to know. Research on the lives of ex-offenders has consistently demonstrated they have difficulty finding jobs and a safe place to live, reconnecting with their friends and families, and making their way in a world where they are branded, often for life, by the stigma of a criminal conviction. Given the broad range of restrictions that stem from a conviction, it is hardly an exaggeration to say that offenders are treated, at best, as partial citizens. Though they are denied the benefits of full citizenship, felons and former felons are nonetheless expected to behave as especially virtuous citizens. In addition to avoiding further illegal activity, many must also meet special conditions of parole or risk being returned to prison.

Felon disenfranchisement laws raise troubling questions about American society in one final way. As we will show later, the adoption and expansion of these laws in the United States is closely tied to the divisive politics of race and the history of racial oppression. Concerns about the role of race are not limited to matters of historical interest. The extraordinarily high proportion of African American men in the criminal justice system today produces the shocking fact that more than one in seven black men is currently denied the right to vote, and in several states over one in four black men are disenfranchised. Just as felon disenfranchisement laws in several states can be traced to patterns of racial exclusion, their current effect in diluting the African American vote is no less significant.

## Rethinking Felon Disenfranchisement

Felon disenfranchisement laws have come under increased scrutiny in recent years, and the question of "what is to be done" has become more pressing. As social scientists, we see our task in this book as bringing empirical evidence about felon disenfranchisement to bear upon the policy, legal, and theoretical discussions that are already under way. We begin by examining the intellectual foundations and historical origins of felon disenfranchisement (chapters 1 and 2, respectively), the composition of the disenfranchised felon population (chapter 3), and the sources of contemporary change in the criminal justice system that are causing it to grow (chapter 4). Next we consider the social and political impact of disenfranchisement, both in terms of offender reintegration (chapter 5), the loss of political voices of disenfranchised felons (chapter 6), and the impact on turnout rates and elections (chapters 7 and 8). Finally, we consider the political and policy implications. Chapter 9 examines public attitudes toward disenfranchisement, while chapter 10 considers a range of policy and political proposals.

Our investigations throughout this book are closely linked through the tripartite lens of democracy, citizenship, and race. The origins of these laws, and their contemporary impact on offenders and communities and the political system as a whole, require a broad investigation that accounts for their complex interplay. We hope that the contribution we make here can help, in a small way, to inform the policy and political debates over the future of felon disenfranchisement laws. We will start our discussion by examining the intellectual and historical foundations of disenfranchisement measures.

# 1 Foundations

From the founding of the United States to the waning years of the twentieth century, the practice of disqualifying criminals from voting was rarely questioned. In the last few years, however, a political debate has sprung up. Felon disenfranchisement—the loss of voting rights following a felony conviction—is now being challenged across the country in state legislatures and in national political debates. Civil rights organizations and public interest lawyers have gotten involved, and numerous editorials and opinion pieces advocating change have appeared. Prominent members of Congress have introduced legislation, and presidential candidates have debated the issue. The *New York Times* even designated restoration of ex-offender voting rights one of the "ideas of the year" in 2003.[1]

In the face of these growing challenges to felon disenfranchisement, there have been surprisingly few voices defending the practice.[2] Usually, when there is a strong push for a significant policy change, there is corresponding resistance from proponents of the status quo. Yet only a handful of politicians and pundits have gone on record as defending disenfranchisement. The lack of creditable defenses of the practice is a puzzle. And dialogue over the merits of the law is confused without a clear set of pro and con arguments to test and probe. Critics of disenfranchisement may feel a bit like a boxer entering the ring only to discover there is no opponent to fight. For the most part, disenfranchisement supporters have spoken up reluctantly, and only when forced to do so when laws are challenged in court or placed on the legislative agenda.

From these occasional defenses, however, it is possible to construct the underlying logics of felon disenfranchisement. One very abstract set of arguments relates to what is sometimes referred to as "the purity of the ballot box," as the Alabama Supreme Court described it in 1884.[3] In contemporary variants of these arguments, the presence of criminals within the polity potentially erodes confidence in elections through a process of contamination in which dirty votes taint clean ones. As Kentucky senator Mitch McConnell commented during a 2002 U.S. Senate debate over disenfranchisement, "states have a significant interest in reserving the vote for those who have abided by the social contract that forms the foundation of representative democracy . . . those who break our laws should not dilute the votes of law-abiding citizens."[4]

A parallel argument concerns the potentially subversive impact of allowing felons to vote. Having violated the social contract on at least one occasion, these arguments suggest, criminals cannot be trusted to exercise the franchise responsibly. Such imagery is powerful. As one disenfranchisement proponent said in congressional testimony, allowing convicted felons to vote "could have a perverse effect on the ability of law abiding citizens to reduce the deadly and debilitating crime in their communities." Noting the "the high percentage of criminals . . . and . . . disfranchised people in some communities," another supporter foresaw "a voting bloc that could create real problems by skewing election results" if (as Senator McConnell put it) such "'jailhouse blocs' band together to oust sheriffs and government officials who are tough on crime."[5]

The argument that criminal offenders could corrupt the ballot box or use their votes illegitimately resonates with a powerful strain in American political history. The fight against electoral corruption in the age of the urban political machines was one of the defining conflicts in the rise of the modern party system. In the late nineteenth century and well into the twentieth, charges of ballot-stuffing and outright fraud were frequently alleged. Although the extent of actual electoral fraud has been debated, *perceptions* of fraud were certainly widespread. Introducing measures to combat such fraud was a central objective of the progressive "good government" movement in the early part of the twentieth century. These included establishing systematic electoral rolls, voter registration requirements, the use of "Australian" style ballots, and other measures. All served to hinder participation.[6]

To be sure, empirical evidence that criminal offenders would be more likely to commit electoral fraud is essentially nonexistent. The sole exception is improper voting by some disenfranchised felons, a matter we explore in chapter 10, but here confusion over eligibility rather than a determined effort to break the law is likely responsible in most cases. Fraudulence might also be expected among those convicted of political crimes, such as violations of election or campaign finance laws. But these make up a very small proportion of all felons, and there is little evidence that serial political offenders constitute a significant actual or potential threat. For the great bulk of criminal offenders who have committed nonpolitical crimes, the claim that they could or would "band together" to loosen criminal laws, elect weak-on-crime sheriffs, or generally "skew" electoral results is clearly an unproved hypothesis.[7]

Justifications of disenfranchisement laws based on states' rights arguments are probably the most straightforward defenses. The Constitution vests the states with the right to decide who can vote, and except for the explicit constitutional exceptions, states are free to decide which criteria they want to use. The Supreme Court has generally sided with such views in this area. Its supporters point to the diversity of state felon disenfranchisement laws, asserting that each state adopts laws consistent with the political ideology of its citizens. For example, in a recent U.S. Senate debate, Jeff Sessions (R-AL) declared: "I think this Congress, with this little debate we are having on this bill, ought not to step in and, with a big sledge hammer, smash something we have had from the beginning of this country's foundation—a set of election laws in every State in America. . . . To just up and do that is disrespectful to them."[8]

Setting aside the response that states' rights arguments have historically allowed for continuing racially discriminatory practices, these arguments—however well grounded in contemporary law and practice—elide the substantive question at stake: whether people with a felony conviction *should* be allowed to vote. To say that the states should decide the question does not justify any particular state's law, and indeed most other state restrictions on the franchise have been abolished since the 1960s. State's rights arguments, in short, do not settle the normative and empirical puzzle.

Another tactic employed against legislative proposals to enfranchise some or all felons is the charge of partisanship—that enfranchisement is a blatant political move by the Democratic Party to gain votes. A recent *New York Post* editorial, for example, declared that a proposal by Senate Democrats to enfranchise ex-felons "appears to be angling, not for the votes of centrists but for the votes of the most dedicated left-wing constituency in America: Criminals." Similarly, on the Fox News Network news show *Hannity and Colmes,* conservative commentator Sean Hannity declared that "the evidence shows this [reenfranchising ex-felons] clearly favors the Democrats. So isn't this simply a political move to help in close races?" Political commentator George Will put forth a more elegant, but equally pointed, version of this same point:

> Sentimentalism and cold calculation combine to make felons' voting attractive to liberals. They know that criminals often come from disadvantaged circumstances and think such circumstances are the "root causes" of criminality. As for the calculation, it is indelicate to say but indisputably true: most felons—not all, not those for example, from Enron's executive suites—are Democrats. Or at least were they able to vote, most would vote Democratic.[9]

Such arguments, however, are problematic for a democratic polity, where the right to vote is not premised on *how* one plans to vote. Pushed to its logical conclusion, this position implies that governments should be free to pick and choose which citizens to enfranchise and which to keep out of the ballot box. Such a policy has no basis in modern conceptions of democracy, and indeed the Supreme Court has ruled repeatedly against discriminating among voters on the basis of how they might vote. For example, in *Carrington v. Rash*, the Court declared that

> "Fencing out" from the franchise a sector of the population because of the way they may vote is constitutionally impermissible. "The exercise of rights so vital to the maintenance of democratic institutions" cannot constitutionally be obliterated because of a fear of the political views of a particular group of bona fide residents.[10]

Here and elsewhere, the Court has ruled—and common–sense understandings of democracy and universal suffrage in the modern world would suggest—that *how* someone might vote has nothing to do with whether he or she *should* be allowed to vote.[11]

Some arguments in support of disenfranchisement zero in on the most heinous crimes or criminals. For example, Florida governor Jeb Bush has argued against restoring civil rights to those who have "committed more serious crimes, such as violent or multiple felonies, or have broken the law after previously having their rights restored."[12] Such arguments have dramatic appeal. Though most Americans are appalled by the idea that a convicted terrorist or a mass murderer would help to decide a presidential election, focusing on the least palatable offenders is disingenuous. As we will show in chapter 3, violent offenders make up a relatively small proportion of the total disenfranchised population; only about one in five felony convictions are for violent crimes.[13] Moreover, the specter of large numbers of murderers and terrorists voting in a polity where all nonincarcerated felons—but not inmates—could vote is pretty much a red herring, given the long prison sentences such offenders typically incur.

To be sure, opponents of felon disenfranchisement employ equally disingenuous strategies when they highlight only the most sincere and deserving former offenders. Such people may have committed unusually minor offenses, or they may have made remarkable efforts to reform their lives and outstanding contributions to their families and communities. Many newspaper and magazine accounts of disenfranchisement, often written by sympathetic liberal reporters, dramatize the apparent injustice of the practice by highlighting the cleanest of such former offenders, and usually in states with the most extreme laws.[14] Given high recidivism rates, however, such inspiring stories are also unrepresentative of the entire disenfranchised felon population.

Finally, some critics of disenfranchisement have suggested that racial considerations underlie disenfranchisement laws. We consider the empirical evidence for the role of racial factors in the origins and contemporary practice of disenfranchisement in chapter 2. It is important to note, however, that these laws are racially neutral on their face, and no serious contemporary advocate defends them on explicit racial grounds. This does not, of course, rule out the possibility that racial factors are associated with disenfranchisement laws, only that contemporary justifications are almost never explicitly racial.[15]

These are the arguments that supporters of felon disenfranchisement have used to frame the public debate. In this book, we will be assessing each of them. But the contemporary arguments in support of felon disenfranchisement do not help us understand how these laws came into existence in the first place. We must instead look to the legal, political, and historical record to understand how we got to this point. The denial of political rights to criminal offenders can be found under very different types of democratic (and protodemocratic) regimes, and the practice has sparked philosophical debates since at least Aristotle. Understanding this history requires exploration of premodern political regimes and legal systems, classical philosophical writings, and their enduring traces in contemporary legal and political discourses.[16] That is the goal of this chapter. But before exploring how and why societies disenfranchise, we must first ask why the right to vote became—and has remained—a bedrock of democratic governance.

## The Right to Vote Revisited

The right to vote rarely generates much discussion among democratic theorists these days, in large part because it appears to be such a settled question. At the beginning of the twenty-first century, almost every country in the world *claims* to have at least some form of democratic governance based on universal suffrage. One survey in the mid-1990s found that 94 percent of countries claimed to be governed through democratic elections.[17] As recently as 1980, by contrast, enormous sections of the globe still lacked any form of democratic governance.[18] To be sure, many contemporary "democracies" are in fact more authoritarian than democratic, with one-party dominance, unequal media access, institutional biases discouraging political challengers, and (in extreme cases) blatant and regular electoral fraud. But the very fact that so many nations feel such claims are necessary provides powerful confirmation of the legitimating function of "democracy." Everywhere we look around the world, we see examples of citizens demanding free and fair elections, and that the results of such elections be upheld.

From the standpoint of political theory, there are virtually no contemporary models of legitimate democratic governance that are not tied to universal participation in some form—or at least none that claim any significant number of adherents today. There were major twentieth-century competitors to democracy in the Marxist tradition, such as Leninism, Maoism, and their diverse manifestations around the world. These once provided a critical alternative to the "bourgeois" model of democracy in the affluent capitalist societies, but they have largely disappeared. There are plenty of critics of representative democracy through mass elections who have highlighted the shortcomings of passive participation and the potential it poses for elite manipulation.[19] The anarchist alternative of fostering means of direct participation and self-governance has, however, also proved problematic when it has been attempted in various institutional contexts. To be sure, many small-scale experiments in participatory democracy will continue, but even the most successful of these are likely to coexist alongside, rather than supplant, mass electoral democracy.[20]

There are, of course, many critics of the contemporary *practice* of democracy, in the United States and elsewhere. But in spite of the analytical and political bite of utopian critics, democratic governance based on universal suffrage and equal representation has become the overwhelmingly dominant model. Perhaps the strongest evidence of the power of the democratic ideal is found in the intensity with which the right to vote has been pursued by the vigorous social movements demanding democratic political processes.[21] Around the world, inspiring examples of recent struggles—in places as diverse as eastern Europe, South America, southern Africa, and Asia—recall the echo of earlier struggles in the American or other democratizing contexts. The very fact that we can now count the holdouts is instructive—China, most of the regimes in the Middle East and Africa, and a rapidly disappearing handful of countries elsewhere. While the right to vote may sometimes provide but a passive and indirect instrument of citizen control, millions of people around the globe remain willing to fight aggressively to win or maintain that right. It is a striking confirmation of the legitimating function of democratic elections that no mass-based revolutionary movement has succeeded in overthrowing a democratically elected government.[22]

### Why Does the Right to Vote Matter?

Voting in democratic elections has many implications, for both individuals and societies. For individuals, voting is the most common act of citizenship. Indeed, our status as "citizens" is defined in large measure by the very fact that we can vote (whether we actually do so or not), and becoming eligible to vote marks an important transition to adult status. It is a low-cost way of making a civic contribution. It provides a means of expressing ourselves politically, thereby affirming an important type of identity through our political choices ("she is a Democrat").[23] Voting also gives us the opportunity to express displeasure with governmental policies and to exert some control, however imperfect, over the policies of the government.[24] Voting is a powerful symbol of political equality: each vote counts the same, and each voter gets one, and only one, vote. Participating in elections gives voters a stake in the outcome, a way of talking about public affairs with friends and family, and excitement from its horse-race dynamics.[25] Finally, voting provides regular concrete evidence that we live in a "good" democratic society, as opposed to a "bad" authoritarian one in which ordinary people cannot choose their government.

Democratic elections with universal suffrage also provide important benefits for entire societies and their rulers. They confer legitimacy on past and future government officials and the public policies they adopt as reflecting "the will of the people." Competitive elections also provide opportunities for minority groups and parties to compete for political influence in future elections. They diffuse the threat of revolutionary upheavals from below, and provide a basis for citizens to assume the legitimacy of the political system as a whole. For all of these reasons, democratic governance with universal suffrage has become a core, indispensable component of legitimate governance today.

### The Rise of Universal Suffrage

The form and content of democracy has varied widely across time and space. The notion, now taken for granted, that universal suffrage is a necessary (if not sufficient) condition for democracy was largely an invention of the late nineteenth and twentieth centuries. In its original meaning, "demos," or rule of the common people, was an epithet implying mob rule.[26] Eventually, however, it came to denote the extraordinary experiment in participatory governance undertaken in the Greek city-state of Athens beginning around 500 B.C. In Athens, as in other early protodemocratic societies, the right of participation was limited: only males with the status of citizen could participate in democratic forums. Slaves and others without full citizenship were excluded from participation. Other early democratic experiments imposed similar kinds of constraints. In the Roman republic, for example, foreign military conquests created vast outposts of subjects who could not meaningfully be incorporated into the polity.[27]

Varieties of democratic governance and models of suffrage have been invented or reinvented throughout human history: in Italian city-states, in regional assemblies in northern Europe in the Middle Ages, in the development of Parliament in England, in the American and French revolutions (and in democratic state-building in the United States after the revolution), in the 1848 revolts in Europe, in the emergence of mass socialist and working-class movements in western Europe in the latter half of the nineteenth century, in the struggle for women's and minority group suffrage in the early part of the twentieth century, and, finally, in the globalization of democracy over the past 25 years.

Standing in the way of all of these democratic experiments was a series of problems: how could societies establish institutions capable of linking small local assemblies together into a meaningful whole?[28] How could they foster group interests through the expansion of "civil society" and political parties, unions, social movements, and interest groups?[29] Finally, how could they develop and protect free speech norms, independent media, and other channels of communication to make it possible for such groups to organize and communicate demands to elites? Alongside these institutional developments was the problem of establishing universal suffrage for all citizens. Without universal suffrage, even the establishment of a free press, a vigorous civil society, durable political organizations, a national legislature, and regular elections would strike modern observers as a weak and incomplete form of democratization at best. Winning universal suffrage has occasioned some of the harshest and most intractable fights. Each newly incorporated bloc of voters typically has required a powerful social movement demanding its inclusion.[30] But once established, universal suffrage has generally proved irreversible, at least so long as overall democratic governance persists.

This is an important point. Reversion to authoritarian rule is by no means uncommon in the history of democracy. One analyst uses the metaphor of "waves of democracy" to describe the ebb and flow between democratic and authoritarian governance since the nineteenth century.[31] Once universal suffrage has been consolidated, however, it has almost never been only *partially* reversed (as opposed to the complete reversion entailed by a shift from democratic to authoritarian rule). The major exception is the case of African Americans, who gained the right to vote during Reconstruction and the adoption of the Fifteenth Amendment only to see it eroded in many states by disenfranchising measures after Reconstruction.[32]

### The American Case

When the Framers met to draft the Constitution, there were no existing models of universal suffrage to draw upon. Some participants wanted to declare the vote a right of citizenship, even a "natural right." Such views were supported by radicals such as Ethan Allen and Benjamin Franklin. Against these ideas were various conceptions of "stakeholder" democracy, in which only property owners or taxpayers would participate because only they had a material interest in the well-being of the community and would exercise the franchise wisely.[33] In the end, the drafters compromised, with the result that the Constitution does not explicitly guarantee the right to vote for all citizens (as do virtually all other democratic constitutions). Instead of a universal guarantee of the right to vote, the states were entitled to set eligibility criteria. Before and after ratification, states devised various restrictions.[34] Given this diversity, political theorist Katherine Pettus has suggested that a better way to think about political citizenship in the United States is that it consists of 51 separate republics, each with the power to determine who is eligible to vote. In relation to felon disenfranchisement, it is the states who decide both who is a "criminal" and whether and when that group of "criminals" can vote.[35]

To be sure, over the past 150 years, a national guarantee of the right to vote has essentially developed. Constitutional amendments have imposed important limitations on the capacity of states for disqualifying citizens from voting. In 1870, the Fifteenth Amendment prohibited the denial of the right to vote based on race. In 1920, the Nineteenth Amendment prohibited denying the right based on sex. In 1964, the Twenty-Fourth Amendment eliminated poll taxes in federal elections. The Twenty-Sixth Amendment in 1971 extended the right to vote to those 18 and older.

Most important of all, in 1868, the Fourteenth Amendment virtually announced a national citizenship:

> All persons born or naturalized in the United States and subject to the jurisdiction thereof, are citizens of the United States and of the State wherein they reside. No State shall make or enforce any law which shall abridge the privileges or immunities of citizens of the United States; nor shall any State deprive any person of life, liberty, or property, without due process of law; nor deny to any person within its jurisdiction the equal protection of the laws.

Nevertheless, in the evolution of Fourteenth Amendment jurisprudence through World War II, the national citizenship norms implied under the "equal protection" clause of the amendment generally did not include a right to vote. This all changed with key Supreme Court rulings in the 1960s. In *Reynolds v. Sims* in 1964, the Court declared that voting was a fundamental right that could not be restricted unless a state established a compelling reason for doing so, and narrowly tailored the restriction to serve that purpose. The Court announced its intention to "carefully and meticulously" scrutinize deviations from a universal franchise.[36] Subjecting voting restrictions to the toughest standard of review—"strict scrutiny"— provided the basis for a series of important rulings that limited state restrictions on the franchise: for example, residency restrictions for members of the armed forces,[37] poll taxes for local elections,[38] long residential requirements as a condition for voting,[39] and others.

These decisions, along with the earlier "one man, one vote" ruling in *Baker v. Carr* in 1962 (which required states to create legislative districts of roughly equal size), are among the most important in American political history. Considered alongside other pathbreaking civil rights decisions in the mid-1960s, they helped establish the enduring reputation of the Warren Court. With the passage of the Voting Rights Act of 1965 (VRA), which finally undermined the disenfranchisement of African American voters in the South, universal suffrage appeared at last to have been established.

## The Disenfranchisement of Criminal Offenders

We now turn from why the right to vote matters in general, and the establishment of universal suffrage, to the specific case of felon disenfranchisement. Of all the restrictions on the right of individuals and groups to participate in democratic elections, the disqualification of criminal offenders stands out in a variety of ways.

Criminal disfranchisement has an extensive history, spanning from ancient Greece and Rome to medieval Europe, to the English law of attainder, and, finally, to the establishment of town hall democracies in colonial America.[40] The penalties of *atimia* and *infamia* in ancient Greece and Rome, respectively, are the ancient precursors to modern disenfranchisement laws. These were among the most severe punishments available in ancient regimes, as they entailed not only the loss of the right to participate in politics but also the loss of many other rights associated with full citizenship.

In Athens and other Greek city-states, the status of *atimia* was imposed upon criminal offenders. This status carried the loss of many citizenship rights, including the right to participate in the *polis* (polity). Of course, only elites had those rights to begin with, so disenfranchisement was a penalty imposed on deviant elites. In ancient Rome, the related punishment of *infamia* could be imposed on criminal offenders. In this case, the principle penalties were loss of suffrage and the right to serve in the Roman legions (a desired opportunity).[41] Application of disenfranchisement differed in Rome and Greece. In Rome, there were finer gradations of citizens, and the application of *infamia* varied according to class of citizenship. In addition, the innovation of the Roman census made possible the bureaucratic registration of *infamia* status.

In medieval Europe, the legal doctrines of "civil death" and "outlawry" carried forward similar notions. As with *atimia*, those punished with civil death generally suffered a complete loss of citizenship rights (in some early Germanic texts, outlaw status meant a "loss of peace" that was comparable to becoming a wolf, since the outlaw had to "live in the forest").[42] In extreme cases, civil death could be injurious or fatal, since outlaws could be killed by anyone with impunity, or have their property seized. In most medieval contexts, political rights held little substantive meaning. But the civil death model carried over into parts of modern criminal law.[43] In England, medical courts could impose the penalty of attainder after conviction. Although varying in severity, attainder, in the extreme, could include the loss of all civil rights. In all cases, though, attainder meant the loss of the right to vote for Parliament for anyone who would be otherwise eligible.[44]

### Early Colonial Statutes

The scant evidence we have indicates that criminals in the colonial era were subject to disenfranchisement. As in other premodern polities, informal exclusion of deviants was possible because political participation occurred in small face-to-face settings. There were attempts at legal regulation as well. For example, an early Connecticut statute declared that

> if any person within these Libberties have been or shall be fyned or whipped for any scandalous offence, hee shall not bee admitted after such time to have any voate in Towne or Commonwealth, nor to serve in the Jury, untill the courte shall manifest theire satisfaction.[45]

Elsewhere, Plymouth denied polity membership to "any opposer of the good and wholesome laws of this colonie." In Massachusetts, disenfranchisement was authorized for any "shamefull and vitious crime," while in Maryland multiple incidences of public drunkenness meant loss of political rights.[46] We do not know how widespread such restrictions were, or how well they were enforced. Most likely, in small colonial gatherings, offenders knew they were not welcome in public forums open to citizens of good standing, and physical recognition provided the mechanism for enforcement. Indeed, in many settled towns, the charter required new citizens to be certified at town meetings. Still, the existence of such traces demonstrates the early transition of criminal disenfranchisement from European to American political institutions.[47]

Although the Constitution barred some medieval punishments, and in this way broke with existing premodern penal models, it did not formally abolish the notion of civil death. Several early state constitutions incorporated civil death statutes, including criminal disenfranchisement and morals clauses.[48] As we discuss in chapter 2, where the states could impose restrictions on citizenship, they frequently did so.

## From Classical Political Philosophy to American Political Culture

Given the long history of restrictions on the political rights of criminal offenders, it is hardly surprising that political philosophers have sought to develop justifications for disenfranchisement. In spite of their other differences, philosophers as diverse as Aristotle, Locke, Rousseau, Montesquieu, Kant, and Mill converged on the view that criminal offenders should not be entitled to full participation in political or civic life.[49]

Ancient political theory explored the issue as it relates to citizenship and the governance of the city-state. In *Politics*, Aristotle developed a theoretical rationale for the exclusion of the *atimia* from the *polis*. He envisioned the *polis* as a community requiring acceptance of certain baseline commitments by all members. As political theorist Zdarko Planinc summarized it, the Aristotelian view rests on the idea that while citizens are capable of rational deliberation, "criminals who break laws cannot govern themselves, and hence are not fit to govern others."[50]

This theme of innate defects precluding membership in the polity is central in the writings of other early modern political theorists. For early republican and utilitarian theorists, the performance defects of criminals are the basis for their exclusion from the polity. In his formulation of the virtues of republican governance, for example, Montesquieu argued, "it is . . . on the goodness of criminal laws that the liberty of the subject of criminal laws principally depends." Individuals who offend must be excluded to avert the dangers of the "spirit of extreme equality."[51]

A similar logic prevails in classical social contract theories.[52] Criminals' innate defects mark them as incapable of respecting the social order. For John Locke, the "law of nature" is undermined by the "corruption and vitiousness of degenerate men."[53] Jean-Jacques Rousseau echoed these concerns: "every offender who attacks the social right becomes through his crimes a rebel and a traitor to his homeland; he ceases to be one of its members by violating its laws, and he even wages war against it."[54]

It is striking that the confident dismissal of political rights for criminal offenders in the writings of early modern theorists had largely disappeared from political philosophy by the second half of the nineteenth century. This shift coincides with the beginnings of the modern democratic polity, and the modern criminal justice system of criminal courts, police forces, and graduated punishments. The problem becomes fundamentally different in a world in which mass participation—and citizenship *rights* defined by birth—emerges alongside notions of the possibility of *rehabilitating* criminal offenders. The former threatens the performative logics of citizenship, replacing them with a view of citizenship as entitlement. In the famous formulation of T. H. Marshall, the evolution of modern citizenship is one in which societies pass through stages, first granting the masses civil rights, then political rights (including the right to vote), and, finally, social rights (including the right to an income).[55] While Marshall's functionalist assumptions are certainly debatable, he nonetheless provides a useful narrative of what actually transpired. Once political rights are made universal, each exclusion becomes harder to justify.

The importance of Enlightenment notions of proportionality in punishment has received relatively little attention outside criminology, but these penological developments are also critical. Cesare Beccaria's influential work *On Crimes and Punishment* applied social contract theory to the problem of criminal law in 1764. Beccaria suggested that the legislator act as a "skilled architect," crafting punishments sufficient to deter or prevent crime. Any punishment beyond this standard, however, would be an unjust abuse of power, breaching the contract between the state and its citizens.[56]

In addition to proportionality sufficient to deter crime, the rehabilitative philosophy that gained momentum in the nineteenth century requires that the punishment, or treatment, reform the offender. Rehabilitation models fundamentally reject the presumption that criminal offenders are inherently corrupted. Once reform of individuals became the orienting goal of the "correctional" system, the sharp line between offender and citizen began to erode. Zebulon Brockway, the influential nineteenth–century superintendent of the Elmira Reformatory, used the return to citizenship as an orienting philosophy. He sought to turn a prisoner's mind to "preparing himself for restoration to citizenship," and "personal fitness for future liberty."[57] The classical view of disenfranchisement was undermined as penal philosophy moved from simple vengeance to a system of deterrence, and finally to one of rehabilitation in modern penal institutions. Once a criminal sentence is completed, the offender gets a "second chance," or opportunity to "start over." In a polity in which the right to vote is universal, restoration to citizenship means, among other things, having the right to vote.[58]

## American Political Culture and the Unique
## Persistence of Felon Disenfranchisement

It has been argued, most forcefully by political scientist Alec Ewald, that the foundations of felon disenfranchisement strongly resonate with the core intellectual traditions of American political culture.[59] Ewald argues that felon disenfranchisement echoes each of three major civic traditions: liberalism, republicanism, and racialized conceptions of identity. For classical liberalism, disenfranchisement serves to prevent the illegitimate use of the ballot by individuals who break the law; for republicans, disenfranchisement screens out morally unworthy individuals; and, for racists, disenfranchisement laws can be used to target undesirable racial or ethnic groups and reduce their political power.

Despite such powerful affinities, however, no leading political theorist in either the liberal or republican traditions has stepped forward to explicitly defend these laws.[60] There are perhaps good reasons for the failure to develop such arguments, as both present sharp theoretical and empirical problems. Theoretically, the classical logics of both liberalism and republicanism have been significantly reformulated.

Empirically, the liberal case ultimately requires some demonstration that offenders would use their voting rights to do bad things. The republican justification requires evidence that felons' participation would negatively influence the polity as a whole (or "contaminate" the ballot box). The liberal case is at best unproved, although some contemporary advocates of disenfranchisement emphasize voter fraud and influence on outcomes. The central tension in this model is that the presumed political preferences of the disenfranchised felon population are simply *not* a viable basis for exclusion in modern liberal theories. The expectation of voter fraud might provide a stronger basis, but no one has advanced any significant evidence that offenders are, in fact, more likely to commit such fraud. The republican claim is based on symbolic, or moral, considerations, and it is essentially nonfalsifiable. But here, too, there is no evidence that democratic political communities are debased in places where offenders can vote, either in the United States or elsewhere. On the contrary, the strife generated by disenfranchisement is considerable (particularly in states with high disenfranchisement rates and a history of race-based disenfranchisement), and is damaging to the sense of the goodness and fairness of civic life that republican virtue requires.

The diverse strands of American political culture may well provide a theoretical foundation for the existence of these laws. And close inspection of some of the rhetoric of modern defenders of disenfranchisement reveals traces of these ideas. But modern liberal and republican theorists have not, for the most part, stood up to defend the practice of disenfranchisement. And it is not clear how they would, if they did. With respect to race-based theories, we evaluate in the next chapter the evidence that the implementation of felon disenfranchisement laws was rooted in racial politics of the past. To persist in the modern, post–Voting Rights Act world, however, felon disenfranchisement laws cannot be justified in explicitly racial terms.

## Legal Foundations of Felon Disenfranchisement

While the foundations of felon disenfranchisement owe much to classical political philosophy, they have their firmest grounding in law, both constitutional and statutory. When Supreme Court decisions drastically extended the franchise in the 1960s, many contemporary observers thought that the time was ripe for felon disenfranchisement laws to fall as well. But quite the contrary: federal courts, most notably the Supreme Court, have reviewed state felon disenfranchisement laws and, for the most part, endorsed their continuance.

### Early Disenfranchisement Cases

The first felon disenfranchisement cases to reach the Supreme Court were the so-called Mormon cases.[61] In 1882, Congress responded to a variety of pressures to curtail Mormon influence in the West by adopting the Edmunds Act, which outlawed bigamy and polygamy in the territories and disenfranchised anyone convicted of either. In 1885, a unanimous Supreme Court upheld the Act, holding explicitly that it was not a retroactive punishment but rather a constitutionally viable test for voting eligibility. An 1890 decision later approved Idaho's antibigamy oath provision in its state constitution allowing the state to disenfranchise bigamists.[62]

These cases stood as the Court's only systematic assessment of felon disenfranchisement until 1974. Lower court cases, however, addressed the issue in the context of the larger prisoner's rights movement of the 1960s and 1970s.[63] Among these cases was *Green v. Board of Elections of New York*. In this case, a former Communist Party activist, prosecuted under the Smith Act (a McCarthy-era law that made membership in the Communist Party illegal), challenged New York's disenfranchisement law. In upholding the state's law, the court colorfully noted:

> A man who breaks the laws he has authorized his agent to make for his own governance could fairly have been thought to have abandoned the right to participate in further administering the compact. . . . It can scarcely be deemed unreasonable for a state to decide that perpetrators of serious crimes shall not take part in electing legislators who make the laws, the executives who enforce these, the prosecutors who must try them for further violations, or the judges who are to consider their cases. This is especially so when account is taken of the heavy incidence of recidivism and the prevalence of organized crime. A contention that the equal protection clause requires New York to allow convicted mafiosi to vote for district attorneys or judges would not only be without merit but as obviously so as anything can be.[64]

This decision, citing John Locke, is often quoted as a canonical statement of the logic supporting felon disenfranchisement, despite nearly contemporaneous Supreme Court decisions rejecting franchise restrictions on the basis of a prospective voter's viewpoint.[65]

### The Current Framework: Richardson v. Ramirez

The landmark Supreme Court decision on felon disenfranchisement is *Richardson v. Ramirez*, which affirmed the right of the states to disenfranchise felons in 1974.[66] The case concerned three California men who had completed their criminal sentences, were denied the right to register to vote, and then sought to challenge the state's law disenfranchising ex-felons.[67] The plaintiffs made two arguments. First, they argued that felon disenfranchisement laws required the same strict standard of review as other voting restrictions. A "compelling state interest" was required to restrict a fundamental right such as voting. Second, they argued that extending the right to vote would serve the goal of rehabilitation by helping to reintegrate offenders back into society. The California Supreme Court sided with the plaintiffs.[68]

The United States Supreme Court reversed and upheld the state's law in a six-to-three decision. The majority opinion, written by then associate justice William Rehnquist, was based on a passage in section 2 of the Fourteenth Amendment, which says: "when the right to vote . . . is denied to any of the male inhabitants of such State, being twenty-one years of age, and citizens of the United States, or in any way abridged, except for participation in rebellion, or other crime, the basis of representation therein shall be reduced."[69] The Court held that the "express language" of "participation in rebellion, *or other crime*" contemplated and permitted states to disenfranchise criminals with felony convictions.

Justice Rehnquist's decision reasoned that ex-felon disenfranchisement did not violate the equal protection clause of section 1 of the Fourteenth Amendment, thereby declining to extend the same analytical framework used in the other voting rights cases to felon disenfranchisement. While the Court declared the plain meaning of the language to be clear, it also cited the Amendment's legislative history in support of its holding. The Court noted that "throughout the floor debates in both the House and the Senate, in which numerous changes of language in [section] 2 were proposed, the language 'except for participation in rebellion, or other crime' was never altered." The majority concluded that the language was "intended by Congress to mean what it says." In support of this proposition, the Court identified the fact that (at the time) twenty-nine states had provisions in their constitutions that disenfranchised ex-felons. Finally, the Court pointed to the internal consistency between sections one and two, noting that

[Section] 1, in dealing with voting rights as it does, could not have been meant to bar outright a form of disenfranchisement which was expressly exempted from the less drastic sanction of reduced representation which [section] 2 imposed for other forms of disenfranchisement.[70]

The dissenting justices provided a very different reading of the legislative history. In his vigorous dissent, Justice Thurgood Marshall emphasized that section 2 of the Fourteenth Amendment was designed to provide the special remedy of reduced representation to address the disenfranchisement of blacks. From this perspective, the majority's reading of the legislative history was fundamentally mistaken.[71] Marshall pointed to the absurd results that stem from the Court's holding, including allowing states to disenfranchise citizens for "seduction under promise of marriage, or conspiracy to operate a motor vehicle without a muffler . . . or breaking a water pipe."[72]

The Court's reasoning surprised many. The Fourteenth Amendment is best known for the equal protection clause of its first section. The obscure second section was largely considered a dead letter in American law. It originally sought to provide a remedy for situations in which the first section was violated, most notably with respect to the franchise. Later analysts have excoriated the *Ramirez* opinion as exemplifying the limitations of the textualist approach. The narrow, literal reading of the wording of section 2 left no room for interpretation that might reflect historical developments or contextual circumstances.[73] Nonetheless, the decision stands as the Court's position on felon disenfranchisement and it has generally been followed by later courts.[74]

Critics have pointed to the numerous anomalies presented by the *Ramirez* decision's reliance on section 2. When the Fourteenth Amendment was adopted, disenfranchisement applied only to those convicted of felonies at common law, a far more limited class of offenses than the modern conception of "felony." Moreover, it did not apply to women, who did not have the right to vote in 1868.[75] Yet despite these flaws the Court has recently declined to hear two cases challenging disenfranchisement, and with one exception, discussed later, this is where matters now stand.[76]

The irony of the interpretation of the Fourteenth Amendment in *Ramirez* is remarkable. The Fourteenth Amendment was intended to *expand* voting rights to previously excluded groups, *not* to allow the states to add new restrictions.[77] Yet, as the next chapter shows, many states did precisely that, expanding felon disenfranchisement laws following the adoption of the Fourteenth and Fifteenth amendments.

What exactly did Congress intend in the second section of the Fourteenth Amendment? Unfortunately, the exact origin of the phrase "or other crimes" is ambiguous, and the legislative record is scant. Since many states had already established felon disenfranchisement, one reading is that Congress simply intended to endorse those laws. But there is nothing in the legislative record to support such a view. At the time of its passage, the Fourteenth Amendment was clearly understood as seeking to turn vague natural rights into something concrete and defendable for African Americans, and to nationalize citizenship to override state-level biases.[78] There is, in short, no clear evidence that the phrase "or other crimes" was intended to have any meaning outside the larger context of punishing the former Confederacy and its leaders.[79]

A key set of issues concerns the exact relationship between the Fourteenth and Fifteenth amendments. Constitutional law scholar Gabriel J. Chin has recently argued that the only plausible interpretation of the relationship between the two amendments is that Congress intended the Fifteenth to supersede the Fourteenth with respect to the right to vote.[80] First, Chin argues, section 2 of the Fourteenth Amendment implicitly gave the states the right to disenfranchise African Americans (although Congress could punish such states by reducing their representation in Congress). By contrast, the Fifteenth imposed a national standard, barring states from disenfranchising based on race. The section 2 penalty has thus never been used.[81]

Further, Chin argues, after the adoption of the Fifteenth Amendment, the punishing mechanisms of the Fourteenth *could not* be used; states could not first discriminate, only to be punished for doing so, once the Fifteenth was in place. The Fifteenth Amendment was adopted soon after the Fourteenth because "the South's emphatic rejection of the Fourteenth Amendment led Congress to recognize almost immediately that Section 2 would protect neither northern political interests nor the rights of the freedman."[82] Radical Republicans and their moderate allies understood that stronger medicine was needed. A striking affirmation of the view that the Fifteenth Amendment superseded the Fourteenth can be seen in an 1873 Supreme Court decision:

> Before we proceed to examine more critically the provisions of this amendment . . . let us complete and dismiss the history of the recent amendments, as that history relates to the general purpose which pervades them all. A few years' experience satisfied the thoughtful men who had been the authors of the other two amendments that, notwithstanding the restraints of those articles on the States, and the laws passed under the additional powers granted to Congress, these were inadequate for the protection of life, liberty, and property, without which freedom to the slave was no boon. They were in all those States denied the right of suffrage. The laws were administered by the white man alone. It was urged that a race of men distinctively marked as was the negro, living in the midst of another and dominant race, could never be fully secured in their person and their property without the right of suffrage. Hence, the fifteenth amendment.[83]

The implications of Chin's thesis are straightforward. If section 2 of the Fourteenth Amendment was repealed by the Fifteenth, then it would simply not be a viable basis for the *Ramirez* decision. The plaintiffs in *Ramirez*, however, did not raise this argument, and the Court never considered it.

## Further Legal Challenges

To date, no court has completely abolished a state's practice of disenfranchising convicted felons. The Supreme Court, however, carved out one limitation in 1985. In *Hunter v. Underwood,* the Court struck down a state disenfranchisement law on the basis of discriminatory racial intent.[84] At the time of the *Hunter* challenge, African Americans in two Alabama counties were 1.7 times more likely to be disfranchised than whites for crimes that did not result in incarceration, primarily because of a law that disenfranchised those convicted of minor "moral turpitude" offenses. The Court invalidated the law on the basis of clear evidence from the state's 1901 constitutional convention that the law was adopted with a racially discriminatory intent. While it explicitly declined to reconsider the *Ramirez* verdict, the *Hunter* Court declared that

> without again considering the implicit authorization of § 2 to
> deny the vote to citizens "for participation in rebellion, or other
> crime," we are confident that § 2 was not designed to permit
> the purposeful racial discrimination attending the enactment and
> operation of [the Alabama law] which otherwise violates § 1 of
> the Fourteenth Amendment. Nothing in our opinion in *Rich-*
> *ardson v. Ramirez* suggests the contrary.[85]

The *Hunter* decision potentially opened the door to challenges to felon disenfranchisement on the basis of race. Indeed in the late 1980s and early 1990s several legal commentators argued for such a tactic. Since then, numerous legal challenges have attempted that strategy.[86] The most frequent of these have been based on the Fourteenth and Fifteenth Amendments, as well as on the Voting Rights Act of 1965 (and its important 1982 amendments).[87] The Supreme Court's *Hunter* decision, however, only addresses intentional racial discrimination, which is generally very difficult to prove in legal proceedings. The burgeoning population of African Americans in the criminal justice system and the changing consequences of felon disenfranchisement may ultimately be a decisive factor in other federal courts, and perhaps ultimately the Supreme Court.[88] But so far, disproportionate impact alone has not been enough. The firmest foundation for felon disenfranchisement remains in the legal realm.

## Is There a Penological Basis for Felon Disenfranchisement?

Disenfranchisement is also interwoven into the larger history of criminal punishment. Today, societies punish criminals for four basic reasons: (1) to exact retribution or vengeance for the victims; (2) to deter offenders and others from committing crimes; (3) to incapacitate or otherwise prevent offenders from committing further crimes; and, (4) to rehabilitate or reform them. To what extent do these forms of punishment provide a basis for felon disenfranchisement laws?[89]

### Retribution

A form of institutionalized vengeance, retribution is founded on the notion that those who have committed crimes should suffer for the harm they have caused others. Modern proponents of retribution argue that the punishment should fit the crime already committed, rather than future crimes that the criminal or others might commit.[90] Retribution thus demands sanctions proportionate to the seriousness of the offense and to the degree of the offender's culpability, such that more blameworthy offenders who cause greater harm face greater punishment. While the denial of voting rights may exact some degree of vengeance from felons, it is not clear that retribution can be the basis for disenfranchisement. In particular, the blanket disenfranchisement of *all* felons—murderers and petty thieves alike—violates the principle of proportionality.

### Deterrence

In contrast to retribution, which is designed to redress crimes already committed, deterrence endeavors to prevent future crimes. Criminologists distinguish between specific deterrence, which punishes to reduce future recidivism among people convicted of crimes, and general deterrence, which punishes criminals to influence others who might otherwise be tempted to engage in crime. To some extent, felon disenfranchisement serves both deterrent purposes, since (as we will show in later chapters) some disenfranchised offenders value the right to vote. But effective deterrents require that the consequences be known to offenders when they are contemplating criminal acts. In the case of felon disenfranchisement, this is problematic for several reasons. First, even criminal justice personnel, politicians, and administrative officials are often uncertain about when and where voting restrictions are imposed in their states. Few potential offenders would possess very specific knowledge about the nature of possible political penalties at the time of the crime. Second, the *marginal* deterrent value of disenfranchisement—over and above that of more immediate and severe penalties—would hardly seem to be sufficient to alter the criminal calculus. Criminal offenders know that they risk a jail or prison sentence. Even if they knew they would also forfeit voting rights if apprehended, that threat pales relative to the wholesale deprivations that accompany incarceration.[91]

### Incapacitation

Removing criminals from society to reduce or eliminate their capacity to commit subsequent offenses is certainly a legitimate aim of punishment.[92] The idea of incapacitation hinges on restraining or isolating offenders. Today, this typically means institutional confinement, though bodily mutilation and death were also widely used in earlier times. To what extent does felon disenfranchisement prevent felons from committing crimes generally, or election crimes specifically? Because disenfranchisement only affects a narrow range of activities, it cannot prevent people from committing crimes unrelated to voting. Even for those convicted of political crimes, felon disenfranchisement is not well suited to restraining repeat offending. Felons convicted of making illegal campaign contributions, for example, would not be restrained from doing so by restricting their rights to cast ballots on election day. In short, while disenfranchisement effectively prevents political participation, it would appear to have little impact on criminal activity.

### Rehabilitation

The final goal of punishment is to create the means to rehabilitate offenders, so that they will not commit future crimes. Theories of rehabilitation have undergone a significant revival in recent years. During the "get tough" period of rising incarceration that began in the mid-1970s, critics successfully challenged the legitimacy and effectiveness of rehabilitation as a correctional philosophy.[93] More recently, however, criminologists have reaffirmed rehabilitation, challenging the "nothing works" dictum and developing new evidence that treatments such as cognitive behavioral therapy reduce recidivism.[94] Reenfranchisement might plausibly be linked to rehabilitation if it is offered as a "reward" for good behavior. Yet restoration of voting rights is rarely conditional on good behavior. Instead, it is triggered automatically when a sentence is completed or a waiting period has passed. The reward logic is perhaps most compelling in states that disenfranchise indefinitely (such as Florida), but in many such states, cumbersome restoration procedures likely diminish the rehabilitative effects (see chapter 3 for further discussion).[95]

More generally, there are reasons to conclude that disenfranchisement hinders rehabilitative efforts. Disenfranchisement cannot help to foster the skills and capacities that will rehabilitate offenders and help them become law-abiding citizens. Indeed, on the contrary, it is more likely that "invisible punishments" such as disenfranchisement act as barriers to successful rehabilitation.[96] It is much more plausible to think that *participation* in elections as stakeholders might reduce recidivism, at least for those former offenders who participate. As a fundamental act of citizenship, voting may foster respect for laws, criminal and otherwise, and the institutions that make and enforce them. We investigate the latter possibility in chapter 5.

## Felon Disenfranchisement in Comparative Perspective

The debate over felon disenfranchisement in the United States does not take place in a vacuum. Considering it in international context provides another important vantage point. The starting point for such an analysis, of course, is the oft-remarked fact that the United States has the highest incarceration and conviction rates in the world, 5 to 10 times that of European countries.[97] As we discuss in chapter 3, current levels of incarceration and criminal conviction are unprecedented not only in a comparative sense but also historically within the United States, with massive increases since the early 1970s. In short, there are a lot more disenfranchised citizens in the United States in large measure because we issue a lot of felony convictions.

The second source of American exceptionalism in regard to felon voting lies in the nature of the laws themselves.[98] Many countries, including a number of European democracies, allow all criminal offenders—even those currently in prison—to vote. Israel, Canada, and South Africa allow current inmates to vote on the basis of recent high court rulings. A group of other European nations, as well as Australia and New Zealand, disenfranchise only some current inmates. In these countries, restrictions on prisoner voting are typically based on either the length of the sentence, the nature of the crime committed, or the type of election. Nine European countries bar all current prisoners from voting, but only a handful place any restrictions on nonincarcerated felons, and most of these apply only to a small minority of offenders. (Details are provided in appendix table A1.1.)

The key point to draw from this comparative survey is that the United States is the only country in the democratic world that systematically disenfranchises large numbers of nonincarcerated offenders (i.e., those who are either on probation or parole, or have finished their sentence). In particular, it is the only country disenfranchising a large number of former offenders who are no longer under any correctional supervision. There are only a few exceptions to this generalization, but none involve large numbers of offenders. In Germany, courts have the power to withdraw voting rights for up to five years after the completion of a prison sentence as an additional punishment, although actual use of this sanction is very rare. One analyst has observed that in a recent year for which she had data, courts applied it in only 11 cases.[99] In France, courts can impose restrictions on civil and political rights that extend beyond the prison sentence, but these are a formal part of the punishment and expire at the end of the sentence. Finland and New Zealand disenfranchise certain ex-felons for political offenses. Some convicted offenders with long sentences can be disenfranchised for life in Belgium. But the existence of a blanket ex-felon voting ban on millions of nonincarcerated citizens in the United States today is unparalleled. In fact, the closest parallels are to the premodern political regimes mentioned earlier, in which criminal offenders were precluded, once marked by legal conviction, from reentering the polity for the rest of their lives.

What explains these enormous discrepancies? Unique aspects of American political and legal institutions and culture, described earlier, are clearly important. But we also cannot understand the spread of felon disenfranchisement in the United States without examining the intertwining of race and criminal justice. We explore these questions in more detail in the next chapter.

# 2 The Racial Origins of Felon Disenfranchisement
*with Angela Behrens*

Felon disenfranchisement laws in United States are unique in the democratic world. Nowhere else are millions of offenders who are not in prison denied the right to vote. How did we get to this point? Because individual states establish eligibility for criminal offenders, there are 50 different, often zigzagging stories to be told. Still, some common dynamics may hold across the states. Some of the earliest felon disenfranchisement measures were holdovers from medieval legal systems. The sequencing of the adoption of felon disenfranchisement laws in many states *after* property and other restrictions were eliminated provides an important clue. However, one factor—race—seems to recur again and again.

Consider the following three moments in the history of felon disenfranchisement. The earliest campaigns to disenfranchise African Americans frequently invoked racial disparities in criminality as evidence that blacks were unworthy of assuming the full rights and duties of citizenship. Colonel Samuel Young, one of a group of leading Jeffersonians in New York who had campaigned on the slogan "Federalists with Blacks United," declared in an 1821 New York state legislative debate that

> The minds of blacks are not competent to vote. They are too degraded to estimate the value, or exercise with fidelity and discretion this important right. . . . Look to your jails and penitentiaries. By whom are they filled? By the very race it is now proposed to clothe with the power of deciding upon your political rights.[1]

New York eventually established a law requiring blacks to own at least $300 of property, effectively disenfranchising almost all African Americans in the state, while abolishing property restrictions for whites.[2]

In 1896, the Mississippi Supreme Court considered a challenge to the state's 1890 constitutional convention, which had explicitly barred individuals convicted of certain petty offenses from participating in elections. The selected offenses were almost exclusively applied against African Americans, while crimes of which whites were regularly convicted (including rape and even murder) did not affect voting rights. In endorsing this seemingly bizarre duality, the court declared that race affects the type of crime to which one is prone:

> The [constitutional] convention swept the circle of expedients to obstruct the exercise of the franchise by the negro race. By reason of its previous condition of servitude and dependence, *this race had acquired or accentuated certain peculiarities of habit, of temperament and of character, which clearly distinguished it, as a race, from that of the whites*—a patient docile people, but careless, landless, and migratory within narrow limits, without afterthought, and its criminal members given rather to furtive offenses than to the robust crimes of the whites. Restrained by the federal constitution from discriminating against the negro race, *the convention discriminated against its characteristics and the offenses to which its weaker members were prone*.[3]

Remarkably, Mississippi continued to allow many violent offenders to vote while disenfranchising many minor offenses until the late 1960s, when all ex-felons were excluded from voting.

Finally, a more recent example. In 2001, South Carolina legislators had several heated exchanges over a bill to further tighten the state's disenfranchisement law. Responding to assertions that he was using race to push the bill through, one of the bill's sponsors rejected any racial motivation by asserting: "If it's blacks losing the right to vote, then they have to quit committing crimes. We are not punishing the criminal. We are punishing conduct."[4] The South Carolina legislature did not, in the end, pass the proposed measure.

While these three anecdotes span a nearly 200–year period, the racial thread connecting them is clear. And in view of the historical connections among race, criminal justice, and disenfranchisement, it should hardly be surprising to find other such traces in the historical record.[5] Indeed, a number of commentators have hypothesized that racial politics provides the hidden glue to understanding the historical origins and persistence of felon disenfranchisement laws.[6] Many scholars have noted in particular that states in the post-Reconstruction era, particularly those in the South, changed their disenfranchisement laws to exclude African American voters by "tying the loss of voting rights to crimes alleged to be committed primarily by blacks while excluding offenses held to be committed by whites."[7]

Most of this previous scholarship and popular commentary, however, has been rooted in either legal and doctrinal analyses of court decisions, or anecdotal historical evidence. Most of the historical work has also focused on the relatively brief period from Reconstruction and its aftermath through the 1890s, when the southern states adopted numerous racially explicit disenfranchising measures which rendered felon disenfranchisement less important for reducing racial threat. But the history of felon disenfranchisement is a national story, and it is not limited to the post-Reconstruction era. Yet we lack detailed historical narratives of the development of felon disenfranchisement laws across the states and over time, as well as a systematic examination of the role of race.[8]

In this chapter, we develop a broad historical overview, subjecting race-based theories about the adoption and development of felon disenfranchisement laws to scrutiny. We developed a systematic quantitative analysis that uses detailed information on the social and political makeup of individual states over a long historical period to examine how various factors affect the adoption and extension of state disenfranchisement laws. Although this approach does not provide a rich, textured set of case studies, it does guard against overinterpreting race-based anecdotes from a handful of states. It also controls for potentially confounding factors such as region, partisan control of government, the punitiveness of a state's criminal justice system, and other institutional factors.

Why is race a logical culprit in the search to explain the development of felon disenfranchisement laws? In recent years, there has been an explosion of scholarship by social scientists and historians fingering race, and racial politics, as principal sources of the peculiar development of American political and legal culture. This scholarship includes three distinct types of argument: (1) arguments about the interaction between race and the development of U.S. political institutions; (2) arguments focusing on the impact of racial attitudes and racism; and (3) arguments that stress the nexus between race (and class) in the political economy of the American South.[9]

## Race and American Political Institutions

Racial factors played key roles in the construction and development of American political institutions. These institutional outcomes have in turn shaped policymaking in general, and voting rights and criminal justice in particular. The most distinctive features of American political institutions are a system of federalism in which significant powers are vested below the national level, procedural rules that require supermajorities to pass new legislation, weak political parties, and an array of institutional "veto points" that are available for opponents of reform proposals.

How is race implicated in the construction of American political institutions? The most important set of enduring institutional innovations can be traced to the compromises at the founding of the republic to ensure support from the slave states when drafting the United States Constitution. The slave states wanted to protect their racial order against northern incursion. A series of safeguards were added to prevent northern interests from challenging or undermining the slave economy. The most famous of these was the "three-fifths" compromise, in which slaves would be counted toward the apportionment of House seats even though they could not vote. Other safeguards included the adoption of the Electoral College system, equal representation in the Senate irrespective of state population (both of which helped give the South disproportionate regional influence on national politics), and the creation of a strong judiciary capable of overturning national policy initiatives that threatened regional interests or "states' rights."[10]

Race has also played a critical role at all of the major institutional turning points in American history. The Civil War was fought over slavery, and the postwar Reconstruction era was largely a battle over whether and to what extent the former slaves would be granted full citizenship. The extraordinary Reconstruction amendments—the Thirteenth, Fourteenth, and Fifteenth amendments to the Constitution—promised to remake the political order by nationalizing male citizenship rights (with the equal protection clause of the Fourteenth having numerous consequences unknowable at the time it was drafted). The efforts of the Radical Republicans to establish political equality for African Americans and bring multiparty democracy to the South foundered, however, on political divisions among northern Republicans with respect to race and constitutional rules that hindered reform efforts.[11]

Important challenges to the dominant political order from below— notably the Knights of Labor, populism, and the industrial labor movement—also ran headlong into a racialized political order. These movements mounted strong challenges, in part by attempting to organize across racial lines. Indeed, much of their potency lay precisely in the prospect of overcoming embedded racial antagonisms. In each case, however, virulent race-baiting by opponents and internal conflicts over race undermined the potential of these movements.[12]

At the national level, the crucial twentieth–century moment of institutional reconstruction was the New Deal. Although racial politics operated somewhat behind the scenes of front-stage New Deal policymaking, the political and racial conservatism of the southern Democrats was crucial. Elected by essentially all-white electorates, southern Democrats supported relief initiatives but had little use for the broader reform initiatives of the New Deal. They resisted the social insurance programs included in the

Social Security Act of 1935, rejected national health insurance (which would have potentially brought whites and blacks into the same system), and ultimately deflated the pro-labor momentum of the 1933–37 period.[13]

It was not until the civil rights era that the combination of pressures from civil rights organizations and growing racial liberalism among northern Democrats in Congress overwhelmed the opposition of southern Democrats, leading to enduring political reforms. The innovative antipoverty and antisegregationist policies of the period had a lasting and profound impact. But even here, implementation of Great Society programs at the local level frequently stalled in the face of racial antagonisms and the reluctance of local officials to challenge existing social arrangements.[14] Political momentum was lost after the late 1960s, and reform initiatives declined markedly.

The existing literature is very clear about the importance of these institutional arrangements and political developments, perhaps nowhere more so than in discussions of the underdeveloped American welfare state.[15] Federal courts hindered certain kinds of policy initiatives, especially before the New Deal. The fragmented system of social benefit administration precluded national standards with equal application for all groups. The long-standing dominance of southern interests inside the Democratic Party precluded that party from evolving into a prowelfare social democratic party along western European lines. As a consequence, political actors and social movements were forced to adapt to this institutional terrain and promote different kinds of reforms.

### Racial Attitudes and Political Outcomes

A second aspect explored extensively in recent scholarship is how the racial attitudes of white Americans have influenced policy and political processes. In the past 15 years, the link between racial attitudes and the policy preferences of citizens and elites has become one of the most widely studied topics among analysts of political psychology and public opinion. These studies agree that, to the extent public policies come to be seen as benefiting African Americans, their popularity plummets; "race-neutral" social policies, by contrast, tend to retain much higher levels of popular support.[16]

The role of racial attitudes and race-based stereotypes has been particularly important in relation to crime (and criminal justice policies). Racial stereotyping about criminality has been pervasive. Theodore Roosevelt, expressing widely held views in the Progressive era, called for "relentless and unceasing warfare against lawbreaking black men" on the grounds that "laziness and shiftlessness . . . and above all, vice and criminality of every kind, are evils more potent for harm to the black race than all acts of oppression of white men put together."[17] Lynching was frequently justified by black criminality. The first woman to hold a Senate seat, Rebecca Latimer Felton of Georgia, told her supporters in 1897 that rapes of white women "will grow and increase with every election where white men equalized themselves at the polls with an inferior race and controlled their votes by bribery and whiskey. . . . If it takes a lynching to protect woman's dearest possession from drunken, ravening human beasts, then I say lynch a thousand a week if it becomes necessary."[18] Similar stereotypes—if not remedies—were applied to waves of newer immigrant groups from Europe, including the Irish, Italians, Greeks, Hungarians, and Slavs, to name just a few.[19]

The ascription of criminal traits to subordinate racial and ethnic groups also defined the early history of criminology. For example, Cesare Lombroso and other early criminologists made reference to "criminal races."[20] By the 1930s, however, the work of Clifford Shaw and Henry McKay had largely dispelled such ideas in academic criminology, showing geographic stability in delinquency rates despite dramatic changes in their racial and ethnic composition.[21] During this long interim, however, scholarly ideas associating criminal propensities with racial characteristics proliferated and had wide popular and scientific influence.

Racism and racial threat, of course, are not static concepts, and they manifest themselves in different forms over time. The history of the nineteenth century and the first half of the twentieth century is replete with examples of open and explicit advocacy of racial segregation and white supremacy. By the time of the civil rights era, however, blatant racism no longer held any scholarly respectability and popular support for the idea was rapidly declining as well. Despite the changes established during the "second reconstruction" of the 1960s, a number of scholars have argued that racial influence on policymaking persists. While structural and economic changes have reduced social acceptance of explicit racial bias, current race-neutral language and policies remain socially and culturally embedded in the discriminatory actions of the past.[22] In contrast to earlier forms of racism based on biological superiority, a "modern" racism rooted in notions of cultural inferiority has come to replace the explicit racism of the Jim Crow era.[23]

### Race and the Political Influence of the South

The final angle on the political impact of race highlights how the former Confederate states used their disproportionate influence to shape American political development in ways that served narrow regional interests.[24] After Reconstruction, the one-party "solid South" routinely elected and reelected conservative southern Democrats who—under the institutional rules of Congress—were able to acquire enormous leverage through seniority in the congressional committee system. These legislators were rigid in their defense of states' rights and the social order of the southern plantation economy.[25] In the 1960s and 1970s, that power would finally break down, as the South became more electorally competitive and seniority rules in Congress were ended after the 1974 (post-Watergate) election.

But the legacies of Southern political influence endure to the present. It is often thought that the Democratic Party cannot capture the White House with a non-Southern candidate, and until very recently the remaining southern Democrats continued to have disproportionate influence in the party leadership.[26] The South has now become the primary bastion of Republican control in the country as a whole, switching from nearly complete Democratic control before the 1960s to almost as thorough Republican domination today. The region may eventually become as important inside the Republican Party as it once was for the Democrats in the heyday of the "solid South."

Especially striking for our purposes is the February 2002 U.S. Senate vote on an amendment to the federal voting reform legislation that proposed to restore voting rights to ex-felons in federal elections. Senators from the 11 former confederate states voted 18 to 4 against enfranchisement (the measure went down by 63–31 floor vote), and the most passionate speeches against it were made by southerners (Jeff Sessions of Alabama, Mitch McConnell of Kentucky, and George Allen of Virginia).

### The Influence of Race

The three prongs identified here—race and institution-building, racial attitudes and stereotypes, and race and region—provide ample grounds for developing hypotheses about the political power of racial factors. When we add to the mix the evident racial disparities in the criminal justice system and race-based stereotypes surrounding crime, the prima facie case for the racial origins of felon disenfranchisement appears to be a strong one. But we still need concrete proof.

## State Felon Disenfranchisement Laws: An Overview

We begin our investigation of the sources of state disenfranchisement laws by documenting the timing of the adoption of those laws. Figure 2.1 charts

**Figure 2.1.**
Percentage of states disenfranchising felons and ex-felons, 1788–2004.

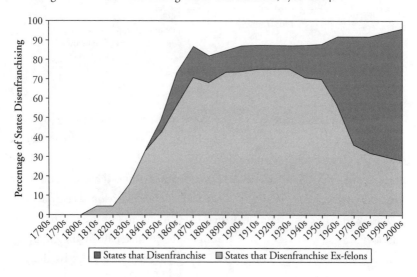

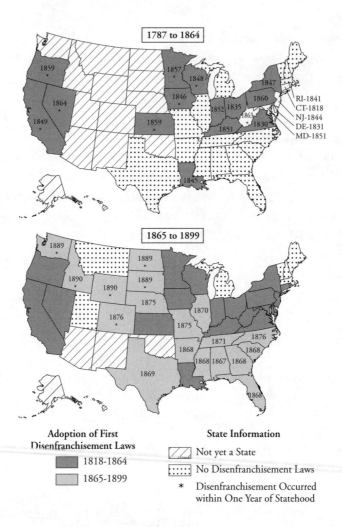

**1787 to 1864**

1859 *
1864 *
1849 *
1859 *
1857 *
1848 *
1846
1852 | 1835
1863 *
1851
1830
1860
1847
1845

RI-1841
CT-1818
NJ-1844
DE-1831
MD-1851

**1865 to 1899**

1889 *
1890 *
1890 *
1889 *
1889 *
1875
1876 *
1875
1870
1875
1868
1869
1871
1868 | 1867 | 1868
1876
1868
1868

**Adoption of First Disenfranchisement Laws**

1818-1864

1865-1899

**State Information**

Not yet a State

No Disenfranchisement Laws

\*   Disenfranchisement Occurred within One Year of Statehood

the development of state laws since 1840. It shows the percentage of states that held a broad measure disenfranchising felons, and the percentage of states that additionally disenfranchise ex-felons after they have completed their sentences. (More details about individual states' laws are shown in appendix table A2.1.) While 11 states had established felon disenfranchisement laws by 1850, 38 states had such laws by the end of the century. That number stayed relatively stable throughout the first half of the twentieth century, with only four more states adding laws in this period. By the year

**Figure 2.2.**
Timeline of statehood and disenfranchisement, 1787–1864, 1865–1899, and 1900–2000.

2000, however, 48 states had some type of law restricting voting rights on the basis of a felony conviction; Maine and Vermont were the only two states with no restrictions.[27] The percentage disenfranchising ex-felons, however, declined sharply after the late 1950s.

Figure 2.2 highlights the geographic clustering of franchise restrictions. It shows two noticeable waves of disfranchisement laws in the nineteenth century. The first wave begins in the 1840s in the Northeast, following on the heels of the decline of property and other restrictions on white male suffrage. Unlike the northern states, several midwestern and western states adopted many of these laws with statehood. The second wave of restrictions occurred in the South after the Civil War, in some cases following passage of the Fifteenth Amendment and extension of voting rights to African American men.

Prior to 1840, four states (Connecticut, Delaware, Ohio, and Virginia) had established broad felon disenfranchisement measures. The first significant wave of disenfranchisement for criminal offenders spans the two decades before the Civil War. Expansive changes in state suffrage rules occurred shortly before and during this period. The first half of the nineteenth century saw the beginnings of the world's first mass democracy, albeit one in which in most states only white men had the right to vote.[28]

Before 1800, most states had established restrictions on the franchise for white men, such as property ownership or payment of certain taxes. In 1790, for example, 10 of the original 13 states had property requirements.[29] States generally required ownership of a certain amount of land (often 50 acres) or of land worth a minimum value. Many states, in addition, enforced durational residency requirements. In Virginia, for example, voters had to own their property for at least one year prior to the election. New Hampshire enforced a poll tax, and Georgia and Pennsylvania both required all taxes to have been paid in the year preceding the election. New Hampshire excluded all "paupers," although the prevalence of property requirements in the other states effectively produced the same exclusion without the formal restriction.

In his authoritative history of voting rights in the United States, Alexander Keyssar argues that the expansion of the franchise in this period resulted from a range of social pressures, including the growth of the propertyless masses, wars, interparty competition for votes, and pressure to increase the population of remote states. The process was uneven, halting, and subject to reversal. In both theory and practice, however, the classical justifications for restricting the voting rights of white men were losing influence during this period.[30] By the middle of the nineteenth century, most states had responded to these various pressures by easing or eliminating voting restrictions. Many states abolished requirements of taxpaying and property ownership through constitutional revisions, while newer states never imposed the restrictions. New York dropped its property requirement in 1821 and its taxpaying requirement in 1826, although in both cases the change only affected whites (as the state's 1826 and 1846 constitutions continued to apply the requirements to "men of color").[31] By 1855, only three of the 31 states had property requirements in effect.[32] Nine states, however, had added or retained pauper exclusions,[33] and Connecticut enforced a literacy requirement.[34]

Having allowed the growth of a mass democracy, elites' concerns about its implications—particularly, the consequences of allowing "undesirables" to participate—were widespread. The most notable of these concerns was a fear of fraud, as well as more obscure fears on the part of some that the integrity of the ballot box would be tainted by the participation of unworthy electors. This included, most obviously, all women, African Americans in most states, and, increasingly, immigrants. For example, in 1790, only 3 of the 13 states excluded nonwhites from voting, but by 1840 20 of the then 26 states had removed nonwhites from the rolls, either by directly specifying that African Americans could not vote or by indirectly disenfranchising them through the implementation of onerous property requirements applicable only to African Americans (as in New York).[35]

Criminal offenders constituted another category of undesirable voters, but unincarcerated former offenders also presented a more complicated enforcement problem than women or voters of color. A comparison with the types of criminal disenfranchisement practiced in the colonial era, described in chapter 1, highlights this problem. In the town hall meeting, the disenfranchisement of offenders was enforceable through direct personal means: the offender was known to the community, and easily barred from attempting to participate. The transition to a modern democratic regime, in which masses of white men could vote in the anonymous environs of the urban polling booth, made direct (and systematic) enforcement more difficult because offenders could not necessarily be identified by sight.

What was the connection between the extension of the franchise and felon disenfranchisement? We have very few traces of information, beyond what can be gleaned from the statutory and constitutional histories of the states. One pattern, however, is strikingly clear. Between 1840 and 1865, all 16 states adopting felon disenfranchisement measures did so *after* establishing full white male suffrage by eliminating property tests (see appendix table A2.2).[36] To be sure, some of the new states in this period adopted restrictive voting laws from the outset. For example, when Nevada became a state in 1864, its constitution gave its state legislature the power to condition voting on payment of a poll tax, and in 1865, the legislature enacted such a statute.[37] West Virginia had no property or taxpaying requirement, but still banned all paupers from voting when it became a state in 1863. The majority of new states, however, had constitutional provisions specifically banning property requirements or limiting taxpaying requirements to special elections, such as those authorizing a city or town to incur debt.[38] It is striking, however, that almost all of the 19 states established after 1850 included *both* near-universal white male suffrage and a law authorizing felon disenfranchisement in their founding constitutions. Of the 19 new states in the post-1850 period, 17 had felon disenfranchisement provisions in place at the time of statehood.

While class-based factors were important, felon disenfranchisement laws before the Civil War are not plausibly tied to race for the simple reason that most states did not permit African Americans to vote at all. On the eve of the Civil War, only six states allowed African Americans to vote, and these states (clustered in the Northeast) generally had very small African American populations.[39] Since most free African Americans were already legally disenfranchised, further targeting of the black vote through disenfranchising measures directed at felons would have been largely superfluous.

It is also important to note that in this early period, the criminal justice system was still quite underdeveloped, although entering a phase of rapid development. There were virtually no professional police forces before 1840, and few jurisdictions had criminal courts to deal with routine offenses. For example, Boston did not establish regular police officers until 1838, with New York City and Philadelphia following in 1845. Most states maintained a single state penitentiary, and incarcerated only a small number of offenders (many of whom had simply failed to pay their debts or taxes). The modern criminal justice system, including the widespread use of prison, formalized probation and parole, and indeterminate sentencing, developed in waves between 1830 and 1920. Nonetheless, the growth of felon disenfranchisement in this period was symbolically, if not substantively, important.

The takeoff period for criminal disenfranchisement laws thus appears to have corresponded with two major developments: primarily, and most important, the spread of suffrage rights to the (white male) masses, and secondarily, the expansion and growth of the criminal justice system. Our evidence here is not as strong as we would like, and later investigators will surely provide a more complete portrait. But already we are beginning to see how the adoptions of disenfranchisement laws were not free-floating events. Rather, they were tied to social dynamics, in this case the spread of voting rights to propertyless white men.

### Felon Disenfranchisement after the Civil War

The second major growth period of disenfranchisement laws occurred after the Civil War. Between 1865 and 1900, 19 states adopted or amended laws restricting the voting rights of criminal offenders (as shown in appendix table A2.1). In the South, during and after Reconstruction, many states expanded their restrictions on the felon population, which began to contain large proportions of African Americans for the first time. These measures included the extension of disenfranchisement to cover a wide range of crimes not previously included among the common-law felonies.[40] For example, South Carolina crafted a law to disenfranchise for crimes of "thievery, adultery, arson, wife-beating, housebreaking, and attempted rape," while excluding murder.[41]

The last half of the decade in particular saw a large number of restrictions put into place. Three states that had not disenfranchised added laws. Nebraska became the 36th state in 1875, disenfranchising felons until the completion of their sentences. By the end of the decade, 28 states had some type of felon voting restriction, most of which disenfranchised convicted felons until they received a pardon. In the 1870s, disenfranchisement laws spread further as four states added laws and two (Arkansas and Texas) expanded their list of disqualifying crimes. In the 1890s, a number of additional southern states also expanded the list of offenses that would trigger disenfranchisement. Four new states added laws that, to varying degrees, restricted felons' right to vote. Wyoming and Montana disenfranchised felons until they received a pardon, whereas Idaho disenfranchised only for the duration of sentence, and Utah disenfranchised only those convicted of election offenses (Utah would not change its law to disenfranchise all prison inmates until 1998).

The beginning of the twentieth century brought fewer, but generally more restrictive, changes. Beginning in 1901, Alabama disenfranchised for crimes of "moral turpitude." Several years later Oklahoma became the 46th state and disenfranchised felons for the duration of their sentence. In 1909, New York disenfranchised felons convicted of a federal offense. In the 1910s, Iowa disenfranchised federal offenders in addition to all other convicted felons, and when Arizona and New Mexico became states in 1912, each disenfranchised felons permanently unless pardoned. At the same time, New Hampshire, which previously had not restricted the voting rights of felons, disenfranchised those convicted of treason, bribery, and election offenses.

What drove the post–Civil War changes? They were substantively as well as symbolically important. It appears likely that felon disenfranchisement laws were poorly enforced prior to the Civil War, and perhaps for some time thereafter as well.[42] In the aftermath of the Civil War, a new and complex dynamic developed around racial politics that appears at first glance to bear a significant relationship to the changing pattern of disenfranchisement laws. In 1868, the Fourteenth Amendment was added to the Constitution, mandating equal protection of the races, and giving states a strong incentive to grant all men the right to vote—a threat of reduced congressional representation.[43] The amendment further redefined citizenship by deeming all persons born in the United States to be American citizens, thereby superseding the Supreme Court's declaration to the contrary a decade earlier in the infamous *Dred Scott* case.[44] (As we discussed in the previous chapter, section 2 of the amendment also contained the clause permitting the states to disenfranchise those convicted of "rebellion or other crimes.") Two years later, in 1870, the Fifteenth Amendment enfranchised African American males, expressly declaring that states could no longer deny the right to vote based on race.

Despite their legal enfranchisement as a result of the Reconstruction amendments, many African Americans remained practically disenfranchised as a result of concerted efforts to prevent their exercise of these rights. The general process of disenfranchising all blacks following the end of Reconstruction would, however, take some time to unfold. The mechanisms through which this was achieved are widely known. Violence and intimidation were widespread, especially until legal measures took hold. Most southern states, as well as some nonsouthern states, implemented some combination of poll taxes, literacy tests, "grandfather clauses," white-only primaries, and discriminatory registration requirements.[45] Such limitations on the right to vote were extremely effective, especially after 1900, relegating most African Americans in the South to the status of nonvoters.[46] It was not until the combination of a series of Supreme Court decisions in the 1960s and the passage of the VRA that these barriers began to fall.[47]

Restrictions targeting immigrants, the poor, and the urban working class also began to appear in this period. These included such measures as preregistration and long residency requirements.[48] More than half the states adopted literacy tests in this period. Further, between the 1880s and the early 1900s, almost all of the states that had previously allowed immigrant voting did away with those provisions.[49] This was a period in which elites stepped back from the universalizing innovations of the first half of the nineteenth century, in the North as well as the South.

Although it was far less widely applied than such general measures, the explicit use of felon disenfranchisement contributed to preventing African Americans and other "undesirable" groups from voting. Disenfranchisement based on criminal conviction provided a useful, and potentially permanent, way to eliminate voters, particularly in light of corresponding changes to the criminal justice system (which became both more expansive and more formalized during the mid- to late nineteenth century).[50] Although this type of voting ban inevitably disenfranchised potential white voters as well, changes in prison populations during this period suggest that the burden fell mainly on nonwhites. In Alabama, for example, nonwhites made up just 2 percent of the prison population in 1850, but 74 percent by 1870.[51] Felon disenfranchisement, therefore, cannot be separated from the larger dynamics of criminal justice and racial politics in this same period.

The case of Alabama is a particularly interesting exemplar. Alabama has formally banned voting for all felons and ex-felons since 1868. The original state constitution of 1819, however, gave the legislature the authority to disenfranchise those convicted of "bribery, perjury, forgery, or other high crimes or misdemeanors" (art. 6, sec. 5). The provision was amended in the 1868 constitution, which disenfranchised for any crime "punishable by law with imprisonment in the penitentiary" (art. 7, sec. 3). Although most felons and ex-felons were disenfranchised by 1868, the state continued to further restrict voting rights with subsequent amendments. In 1875, larceny was added to the list of crimes resulting in disenfranchisement (art. 8, sec. 3), regardless of whether the larceny was a felony or a misdemeanor. The state's supreme court held that the law could be applied retroactively to include people convicted of larceny before 1875, citing the state's need to "preserve the purity of the ballot box."[52] More substantial changes were adopted during the state's 1901 constitutional convention, when the vague phrase "crime involving moral turpitude" was added. Participants at the all-white convention openly sought to "establish white supremacy," using suffrage as a key mechanism to achieve the goal. John Fielding Burns, sponsor of the new disfranchisement bill, boasted that "the crime of wife-beating alone would disqualify sixty percent of the Negroes."[53]

The Alabama case provides an example of how subtle changes in a state's law may be driven by a clear racial purpose. The moral turpitude clause lasted nearly 85 years, and permitted the state to target African Americans for acts beyond the reach of other disenfranchising measures. Indeed, historical evidence presented to the Supreme Court in 1985 suggested a sufficiently clear racial bias to warrant a conservative Court to strike it down.[54] But whether we can finger race in other states, or for the overall national pattern, remains unclear.

### The Great Liberalization: Felon Disenfranchisement during the Civil Rights Era

Between 1920 and the late 1950s, relatively few changes in felon disenfranchisement laws were enacted, or indeed laws regulating the right to vote more generally.[55] The final key period visible in figure 2.1 begins in the late 1950s and runs more or less to the present, though reaching high tide in the early 1970s. During this period, a large number of states (23 in all) amended or did away with laws barring some or all of the ex-felon population from access to the ballot box. To be sure, even in the midst of this general period of liberalization, two states (Michigan and New Hampshire) became more restrictive, but the clear direction of change was toward liberalization. Some states reduced the scope of their laws by allowing probationers to vote and by automatically restoring voting rights upon completion of sentence. During the peak of this liberalization phase, voting was increasingly extended not only to ex-felons but also to those nonincarcerated felons on probation and, in some cases, parole. Five states changed their laws to automatically restore voting rights upon completion of sentence and five more to disenfranchise only inmates between 1970 and 1975.

Since the mid-1970s, the pattern of change has slowed, but of those states changing their laws far more have liberalized (see chapter 10). These liberalizing measures have also affected far more individuals than the restrictive measures. We will discuss the sources and implications of liberalization more extensively in chapter 10.

### Did Racial Politics Drive Felon Disenfranchisement?

On the eve of the Civil War, only a handful of states allowed African Americans to vote. But in the period after 1865, anecdotal evidence suggests race might have played a critical role. In this section we consider that possibility more systematically. Variation across the states affords the opportunity to compare contexts where racial factors are likely to matter a great deal to those where they are unlikely to have played a significant role in explaining felon disenfranchisement. We can use state-level variation to compare racial *and* nonracial factors, and can also examine the broad national pattern by looking at all states rather than focusing on a few notorious cases. (For further descriptions of the methods employed in this analysis, see the chapter's methodological appendix at pp. 236–38.)

### Varieties of Racial Threat

Our starting point is sociological theories of racial (or ethnic) threat.[56] Racial group threat theories assert that dominant groups perceive subordinate groups as a threat when subordinate groups gain power to the detriment of the dominant group. When the dominant group perceives that a subordinate group is gaining power in a sphere previously under the control of the dominant group, such as the political realm, that perception may spark actions to diminish the perceived threat.[57] Legal barriers may be erected, such as Jim Crow laws, and other forms of racial discrimination. Whites, for example, may fight for political restrictions if they perceive that minority groups can mobilize and gain political power. A dominant group may therefore decrease the size of the minority's potential electorate, thereby sapping the political strength of subordinate groups and sustaining the established social structure.

Racial threat theories can take many forms, emphasizing factors such as economic competition, relative group size, and political power to varying degrees. The most common formulation of racial threat is based upon economic relationships in which groups compete over scarce resources. Members of the dominant group may feel that their livelihoods are threatened by the growth of a subordinate group, particularly when the dominant group has a marginal economic status.

Using theories of economic threat to explain the rise of felon disenfranchisement may present a few problems, because disenfranchisement is situated within the *political* realm rather than the market. Models of racial antagonism in general have tended to give less attention to the political sphere in the area of group threat, but those that do underscore a political power threat highlight the size of subordinate groups within specific geographic contexts.[58] Growth in the relative size of a subordinate group increases that group's ability to use democratic political institutions for their benefit and to the detriment of the dominant group. With universal suffrage, in which each person's vote counts the same as any other's, the potential to disrupt existing power relations in a race-based social order is ever present. The use of formal and informal measures to bar or inhibit members of subordinate groups from voting creates an opening to neutralize racial threats and preserve the status quo.[59]

Many previous studies have shown that the size of the racial minority population in a region intensifies concerns among whites. For example, sociologists Lincoln Quillian and Devah Pager have found a link between the perceived racial composition of the neighborhood and perceptions of criminality in the neighborhood.[60] Higher proportions of African Americans in a region appears to increase both traditional white prejudice and white opposition to public policies designed to promote racial equality.[61] And when former Ku Klux Klan leader David Duke ran a close race for a U.S. Senate seat in Louisiana in 1990, his support among whites was strongest in those parishes with the largest African American populations.[62]

Such research focuses on theories of racial threat based on either economic competition or relative group size. However, there is a third, and perhaps more direct, measure of racial threat to apply to the specific case of felon disenfranchisement: the racial composition of the convicted felon population. Imprisoning racial minorities reduces economic threat to whites, but not necessarily the political threat, unless formal disenfranchisement attaches to a criminal conviction.[63] Because felon disenfranchisement laws affect only persons convicted of a felony, the racial composition of a state's prison population is more closely related to felon disenfranchisement than is the racial makeup of a state's population.[64] In other words, the racial composition of state prisons may reveal a direct link to voting restrictions that is less apparent when looking only at the relative size of the nonwhite population within a state.

The analysis we develop considers all three types of racial threat, within the limits of the available data. We tested whether economic competition affects adoption of felon disenfranchisement laws by including a measure of the rate of white male idleness and unemployment in each state. Using historical data from the U.S. Census Bureau, we calculated this rate by dividing the number of white males aged 15 to 39 who were either unemployed or "idle" (defined as neither attending school nor participating in the labor force) by the total white male population aged 15 to 39.[65] To account for more general economic conditions, we included an indicator of national economic contraction or recession.[66] The latter measure supports the literature on ethnic competition because it captures economic fluctuations, which may trigger feelings of economic threat.[67]

To test whether political threat in the general population drives disenfranchisement laws, we evaluated the effect of the African American and non–African American populations across the states and years. We also consider a measure of the percentage of nonwhite males in a state's total population, in light of some research suggesting that nonwhite male populations pose a larger threat than the total nonwhite population.[68]

Finally, we consider the racial composition of state prisons by including a measure of the percentage of nonwhite inmates in state prisons.[69] While we would prefer broader information about the racial composition of *all* convicted felons (not just those in prison), a prison-based indicator is the only available information over the long historical period of our investigation. Fortunately, data in recent years show a high correlation between the two measures (all felons and incarcerated felons) across time and space.[70]

### Alternative Explanations

To conclude that one or more racial threat explanations provide the best available theory of how disenfranchisement laws developed across the states, we need to test them against plausible alternatives. Other factors we suspect could influence legal change include region, partisan control over state government, and the level of criminal justice punitiveness in a state. Region may play a particularly important role in this context. Following the Civil War, most states imposed various restrictions on suffrage, but states in the South typically adopted laws that were more comprehensive and detailed.[71] A statistical control for region allows us to examine whether our conclusions about the national patterns were driven by developments in the South.

A measure of partisan control of government is another key factor to consider. Political actors must formally introduce, propose, and vote on the creation of, or amendments to, disenfranchisement laws.[72] Throughout the post–Civil War era, and until at least the New Deal, Republicans generally supported African American suffrage, while southern Democrats (and frequently their northern allies) opposed it. (Later, of course, this pattern reversed, as northern Democrats became increasingly reliant on African American votes and shifted toward a pro–civil rights position.)[73]

Key historical turning points, in addition to data limitations, complicate our analysis of partisan effects on the passage of felon disenfranchisement laws. For example, data on the political party compositions of state legislatures are not available for the entire period. We are therefore only able to represent political power in our analyses with gubernatorial partisanship (a clearly imperfect measure of state partisan control). To account for partisan racial dynamics across the years of our study, as well as for potential interactions between region and partisanship, we tested whether political effects varied over time, using three time periods to represent gubernatorial leadership: prior to 1870, 1870–1960, and 1960-present.[74] These time periods capture the effects of Reconstruction in the first and second periods, while the third period captures the shift of racially conservative southern Democrats to the Republican Party beginning in the early 1960s.[75]

To isolate the effects of racial threat from the effects of overall state punitiveness, we also considered state incarceration rates.[76] It may be that some states are simply more punitive and, as a result, more readily adopt or extend disenfranchising measures alongside other forms of punishment. Finally, to account for the likelihood that new states would adopt disenfranchisement provisions as part of their initial constitutions, we included a measure tracking the number of years since statehood. (A summary of the key variables we used for this analysis, and a brief description of their measurement, is provided in appendix table A2.3.)[77]

### Changes in State Felon Disenfranchisement Laws

The dependent variable—the variation we are attempting to account for in the statistical analyses we will discuss shortly—is passage or extension of disenfranchising measures. States impose disenfranchisement for varying periods, generally following one of four schemes: (1) disenfranchisement only while incarcerated; (2) disenfranchisement while incarcerated and while on parole; (3) disenfranchisement for the length of sentence (until completion of probation, parole, and incarceration); and (4) disenfranchisement after completion of sentence (ex-felons). We examined changes within state disenfranchisement laws and considered a new law to be a more restrictive change if it disenfranchised a new category of felons.[78] (The exact timing of these changes in each state is shown in appendix table A2.1.)

## Results

### Bivariate and Multivariate Statistical Analyses

We first examine state-level predictors of when a state adopts its first felon disenfranchisement law in simple bivariate models, which consider the impact of one factor at a time (see appendix table A2.4, middle column). We label these "bivariate" because they show the effects of one variable on another variable, passage of a strict felon voting law, without statistically controlling for anything other than time. The statistically significant predictors of felon disenfranchisement laws in these models are the racial composition of state prisons, southern and western regions (relative to the Northeast), the time since statehood, and the decades of the 1860s, 1870s, and 1880s (relative to the 1850s).[79]

Racial threat, as measured by the percentage of nonwhites in state prisons, is clearly associated with adoption of state felon disenfranchisement laws.[80] Regionally, relative to states in the Northeast, southern and western states were more likely to pass a felon disenfranchisement law. Perhaps surprisingly, we found little effect of political partisanship. States were most likely to adopt felon voting bans at the time of statehood or in the years immediately thereafter.[81] Finally, when time is modeled by decade (as dummy variables), we find that states were especially likely to adopt a first law in the late 1860s through the 1880s, during the post–Civil War and post-Reconstruction eras.[82]

We next introduced systematic controls to test whether some of these factors are in fact explained by others (and thus there is no underlying causal relationship). We do so by estimating a series of multivariate models that introduce variables corresponding to the alternative explanations for disenfranchisement laws discussed earlier (see the righthand column of appendix table A2.4, which shows the multivariate results for the final model, which statistically controls for the estimated effects for the presence of all other factors).

Although the bivariate results showed strong regional effects, these were diminished once we accounted for the effects of the racial composition of prisons and economic and political forces. Restrictive changes are less likely to occur during times of Democratic political control.[83] Finally, time since statehood remains a strong negative predictor in the full model, suggesting that the likelihood of states adopting felon disenfranchisement provisions declines precipitously with time. We should note that adding the indicator of time since statehood diminishes the effects of the individual decades, region, and recession (and inflates their standard errors) because of their mutual association. The key racial threat effect, by contrast, is somewhat larger in magnitude in models that also include a measure of time.

### Laws Disenfranchising Former Felons

We repeated our analyses to test the effects of the same independent variables on adoption of a state's first *ex-felon* disenfranchisement law, the most severe ballot restriction. We again found a positive and significant effect of the nonwhite prison population.[84] Taken together, these analyses show a strong and consistent relationship between racial threat, as measured by the percentage of nonwhite state prisoners, and laws restricting the voting rights of people with a felony conviction. States in the Midwest, South, and West are also more likely to pass ex-felon disenfranchisement laws than states in the Northeast. The effect of the South, however, again diminishes when controlling for the nonwhite prison population, indicating that race is particularly important in the South.

### Are There Differences across Historical Periods?

Our results thus far have considered the effects of selected racial threat indicators and other characteristics measured over a long undifferentiated historical period. How robust are they? In particular, what happens if we allow those effects to vary across historical periods? Because states had unchecked power to restrict suffrage before the Fourteenth and Fifteenth amendments, many nonwhite citizens were disenfranchised throughout most of the nineteenth century, regardless of whether they had a felony conviction in their past.[85] We therefore expect the effects of racial threat on felon disenfranchisement to *increase* after adoption of the Fifteenth Amendment in 1870, which prohibited states from denying suffrage based on race.[86] We explored this possibility by allowing the effects of racial threat to vary across historical periods (see appendix table A2.5, which uses 1870 as a historical cut-point to consider the influence of several indicators of racial threat across these periods, including the nonwhite population, the nonwhite male population, the nonwhite prison population, and the idle white male population).

Our primary interest is in comparing the pre-1870 period in panel A with the 1870–2002 period (see appendix table A2.5). For each period we identified the predictors that had a significant effect on passage of a first felon disenfranchisement law. All models controlled for decade, region, gubernatorial partisanship, idle white males, population, incarceration rate, and time since statehood. In the earlier period, only the nonwhite prison population is a significant predictor of passage of a felon disenfranchisement law. As expected, however, each racial threat predictor becomes much stronger (in magnitude as well as statistical significance) after passage of the Fifteenth Amendment. The nonwhite population, the nonwhite male population, and the nonwhite prison population are all significant positive predictors of passing a felon disenfranchisement law after 1870.

As expected, racial threat has more pronounced and consistent effects in the post-1870 period. That the nonwhite prison population remains a strong predictor in the earlier period is perhaps not surprising in models predicting *felon* disenfranchisement, because the racial composition of state prisons likely represents the most proximal measure of racial threat. Racial challenges to political power were much more visible during and after Reconstruction, but it is important to note that they predated 1870. Recall that several states allowed nonwhites to vote before the constitutional amendments of the Reconstruction era. When Rhode Island passed its first felon disenfranchisement law, for example, it had no race requirement for voting. Similarly, Indiana and Texas excluded African Americans from voting but not other nonwhites. While an 1870 cut-point seems justified based on the historical record, racial threat was also likely to be salient in the 1868–70 period between adoption of the Fourteenth and Fifteenth Amendments. During this time, six states adopted their first felon disenfranchisement law.

## Conclusion

When African Americans make up a larger proportion of a state's prison population, that state is significantly more likely to adopt or extend felon disenfranchisement. To be sure, many states adopted an initial felon disenfranchisement measure after property and other restrictions on lower-class white men were lifted (and before blacks could vote). Individual state histories may be more complex than our race thesis implies. But the overall evidence we have presented supports a strong conclusion about the political significance of race in driving the adoption of felon disenfranchisement laws.

This finding, along with other evidence presented in this chapter, clearly fits the broader patterning of race and voting rights in America. The right to vote for African Americans has moved in waves throughout the course of U.S. history.[87] Free blacks were often permitted to vote in the early years of the new republic, even in some of the slave states, until the states began taking explicit measures to block them from voting in the early nineteenth century. By the onset of the Civil War, only a handful of states (all with small black populations) allowed African Americans to vote.

Following the war, the adoption of the Fourteenth and Fifteenth amendments established formal racial equality in terms of access to the ballot box. The spirit of these amendments was simultaneously undermined in various ways across the country. In the South, methods included the implementation of grandfather clauses, poll taxes, and literacy tests. These devices were coupled with aggressive gerrymandering to ensure that even African Americans who managed to vote did so in legislative districts where they did not constitute a majority of the electorate. In the North, blatant discrimination was less overt, but states periodically employed subtle means to hinder participation by African Americans and newer immigrant groups, most notably through the institution of literacy tests and voter registration requirements. Throughout the country, felon disenfranchisement constituted another means through which the African American vote was restricted.

Felon disenfranchisement thus has to be viewed as one of the many side effects of the peculiar history of racial politics in the United States. In the abstract, felon disenfranchisement can be separated from race: state laws are literally race neutral, in that all who are convicted of felonies are subject to the same sanction. Moreover, modern defenders of the practice certainly draw upon nonracial reasons for their position, and we do not intend by this analysis to imply anything to the contrary. This does not, however, mean that there is no connection between race and felon disenfranchisement. Indeed, when we ask the question of how we got to the point where American practice can be so out of line with the rest of the democratic world, the most plausible answer we can supply is that of race.

# 3 The Disenfranchised Population

In chapters 1 and 2, we endeavored to describe and analyze the origins of modern felon disenfranchisement laws, as well as highlight the peculiarities of the American case. It is time now to ask who these disenfranchised citizens are. How many are there? How and when are their rights restricted? When are they restored? And do the laws have a disproportionate racial impact today?

## What Is a Felony Conviction?

The term "felon" is derived from the legal classification of crimes. "Felony" is a generic term, historically used to distinguish certain "high crimes" or "grave offenses" such as homicide from less serious offenses known as misdemeanors.[1] In early English law, the distinction was tied to forfeiture, with a felon forfeiting "life and member and all that he had" while a misdemeanant could retain citizenship and property rights.[2] In the contem-

porary United States, felonies are considered crimes punishable by incarceration of more than one year in state or federal prison, and misdemeanors
are considered crimes punishable by local jail sentences, fines, or both.
While some felons go to prison, however, many others serve time in jail
or on probation in their communities. Misdemeanants generally do not
formally lose the right to vote, although a recent canvass of state practices
finds that at least some states disenfranchise misdemeanants as well.[3] It is
also important to note that most states have made little provision for those
incarcerated on Election Day to vote from jail.

What types of crimes result in a felony conviction? In 2002, U.S. state
and federal courts convicted over 1.1 million adults of felonies.[4] Figure 3.1
provides a breakdown of those convictions that occurred in state courts
that year (approximately 90 percent of convictions are in state courts).
Drug offenses make up almost one-third of the total. The next most common offenses are the property crimes of larceny-theft, burglary, and fraud,
each of which accounts for more than 9 percent of all felony convictions.
Finally, violent offenses make up about one in five felony convictions, with
aggravated assaults accounting for about half of all violent crimes. In many
cases, the latter are simply fights that get out of hand. The crimes of greatest

**Figure 3.1.**
Felony convictions in state courts, 2002. Source: *Felony Sentences in State Courts, 2002* (Washington, D.C.: Government Printing Office, 2004).

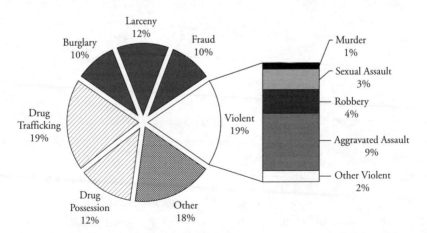

public concern—murder, rape, and robbery—together made up just 8 percent of all felony convictions.

In 2002, about 41 percent of felons were sentenced to prison, and 28 percent were sentenced to serve time in a local jail, typically for a period of less than one year. The remaining 31 percent were sentenced to "straight probation" without any jail or prison time required. Regardless of the type of sentence, all felonies result in the loss of voting rights in almost every state. In many states, even nonincarcerated offenders—who live in their communities and are expected to abide by the laws made by the government—lose voting rights. As we noted in chapter 1, this practice represents one of the critical differences between the United States and the rest of the world.

All categories of correctional populations—prisoners, jail inmates, parolees, probationers—have grown at astounding rates in recent years. United States prisons and jails now house over 2 million inmates, an overall incarceration rate of 714 per 100,000 people.[5] By comparison, in 1972 fewer than 200,000 Americans were imprisoned, and the prison incarceration rate was only 94 per 100,000. The number of probationers and parolees has grown rapidly as well. As of 1976, there were only 455,000 felony probationers and 161,000 parolees, compared to over 2 million felony probationers and 775,000 parolees in 2003.[6]

These increases are unprecedented. Yet their full impact is further magnified because the felon population is not drawn at random from the entire U.S. population. Rather, it is highly concentrated among some subgroups. Young African American men are vastly more likely to be incarcerated than any other group. According to the Bureau of Justice Statistics, if current incarceration rates remain unchanged, about 32 percent of African American men and 17 percent of Latino men will go to prison during their lifetimes, compared to less than 6 percent of white men.[7] Sociologists Bruce Western and Becky Pettit have shown that the cohort of African American men born from 1965 to 1969 are more likely to have prison records (22 percent) than either military records (17 percent) or bachelor's degrees (13 percent).[8]

## The Felon Population: A First Look

The Department of Justice has conducted a large-scale, nationally representative survey of state prison inmates at approximately five-year intervals since 1974. These inmate surveys afford a unique demographic portrait of the convicted felon population and its changes over time. (It is important to keep in mind that this is a survey of *inmates*, who are younger and more disadvantaged than the entire felon and ex-felon population.) The surveys show that men and racial minorities are vastly overrepresented in the prison population relative to the general population. By the late 1990s, approximately 94 percent of all prison inmates, 90 percent of parolees, and 79 percent of probationers were males. African Americans make up almost half of the prison and parole populations and almost one-third of the felony probation population, as compared with 12 percent of the general population and 13 percent of the population aged 25–34 (see appendix table A3.1 for more detailed information).

The rate and absolute number of offenders entering prison on the one hand, and ex-inmates leaving prison on the other, has changed dramatically over this period. In 2003, over 600,000 individuals departed from America's state prisons, up from approximately 400,000 in 1990.[9] Another important change is the most serious offense for which prison inmates have been convicted. Drug offenders have increased dramatically from about 10 percent of all state prison inmates to over 26 percent. Property offenders have declined from 33 percent to 14 percent, and violent offenders have declined from 53 percent to 46 percent (and here, the increase in the amount of time served for violent offenders is an important factor preventing a further decline in the violent offender share).

The average age of prison entry has risen steadily over this period, with prisoners now averaging over 30 years of age at the time of admission. Despite their advancing age, however, prisoners remain seriously disadvantaged relative to the general population. They have low levels of education: fewer than one-third had received a high school diploma. Full-time employment levels—at the time of conviction—have declined gradually since 1974, although a majority (56 percent) still held a full-time job prior to their most recent arrest in 1997. By comparison, over three-fourths of males of comparable age in the general population held full-time jobs, and 87 percent had attained a high school degree. Nevertheless, far more prison inmates are employed at the time of their conviction than is commonly assumed.

The percentage of married inmates has declined over time, from 24 percent in 1974 to 18 percent in 1997. The comparable figure in the general population is 53 percent for males in this age range. Despite low rates of marriage, most inmates are parents: 56 percent reported having one or more children in the most recent survey. Although trends such as declining rates of marriage and nonmarital births mirror shifts in the larger society, the characteristics of the inmate population have remained relatively stable over the past 25 years. Prison and jail inmates lag the farthest behind their contemporaries in the general population, while probationers and parolees are somewhat better off socioeconomically. All, however, face challenges in rebuilding their lives after they have served their sentences.

## Growth of the Disenfranchised Population

The rise of mass incarceration and mass conviction provides a critical backdrop to understanding the growth in felon disenfranchisement. As correctional populations have risen since the 1970s, so, too, has the number of felons who have lost the right to vote. Estimating the size of the disenfranchised felon population is not a simple task. Both state laws and the affected population change over time. The first available estimates of the disenfranchised felon population were developed in the late 1990s by the Sentencing Project, a policy research and advocacy organization based in Washington, D.C. Their figures provided a useful and widely publicized baseline estimate. But more reliable numbers require application of demographic techniques to criminal justice data. In particular, it is essential to adjust estimates for recidivism (to avoid double-counting) and mortality (to take into account that some disenfranchised felons die).[10]

Our first investigation, making such adjustments, found that there were 4.7 million disenfranchised felons at the time of the 2000 election. That estimate has been repeated many times in news reports and by other commentators, but enough time has passed that that figure is now significantly out of date.[11]

The starting point for our new estimates—as with our estimate of the disenfranchised felon population at the time of the 2000 presidential election—is the differing state laws. To establish which correctional populations to count among the disenfranchised population, we carefully examined the elector qualifications and consequences of a felony conviction as specified in state constitutions and statutes, and we referenced secondary sources detailing the voting rights of offenders.[12] Current state-by-state restrictions are shown in figure 3.2 (further details are available in appendix table A3.2).

Only two states, Maine and Vermont, currently allow all felons to vote, including those serving time in prison. At the other extreme, 13 states bar ex-felons from voting for life, unless their rights are restored. Between these most and least restrictive ends of the continuum, a variety of intermediate policies exist. Some states, such as Arizona and Maryland, disenfranchise only recidivists (those with multiple felony convictions) after completion of the sentence. Delaware and Nebraska (as of 2005) impose waiting periods, of five years and two years, respectively. Washington and Tennessee no longer disenfranchise ex-felons but continue to restrict the voting rights

**Figure 3.2.**
Felon disenfranchisement restrictions by state, 2004.

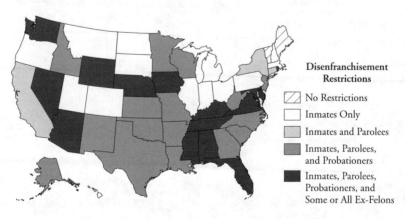

of those convicted prior to a series of legal changes beginning in the mid-1980s. Our calculations of the number of persons disenfranchised in a given state in a given year must therefore account for each of these administrative complexities.

To establish the number of disenfranchised felons currently under supervision, we added up current prisoners, parolees, felony probationers, and convicted felons serving jail sentences.[13] We estimate that on December 31, 2004, 3.2 million felons currently under supervision were legally disenfranchised, or slightly less than half of the 6.9 million adults under correctional supervision.[14] For most states, this calculation involves a rather straightforward accounting of the current correctional (i.e., prison, parole, and felony probation) populations.[15] These "head counts" are based on excellent data. Estimating the number of disenfranchised ex-felons not currently under supervision, however, is a much greater challenge. Existing estimates vary with the assumptions made by researchers. The first available estimate, for example, of the Sentencing Project in 1998, was based on national felony conviction data and state-level reports of criminal offenses between 1970 and 1995.[16] The use of such procedures makes somewhat untenable assumptions about the stability and uniformity of felon populations across space and time (such as applying national information on racial composition and criminal convictions to individual states). Moreover, it does not account for deceased felons, nor does it consider those convicted before 1970 or after 1995. These factors are particularly important for estimating the size of the ex-felon population in those states disenfranchising for life.

Given these limitations, we set out to develop an alternative estimate based on exits from (rather than entry into) correctional supervision. We made a number of simplifying assumptions to obtain our estimates, but in each case used *conservative* assumptions to reduce the risk of exaggerating or overstating the disenfranchised population.[17] First, our estimates assume an average prisoner and parolee reincarceration rate of 18.6 percent at one year, 32.8 percent at two years, and 41.4 percent at three years after release. For probationers and jail inmates, the corresponding three-year failure rate is 36 percent. To extend the analysis to subsequent years, we computed a trend line based on the ratio of increases in a study of federal prisoners. By year 10, we estimate a 59.4 percent recidivism rate among former prisoners and parolees, which increases to 65.9 percent by year 56 (the maximum duration in the analysis). Because these rates exceed those of most long-term recidivism studies, they yield conservative estimates of the disenfranchised ex-felon voting base. Second, we calculate mortality based on the expected number of deaths for African American males (the group with the highest mortality rates) at the median age of release for each state, multiplied by a constant factor of 1.46 to match the high death rates observed in the Justice Department's recidivism study.[18] Again, because African American males are less than half of the disenfranchised population, we have imposed very conservative assumptions.

In addition to adjusting for recidivism and mortality, these ex-felon estimates also account for the fact that some states restore the civil rights of many releasees or only disenfranchise certain ex-felons. Florida, for example, has restored voting rights to over 160,000 disenfranchised felons since the 1960s and does not impose felony adjudication for some probationers who successfully complete their sentences. Although state disenfranchisement rules have grown increasingly complex in recent years, we have attempted to take each legal development into account in estimating the disenfranchised population in each state.[19]

### Disenfranchised Felons in 2004

With these background points in mind, we can now turn to the bottom line. Overall, we estimate that there were 5.3 million disenfranchised felons on Election Day in November 2004. This represents about 2.5 percent of the voting age population, and 2.7 percent of the "voting eligible" population.[20] Considering the approximately 600,000 jail inmates and pretrial detainees who were practically, if not legally, disenfranchised on Election Day, almost 6 million Americans were prevented from voting in the 2004 election because of a criminal conviction.

The estimates are unadjusted in two important ways. We have not taken into account the possibility that some legally disenfranchised voters will nonetheless manage to vote. Some commentators have asserted that illegal voting among felons is common.[21] However, while some ineligible current or former felons have voted, the best national evidence from around the country suggests that the numbers are very small, even when considerable efforts are undertaken in closely fought elections to identify improper votes. We also have not taken into account *eligible* former offenders who would like to vote but do not realize they are able to do so. There is troubling evidence that many eligible individuals with criminal records do not understand—or have been misinformed by criminal justice or voting officials—about their political rights. In chapter 8, we will review some of that evidence more carefully, but it is clear that far more individuals do not vote who could than do so but should not. The figure of 5.3 million disenfranchised felons in 2004 thus should be taken as a conservative estimate of the full size of the effectively disenfranchised population.

The distribution of the legally disenfranchised population by correctional status is striking. As figure 3.3 shows, only a little more than one-fourth of the estimated 5.3 million disenfranchised felons were actually incarcerated in prison or jail. The rest were either living in their communities as felony probationers (25 percent), parolees (9 percent), or *former* felons (39 percent).

How have these numbers changed in recent years? Although the total number of disenfranchised declined from 1.8 million in 1960 to 1.2 million in 1976, due in large part to the democratizing changes of the civil rights era, the number began growing thereafter, reaching 5.3 million by 2004 (see fig. 3.4).

**Figure 3.3.**
Disenfranchised felons by supervisory status (estimated total = 5,259,530).

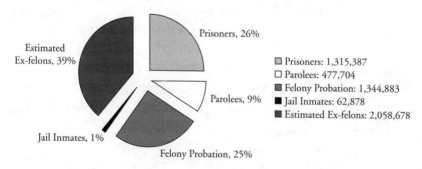

Prisoners, 26%

Estimated
Ex-felons, 39%

Parolees, 9%

Jail Inmates, 1%

Felony Probation, 25%

☐ Prisoners: 1,315,387
☐ Parolees: 477,704
■ Felony Probation: 1,344,883
■ Jail Inmates: 62,878
■ Estimated Ex-felons: 2,058,678

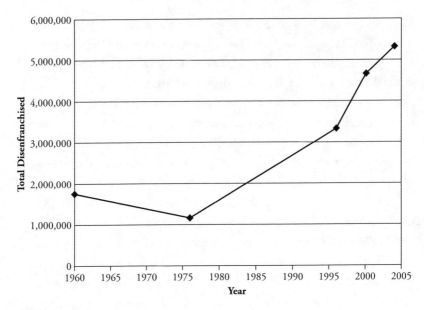

**Figure 3.4.**
Historical changes in felon disenfranchisement, 1960–2004.

The distribution of disenfranchised felons and ex-felons across the states is shown in appendix table A3.3. As one might expect, states that disenfranchise more categories of felons show the greatest rate and number of disenfranchised citizens. Florida is the clear leader in the number of disenfranchised, with an astounding 1.1 million—almost 10 percent of its voting age population. In states that disenfranchise prisoners alone, such as Illinois, Ohio, and Oregon, voting restrictions affect about one-half of 1 percent of the voting age population. Among states that disenfranchise parolees as well, such as California, Connecticut, and New York, approximately 1 percent of adults are barred from the ballot. For states that additionally impose franchise restrictions on probationers, such as Arkansas, Minnesota, and Wisconsin, about 1 to 3 percent of the voting age population is affected. The laws have the greatest impact, however, in states that restrict voting rights indefinitely, such as Alabama, Kentucky, and Virginia, where over 5 percent of adults are prohibited from voting.

Our earlier discussion of the passage of felon voting restrictions highlighted their racial origins in many states. Because African Americans are far more likely to be subject to criminal punishment than are other groups, such laws continue to have a vast racial impact as well. Today, felon disenfranchisement affects a far greater proportion of the African American electorate than of any other group. The small African American base population in states such as Iowa (whose governor granted clemency to ex-felons by executive order in 2005), Rhode Island, and Wyoming leads to volatility in estimating the percentage of the voting age population that is disenfranchised. Moreover, we must caution that in states that disenfranchise ex-felons we cannot be certain that mobility across states has not affected the estimated disenfranchisement rate.[22] Nevertheless, it is noteworthy that in 14 states, more than 1 in 10 African Americans have lost the right to vote by virtue of a felony conviction, and 5 of these states disqualify over 20 percent of the African American voting age population. (State estimates for African American disenfranchisement are shown in appendix table A3.4.)

**Figure 3.5.**
Total felon disenfranchisement as percentage of voting age population by state, 2004.

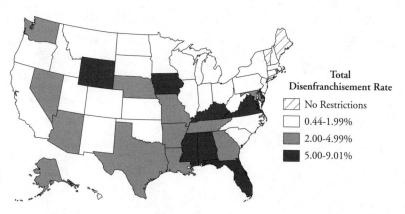

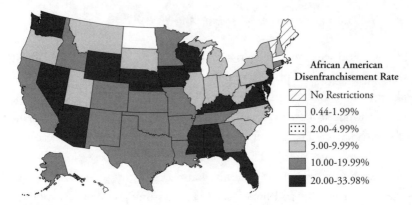

**Figure 3.6.**
African American felon disenfranchisement as percentage of African American voting age population by state, 2004.

The contrast between the total disenfranchisement rate and the African American rate can best be appreciated by comparing figures 3.5 and 3.6. These maps show (by the gradient of shading) the estimated extent of disenfranchisement. Figure 3.5 shows the total disenfranchisement rate. Only a few states, primarily clustered in the South, have a disenfranchisement rate of over 5 percent. Figure 3.6, by contrast, shows that almost the entire nation has an African American disenfranchisement rate of 5 percent or higher. The extensive darker regions exceed 10 percent and, in some cases, 20 percent.

The specific impact on African American men is even greater. As noted earlier, the vast majority of convicted felons are men (over 90 percent of prisoners and parolees and over 75 percent of felony probationers). One widely quoted statistic notes that at least one in seven black men nationally have lost the right to vote, and as many as one in four in those states with the highest African American disenfranchisement rate.[23] Such figures are especially startling, and troubling.

## The Ex-felon Problem

Clearly the size of the disenfranchised population is greatly increased by the fact that many states do not automatically restore voting rights upon completion of their sentences. Not surprisingly, opponents of felon disenfranchisement often call special attention to the case of these disenfranchised "ex-felons," 2 million strong in 2004. Even the hardiest supporters of disenfranchisement face an awkward dilemma when it comes to people who, by any other measure, have "paid their debt to society." Some commentators have argued that continuing or lifetime voting bans on ex-felons are justified for repeat offenders who continue to exhibit a lack of respect for the law, or because of the nature of their crimes (highlighting violent or sexual offenders). Few are willing to endorse blanket restrictions, however, particularly for those ex-felons convicted of relatively minor crimes.

Yet in some jurisdictions, many individuals do indeed lose the right to vote indefinitely following a felony conviction, even for relatively minor offenses or one-time occurrences. Faced with the dilemma of justifying such extreme punishments, those who favor it point to an existing remedy: the institutionalized system of clemency that allows individuals to seek restoration of their voting rights.

Through clemency, "deserving" former felons avoid civil death, at least in principle. The possibility of receiving clemency potentially provides an escape hatch for those who have reformed, or those who committed minor offenses for which a lifetime penalty seems to violate our sense of propriety and fairness. The availability of this remedy is sometimes invoked in defense of ex-felon restrictions. For example, in the February 2002 Senate debate over a measure to restore the voting rights of ex-felons in national elections, Senator George Allen (R-VA), the former governor of Virginia, suggested the following.

> Virginia is one of ten states [*sic*] that permanently prevent . . . ex-
> felons from voting. That does not mean their rights can never
> be restored. Their rights can be restored . . . many ex-felons did

get their rights back. There is the record of my successor, who restored the rights of 210 people during his 4-year term. That is less than half of what was restored during the previous three administrations. While I was Governor, I restored 459 ex-felons' right to vote. . . . The things most Governors would look at, regardless of party, are what kind of life has the ex-felon led since serving their time? I would consider whether or not they were involved in wholesome community-based activities, or just leading the life of a law-abiding citizen and not committing any crimes.

Later in the discussion, Allen had a friendly exchange with Senator Mitch McConnell (R-KY) over the restoration process:

> *Mr. McConnell:* Is it true that in every State there is an opportunity for someone who has served their time to get those rights restored?
>
> *Mr. Allen:* Correct . . .
>
> *Mr. McConnell:* There is a procedure, so it is not hopeless.
>
> *Mr. Allen:* Absolutely, there is a procedure.
>
> *Mr. McConnell:* It is not a hopeless situation.
>
> *Mr. Allen:* It is not a hopeless situation.[24]

But do existing clemency procedures really provide an alternative to the "hopeless situation" of disenfranchisement? Does clemency really provide, as senators Allen and McConnell implied, an appropriate alternative to automatic restoration? Or does it actually impose such a high burden on ex-felons that only a few are likely to seek restoration? Moreover, even for those who are able to navigate state procedures for seeking clemency, how many actually regain their rights?

We can answer those questions by examining state requirements for restoration in the ex-felon disenfranchisement states. But before doing so, it is important to put restoration via clemency in the context of the *other* barriers to participation that all voters in U.S. elections must navigate.

*The Existing Burdens of Voting*

Voting in the United States is not as easy as it is elsewhere. There are a variety of unusual institutional hurdles placed before American voters, and these have been shown to significantly depress turnout.[25] These hurdles include requiring voters to engage in the two-step process of first registering to vote before the election and then voting in elections that take place on working days (as opposed to weekends or national holidays). Voter registration requirements before elections reduce turnout, with the size of the estimated effect ranging from between 8 to 15 percent in most studies.[26] Requiring most citizens to register prior to elections is unique among post-industrial democratic countries. In most other countries, the national government takes responsibility for registering voters, and there is no distinction between citizens and registered voters.[27] For all of these reasons, voting is already more difficult in the United States than in other countries. Many voters, particularly members of disadvantaged groups, may be unable or unwilling to surmount these hurdles.[28] And in large part because these hurdles are so considerable, decades of legal rulings have nullified many state-level restrictions on the right to vote. The Supreme Court established that, consistent with the principle of universal suffrage, states cannot adopt laws that place unnecessary burdens on exercising the right to vote.[29]

Now consider felons who have been stripped of their voting rights. Adding the burden of a separate clemency procedure to these registration requirements places extraordinary demands on people who have done their time and are merely seeking to vote. As we describe in this section, the requirements for obtaining clemency extend far beyond those ordinary voter registration requirements that all voters must surmount. Moreover, this additional step is subject to a far greater level of governmental discretion than simple voter registration. It creates a *three-step* process to vote for ex-offenders who do not automatically regain their rights: restoration, registration, voting.

The underlying presumption of the Supreme Court decisions loosening restrictions on voting is that high barriers reduce political participation. The logic is impeccable, and indeed a small army of rational choice theories of low voter turnout have stressed a cost-benefit analysis in which it is rational to "free ride" and not vote. Requiring ex-felons to navigate a formal process for restoring their voting rights imposes high additional costs of participation upon them. And in extreme cases, ex-offenders must first pay outstanding court costs, restitution, and other penalties before they are even permitted to apply to have their voting rights restored.[30]

### State Procedures for Restoring Voting Rights

As proponents of ex-felon disenfranchisement have pointed out, each state disqualifying ex-offenders after the completion of the sentence has developed a process for restoring the right to vote. It is for this reason that they object to characterizing these voting restrictions as "permanent" or lifetime bans.

We conducted a state-by-state canvass of clemency procedures to understand how they work. The process was daunting. Calling state clemency offices, we were often transferred from one administrative office to another, or confronted with two official documents that seemed to make contradictory statements about just who is eligible for clemency and what the appropriate procedures are for application.[31] Not surprisingly, ex-felons also find the process confusing, especially those who have moved from one state to another since their original conviction or whose conviction occurred prior to a significant legal or administrative change in state procedures. In fact, we continue to get calls and email correspondence from former felons who routinely stump us with questions about their own voting status. Although a number of useful resources are emerging to explain the general requirements in each state, the rules governing reenfranchisement are complex enough to require individualized legal assistance in many cases.[32]

While each state has its own set of laws and rules relating to restoration of rights, some parallel features exist among most states that disenfranchise beyond completion of sentence. Who is eligible to seek restoration of voting rights, who makes the decision to restore these rights, and the information that is considered in this decision are all characteristics that are similar across states.[33]

The first factor that channels people out of automatic restoration of rights after they finish their sentences stems from criminal history. Several states make distinctions between first-time offenders and recidivists, and between people convicted of violent versus nonviolent crimes. In Arizona, for example, first offenders regain voting rights as soon as they complete their sentences, as long as they have paid all financial obligations to the state. Nevada limits automatic restoration to first-time, *nonviolent* offenders, so that anyone convicted of a violent felony must obtain a pardon.

For people who do not regain voting rights after finishing all correctional supervision, states next draw lines based on *when* rights can be restored. In Delaware, people can either apply for a pardon or wait five years, at which time their voting rights will be restored automatically. Those convicted of murder, manslaughter, sex offenses, or offenses against public administration, however, can regain rights only through a pardon. Maryland restores rights to first-time offenders upon completion of their sentences and to nonviolent recidivists three years after completion of sentence, while all others must apply for a pardon. In Arizona, recidivists whose sentences include prison time must wait two years after being released (unconditionally from prison or conditionally from parole) to *apply* for restoration of rights. Wyoming began restoring voting rights to first–time nonviolent offenders after a five-year waiting period in 2003. Repeat offenders and violent felons in Wyoming, however, must continue to seek a pardon from the governor.

In spite of the exchange between senators Allen and McConnell, Virginia has historically been very sparing in reenfranchising its citizens convicted of felonies. Only 238 applications were granted from 1998 to 2002.[34] After a flurry of changes in recent years, however, Virginia now routinely restores voting rights for increasing numbers of former felons. Alabama has also very recently streamlined its restoration process, restoring the rights of several thousand people in the process. In each of these states, the barriers to restoration have been eased, but not eliminated. All continue to require that former felons submit formal applications for restoration of voting rights.

Applicants for restoration must typically appeal to a formal board that can restore the right to vote (often titled a "Board of Pardons," "Board of Parole," or "Board of Executive Clemency") or directly to the state governor. In Mississippi, the state legislature can also restore individual voting rights, if a legislator introduces a bill on a person's behalf and it passes by a two-thirds majority. A few states, such as Nevada and Arizona, also allow a court to formally restore the right. Most states require the person seeking rights to initiate the application process.[35] Several states, such as Virginia and Florida, provide "short forms" and "long forms," for persons eligible (or ineligible) for streamlined restoration procedures.

Regardless of how the restoration process is initiated, states generally seek the same type of information. Often this information extends far beyond one's criminal record. Initial applications for restoration may appear simple at first, but the information they require, or the follow-up information demanded during the state's subsequent investigation, can be quite intrusive. First, those applying for restoration must often obtain certified copies of all documents relating to any criminal offenses and notify the board of any other encounters with law enforcement (including arrests and traffic offenses). Other inquiries include questions about applicants' home lives, their job statuses and employment histories, and any child support obligations. Further, some states require written references on the applicant's behalf. The idea of asking such questions of the general public when they register to vote is unimaginable.

Some states have even more burdensome requirements. In Delaware, those who seek a pardon must also submit a current psychological or psychiatric evaluation. While this obligation is limited to those convicted of certain offenses, a surprising range of crimes triggers the requirement.[36] Even more intrusively, some felons convicted in Alabama were required, until very recently, to submit a DNA sample as a mandatory condition of the pardon.

Upon receiving an application, state officials typically investigate the person applying for rights. Beyond any questions directly asked, applicants typically must sign a general catchall release form authorizing the state to obtain any relevant records (including medical) and to interview anyone who knows the applicant (including neighbors and employers). Iowa, for example, permits its Board of Parole to conduct any investigation it deems "is appropriate."[37] There is little privacy for people wishing to keep their past in the past. Further, most states notify many others that an individual is seeking restoration of civil rights, including the victim or the victim's family and officials from the jurisdiction where the conviction occurred. These parties may then voice their concerns about whether the applicant's voting rights should be restored.

After the initial investigation, states generally conduct a hearing in which the applicant may speak before the board. Hearings are typically held in the capital city, often requiring lengthy travel for those who wish to attend their own hearing. States vary as to the frequency of hearings; some hold them monthly, and others, such as Florida, hold them quarterly. In Florida, some former felons now qualify for an automated restoration procedure that does not require a hearing, but those who have committed any of more than 200 disqualifying offenses are not eligible for this streamlined process. Moreover, if any two members of the Board of Executive Clemency object to restoration without a hearing, the applicant can regain rights *only* after a formal hearing.

What goes on in one of these hearings? *New York Times* reporter Abby Goodnough attended one of the hearings in Florida (on March 18, 2004) and filed the following dispatch.

> Gov. Jeb Bush looked out over a roomful of felons appealing to him for something they had lost, and tried to reassure them. "Don't be nervous; we're not mean people," the governor said as some fidgeted, prayed, hushed children or polished their hand-written statements. "You can just speak from the heart." And they did: convicted robbers, drunken drivers, drug traffickers and others, all finished with their sentences, standing up one by one in a basement room at the State Capitol and asking Mr. Bush to restore their civil rights. Their files before him, Mr. Bush asked one man about his drinking, another about his temper, and so on. Four mornings a year, this unusual scene unfolds in front of the governor and his cabinet, as they review the requests of some of the thousands of felons whom Florida has stripped of their right to vote, serve on a jury, and hold public office. . . . The clemency board, which consists of the governor and his three cabinet members, has files on each applicant. The State Parole commission recommends before their hearings

whether to accept their applications, based partly on investigations that might include interviews with employers, neighbors, and victims. But the board does not always follow the recommendations. "How's the anger situation going?" Mr. Bush asked one man after leafing through his file on the most recent hearing day, March 18, when the clemency board considered 57 voting rights cases. "You've stayed clean?" the governor asked another. Over the course of that morning, board members seemed especially interested to know whether former alcohol and drug abusers were now sober. They had little patience for multiple traffic violations, domestic violence records, and blame passing. They rejected the application of a man convicted of killing a pregnant woman while driving drunk in 1989 (her mother was there, tearfully saying that he had never apologized) and a man convicted of a lewd act against a child in 1993. They restored the rights of a former drug addict who now helps AIDS patients and a convicted drug trafficker who said he wanted to make his young daughter proud by voting. In all, the board restored the rights of 23 felons, rejected the applications of 30, and delayed decisions on 4.[38]

The final decision as to restoration of rights is usually vested in the board, but in some states the board only makes a recommendation to the governor, who is free to disregard it. One of the greater mysteries of restoration is the basis for decisions to grant or deny requests. Some states do not require any sort of rationale for the decision, and others require a written reason for a decision to restore rights with no corresponding obligation for denials.[39] For applicants who are denied restoration, many states require a further waiting period before they are permitted to reapply.

As this brief survey suggests, states have clearly devoted a fair amount of attention to developing elaborate restoration procedures. How many people actually emerge from these procedures with the right to vote? A 2005 report by Marc Mauer and Tushar Kansal of the Sentencing Project, estimating the number regaining their voting rights in recent years, suggests that in most states relatively few ex-felons have benefited (see appendix table A3.5 for details). Although the states did not provide consistent information spanning the same period, and some caution should be used in interpreting these numbers, examining this data closely suggests just how little overall restoration has occurred in recent years. Florida has restored the voting rights of approximately 48,000 over the past few years, but this represents only about 5 percent of the total disenfranchised population in that state. When considered as a percentage of the felons released from supervision over the period, the "reenfranchisement rate" varies dramatically, from less than one-tenth of 1 percent in Wyoming and Mississippi to a high of about 17 percent in Delaware.[40] In light of the large numbers of people disenfranchised in states requiring formal restoration, clemency processes simply do not appear to provide a viable remedy for most ex-felons. Compared to the overall disenfranchised population of ex-felons in these states, the number regaining voting rights is very small.

Some might interpret the fact that few ex-felons even *apply* for clemency as evidence that they have little interest in voting. While it seems reasonable to believe that applicants may have more intense political interest than do nonapplicants, we must again place these results in the context of political participation more generally. Whenever any group of citizens must overcome a set of burdensome, confusing, or invasive prerequisites, their participation rates are likely to decline. All of the same reasons why voter registration keeps people from participating apply with much greater force to the even more burdensome requirements of seeking restoration.

### Other Persisting Problems in Ex-felon Restoration Procedures

In addition to the substantive difficulties in regaining voting rights, the process is beset by other problems. Many state officials are poorly informed about who can vote, and even those whose rights have been restored have been placed on erroneous purge lists. There is ample evidence of confusion, and even contradictory laws or administrative practices.[41] In the recent controversy over the 2004 gubernatorial election in Washington, for example, some of the ineligible ex-felons identified in a lawsuit brought by the losing Republican candidate had in fact successfully had their rights restored, but the appropriate documentation was not placed in their file. Others who should have had their rights automatically restored were listed as ineligible. Administrative responsibility for establishing eligibility sits uneasily between the Department of Corrections and county election officials.[42]

Second, states are not well equipped to keep pace with those seeking restoration of their voting rights. As we discuss in the next section, Florida is among the most notorious in this respect, with a backlog of applications estimated to be in the tens of thousands. Even states striving to streamline the process still face problems. Alabama recently changed its law to permit certain people to bypass the pardon process and seek a certificate of eligibility to register to vote. While the investigation is supposed to be completed and a decision reached within 45 days, the state lacks adequate staff to process applications within that deadline.

Third, the secretive nature of some board decisions and the negative outcomes for those who are ultimately denied clemency leave many feeling dejected. Although applicants have moved on with their lives and past the offense that resulted in their conviction, state officials are adopting the role of what one state legislator terms "virtuecrats."[43] Despite fulfilling the requirements of their sentence, former felons have to prove their worthiness to vote. Governor Bush's quizzing of applicants about their drinking habits or anger management issues suggests criteria for voting eligibility that would be unthinkable if used as a general basis to decide who should be allowed to vote.

### Florida: A Case Study

Florida is "ground zero" for discussing ex-felon disenfranchisement. The Sunshine State has both the largest disenfranchised ex-felon population and the largest number whose civil rights have been restored by a Board of Executive Clemency. By year-end 2004, the size of Florida's disenfranchised population exceeded 1.1 million people, including about 957,000 who had completed their sentences.[44]

Florida has two tracks for regaining voting rights: restoration without a hearing, and restoration with a hearing. In the early 1990s, then governor

Lawton Chiles amended clemency rules to make it more difficult to regain rights without a hearing. Data from the State Department of Corrections show a significant decline in the number of successful restoration cases thereafter. By the end of the decade, however, many of these new rules had been relaxed. Yet when current governor Jeb Bush took office in 1999, many of the older rules were restored, and some 200 new crimes were added to the list of offenses requiring a full-blown hearing. Even cases not requiring a full administrative hearing may take a long time to resolve, and protracted administrative delays are normal. At present, it typically takes a year for the Florida Parole Commission to rule on whether an applicant is eligible for automatic restoration; if found ineligible, the case must go through the Clemency Board for a full hearing.[45] Parole examiners report being significantly understaffed, and one examiner told the *Miami Herald* that "we were always told this was a low priority."[46] Requests for the increased staffing necessary to handle the backlog have been rejected by the governor, and the Parole Commission estimates it is 20 staff members shy of the number needed.[47]

When a case requires a hearing, further long delays can be expected. As of the end of October 2004, over 4,000 people were awaiting a hearing, which the *Herald* noted was "triple the number heard by the board in all of the last 16 years."[48] Clemency officials also notify victims that the applicant is seeking to regain voting rights, providing opportunity for them to testify at the hearings.[49] While a majority of the cases heard by the board are eventually approved, many are denied, and the board is not required to provide any reasons for its decisions.

A recent *Herald* investigation reported that Governor Bush had quadrupled the number of disqualifying offenses that prevent restoration without a hearing. The newspaper concluded that from 2001 to 2003, the crime rule change alone disqualified nearly 27,000 people.[50] Further, 40 percent of the cases reaching the Clemency Board are for nonviolent offenses. The Sentencing Project has estimated that fewer than 15 percent of people released from prison are eligible for restoration without a hearing.[51]

In the face of a wave of lawsuits and negative publicity, the state has recently changed the rules to allow more people to qualify for restoration without a hearing, even offering an online application option for this group. Yet the changes still impose long waiting periods: people convicted of nonviolent crimes must be arrest free for five years and fulfill any restitution requirements; people convicted of violent crimes must be arrest free for 15 years and fulfill any restitution requirements.[52] Further, whether and how the state will speed up the certification process for automatic restoration and reduce the large backlog of cases remains unclear. The situation has gotten so bad that some senior Republicans are reported to favor a statewide vote on automatic ex-felon restoration.[53]

### Race, Class, and Restoration in Florida

African Americans are not only disproportionately disenfranchised but are also less likely to have their voting rights restored, at least in the critical stqate of Florida. In Florida, of the 293,000 African Americans who are disenfranchised, about 205,000 of whom have completed their sentences. This means that about 19 percent of the African American voting-age population in Florida is disenfranchised because of a felony conviction, more than double the overall rate of disenfranchisement in the state. Charges of racial bias in the clemency process have been raised.[54] Close examination of these allegations provides a clearer picture of who applies for restoration of their rights and how factors such as race and class factor into the decision to restore these rights.

Who applies for restoration of rights in Florida? We explored this question by examining a random sample of 1,217 application case files.[55] Our investigation found that the typical applicant is a married white male in his forties who has a high school (or equivalent) education, and earns about $24,000 a year. Less than one-fourth have committed a violent crime. Compared to those convicted of felony-level crimes in Florida, African Americans, women, and younger people are significantly underrepresented among clemency applicants in the first place.

Voting rights are clearly important to clemency applicants in Florida, for (as we shall discuss in later chapters) many felons link political participation to their ability to be a fully participating member of their communities. Nevertheless, it is important to note that people have other reasons to apply for restoration of civil rights. In addition to voting rights, a felony conviction also removes the right to carry a firearm and to obtain many occupational licenses. People often seek restoration of each of these rights, but there appear to be race differences in the primary reasons for requesting clemency. We found that about 21 percent of African American applicants mentioned voting as their primary reason for seeking clemency, compared to 13 percent of non–African Americans. In contrast, only about 5 percent of African Americans mentioned regaining the right to carry a firearm in their application, whereas close to 18 percent of non–African Americans did so. Voting appears to be especially salient to African American applicants.

Most clemency seekers fail to regain the right to vote, but not necessarily because they are denied by the Clemency Board. In fact, most applications never get that far. Of all applications we analyzed, over 60 percent were returned as "ineligible." Money was the most common reason cited for returning the applications: anyone who owed outstanding court fees, restitution, or other pecuniary penalties was automatically ineligible for consideration. African American applicants were especially likely to be ineligible because they owed money to the state. As one might expect, the people most likely to be denied clemency are those with more serious criminal histories. Yet surprisingly few of the felons completing sentences for any category of crime will regain their rights. There are, however, even more troubling differences between those applications that are granted and those that are denied. African Americans are significantly less likely to have their rights restored, as are those of lower socioeconomic status, those who are not married, and those who do not own their homes. Further, people with a history of mental health treatment are less likely to regain their rights. Differences in criminal history account for some portion of these differences, but do not fully account for the race and class effects on restoration outcomes.

Overall, these details reveal clear racial disparities in the process of restoring voting rights to former felons in Florida. African Americans have been less likely to apply for clemency, more likely to have their applications returned as "ineligible" because they owe money to the state, and less likely to have their voting rights restored than whites. Even among the extremely disadvantaged pool of former felons seeking to vote, those with *relatively* greater income and opportunities appear to come out ahead.

Florida, like many ex-felon disenfranchisement states, is in a process of reassessing its policies and practices concerning restoration. It is possible that in the near future, many of these states will significantly ease their rules for those ex-felons seeking to regain the right to vote. In June 2001, Florida, for example, relaxed some of the rules that disqualified ex-felons owing outstanding court costs from applying for restoration.[56] These changes, made in response to a pending legal challenge, may reduce some blatant race-based disparities. We summarized some of the other changes made in states like Alabama and Virginia earlier. Whether these states will go further to make restoration automatic, however, remains to be seen.

## Conclusion

The overall size of the disenfranchised felon population has reached 5.3 million people—a potentially significant number of voters in a competitive two-party system. The size of this group reflects the disenfranchisement of not just current inmates—who in fact are only about one-quarter of the disenfranchised population—but also the disenfranchisement of nonincarcerated felons (out on parole, or sentenced to probation) and ex-felons.

Voting is supposed to be easy, not hard. Yet once we put the restoration process in the larger context of voting rights in the United States, it is clear that these procedures operate as a de facto institutional barrier to participation. If the status quo remains unchanged, many former felons will never regain their right to vote. Avenues to restoration are frequently narrow, dimly lit, and poorly traveled.

The challenges to regaining voting rights presented in this chapter are clear. But we have not yet addressed the question of how the disenfranchised felon population got so large in the first place. How has this population been growing, and why? The answers to these questions are the subject of the next chapter.

# 4 The Contemporary Disenfranchisement Regime

*We're becoming a big jail.*
—Roger, *54-year-old prisoner in Minnesota*

The numbers are shocking. The incarcerated population in the United States has grown sixfold over the past 30 years. Every six months, the Department of Justice issues a report on the number of inmates and felons in America's criminal justice system. For 30 years now, that number has been rising silently but steadily. To be sure, when a particularly big threshold is reached (1 million people in America's prisons and jails in 1989, or over 2 million in 2002), it may be duly reported in the media and become the subject of public commentary.[1] But the size of the felon population has been growing for so long now that mere numbers have lost the power to move us. After a while, they become numbing facts, yesterday's news, something that it is all too easy to take for granted. The news cycle moves on.

But behind the numbers lie two extraordinary puzzles. The first puzzle emerges when we look at comparative crime data. According to comparable national victimization surveys, the United States has crime rates that are close to the average of similar nations, with the exception of a relatively high rate of murder—a rare crime in any society. The second puzzle is that conviction rates have continued to rise while crime rates have fallen, in some cases drastically, since the early 1990s.[2] In 2002, state courts convicted over 1 million adults of felonies, an increase of more than 50 percent since 1988. While it is not at all clear that crime rates are any higher today than in the mid-1980s, there were twice as many felony convictions in the United States in 2002 as in 1986.[3]

Incarceration, once reserved for the most extreme violators, has now become a truly mass phenomenon. Scholarly books and articles now routinely talk about "mass incarceration" as a grand experiment in social policy.[4] Sometimes such rhetoric is overdone. But these commentators also have an undeniable point. We have estimated in other work that about 16 million Americans—over 7 percent of the adult population—have received a felony conviction at some point in their lives.[5] That group is bigger than the population of many midsized states or small countries.

There is nothing in these developments that is "natural": societies choose how much or how little to punish their citizens for criminal activity. There is no rulebook for how many people have to be given felony convictions, and no close connection to actual levels of criminal activity. In fact, there is a lot of variation in punishment rates in different times and places. Yet the United States today has conviction and incarceration rates that are vastly higher than those ever seen in any of the countries most similar to it (e.g., western Europe and Canada).[6]

When we turn to the closely related question of felon disenfranchisement, the relationship between changing criminal justice policy and political disenfranchisement is clear. In almost every case, felony convictions carry with them the loss of voting rights. Any attempt to understand the growth of disenfranchisement thus requires examining the rapid growth of criminal punishment. It is to that story that we now turn.


## A Closer Look at Crime Rates and Criminal Punishment

As figure 4.1 shows, U.S. incarceration rates were fairly stable for the first three-quarters of the twentieth century, except for a notable increase during the depression years of the late 1930s. The dominant view in this era was

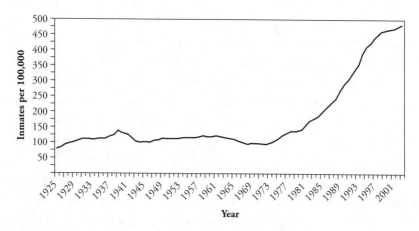

Figure 4.1.

United States prison incarceration rates per 100,000 population, 1925–2003. Source: *Prisoners in the United States* series (Washington, D.C.: U.S. Department of Justice) (see *Prisoners in 2001*, p. 5, for 2000 census adjustments).

that the rehabilitation of offenders was the primary goal of incarceration.[7] The jump in incarceration rates began in the early 1970s, but it took some time before the trend became clear. The peak rate of 137 per 100,000 in 1939, for example, was not surpassed until 1980. But since that time, rates have surged.

The first question to ask is whether rising incarceration is a reflection of rising crime rates. Criminologists generally rely upon two sources of data to understand trends in the crime rate: the FBI's *Uniform Crime Reports,* which detail offenses reported to the police, and the National Crime Victimization Survey, a representative survey of American households that captures unreported as well as reported crimes. When the two measures track one another closely, as they have for the past decade, criminologists have greater confidence about trends in the crime rate. When the two measures tell different stories about the crime rate, however, the victimization surveys provide a more reliable indicator, because the *Uniform Crime Reports* may confound changes in recordkeeping and policing with changes in the crime rate. As police forces have professionalized with the widespread use of computer technologies, they are simply much better at accurately recording crimes than before. But this often gives the appearance that crime has gone up. Victimization surveys, by contrast, are unaffected by any changes in police administration. They are based on a nationally representative sample of households, in which individuals directly report whether they have been the victims of different types of crime in the past year.

To dissect the trends reflected in these data sources, let's start with violent crimes. Americans generally express greater concern with violent offenses than with property, drug, or other types of crime, and for good reason. An increase in violent crime would be cause for concern, even if other types of crime were falling. Figure 4.2 reports trends in rates of serious violent crime—murder, rape, aggravated assault, and robbery—using both data sources during the period of rapid growth in incarceration. The graph shows an increase in the rate of violent offenses reported to the police from 1973 to 1991, but a steady decline thereafter. The more reliable violent victimization data, however, show no consistent pattern in the 1970s and 1980s. The survey suggests a rate of somewhere between 4,000 and 5,000 violent crimes per 100,000 people, before beginning a precipitous decline in 1994. By 2003, the violent victimization rate had reached the lowest level ever recorded.

**Figure 4.2.**
Rate of violent offenses reported and violent victimization, 1973–2003. Source: *Crime in the United States* series (Washington, D.C.: Government Printing Office); *Criminal Victimization* series (Washington, D.C.: Government Printing Office).

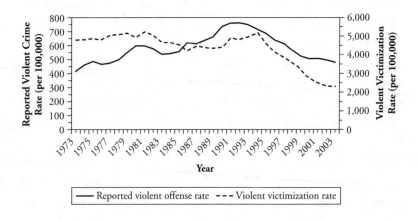

Rates of violent crime thus cannot account for large increases in incarceration. First of all, violent crime rates did not increase exponentially after 1972. There was a well-documented rise in the murder rate in the 1980s, but that increase was small relative to the sharp drop of the 1990s. Homicide is generally among the most well-reported crimes and certainly the crime of greatest concern. Yet the murder rate was actually far lower at the end of the mass incarceration era than it was at the beginning of this period. Second, as discussed earlier, most people are not in prison for violent offenses, although the average sentence for violent offenders has increased in length. Third, most people caught committing serious violent offenses have always been incarcerated and punished, as much in 1972 as today. This is an important point worth reflecting upon. Conviction for serious violent crimes has, with few exceptions, meant a prison sentence since the advent of the modern criminal justice system. Violent offenders continue to be incarcerated, although today we also imprison a much larger number of nonviolent offenders.

Figure 4.3 shows that violent crimes are not the only ones in decline. Property crime victimization, as measured by burglary, theft, and motor

**Figure 4.3.**
Rate of property offenses reported and property victimization, 1973–2003. Source: *Crime in the United States* series (Washington, D.C.: Government Printing Office); *Criminal Victimization* series (Washington, D.C.: Government Printing Office).

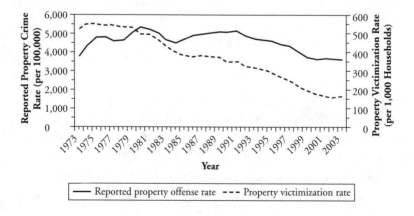

vehicle theft, has also been declining steadily throughout almost the entire mass incarceration era, from a high of over 550 victimizations per 1,000 households in 1974 to a low of 163 per 1,000 in 2003. It is therefore clear overall that crime rates have trended *downward*, rather than upward, in the United States during the past 30 years.

### If Not Crime Rates, Then What?

How can a declining number of crimes produce a rising population of convicted criminals? The likelihood of an arrest leading to a conviction is increasing for most offenses. Surprisingly, neither the percentage of people convicted who are sentenced to prison nor the average sentence length has increased much over these years. But the likelihood that an arrest will lead to a conviction has increased significantly, and convicted felons are now serving a significantly greater *portion* of their sentences prior to release. This pattern is drawn into sharper relief if we view the trends in punishment for a specific offense. In drug trafficking, for example, the "conviction rate," or probability that a felony arrest would lead to a conviction, increased from 52 percent in 1994 to 80 percent in 2002. Those convicted of drug trafficking in 1994 could have expected to serve about 32 percent of a 66-month sentence, or one year and nine months. In 2002, however, those convicted of the same offense could expect to serve about 45 percent of a 55-month sentence, or two years. Considering that there were over 266,000 arrests for drug trafficking in 2002 alone, even a very slight change in the probability of conviction or the proportion of time served can have a dramatic influence on rates of criminal punishment.[8]

The introduction of sentencing guidelines and mandatory minimum sentences has also played a key role. In the federal system, the Federal Sentencing Reform Act of 1984 lengthened prison sentences, as well as time actually served.[9] Moreover, the number of congressional changes to mandatory minimum statutes rose from 61 in 1983 to 168 in 2000, with Congress tending to escalate mandatory minimum sentences in the weeks immediately preceding biennial elections.[10]

State courts have also had very strong incentives to increase the amount of time served by those convicted of felonies. In 1994, Congress passed a measure called the Violent Offender Incarceration and Truth-in-Sentencing Incentive Grants Program as part of the 1994 Crime Act.[11] In order to qualify for grants to build or expand prisons, most states adopted "Truth in Sentencing" laws that require many categories of felons to serve a full 85 percent of their sentences, irrespective of individual circumstances. Although state laws differ in the types of crimes covered and the percentage of time mandated to be served, their undeniable effect has been to prolong the *length of time* under supervision and to thereby expand correctional populations.[12] This development has greatly increased the scope and impact of felon disenfranchisement, as felons convicted under Truth in Sentencing are prohibited from voting for longer and longer periods of time.

Finally, it is important to note that there has also been a marked shift in the "offense mix" of the felon population, or the *types* of crimes that make up the bulk of felony convictions. In 1988, about 17 percent of felony convictions in state courts were for drug trafficking. By 2002, this figure nearly doubled, to over 32 percent.[13] The proportion of violent and property offenses has also increased to some extent over the period, with a corresponding drop in the "other" category (which includes crimes such as receiving stolen property). In sum, a combination of rising conviction rates, longer sentences, and a changing mix of offenses (and in particular, rising drug-related convictions) has placed more Americans than ever before under correctional supervision.

These developments have created a cycle in which punishment begets more punishment. For example, an increasing number of new prison admissions today are people who have violated terms of their conditional release on parole. In some cases these are new crimes, but in others they are "technical violations." Former National Institute of Justice director Jeremy Travis has noted that the 200,000 parole violators who returned to state prisons in 2000 approximates the *total* number of admissions to state prisons in 1980, when only 27,000 parole violators were admitted to prison.[14] California alone returns about 80,000 parole violators to prison each year, accounting for approximately two-thirds of that state's prison admissions in recent years. The rising number of people under criminal justice supervision are thus subject to far greater scrutiny than other citizens, leading to correspondingly higher correctional populations.

The United States has the highest incarceration rate in the world, and the gap has been growing over time. Figure 4.4 shows international incarceration rates for 2003. Of the 14 nations shown in the figure, and for whom reliable recent data are available, Russia and South Africa are the only nations that incarcerate even *half* as large a percentage of their citizenry as the United States. Combining prison and jail populations, our U.S. incarceration rate of 714 per 100,000 population is *four* times that of Mexico, *five* times that of England, *six* times that of Canada and Australia, *seven* times that of Germany and France, and *twelve* times that of Japan.

How about crime rates? Data on crime and victimization are notoriously difficult to compare across societies because definitions of particular criminal offenses differ so greatly in different criminal justice systems. Some excellent recent work, however, shows that U.S. crime patterns are unlikely to explain the large gaps in incarceration. David Farrington, Patrick Lan-

**Figure 4.4.**
International incarceration rates, 2003. Source: *New Incarceration Figures* (Washington, D.C.: Sentencing Project, 2004), and *World Prison Brief* (London: International Centre for Prison Studies, 2004).

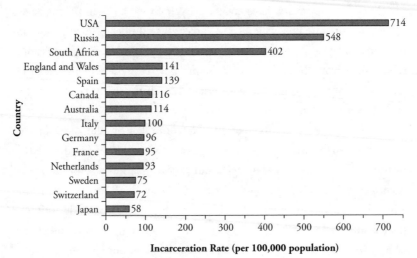

gan, and Michael Tonry compiled comparable crime and justice data from several nations for the period from 1981 to 2000.[15] Because robbery is among the most common and most consistently measured violent crimes, it provides a useful starting point for comparison, although similar comparisons could be made for burglary or other crimes.

Figure 4.5 adapts the Farrington, Langan, and Tonry data for robbery crime rates for the United States, the Netherlands, Switzerland, England and Wales, Australia, and Scotland. Consistent with the overall patterns discussed earlier, U.S. robbery rates have declined over the past 20 years. They now rank among the *lowest* of the six nations. Conviction rates (the number of convictions per 1,000 robbery offenders), by contrast, are comparatively high in the United States. In part, this reflects the efficiency of the U.S. criminal justice system, as well as differing policies and procedures

**Figure 4.5.**
Robbery crime rates by nation, 1981–2000. Adapted from David P. Farrington, Patrick A. Langan, and Michael Tonry, eds., *Cross-national Studies in Crime and Justice* (Washington, D.C.: U.S. Department of Justice, 2004).

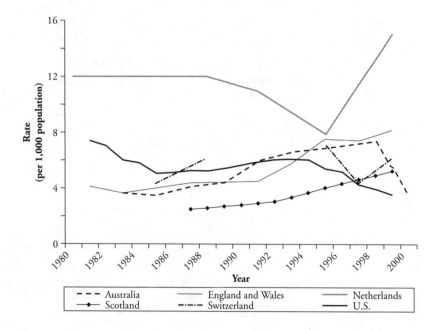

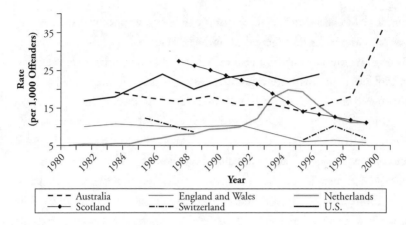

**Figure 4.6.**

Robbery conviction rates by nation, 1981–2000 Adapted from: David P. Farrington, Patrick A. Langan, and Michael Tonry, eds., *Cross-national Studies in Crime and Justice* (Washington, D.C.: U.S. Department of Justice, 2004).

**Figure 4.7.**

Length of incarceration for robbery by nation, 1981–2000. Adapted from David P. Farrington, Patrick A. Langan, and Michael Tonry, eds., *Cross-national Studies in Crime and Justice* (Washington, D.C.: U.S. Department of Justice, 2004).

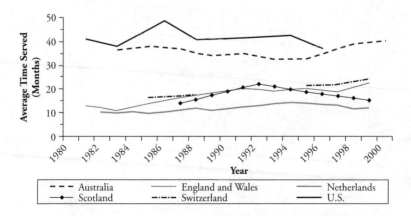

in the administration of justice. In 1996, the most recent year for which data are available for all nations, the U.S. robbery conviction rate of 24 per 1,000 offenders was more than double the Swiss and English rates and significantly higher than Australian, Scottish, and Dutch conviction rates (fig. 4.6).[16] Finally, those convicted of robbery in the United States (and Australia) tend to serve far longer prison sentences than those convicted of the same offense in Sweden, Switzerland, the Netherlands, and England and Wales (fig. 4.7).

## Politics, Culture, and Criminal Justice

If crime rates cannot account for recent trends in punishment practice, then we must look to political and cultural factors. As the American system of criminal justice developed in the nineteenth and twentieth centuries, features such as probation, parole, and indeterminate sentencing were introduced as reforms to rehabilitate offenders and reintegrate them into their communities. The popularity of the rehabilitation model in the middle of the twentieth century marked the high tide of what David Garland has referred to as "penological modernism": the attempt to create a criminal justice system capable of reforming offenders and returning them to society as law-abiding citizens.[17]

The model began to break down in the 1960s, however, as Republican presidential candidates Barry Goldwater (in 1964), Richard Nixon (in 1968), and other conservative and moderate politicians (such as Nelson Rockefeller in New York) successfully promoted more punitive criminal justice policies.[18] Each of these dynamics has been exhaustively explored by others, and it would take us beyond the scope of this book to do each of them justice here. We can, however, outline some of the main points.

### The Punishment Consensus

The period from the late 1960s onward saw the convergence of four important trends that would fundamentally transform the criminal justice policy environment: (1) a conservative backlash in response to the policy initiatives of the Great Society and the shifting mood of the mass public; (2) an economic downturn that precipitated a search for reasons, and scapegoats, for social problems after 1973; (3) urban riots signifying decline and disorder, which made urban crime the focus of intensive media campaigns; and, more generally, (4) the shifting importance of race in American political life, and the reemergence of a sharp link between race and crime. Since the early 1970s, changes in crime policy have been steady and, in total, massive in their impact. The most careful research suggests that Republicans moved first and fastest on crime, with the Democrats following suit later in a desperate effort to prevent crime from becoming a dreaded "wedge issue" in national (or state) politics. Coming out of the bloody political battles of the 1960s, Republican politicians found political space for platforms calling for tough penalties. Where Republicans dominated state governments, incarceration rates rose fastest.[19]

Bill Clinton and other centrist Democratic Party leaders decided by the late 1980s that they could not allow Republicans to be perceived as the party that is tougher on crime, especially as the Democratic Party feared being portrayed as overly sympathetic to African Americans. The historic linkage between race and crime that we noted in chapter 2 makes crime especially likely to hurt a party in a racially divided polity that is already perceived by whites as too sympathetic to African Americans.[20] Although liberal Democrats remained reluctant to support a strategy of mass incarceration, their power base inside the party eroded in the Clinton years. Delaware senator Joe Biden announced the coup de grâce for Democratic Party moderation on criminal justice in 1994, declaring that "the liberal wing of the Democratic Party is now for 60 new death penalties. . . . The liberal wing of the Democratic Party has 70 enhanced penalties. . . . The liberal wing of the Democratic Party is for 100,000 new cops. The liberal wing of the Democratic Party is for 125,000 new state prison cells."[21]

As Democrats stepped up their support for harsh punishment in the 1980s and 1990s, the most intensive incarceration campaign in world history would unfold with bipartisan support. The increases during the 1990s are all the more remarkable because the base rate was so high—the United States was already a world leader in imprisonment when Bill Clinton took office in 1992. Anti-crime measures reached high tide in the 1994 crime bill, which, among other things, provided revenues to support the hiring of 100,000 *new* police officers, new funds for prison construction, and new crimes to be added to the list of offenses punishable by death. These measures were adopted even though America's prison population had been growing steadily for two decades and the actual crime rate was beginning a substantial descent.

Special note must be made of the war on drugs. Most of the master trends were already under way when, in the mid-1980s, the Reagan Administration announced the beginning of a new moral campaign against drugs. Twenty years on, it is clear that the campaign has done little to influence actual drug use, but it has been a remarkable political success story. It unified conservative political forces and put liberals on the defensive. Its vast substantive impact can be very clearly measured by the rapidly rising rates of felony conviction for drug-related offenses we have noted earlier. The drug war peaked during the first Bush Administration but continued during the Clinton years and carries on to the present. Its impact has fallen particularly heavily on African Americans, who are significantly more likely to be convicted of drug-related offenses than are whites.[22]

More recently, since the turn of the millennium, there has been a moderation of the 30-year pattern of ever-growing incarceration. For the first time since the early 1970s, the total prison population has not grown significantly in the last two years, and in some states early release programs have actually helped to push down prison populations. However, the recent stabilization appears to be driven more by cost-cutting concerns on the part of state governments than by any large-scale political or cultural shift or changes in penological policy. With crime rates at historic lows in many parts of the country, the potential for a new mobilization of public fears remains substantial if rates were to again trend upward.

The intellectual side of the transformation of criminal justice policy is also worth noting. By the mid-1970s a rising chorus of conservative scholars, policy analysts, and politicians were advocating punitive strategies of deterrence and incapacitation, and dismissing the rehabilitative model as an "anachronism."[23] David Garland describes this process as a move from a "penal-welfare" model of rehabilitation to one of "punitive sanctions and expressive justice." Garland argues that the harsh justice policies emerging in both the United States and Britain since 1975 grew out of heightened public concerns with crime and the politics of managing risk and uncertainty.[24] Some comparative and historical research on punishment highlights the distinctiveness of the American case. For example, sociologist Joachim Savelsberg suggests that punishment has been much more stable in Germany than in the United States because there is far greater stability in academic knowledge and public opinion in the former nation.[25] Other work suggests that institutional features and political forces in the United States help to explain its high incarceration rates. John Sutton, for example, points to labor markets, welfare spending, and the strength of conservative parties to account for different levels of punishment in common-law democracies such as Australia, Canada, New Zealand, and the United Kingdom versus the United States.[26]

### Sources of Political Change

Changing criminal justice policy has a political foundation. The character and perception of public opinion about crime and punishment is one important component. Figure 4.8 graphs an open-ended question that has been asked of poll respondents every month since the early 1960s: What, in their opinion, is the "most important problem facing the nation"?[27] The remarkable volatility in the importance of crime to the public is a puzzle. Compared to macroeconomic indicators, for example, crime rates are relatively stable from month to month or year to year, yet public concern shifts—often violently—over short periods of time. As Katherine Beckett and others have pointed out, fear of crime appears to be uniquely responsive to mobilization by political leaders.[28] The rapid spike in concern with crime and violence from 5 percent in 1992 to 37 percent in 1994, for example, tracks the fanfare surrounding public debates of President Clinton's crime bill of that year. Similarly, public concern over drug use as the nation's most important problem rose rapidly in the late 1980s to a peak of 27 percent (and even in one month, September 1989, reaching an astonishing 64 percent after a major speech by President George H. W. Bush).

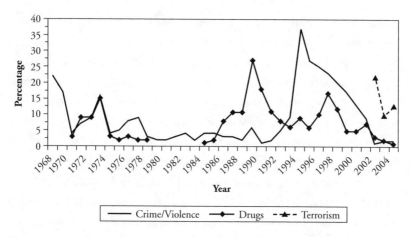

**Figure 4.8.**
Public concern with crime: percentage of Americans naming crime/violence or drugs as the most important problem facing the country, 1968–2004. Source: *Sourcebook of Criminal Justice Studies* series (Washington, D.C.: Government Printing Office).

But it diminished rapidly thereafter, to just 6 percent by 1993 and negligible proportions more recently.[29]

Analysts of crime politics have usually focused on the role of the mass media in shaping fears and influencing public support for harsh punishment practices. The nightly news programs aggressively cover crime stories, exaggerating the problem and feeding public fears. And widespread media depictions of the race of offenders are thus particularly important in the overall s tory and in magnifying public fears. Although African Americans may commit proportionately more crimes than whites, media coverage vastly exaggerates the extent to which blacks are the perpetrators. A political and cultural model that incorporates race is likely the best explanation for rising levels of criminal punishment in the United States.[30]

One piece of evidence supporting media impact can be seen in the difference between fears of crime in general versus fears of crime in one's own community. We learn about the nation's (or a state's, or a metropolitan area's) crime problem from the mass media, but we "know" our neighborhood's crime problem from lived experience. Unlike the sharp peaks shown in the "most important problem" nationally, fear of crime in one's own neighborhood has been far more stable over the past three decades. We can see this in figure 4.9, which plots an indicator from the National Opinion Research Center's General Social Survey against the rate of serious Index Crimes reported in the FBI's *Uniform Crime Reports*. Fear of neighborhood crime tracks the reported crime rate far better than public opinion indicators such as the "most important problem." People are far more likely to perceive a worsening crime rate in the nation as a whole than to perceive a worsening crime rate in their own neighborhoods. In sum, most Americans do *not* fear crime in their immediate environment but do fear it elsewhere. Even more striking, there is some evidence that reported experiences with crime in people's own neighborhoods actually tracks the aggregate crime rate rather closely, trending downward sharply in the 1990s.

**Figure 4.9.**
Crime index rate and fear of crime in neighborhood and country, 1974–2003.
Source: *Sourcebook of Criminal Justice Studies* series (Washington, D.C.: Government Printing Office) and *Crime in the United States* series (Washington, D.C.: Government Printing Office).

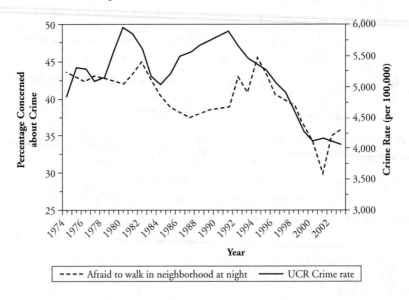

*State Trends*

While our discussion has focused on national increases in criminal punishment, overall trends in the United States are the aggregate result of political decisions made at the state level and criminal justice practices at the local level. National political leaders set the tone, of course, but the vast majority of people are actually sentenced under state law. There is thus tremendous state-by-state variation in incarceration rates over space as well as time. The seven states with the greatest prison incarceration rates are all located in the South, ranging from 539 per 100,000 in Georgia to 801 per 100,000 in Louisiana (these figures do not include jail inmates). The eight states with the lowest incarceration rates are all found in the Northeast and Midwest, ranging from 149 per 100,000 in Maine to 233 per 100,000 in Massachusetts. (Further details are provided in appendix table A4.1.) Given such variation, a political explanation of the sort we are advancing must also examine factors that produce variation in state- or regional-level criminal justice policies.[31]


## Punishment without Crime?

In this chapter, we have analyzed the sources of rising rates of felon disenfranchisement and outlined some explanations for the growth of American correctional populations. The largest part of this growth is due to larger changes in the criminal justice system. We have explored the contours of growing rates of punishment in America, and noted how the nation's policies are remarkably out of step with the rest of the world. Perhaps surprisingly, this has not always been the case. Incarceration rates in the United States were quite stable for most of the twentieth century. It has only been in the final quarter of the century that dramatic changes have taken place, with incarceration and conviction rates skyrocketing in a short span of time.

Finally, although we do not attempt to fully account for the factors driving mass incarceration here, there is one thing of which we can be certain: rising levels of felon disenfranchisement have not been driven by the necessity of combating a massive crime wave. Social and political choices, rather than the response necessitated by soaring crime rates, must play a role in any viable explanation of trends in punishment. Other countries with similar crime rates punish far less harshly, and with far fewer political consequences. We choose to punish—and disenfranchise—for reasons other than social necessity. That social choice, as we will show in the following chapters, has not been without costs for millions of citizens and for American democracy.

# 5 Political Attitudes, Voting, and Criminal Behavior

A felony conviction may come at the conclusion of a public trial or, far more typically, after a behind-the-scenes bargaining session among the accused, the prosecutor, and a defense attorney. In either case, the conviction is a defining moment, marking an individual's formal transition to "felon" status. For those who are incarcerated, it will mean physical removal from their previous life, including their families, their livelihoods, and their neighborhoods. For all convicted felons, it will mean a dizzying array of sanctions—both legal and social—that will make them second-class citizens. Increasingly accessible public databases in many states make their offenses visible to all, a "negative credential" that can last a lifetime.[1] And unlike New York Yankee owner George Steinbrenner, most felons cannot take solace in the victories of their famous baseball club or expect to have the president of the United States step in to issue a pardon.

As more people are released from prison and placed back into their communities each year (some 656,320 in 2003), researchers have turned their attention to prisoner reentry and reintegration. This scholarship details the problems that felons face in attempting to restart their lives, as well as the factors influencing whether they commit further crimes.[2]

Is voting one such factor? Does losing the right to vote matter to individual offenders, and if so, how and why? In this chapter, we use survey data to explore felons' political beliefs and the consequences of political exclusion for individual behavior and public safety. We will look at what felons believe, whether they vote, and how voting at one point in time influences the likelihood of *subsequent* criminal activity. If those who vote are actually less likely to commit new crimes—to "desist" from criminal activity—extending the franchise to felons could reduce rates of recidivism.[3]

To examine these questions, we will make use of an important data source—an ongoing panel study of former public school students in St. Paul, Minnesota (the Youth Development Study [YDS]). By comparing criminal offenders with the nonoffenders in the study, we can make some broad generalizations about differences in political attitudes and participation, and even about the effect of participation on future crime. These data are unique—the YDS is the only source of survey data that includes information about both respondents' criminal histories and their political participation and attitudes.[4] (See appendix table A5.1 for more details.)

One important caveat should be noted at the outset. The YDS research was conducted almost entirely in Minnesota, which is an unusual state in several ways. It typically has one of the highest turnout rates in the country. Minnesota also has a unique political history because of its strong Democratic-Farmer-Labor (DFL) party tradition, which meant there was a consistent social-democratic presence in state politics between the 1920s and the 1970s.[5] Moreover, Minnesota's incarceration and high school dropout rates are among the lowest in the nation, and the state's population is relatively homogeneous, with almost 90 percent of residents white (albeit a much smaller proportion of felons).[6] Finally, it is important to note the impact of Jesse Ventura's successful independent campaign for governor in 1998. As we fielded the YDS survey in 2000, Ventura's actions as governor and his antipolitical rhetoric and attacks on the major parties were widely reported and discussed in the state.[7] In light of Minnesota's unusual characteristics and political environment, we would expect to find some significant differences between our YDS respondents and those in the rest of the country.

The results we present in this chapter should therefore be considered suggestive rather than definitive. Nevertheless, these data represent a major advance over existing sources of information about the political dispositions and behavior of criminal offenders.

## A Comparative Perspective on Felons' Political Engagement

Before we get to our analyses, we must first place the political and policy interests and views of felons into an appropriate context. It is widely assumed that when it comes to politics, felons' low levels of education and (presumably) low citizenship norms make them a "low-information" group with high levels of apathy and distrust, and limited knowledge about politics.

But before jumping to premature conclusions about the character of felons' political consciousness, it is important to keep in mind some well-documented aspects of the American electorate. First, consider political participation. Compared with other postindustrial democratic countries, turnout rates in U.S. national elections are shockingly low. Levels of political participation and involvement by criminal offenders may be low, but so, too, is participation among the American electorate as a whole.

Next, consider political knowledge. Low levels of political information among the mass public have been widely documented since the pioneering work of the Michigan School in the early 1960s.[8] It has sometimes been thought that rising education levels should push up both knowledge and participation, but systematic research on the question has generally not supported such claims. Surveys asking random samples of Americans to identify basic political facts or issues find woeful levels of confusion or outright ignorance. For example, one survey found that only 20 percent of respondents understood the meaning of the First Amendment, just 30 percent could identify Supreme Court chief justice William Rehnquist as a conservative, only 40 percent could get within 3 percent of the correct unemployment rate, and only 15 percent correctly answered four out of five simple questions about current events in international affairs. As one authoritative text aptly summarized the evidence, "many—often most—citizens are ignorant of rather basic facts . . . the data suggest massive public ignorance."[9] Low levels of political information among offenders, then, only parallel those of the nonoffending mass public.

Next, consider distrust of government. Our survey data reveal very low levels of trust in government on the part of criminal offenders, yet such views are also not necessarily different from those of the public as a whole. There is good survey evidence that distrust of politicians and government in general has risen dramatically in recent years. In the early 1960s, about 7 in 10 survey respondents claimed to trust the government in Washington; in recent years, only about 1 in 3 indicate such trust. Other measures of trust, such as the belief that politicians are honest, have also declined precipitously in recent years.[10]

Finally, consider political apathy. A wide range of analysts have emphasized the need to increase deliberation among citizens as a way of reviving democratic practice, based on the underlying widely shared assumption that current levels of political talk are very low.[11] Even Americans who participate in local civic groups or social movements often make little connection between their activism and the larger political environment.[12] In sum, avoidance of politics and distrust among criminal offenders is hardly unique to that group.

### Politics in Prison?

In addition to properly situating the political consciousness of offenders alongside that of the mass public, it is also worth noting that incarceration may encourage or enable some inmates to develop political knowledge and interests. Although rehabilitation and education programs have eroded in recent years, many inmates continue to pursue education in prison and find time to reflect about the outside world in ways that they did not while on the street.[13]

In more unusual cases, prisoners have used their time for intensive study and activism. As Malcolm X put it, "where else but in a prison could I have attacked my ignorance by being able to study intensely sometimes as much as fifteen hours a day?" The Norfolk Prison Colony afforded Malcolm X other opportunities for political action, including a forum for educating or radicalizing other inmates and a weekly debating program that provided a "baptism into public speaking." Upon entering San Quentin a generation later, Sanyika Shakur was told, "You'll feel the comrade strong here. Bro, you'll read books here, see things that are gonna change the way you walk, talk, and think. This is the best place for an aspiring young revolutionary. This is repression at its best."[14] Progressive or radical politics are embedded in several first-person accounts of prison life, both because such messages echo the experiences of "caged-up" men, as Malcolm X put it, and because the radical press is viewed by prisoners as more trustworthy in describing prison conditions and events outside. More typically, perhaps, many inmates simply develop greater interest and participation in politics and the larger world around them as they consider how they will rebuild their lives upon release.[15]

Various forms of collective action among prisoners, including riots, may also stimulate a broader sense of political engagement and power. The prisoners' rights movements of the 1960s and 1970s drew many inmates into political activism. Although some of these activities have faded in recent years, prisons remain places where politics erupts in various forms.[16] In 1997, inmates in Massachusetts even set up a political action committee, a step that may, however, have contributed to passage of a state referendum in 2000 that disenfranchised inmates in that state.[17] Finally, many inmates acquire or reconnect with religion, which in turn can inspire moral and political engagement.[18]

### Political Interest and Participation: The 2000 YDS

In view of the considerations in the previous section, it is important not to assume or exaggerate a high degree of political apathy, disinterestedness, and distrust on the part of criminal offenders. Rather, we will treat these as questions to be interrogated. To identify offenders in the YDS survey, we used self-reported crime and arrest data collected between 1988 and 1998.[19] For political participation questions, we used the 2000 survey, when

757 respondents, aged 26 to 27, remained in the sample. We consider arrestees as well as inmates because, as noted in chapter 4, many disenfranchised felons are never incarcerated. The larger number of arrestees also provides greater statistical power to detect differences across groups. Many of the questions we used were identical to longstanding items on the biennial National Election Study (NES); incorporating these established measures helps us make comparisons to national election survey results. Appendix table A5.1 provides methodological details about the YDS, along with our specific questions on political beliefs, participation, and voting behavior.

The YDS data allow us to distinguish three groups of respondents: those who had never been arrested (about 75 percent of the sample); those who had been arrested but not incarcerated (about 15 percent of the sample); and those who had been incarcerated in jail or prison (about 10 percent). The latter figures are higher than we would expect from a representative sample of all Americans in their midtwenties, reflecting the urban public school backgrounds of the YDS sample.[20] Basic demographic information about each of these groups is included in appendix table A5.2.

Youth Development Study arrestees and inmates were much less likely than nonarrestees to be female, white, and married. Similarly, these arrestees and inmates report lower levels of education than do other respondents. When offenses are ranked by severity (with violent ranked as most severe, followed by property, drug, and other offenses), the most serious offense among YDS arrestees was a violent crime in 19 percent of cases, a property crime in 39 percent, a drug crime in 24 percent, and some other offense (such as a weapons or public order violation) in 17 percent, with a similar distribution observed among those who had been incarcerated. Overall, those who had experienced criminal sanctions were generally less advantaged than the Minnesota cohort from which they were drawn.[21]

### Political Attitudes and Engagement

The figures that follow show our main findings about the political orientations and attitudes of the three groups. The results underscore the extent to which the political beliefs of respondents who have been arrested or incarcerated conform to our starting assumptions—but also reveal that not all of the differences are statistically or (perhaps) practically significant. Although the specific scores of respondents may be different in a different population, we can still make meaningful comparisons between offenders and nonoffenders *within* this particular context.

Arrestees and inmates are significantly more likely to claim independent partisan identification than the rest of the sample, though this result must be interpreted cautiously in view of the strong attraction of Jesse Ventura's 1998 independent gubernatorial campaign (which we discuss later). Fully 54 percent of the incarcerated or formerly incarcerated respondents said they "do not lean toward either the Republican or Democratic Party" (see fig. 5.1). Lack of partisan identification among the remaining sample is also high by comparison with the national mean.

We posed two other questions about general political orientation: a standard ideological self-identification item (asking respondents to place themselves on a five-point scale ranging from "extremely liberal" to "extremely conservative") and whether they identified themselves as "part of

**Figure 5.1.**
Political orientation and criminal history—YDS.

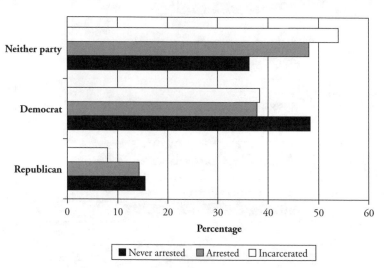

the Christian Right." For the most part, we find that these differences are not significant across groups, though incarcerated respondents reported greater conservatism than the rest of the sample (as shown in appendix table A5.3). The latter may be somewhat surprising at first glance, but the interviews reported in the next chapter lead us to think two factors may account for this result: the comparatively low levels of education of the offender respondents (and knowledge of political labels such as "liberal" and "conservative"); and the use of the term "conservative" to reflect caution or moderation rather than political orientation.

The most striking and consistent differences between inmates, arrestees, and the remainder of the sample are found in attitudes toward government. Youth Development Study respondents were asked several questions about how much they trust politicians and their government. On all of these items, arrestees and inmates expressed significantly less trust than those who had not been arrested or incarcerated (see fig. 5.2). They were

**Figure 5.2.**
Efficacy, trust, and criminal history—YDS.

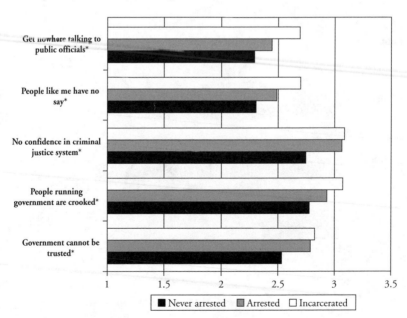

also much less likely to express confidence in the criminal justice system. This not entirely surprising result could be viewed as consistent with some concerns raised by proponents of felon disenfranchisement: that enfranchisement would potentially undermine support for the criminal justice system. But as we discuss in chapter 6, most offenders believe in the virtues of prisons and the importance of laws punishing criminal activity.[22] A wider range of motivations lies behind the reduced confidence found in the survey data, including general distrust in any government institution and, frequently, specific dissatisfaction about the administration of the respondents' own case.

We also probed for respondents' beliefs about the meaning of political action. A sense of political efficacy has long been identified as stimulating participation in civic life.[23] Arrestees and inmates are significantly less likely to think that they can influence public officials, or even have some say in politics. The differences between those who have been incarcerated and those who have not (over one-third of one point on a four-point scale) are statistically and, we suspect, practically significant.

Our final measures of political engagement address political talk (see fig.

**Figure 5.3.**
Political talk and criminal history—YDS.

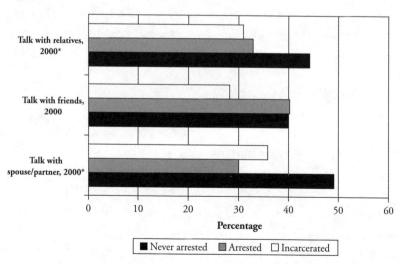

5.3). Conversations with friends, coworkers, and family members are an important source of political information and stimulate interest in politics. These go to the heart of the longstanding idea that an individual's social networks provide an impetus for developing and maintaining an interest in politics.[24] Although inmates may discuss political issues with staff or among themselves, their access to friends, relatives, and coworkers is sharply restricted during periods of incarceration. When it comes to discussing politics, those who have experienced criminal justice sanctions are indeed somewhat less likely to engage in such conversations, particularly with spouses and relatives.

### Political Participation and Voting Behavior

In addition to exploring general political orientations and engagement, we are interested in examining political participation and voting behavior among felons and non-felons. Because individual self-reports of voting always produce inflated estimates, it is the gap—rather than the percentages reporting voting—that is of greatest interest. In the 1996 election, arrestees were 18 percent less likely to vote than nonarrestees, and inmates were 27 percent less likely to vote than nonarrestees (see fig. 5.4).[25] The turnout gap between arrestees and nonarrestees is smaller for the 1998 midterm elections, when participation is much lower overall, and for the item asking respondents (in summer 2000) whether they expected to vote in the November election. The gap between those who had been incarcerated and those who had never been arrested remains consistently high across the different electoral contexts.[26]

We also looked at YDS respondents' voting behavior, focusing on two recent elections, the 1996 presidential election and the 1998 Minnesota gubernatorial race. In 1996, the former urban public school students exhibited strong overall support for the Democratic incumbent Bill Clinton in the 1996 election, so much so that there were only small differences between arrestees, inmates, and the remainder of the sample (fig. 5.5).

More startling differences register in the unusual 1998 Minnesota governor's race, where those who had been arrested exhibited significantly greater support for former professional wrestler Jesse Ventura (see fig. 5.6).

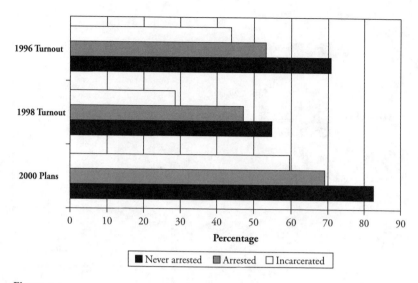

**Figure 5.4.**
Political participation and criminal history—YDS.

**Figure 5.5.**
1996 preference and criminal history—YDS.

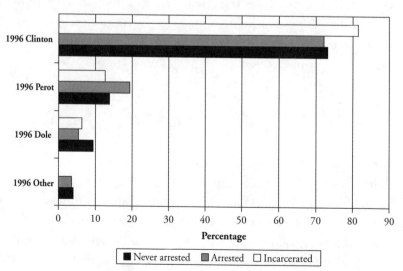

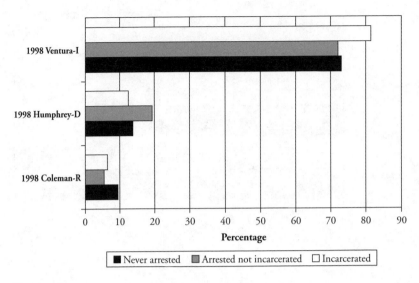

**Figure 5.6.**
1998 preference and criminal history—YDS.

Among those who reported voting, fully 74 percent of arrestees and 70 percent of inmates supported Ventura. The defections tended to come from the Democratic candidate in that race, Skip Humphrey, who received 10 percent and 8 percent fewer votes from arrestees and inmates, respectively. Ventura, like Clinton, drew strong support among this entire sample of young Minnesotans, but his appeal is even higher among those who have been arrested or incarcerated.

## Voting and Crime

We now know something about felons' political views, and about how their political preferences compare with those of nonoffenders. But regardless of how they vote, does the very act of voting affect them? Does it alter their views about citizenship and civic duty? Most important, does it change the likelihood that they will engage in further criminal behavior in the future? The YDS data can once again help us to answer these questions.

Before turning to our analyses, however, we first describe how "civic reintegration" might serve as a link between voting and desisting from crime.

### Crime and Civic Reintegration

The question of how to foster the reintegration of former felons into their communities stands front and center in current debates over criminal justice policy. While the two processes are closely connected, it is useful to distinguish between social reintegration on the one hand and desistance from crime on the other. Criminologists have long known that "reintegration" and the successful transition to adult roles is tied to "desistance" or cessation from crime.[27] Not surprisingly, people in strong marriages with stable work histories are more likely to leave crime behind than are people who have yet to make such transitions.[28] Simple aging is part of the story, but taking on adult responsibilities reduces crime independent of age. Understanding how former criminals make a smooth transition to these roles is thus a critical question for criminology and for public policy.[29]

Taking the lead from the foundational work of criminologists Robert Sampson and John Laub, much of the scholarly literature has focused on changes in work and family roles.[30] Reintegration into the political community of citizens, by contrast, has received comparatively little attention.[31] Yet felons are defined by their legal relationship with the state and their separation from their fellow citizens.[32] We therefore propose *civic reintegration* as a third domain, central to weaving former criminals back into the fabric of law-abiding society.[33]

As we suggested in chapter 1, British sociologist T. H. Marshall's concept of citizenship helps us to understand how felons are set apart from others. Marshall viewed citizenship as "a status bestowed on those who are full members of a community. All who possess the status are equal with respect to the rights and duties to which the status is endowed."[34] If citizenship implies "full membership" in society, what happens when felons lose the basic rights and capacity to perform the duties of citizenship, such as the right to vote, the right to hold elective office, and to serve on juries?

If these limitations and disqualifications hinder reintegrative efforts, they can also affect recidivism. As discussed in chapter 3, most felons occupied marginal social positions even before they landed in the criminal justice system. Relatively few had attained standard markers of adult status, such as finishing school, getting married, and holding a steady job.[35] And for those who had attained such markers, their criminal record would communicate to others that they had not always followed the path of the "good citizen."

As our interviews will show in the next chapter, people with felony convictions express desires to become productive citizens at work, responsible citizens with their families, and active citizens in their communities. With regard to civic life, criminologist Shadd Maruna described the "tragic optimism" of offenders in his Liverpool study, who voiced plans to make great contributions to their communities and families.[36] Similarly, Kathryn Edin and colleagues showed how some low-income fathers recommit to their families in prison, even as their family ties are stretched to the breaking point.[37]

However sincere their desires to take on these new roles, convicted felons often lack the personal resources and the social relationships needed to sustain them. They may also have an unrealistic sense of what the roles themselves entail. Nevertheless, these big plans are more than storytelling or "fantasizing."[38] Trying on roles as productive, responsible, and active citizens provides, at a minimum, an imaginative rehearsal for later assuming these roles.

When they are released, the combination of preexisting personal or social deficits and the stigma of conviction undercut attempts at reintegration. Continuing punishments—including occupational restrictions, loss of parental rights, and disenfranchisement, to name a few—put up further roadblocks. As these barriers are experienced and recognized, it becomes difficult, and sometimes impossible, for former felons to see themselves at the table with other citizens in good standing.

With reintegration and commitment to new work, family, and civic roles, however, former felons are likely to cast aside criminal behavior that is inconsistent with these roles.[39] As our interview data suggest in the next chapter, these domains are mutually reinforcing: work and family combine in the breadwinner role, work and community combine in the volunteer role, and community and family combine in the informal "neighboring" role. As they perform the role behavior expected of productive, responsible, and active citizens—law-abiding citizens—their likelihood of desisting from crime should correspondingly increase.[40]

### Linking Citizenship and Desistance

Our discussion thus far has identified core elements of citizenship and desistance. The argument is straightforward: the full range of civil penalties and informal stigmas that are imposed with a criminal conviction effectively deny individuals the *rights* of citizenship. This denial, in turn, makes performing the *duties* of citizenship difficult. Simply put, people convicted of crimes do not have the same citizenship rights or opportunities as other citizens.

Postincarceration penalties imposed on felons include restrictions on housing, jury service, and educational assistance, in addition to restrictions on work and family life.[41] As Jeremy Travis has pointed out, these "collateral sanctions" are much less visible than the penitentiary, though their consequences to felons may be equally profound.[42] The research literature has only begun to explore the independent contribution of each sanction to the problem of reintegration, although several scholarly volumes on "invisible punishment" and "civil penalties" have recently appeared.[43]

Together these penalties form the legal context within which felons must operate when trying to perform roles as adult citizens. In addition to these formal restrictions, however, there are wide-ranging informal barriers as well. Prospective employers need not hire felons, even if they are qualified; family members, friends, or acquaintances may not necessarily welcome them back; and, as we discuss later, the stigma of a felony conviction may be introduced in many different social contexts.[44]

Looking at the big picture, there appears to be a dialectical relationship between citizenship and the prospect of leaving crime. People convicted of felonies are usually embedded in a set of social institutions that provide little support for reintegration. Even the most ambitious felons striving to "give something back" to their communities face an uphill battle. If felons had greater access to the rights of citizenship, would they be more likely to desist from crime?

## Does Voting Affect Recidivism?

A link between civic participation and virtuous behavior has long been hypothesized by democratic theorists.[45] Conventional theories of democracy typically emphasize its uses as an instrument for citizens to control their government—through elections, public opinion, or popular revolts. But the benefits for the individuals who participate in democratic processes have also been passionately asserted by some democratic theorists.[46] In the latter view of democracy, individuals become citizens in part through the "educative" or "constitutive" impact of political participation.

This view was central to the models of political society in the writings of Alexis de Tocqueville and John Stuart Mill.[47] For Mill, when citizens participate regularly in politics, they develop an explicit identification with the polity and its norms and values. In this sense, democracy fosters citizenship. In the narrowest reading of the constitutive argument, political participation produces citizens with a generalized sense of efficacy, who believe they have a stake in the political system. This, in turn, fosters continued political participation. Some classical studies have provided evidence in support of this view.[48]

Theories of "expressive voting," as well as communitarian and republican theories of government, hold that the right to vote is important precisely because it helps mold individuals into virtuous citizens.[49] In the words of one legal theorist, "the vote should be protected not simply because it enables individuals to pursue political ends, but also because voting is a meaningful participatory act through which individuals create and affirm their membership in the community and thereby transform their identities both as individuals and as part of a greater collectivity."[50] Expressivist theories are today a leading response to rational choice models of voter turnout, suggesting that people participate in part because elections give them an opportunity to develop and express a civic identity.

Even more expansive views of the impact of participation have also been developed, but typically in relation to forms of participation that extend beyond voting. In her modern reconstruction of the idea of participatory democracy, for example, Carol Pateman argues that

> the major function of participation in the theory of participatory democracy is . . . an educative one . . . including both the psychological aspect and the gaining of experience in democratic skills and procedures. . . . For a democratic polity to exist it is necessary for a participatory society to exist, i.e., a society where all political systems have been democratized and socialization through participation can take place in all areas.[51]

Indeed, the essentially limited and passive nature of the act of voting has long been viewed as a trivial form of participation. Advocates of "strong" or deliberative democracy argue that meaningful forms of participation must go beyond the "mere" act of voting.[52] Sociologist Doug McAdam's influential analysis of the impact of social movement activism on the lives of activists and nonactivists contrasts the constitutive and life-changing experience of high-risk activism with more passive forms of support for the civil rights movement.[53] So the case for an impact of voting on other kinds of behavior—including criminal behavior—remains unclear. Yet it is an important question. If those who vote are actually less likely to commit new crimes, extending the franchise may facilitate reintegration efforts and perhaps even improve public safety.

Establishing a causal relationship between voting and recidivism would require a large-scale longitudinal survey that tracked released felons in their communities and closely monitored changes in their political and criminal behavior. At present, no such data exist.[54] Nevertheless, information available in the YDS allows us to bring some empirical data to bear on the question.[55]

## Exploring the Link between Polity Membership and Desistance

As with our analysis of political attitudes and behavior, we use self-reported crime and arrest data collected as part of the YDS. We measure criminal behavior with self-reported indicators of property crimes and violence (reported in 1998 and 1999 for the years 1997 and 1998) and arrest and incarceration (reported in 2000 for 1997 to 2000). Information on marital status, employment, and educational attainment were taken from the 1995 survey so that these background characteristics would precede both the 1996 voting data and the 1997–2000 information on subsequent criminal behavior. Finally, self-reported crime and arrest data prior to 1996, important statistical controls in this analysis, were taken from earlier retrospective reports of arrests, drunk driving, shoplifting, and violence.

These longitudinal data are important because a negative statistical association between voting and arrest may be a statistical artifact. That is, the correlation may be due to some unmeasured characteristic, such as an antisocial attitude or propensity toward bad citizenship that is reflected in both crime and (non)voting. We therefore exploit the longitudinal nature of the YDS to examine the effects of voting on subsequent arrest after statistically controlling for measures of self-reported deviance that would indicate antisocial propensity. In addition to race, sex, education, marital status, and employment, we control for arrest prior to 1996 and for three indicators of common self-reported deviance: drunk driving, shoplifting, and hitting or threatening to hit another person. Our goal is to determine whether voting is really signaling civic reintegration or whether it is simply capturing stable, underlying differences in the social background and criminal history of our survey respondents.

We first examine the simple correlation between voting and crime, asking whether those who voted in the 1996 presidential election had lower rates of arrest, incarceration, and self-reported criminal behavior in the years following this election than those who did not participate. We then statistically control for prior criminal behavior and background factors in order to estimate the *net* effect of voting on crime.[56]

As discussed earlier, self-reported turnout rates were high for this sample, with 65 percent of respondents reporting that they voted in 1996, as against 59.6 percent of people aged 18 to 24 in that election in Minnesota.[57] At the time of data collection in 2000, approximately 57 percent of the remaining sample was female and about three-fourths of respondents were white.[58] By 1995, the cohort had achieved an average of 13.6 years of ed-

ucation, and a good number were currently enrolled in postsecondary education. Only 12 percent were married by 1995, and approximately 82 percent were employed. (Other descriptive statistics are shown in appendix
table A5.2.)

With regard to crime, about 9 percent reported being arrested and 7
percent reported being incarcerated at some point in the four years after
the 1996 election. Before 1996, about 19 percent reported an arrest. Levels
of self-reported criminality are typically much higher than levels of arrest.
About 38 percent in our sample indicated that they had committed at least
one property crime or act of violence from 1997 to 1998. Our property
crime indicator flags those who reported shoplifting, theft, forgery, and
burglary. Overall, approximately 13 percent of the sample reported at least
one of these offenses. The violence indicator measures those reporting hitting or threatening to hit someone, being involved in a physical fight, or
robbing someone by force. The combined prevalence of these behaviors is
about 38 percent overall.

### Basic Correlation between Voting and Crime

We first examine the most basic question about the relationship between
political participation and criminality. Is there any correlation between voting and crime, arrest, and incarceration? Figure 5.7 shows clear differences
in arrest and incarceration by levels of political participation. Approximately 16 percent of the nonvoters were arrested between 1997 and 2000,
relative to about 5 percent of the voters. Similarly, approximately 12 percent
of the nonvoters were incarcerated between 1997 and 2000, relative to less
than 5 percent of the voters. Both of these contrasts represent statistically
significant differences.

The YDS is diverse with regard to criminal history, but approximately
80 percent of the respondents had no prior arrests at the time of the 1996
election. We therefore split the sample to distinguish those with a prior
arrest history from those with no such history. This allowed us to learn
whether the simple correlation shown above holds across levels of criminal
history. Figure 5.8 suggests that this is indeed the case. Among former
arrestees, about 27 percent of the nonvoters were rearrested, relative to 12

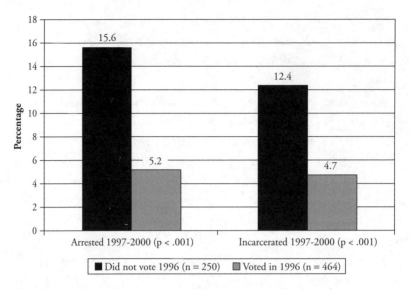

**Figure 5.7.**
Arrest and incarceration among voters and nonvoters.

**Figure 5.8.**
Arrest among voters and nonvoters, by arrest history.

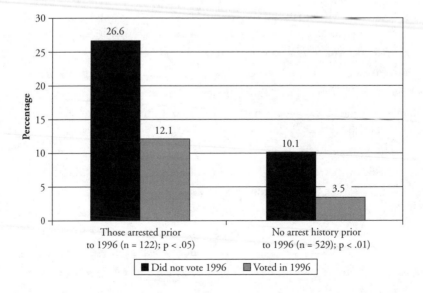

percent of the voters. There is thus at least a correlation between voting in 1996 and recidivism from 1997 to 2000 among people who have had some official contact with the criminal justice system.

As we noted earlier, those convicted of felonies in Minnesota may not vote until they have completed all prison, parole, or probation supervision. Therefore, it may be the case that differences in rearrest by voting status are due to *legal* restrictions on the ability of arrestees to vote—some of them may have been ineligible to vote in 1996. The contrast shown on the right side of figure 5.8, however, suggests that this is unlikely to explain the correlation between voting and subsequent arrest. Even among those with no prior arrest history, about 10 percent of the nonvoters were arrested, compared to less than 4 percent of the voters. Both of these contrasts are again statistically significant. Therefore, the relationship between voting and subsequent arrest does not appear to be a simple function of criminal history.

Arrest is an important measure of official contact with the criminal justice system, but a flawed measure of criminal behavior.[59] Many crimes go unreported, and official arrest data may be subject to biases relating to class, race, and other factors. If civic participation is truly related to desistance from crime, however, voting effects should be visible on self-reported criminal behavior as well as arrest and incarceration. Here, too, we see statistically significant relationships between voting and self-reported property and violent crimes (see fig. 5.9). About 11 percent of the voters reported committing a property crime, compared to approximately 18 percent of the nonvoters. Similarly, about 27 percent of the voters reported violence or threats of violence, relative to about 42 percent of the nonvoters.

The answer to our first question about the basic relationship between crime and voting is now clear: Those who vote are less likely to be arrested and incarcerated, and less likely to report committing a range of property and violent offenses. Moreover, this relationship cannot be solely attributed to criminal history; voting is negatively related to subsequent crime among those with and without a prior criminal history.

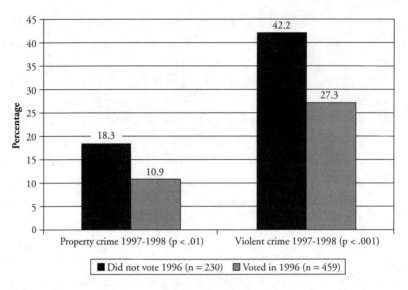

**Figure 5.9.**
Self-reported property and violent crime among voters and nonvoters.

### Controlling for Other Factors

Although the preceding findings are intriguing, they show a correlation that may or may not indicate an underlying causal relationship. Voting is correlated with other factors that are closely related to arrest. For example, race and sex are related to both processes. Women and whites had significantly higher turnout rates than men and African Americans in the 1996 election, as well as much lower rates of arrest.[60] Education is similarly a strong predictor of both voting and arrest in these data.[61]

When we statistically control for the effects of these factors, we do find some important differences in the results. Before introducing statistical controls, the probability of arrest was about one-third as high for voters as for nonvoters. Our full model shows that a good portion of the voting effect on arrest is explained by differences in criminal history and in race, sex, and education differences between voters and nonvoters.[62] In general, whites, females, those with greater education, and those with little criminal history are unlikely to be arrested, relative to nonwhites, males, those with fewer years of education, and those with greater criminal histories. After we adjust for all of these factors, the effect of voting in 1996 on arrest from 1997 to 2000 falls just below standard significance levels ($p = .110$). This more stringent test suggests that the voting effect is at least partially a product of preexisting differences between voters and nonvoters—insofar as we can name and measure these differences.

On the basis of this multivariate model, we calculated the predicted probability of arrest for two hypothetical voters and nonvoters. For an unmarried, African American male with 11 years of education, an income of $19,000, a prior arrest, and no prior self-reported offenses, our model predicts a probability of subsequent arrest of about .47 for voters and about .33 for nonvoters. Although voting is no longer a statistically significant predictor of arrest, this does not necessarily mean that voting is irrelevant to subsequent crime. In predicting a relatively rare event such as arrest in a sample of this size, a large effect would be required to obtain a statistically significant result.

We next considered the relation between voting and self-reported acts of deviant or criminal behavior. Although the voting effect is reduced after adjusting for background characteristics and prior criminal behavior, political participation remains a statistically significant predictor. In the full model, the probability of committing any self-reported crime is reduced from .71 to .59 for unmarried African American men with low educations and from .38 to .26 for married white women with college degrees.[63]

The foregoing results are suggestive, but insufficient to establish a causal link between voting and desistance from crime. A longitudinal panel design that spanned several election cycles would be needed to fully assess such claims, perhaps establishing that *changes* in voting are linked to *changes* in criminal activity. Nevertheless, the strong correlation between voting and subsequent crime raises important questions about the connection between the two phenomena. How do felons themselves think about voting? What, if any, link do *they* make between their participation as citizens in their communities and their participation in crime? The best way to answer these and other questions about felons' political beliefs and behavior is simply to ask them. We turn to an examination of their answers in the next chapter.

# 6 Disenfranchisement and Civic Reintegration: Felons Speak Out

*with Angela Behrens*

*I have no right to vote on the school referendums that . . . will affect my children. I have no right to vote on how my taxes is going to be spent or used, which I have to pay anyway whether I'm a felon or not, you know? So basically I've lost all voice or control over my government. . . . People don't want to recognize that we can still be citizens and still be patriotic even though we made a mistake. And that's a hard pill to swallow. And that's something when I get out there and I start hearing about, you know, politicians and government and things that I could vote on and ideas, it's like I get mad because I can't say anything because I don't have a voice. Or 'cause I can't vote about it.*

—Paul Ferguson, *imprisoned for a sex offense*

The survey results we described in the last chapter provide useful information about the political orientations of people who have had contact with the criminal justice system. Yet those results also suggest new questions: *why* offenders hold the political views they do, and *how* are those views driven by underlying values or dispositions, are not well captured by a survey instrument (however well designed). In this chapter, we begin to address these issues using information from in-depth interviews we conducted. These interviews allow felons to articulate their views within their own frames rather than those provided by survey questions.[1]

In the spring and summer of 2001, we conducted 33 semistructured interviews with Minnesota prisoners, parolees, and probationers. The questions we posed addressed political participation, partisanship, trust in government, and probed for their attitudes about voting restrictions and other penalties typically imposed on felony offenders. We also asked more general questions about felons' communities, employment prospects, and future aspirations. Our primary interest, however, was the deeper significance of losing the right to vote. We asked respondents questions such as the following: What kinds of political experiences have you had? Do you expect to participate in the future? Are any political issues especially salient to you, and if so, why? How did losing the right to vote affect your ideas about being a part of a community, and about your government?

We carried out these interviews at two state correctional facilities and one county community corrections office. Although the interviews took place within these facilities, we arranged for a private room with a closed door where correctional and administrative staff could not overhear the interview questions or responses. (Details of the interview procedures and a copy of the interview guide are included in the chapter appendix, at pages 261–65. Statistical information about the respondents is included in table A6.1.)

Respondents varied in race and gender, ranging from 20 to 54 years of age. Relative to national or Minnesota prison populations, women are significantly overrepresented among our interviewees. In view of the broader questions about citizenship and political rights we are posing, however, we did not necessarily anticipate large gender differences in respondent preferences on many topics.[2] Reflecting in part the unusual demographic profile of the felon population in Minnesota, white respondents constituted a majority (67 percent) of the interviewees, and Native Americans made up an additional 15 percent. On the concrete question of who they preferred in the 2000 presidential election, 24 percent of our small sample expressed a preference for George W. Bush, as compared to our estimate of about 30 percent nationally (according to the statistical evidence presented in chapter 8).

## Views about Government and Public Policy

Our survey findings suggested that arrestees and inmates lack confidence in government and the political system. Such views were widely voiced by many of our respondents in our in-depth interviews. We heard some colorful descriptions of how the *real* crooks were politicians and government bureaucrats. We asked each of our respondents to define in his or her own words what "politics" meant to them, and many of the responses emphasized the idea that "politics" is about politicians who are corrupt or greedy. For example, Thomas, an African American former gang member convicted of drug and weapons charges, told us that, to him, politics is

> Crap. Or, as in my man, he says, "Who wants to be a millionaire?" 'Cause in politics everyone wants the prize. You know? I know a lot of things cost money. . . . Just to make that next dollar. So I'm going to politics, Congress, it's *money*, yeah. Nobody goes to Congress, or into politics just to go "Okay, I'm gonna make a lot of laws." No, it's too much money. It's too much money.

Such blanket dismissals leave little room for a positive appreciation of government as a valuable social institution. But as we probed deeper into these sentiments, we also heard more nuanced explanations of *why* our respondents viewed the political system as untrustworthy. These narratives suggest caution in assuming a simple hostility to all things political among even the most cynical of our respondents. This came across in a number of ways. For example, other respondents who endorsed a similar view of corruption to Thomas's provided substantive *reasons* why the political system falls short of an ideal democracy. Consider the views of Nathan, a white sex offender who is appealing his conviction:

> To me a politician's nothing but a crook, you know? They're making laws, but I never thought it would never affect me, and I [think] "go make your laws." Because I believe the government's all wrong. We've gotten so much with politicians and with the governor, but yet they don't hear what the people have to say. I mean I thought we were based on the Constitution and "we the people" have the say over what the government has to say . . . they're . . . supposed to look up to us and say, "What do you want us to do? We're working for you. What do you want us to do?" . . . It's like, "Well, if they're working for us, why aren't they in my community asking what we want?"

Nathan's broad characterization of politicians as "crooks" is combined here with a real and substantive conception of what a noncriminal democratic politician would do: go to the community and "ask what we want," and then act as an honest delegate. Such a vision of democracy, in which politicians act as brokers of majoritarian opinion, is a model that some sophisticated models of democracy embrace. Diana complained in a similar manner about the lack of openness in the political system as undermining her trust in government:

> I don't know, I think they should do something every, instead
> of every four years, they should have something—I think the
> government should open up and feel what the people need.
> Some countries don't have any say in the matter at all. But
> United States, we're supposed to be more open and more free-
> dom, and more proud, we should be able to open up more, and
> expand more. You know there's a lot out there that the govern-
> ment's not taking care of, and people aren't able to voice their
> opinion.

For those whose primary contact with the state occurs through the criminal justice system, levels of trust and confidence in the government are undoubtedly shaped by that engagement. Scott, an African American probationer in his twenties, described how his experiences with the police reduced his trust in government:

> Who can you trust anyway? 'Cause I think a lot of it's superfi-
> cial. . . . I grew up where the police, you know, the police beat
> up people. And that didn't happen in every instance, you know,
> but you learn to not have trust, you know? . . . I don't think I
> have a say about what the government does. They look good for
> awhile, then they get elected and you hear all kind of junk.
> [The police,] that's the *immediate government* right there. [Em-
> phasis added]

Mary, a Native American woman in her forties who believes she was wrongly convicted on a drug charge, explained how her views of government had changed after experiencing the criminal justice system:

> Five years ago I was sitting on the streets, and I was, you know,
> doing my own thing and I was a law-abiding citizen, and I

didn't have these problems, I didn't have these concerns, I didn't even think about things like that you know, you know? I thought, well, you know "Geez, believe in the judicial system. Believe in the politics of the system because they're what's going to support you." That's a mistake.

Such accounts suggest one unintended consequence of the "war on crime": by subjecting an ever greater number of citizens to the repressive arm of the state, criminal justice policy has created a subgroup in the population with strong reason to dislike their government. We can only speculate as to whether such criminal justice contacts also shape the views of their family and friends.

Disgust with politics was also sometimes accompanied by a preference for local or subnational politics. Consider the views of two respondents, the first from Karen and the second from Andrew, a college-educated white probationer in his twenties:

> Since I've been incarcerated, and even more so, not as strongly would I focus on national politics as I have always been far more concerned about the politics right here and now. You know, more *grassroots*. How it affects—I don't want to say small-town community, because I think that small-town communities, farming communities, all those types of things, you know—have a lot of power, but I think more things like the sheriff being elected, appellate court judges, Supreme Court judges, legislators, you know . . . maybe because it was just closer to home for me. . . . [I'm] closer to Democrat, and I think, a good chunk of that is the born and raised, Iron Range [a Minnesota mining region with a reputation for prolabor politics] union person inside of me.

> I think it's easier to trust the *local* government, which is why my beliefs are as they are. National government, I just think there's so much money involved that corruption might be a little more likely. Not saying that it's, you know, ruined society. I'm not that big of a naysayer, but I just think accountability is

a little easier locally. I think we can trust our local governments more.

Preferences for local government, or governing units below the federal level, are quite common in American society. In the comments of Karen and Andrew, we see two quite different underlying theories of why localism is preferred. For Karen, a more viable democracy with higher levels of citizen activism is more likely at the local level. For Andrew, local governments are more trustworthy and accountable. Both accounts are reasoned understandings of the potential advantages of democratic governance on a smaller scale.

### Policy Views and the Criminal Justice System

As they explained their attitudes about political and policy issues, many respondents stressed *specific* policy questions as their main motivation for paying attention to politics. Sally, a white single mother concerned about finding a good job upon release, commented:

> Here amongst us, we don't do a lot of talking about like politics type stuff. We just . . . don't really do it that often. We talk more about specific issues that have to do with politics, but we don't sit and talk about "Are you a Republican, are you a Democrat, who would you vote for?" We talk about specific issues, you know? . . . We talk about same-sex marriages or raising children . . . the rights of same-sex couples, stuff like that. Well, I've mentioned the welfare stuff. Sex offenders. You know the laws with the sex offenders. . . . Those are mainly the three issues that we talk about that have a lot to do with the government, the political stuff.

Particular areas of concern that came up in our interviews included new time limits on receipt of public assistance (especially among female inmates), education, health care, and, more generally, inequality in American society.

Not surprisingly, given their direct connection to the criminal justice system, numerous interviewees expressed strong and articulate views about criminal justice, and not all of these views inclined toward leniency for their fellow inmates. James, a young African American probationer, explained his opposition to George W. Bush: "I heard he's supposed to hire more police officers and all that, and I think Bush would have been looking out more for the rich and less for the poor." Others discussed specific laws. Minnesota applies restrictive civil commitment laws to certain sex offenders, under which "sexually dangerous persons" may face an indefinite and involuntary period of confinement far exceeding their court-imposed criminal sentence.[3] The anomalies of these laws occasioned comment by several of our interviewees who were serving time as sex offenders. Alan, for example, said: "One of my projects is to try and overturn the Sexually Dangerous Predator law because right now it's so broad. The legislature has worded it so broad that you could have five parking tickets and be committed." Alan also made clear, however, that he had actively lobbied for tougher child pornography laws: "One of [the] things I'm doing is calling, there's a guy named [*state legislator*], I think his name is, and he's trying to get a child pornography law through. You know and I've been calling there a couple times a week going, 'Yeah, I still support it. Keep pushing.' "

Others drew similar distinctions, criticizing the apparent irrationality of particular laws and policies (including disenfranchisement) and advocating more reasoned—though not necessarily more lenient—approaches in their place. Michael, a probationer in his late twenties, pointed to legal changes and technological innovations in policing:

You know how people stand on the corner and sell drugs . . .
stand in one spot, they, that, that code red and that CODE-
FOR [computer-optimized police deployment system] could
change a lot of stuff this summer. Yeah, I think it's a good thing
. . . it's been lot of kids getting killed. You know, I don't like
that 'cause I love kids, you know. So that CODEFOR should
crack down on a lot of drug business, stuff like that, man. . . .

It's good they're making laws, they probably won't be, probably won't be, those loitering laws, you never know, could save somebody from getting killed.

Alan similarly suggested "tougher laws, but fair laws," such as a 10-year period of sex offender registration rather than the current lifetime requirement. Like many other prisoners, Larry, who was serving a long murder sentence, viewed prisons as necessary institutions. Nevertheless, he wished that inmates' time was structured to permit more productive activity:

Most people in here definitely need to be in prison. Definitely most. Up, maybe 90-some percent, 95, 98 percent. Almost everybody . . . where they're going wrong is just putting people away. You know something needs to be done to change the people. And these little treatment programs they have down here aren't changing anybody, you know? . . . So they need to be in here, but it would be so much better if while they're in here, something was done to change them so that, you know, they don't come back. And I think moving people, you know, or educating people is the answer.

Even if they disagreed with the particular punishment they received, or the way they were treated by police, lawyers, judges, or correctional officials, none of our respondents expressed extreme views about eliminating or fundamentally transforming the system. In fact, a number highlighted instead the new knowledge they had gained in prison about just how bad *other* criminals are. We found no evidence that if they could, reenfranchised felons would seek to use their political power to do away with the criminal justice system, as some have feared (and as the federal judge speculated in the *Green* case discussed in chapter 1).[4]

### Political and Partisan Preferences

Some of our respondents articulated clear political and partisan identities. We asked each about the hotly contested 2000 presidential election, and for those who indicated a preferred candidate, why they supported that candidate. Among the supporters of Democrat Al Gore, a number invoked class- or race-based themes similar to those that Gore emphasized during the campaign (in particular when attacking Bush's proposals for a large tax cut). For example, Sally told us:

> My opinion of Bush basically is that he . . . just doesn't care about lower-class people. He's, to me, seems more about people who have money. I just don't see that—I see that there's more middle and lower class people than there is, you know, upper-class. . . . Listening to [Gore] speak, he seems like a more caring, a more caring person. Like he cares about the people.

For Sally, as for many others, Bush's upper-class origins contrasted sharply with her perception of Al Gore as "for the average person." Steven, an older white probationer with a history of substance abuse, invoked similar themes in describing his support for Gore:

> Gore's more for the people and the average person, and, Bush, he's more for the rich. And I have nothing against rich people if they make it fair and square, but there's a lot of things that are going on that ain't right. But I got nothing against rich people otherwise but you gotta, you know, you gotta care about people . . . even if they're not rich.

Similarly, Marvin, a young sex offender who was crusading against hate crimes in prison, said he supported Gore "because Gore seems like a person that's there for the people."

We also found a sampling of support for George W. Bush among our respondents. As with Gore, the themes endorsed by the Bush supporters often paralleled those invoked by Bush on the campaign trail. Jerry, a young white prisoner serving time for manslaughter, said, "Since this incarceration I'm kind of anticriminal. And [Bush] did some good stuff in Texas." Daniel said:

> I liked a lot of what Gore had to say, but his politics on guns kind of turned me off that. So I was more Bush for his . . . education. . . . 'Cause some areas do get more money allocated to them than poor areas. I kind of like his voucher system.

In talking about politics and elections, we also heard numerous references to the individual characteristics of political candidates. Many observers suggest that "candidate-centered politics" have become increasingly central in contemporary American political life.[5] For example, Pamela, the prisoner convicted of drug offenses we met in the introduction, told us that "character" was important in shaping her views of Bush as a candidate.

> Bush . . . absolutely. Mainly because the issue, his opinion on abortion. I found him much more real as a person. It's a character thing. I just felt like he had so much more character and he was much more consistent. He wasn't like a chameleon like changing. . . . I just felt that Bush was more honest and, uh, I liked his wife. . . . He has an honor for our original amendments and everything, you know, that I haven't seen in anyone for awhile. I didn't see it in Clinton. . . . Or an honor looking at how our forefathers really set up the country 'cause it was all about God. It was all about God. And it just got neutralized, neutralized, neutralized as the time went on.

Ideological labels, however, appeared less salient. Only about half of our respondents identified themselves as "liberal" or "conservative," and in many cases these broad labels were given meaning in personal rather than political terms. For example, the term "conservative" connoted maturity, sophistication, or an aversion to risk for many respondents rather than the economic and social approaches of the Republican Party or the preservation of existing political institutions. For example, Thomas, a young African American parolee, Dennis, a Native American prisoner, and Steven, a white probationer, described themselves as "conservative" in the following terms, respectively:

> [I think of myself as] conservative, definitely. Definitely. Because I look at myself as a more mannerable and very conscious man. I wouldn't become more disrespectful. . . . Can't no man make me mad. Can't nobody make me mad, but myself. I become angry of mistakes I've made and try again to be a more conservative type person.

I'd probably put myself as a conservative 'cause I'm a very casual, respectable type person. When I'm out there in the real world, and freedom, I—Suits—gotta look good. Very respectable looking. You know very respectful towards other people and carrying myself very proper. It's a little different in here. . . . But otherwise, I'm a very casual, respectable kind of person.

I was a liberal Democrat most of my life, but due to my problems I have to be conservative 'cause I can't cope with my problems and be liberal . . . like when I got drunk and became sexual act-, sexually prone, you know? . . . I grew up in a liberal environment . . . in the sixties when a lot of changes in this country happened . . . even though alcohol affected me so severely, I was liberal, you know, and I didn't, I wasn't proud of not drinking. I was "If I want to go out and get drunk with the guys, well, so what?" . . . But being, switching to conservatism, now I, you know, I have to be conservative 'cause I- With my medications and stuff, and my mental problems, if—without being conservative, I'll be in trouble.

By contrast, party labels held greater meaning for most respondents, as a negative heuristic if nothing else. Eighteen of the 33 interviewees identified with the Democratic Party, most doing so in terms of class or race. James and Mary, respectively, present typical class-based perceptions about the parties in explaining why they identified with the Democrats:

I would probably prefer the Democrats more because I feel they look out more for the poor. And Republicans, you know, they gonna look out more for the rich, and less for the poor really. That's how I see it.

I feel that the little people is what needs the help. Not the big businesses and the big people, you know? And that's what the Republicans represent, you know, I feel essentially. You know the rich get richer and the poor get poorer and there's really no in between.

Not surprisingly, race drove Democratic Party preference for some African American respondents, with several suggesting that disenfranchisement laws are intended to dilute the votes of racial minorities. Michael characterized the different social bases of the two parties, and his reasons for supporting the Democrats, in the following terms.

> The Republicans don't really be for the minorities, they're like for the majority. And the Democrats seem like they, you know, more minority-based, trying to help, you know, better the community, our community. . . . Well, I think the Republicans [are] more based in the middle-class area. . . . They try to do for them. But the Democrats, you know, try to help out with child care . . . they try to help you get off welfare and get a stable job. Whereas, the Republicans, they just, they just want you to be based how you already is, you know . . . that's my view, that's my opinion, I really don't know too much about politics, but from what I be seeing . . . Democrats can more help, you know, my people out more.

Other people cited a family history of support for one of the major parties. Lynn told us:

> I'm not ashamed to say it, I'm a Democrat . . . from what I've gathered through the years and what I guess I grew up with, my parents were, are both Democratic, it always seems that the Democrats fight a little harder for the middle-class, the underdogs. Their, the education issue, the welfare thing was [a] big thing . . . you know, and I've used the system, but only when I've needed to so I think the five years and off is great, and it's not just a kick-you-off program. They go out of their way to try and help you get jobs, to make you self-sufficient. . . . Basically any issue that is on the Democratic side, I'm pretty much, pretty much with. It's, you know, the health care, that was a big one.

A perception that the Republicans are less receptive to the needs and interests of low-income urban communities provided some with another basis for identification with the Democratic Party. Thomas described his experiences with party politics in Chicago:

> I look at myself more as a Democrat. . . . Where I come from, Chicago . . . you know, men organizations, that I was in. . . . A lot of people would say gang, but I call it organization. We did a lot of, you know, there's like a lot of community work. . . . In Chicago, they came, and you know there's a lot of Democrats, you know what I'm saying? With, not that we have anything against them, but we more like, speak out more. Democrats gonna speak out more. The Republicans gonna, in my eyes, is gonna be like a snake, a serpent. You know, reach out for the weak. And they're gonna use you, twist you, spit you out whatever. They don't need them, throw them away. That's why so many people are in prison now, you know? Anything to send a person to prison.

Those who identified with the Republicans (roughly a quarter of the respondents) frequently cited their preference for limited government. In the words of Larry, the white prisoner serving a long murder sentence,

> I like the idea that Republicans are more in favor of the smaller government and they're not so interested in the push towards socialism that our country seems to be heading for right now. You know like socialized medicine and, you know, trying to take control of everything. . . . One thing that would make me lean toward the Republican viewpoint is their, they think that, you know, the government shouldn't have so much money and, you know, shouldn't be as big as it is and have so much power and authority, which all really comes from money, I guess. But they think it should be more of the people.

Finally, we also asked respondents who characterized themselves as political "independents" why they did not identify with the major parties. These individuals often expressed a basic distrust of each major party, or disaffection from political life more generally.[6] These views were often accompanied by a pragmatic nonpartisan approach to politics, although in practice these two meanings of political independence overlapped.[7] Roger, an older white probationer convicted of fraud, characterized his political independence in candidate-centered terms:

> I consider myself to be an independent voter. . . . I let the man dictate how I vote and not the party. I would have voted for Jesse Ventura had I been able to vote. 'cause he made the most sense. . . . I supported Jimmy Carter. I supported Ronald Reagan. Especially John Kennedy. Because he was a mover and a shaker. And I tend to probably vote more so that way. Towards the movers and the shakers. . . . [Ventura's] antics I'll put up with because you see him doing some stuff that is, so to speak, against the political machinery. You know, myself I'm middle-income and I would say that we been, basically, we've been the class of people that have been where everything falls onto. . . . You've got the Democrats, of course, for the working person, you've got the Republicans, so to speak, for the upper class, and, you know, in the midst of that, the middle class gets trampled.

By contrast, Craig, a young white prisoner incarcerated for burglary, said he supported independents because their nonpartisanship cut "against the grain" of conventional politics:

> I do like some of the independents and the alternatives just because it's just that. It's not so polarized. So I do tend to side when it will come to voting with Independent or somebody that at least sounded like they were against the grain. And not just the same old talk. Somebody that sounded genuine and didn't sound like maybe a career politician.

Political independence allowed these respondents to choose whether to support major party candidates rather than to be forced to do so out of habit or convention.

## The Experience of Second-Class Citizenship

In contrast to images of offenders as an ill-informed, apathetic group with low citizenship norms, our respondents shared plenty of reasoned and even sophisticated views about politics, rights, and public policies. Far from being the politically deviant or incompetent citizens imagined by those who would protect the "purity" of the ballot box, they expressed the same types of political hopes and fears, and policy preferences, as other enfranchised groups. Our interviews also showed quite clearly that felons do not speak with one voice. Even within the same institution, we were struck by the diversity of political views and concerns expressed. We also learned that labels such as "liberal" and "conservative" have far different connotations among convicted felons than among the general population. In a correctional setting, it is vitally important to present oneself as "conservative" in manner and dress, regardless of political beliefs. Indeed, this underlying conservatism might provide conservative political forces with an important opening in appealing to ex-inmates.

The interviews also show how social divisions along race, class, and gender lines remain important for understanding the political attitudes and behaviors of convicted felons. In particular, our African American respondents generally expressed much less faith in the criminal justice system and in government more generally.[8] Our discussions showed substantial variation in the sort of class-based themes invoked on behalf of particular parties and candidates. With regard to gender, the women we interviewed consistently expressed greater concern for issues such as welfare reform, education, and health care than did the men. Despite important differences in the orientations and positions of our respondents, however, it is important to reiterate that a disproportionate number of the lost political voices in the United States are those of young men of color. Criminal punishment and disenfranchisement directly dilute the political power of African Americans, males, and poor and working-class U.S. citizens.

Most important, the interviews helped us understand how much voting matters to felons with more pressing security and survival needs. The denial of voting rights was perceived as "another loss to add to the pile," as Pamela put it, one that still carries a sting for citizens convicted of crimes. Steven also used the image of a pile: "On top of the whole messy pile, there it was. Something that was hardly mentioned, and it meant a lot." The "messy pile" of losses is, of course, enormous and enduring. Many of our interviewees felt permanently marked or "branded" by their conviction. Thomas referred to the "F" on his record:

> You are labeled as a felon, and you're always gonna be assumed and known to have contact with that criminal activity and them ethics. And even when I get off parole, I'm still gonna have an "F" on my record. I can have twenty million dollars just sitting in an account. I'm still gonna be a felon.

Karen discussed how the label permeates virtually every area of her life:

> When I leave here it will be very difficult for me in the sense that I'm a felon. That I will always be a felon . . . a felon is a term here, obviously it's not a bad term . . . for me to leave here, it will affect my job, it will affect my education . . . custody, it can affect child support, it can affect everywhere—family, friends, housing. . . . People that are convicted of drug crimes can't even get housing anymore. . . . Yes, I did my prison time. How long are you going to punish me as a result of it? And not only on paper, I'm only on paper for ten months when I leave here, that's all the parole I have. But, that parole isn't going to be anything. It's the housing, it's the credit re-establishing . . . I mean even to go into the school, to work with my child's class— and I'm not a sex offender—but all I need is one parent who says, "Isn't she a felon? I don't want her with my child." Bingo. And you know that there are people out there like that.

Susan, imprisoned for murder for almost her entire adult life, raised more general questions about stigma and the prospects for reintegration:

> Right now I'm in prison. Like society kicked me out. They're like, "Okay, the criminal element. We don't want them in society, we're going to put them in these prisons." Okay, but once I

get out, then what do you do? What do you do with all these millions of people that have been in prison and been released? I mean, do you accept them back? Or do you keep them as outcasts? And if you keep them as outcasts, how do you expect them to act?

Even as "outcasts," felons must nevertheless manage the stigma and take on the rights and responsibilities of law-abiding citizenship. But they face formidable difficulties. The first problem is making a living and overcoming employers' reluctance to hire them, restrictions on the types of jobs they can hold, and their limited social networks.[9] While Rita knew little about getting a straight job, for example, she was embedded in a dense network in the illegal economy that made selling drugs or disposing of stolen property an all-too-attractive alternative.[10]

A felony conviction also complicates family life. Incarceration creates a physical barrier, and extended absences from family members can make homecomings problematic.[11] The acute pain experienced by the temporary or permanent suspension of parental rights has been repeatedly documented, and is one of the hidden social costs of incarceration.[12] Several of our respondents also noted how entire families are affected when one member is incarcerated and how they wanted to become a role model to prevent their children from repeating their own difficulties.

As with work roles, taking on family roles as responsible citizens—as parents, partners, adult children, or siblings—is a central task of reintegration. Our primary interest, however, is the task of civic reintegration.[13] How do felons resume or begin lives as active and law-abiding citizens in their communities? A felony conviction and a history of problematic behavior create barriers to community participation. According to Paul, the politically active inmate doing time for a sex offense, "there's too many sanctions against me for me to be an active part of the community." Others lamented the continuous and critical scrutiny of others. Roger, whose first felony conviction came late in life, aptly summarized the problem:

They say, "Okay, I want you back into the community," and then you point your fingers at them and keep your fingers pointed at them and say, "This guy did a bad thing." . . . Make

it easier to come back into society instead of saying, "We're accepting you back, but you can't do this and you can't do that,
and you can't do this. You can walk around our streets, but after 9:00 at night, I want you to be out of sight so the good
people of, you know, Pleasant Acres, won't see you."

Thomas and Henry, much younger African American men, felt the
same sort of scrutiny, respectively:

> For you to make a transition from prison and come out here
> and they expect you, "You need to do this" and "You need to
> do that." You know, you're telling me to do so much, and
> there's only so much that I can do. I don't have too many op-
> tions. I'm a felon.

> [It's like] you broke the law, you bad. You broke the law, bang—
> you're not a part of us anymore.

For women, a felony conviction is more rare, and perhaps as a consequence
even more stigmatizing. Rachel, imprisoned for a violent assault, was
acutely aware of her deviant status: "People just look at you like, 'I can't
believe you. I can't believe you. Look at her. Oh my God, she went to
prison.'"

Such public scrutiny and constant judgment complicate efforts at reintegration. Susan was concerned about her privacy and personal safety:

> It's kind of scary now for felons, with the internet . . . people
> can know my address and stuff. That kind of makes me want to
> go back underground in a criminal element. I mean, I was—I'm
> a—I committed a murder. I'm not a murderer 'cause that's not
> what I am. But I did do a big mistake once, and, you know, a
> lot of people like to judge you on your past mistakes. And they
> like to label you and not see you, but that's not the totality of
> my being, you know? I'm, I'm a really good person. I have a
> good heart, and a lot of people are like [sarcastically], "Yeah,
> right." But what if it's true? . . . You're going [to] squelch that,
> you're not going to let that happen, you're not going to let me

be good because you have these labels on me? And you're going to make it hard for me to get a job, and you're going to make it hard for me to get a place to rent? And if my address is on the internet, what if some local renegade kind of, I don't know, people, just want to go kill an ex-con, or something or go harass them? I mean . . . that's scary to me.

Those formally classified as sex offenders face even greater scrutiny and stigma. Their situation raises unique concerns because of registration and notification laws that create a hyperstigmatized status. Alan said that this stigma is so powerful that "a person would rather have a murderer living next door than me." Dennis, a sex offender in his twenties, discussed how public attention hinders attempts to assume the role of a law-abiding citizen: "They notify everybody—your community, all the schools, all businesses, everything. They just blurt you out there to everybody. And it really screws your chances up."

The hostile community reaction to people with a felony conviction instills a sense of ongoing punishment that lasts far beyond anything court-imposed. While their reception in the community restricts informal neighboring and other civic participation, they must also contend with literal disenfranchisement. Losing the right to vote incited a range of emotion. Even felons who had never voted viewed the right to vote as fundamental to citizenship and reintegration. Because voting is something that adult citizens are simply supposed to do, disenfranchisement left many feeling "exiled" from their fellow citizens. Without the right to vote, Rachel felt she was "less than the average citizen." Karen, who had been an enthusiastic voter before incarceration, discussed how losing the right to vote conflicted with her plans to be an active citizen upon release:

I voted every single solitary year from the day I was granted voting privileges when I was eighteen until I was convicted. . . . For me it's important because I like to know that when I leave here, I will start—I will continue my life because I won't start it over—although there's a whole new part of me coming out of here—I will continue my life, and I would like to have that position back. To be able to vote.

We found great variation in respondents' self-reported political participation prior to their most recent felony conviction. Of the 33 interviewees, 22 reported having voted at least once in the past, and a few had been active and enthusiastic voters prior to their conviction. For example, Lynn, a small-town mother of a teenager, was passionate about voting and tried to impress its importance upon her disinterested son:

> I take [voting] very seriously. . . . This was the first year my son
> was able to vote, and he wasn't going to and I literally put him
> in the car and took him to vote. I mean it was "You're living in
> my house, you're going to vote" kind of thing because I can't,
> so. . . . I've voted every time I can since I've been eighteen, and
> I think this is the worst, one of the worst things about being a
> felon, having a felony, is not being able to vote.

It is awkward to admit that one does not vote, as it represents a failure to fulfill basic citizenship duties. This is reflected, for example, in the over-reporting of turnout by survey respondents (such as those in the YDS). Of those who had been old enough to vote in a previous election but volunteered that they had not, justifications for the failure to participate were similar to those that other Americans express. Henry had never been eligible to vote because he was never "off paper" at the time of an election. Even so, he feels that his one vote is unlikely to make much difference anyway.[14]

> I'm not too involved [politically]. The reason I say that is 'cause
> I feel one person doesn't have enough power. It takes a group.
> A majority, you know? And I've kind of lowered my standards
> on how much to give off. I figure if I don't count for much,
> why get involved, you know? But they say one can make [a]
> difference sometimes. So either way, you can look at it either
> way, but I look at it as I wouldn't make a difference politically.

Ironically, however, Henry also told us that he *did* attempt to vote in the 2000 presidential election but was turned away at the polls because of his current parole status (Minnesota is one of several states that allows Election Day registration). Other respondents conceded that they might not have voted even if they had been eligible. Michael explained, "I never voted.

Never. . . . I couldn't 'cause I just caught that felony [in 1996]," before adding, "I really don't think I'd vote anyway."

Others told us that although they had never voted before, they resolved to do so once they regained eligibility. Travis, a white parolee in his twenties, felt that he had benefited from the "structure" of prison and was now able to take on greater responsibilities. He recalled not voting in the one presidential election for which he was eligible, commenting, "I don't think I even cared about it then." Louis, an African American recently imprisoned for a drug conviction, said his views about participation had evolved since being imprisoned.

> No [I've never voted in an election]. Due to a lot of things. Environment, never been encouraged, but after being incarcerated and having that time to reflect on all issues, I see how important it really can be. Well, as I look at it now, to not vote is to not be heard.

Our interviews also suggested an interaction between the right to vote and the willingness to invest in political knowledge, awareness, or interest, which might stimulate participation in the first place. Susan told us her disenfranchisement discouraged her from thinking about politics:

> I was thinking about getting involved with politics when I get out, and how I'd love to, and then I'm like, "Well, I can't vote," so it's so discouraging. I'm not gonna read this article on this candidate's views or, you know, I'm not going to research on it. But then the only thing th[at] motivates me is that the people around me don't know I'm an ex-con and can't vote, and so I don't want them to think I'm just lame and ignorant because I can't participate in their political conversations. So that's like my only motivation, and that's not a lot of motivation because, I mean, being able to vote, my vote making a difference would be more motivation than the rare political conversation.

In addition to these disincentives, felons felt disconnected from the outside world while in prison. Most had limited interaction with family and friends, had no internet access, could only watch television in common areas where the daily news was a low priority; and, of course, had little access to political life outside prison walls. Lynn, the politically enthusiastic mother quoted earlier, describes some of these problems:

> I [used to] go to city council meetings. I want to know what's going on. That's the one thing I hate about being in here. Nobody wants to watch the news. And so I . . . broke down and spent the $250 and got a TV [in my cell]. . . . I'm part of this world, whether I'm in here or not. I'm not going to be here that long, I'm still going to be out in the real world. I want to know what's going on, and I want to know what's changed since I've been in here. You try to watch news in here, oh no . . . that really irritates me.

Despite these barriers, prison is not a simple roadblock to political interest and consciousness. Many of the inmates with whom we spoke told us that time in prison made them *more* interested in political issues. Dylan, incarcerated for murder since his late teens, was trying to "make the best" of the limited opportunities that prison offered. He described how his interest in politics gradually took root:

> Early on when I was a teenager and I was first incarcerated, obviously, if it ever came to mind, it was, "I don't care." You know? Or "It doesn't affect me," and the whole attitude of that, I suppose. But as I've matured over the years in prison, and started looking forward to all the trappings of society and what it's going to mean to be free again, and that was one of the considerations that, you know, I start forming actual political opinions about these—you watch these politicians on TV and say, "This guy's a scumbag. I wouldn't vote for him," or whatever. Or you see someone that actually has a good agenda. And, I don't know, I've gotten more and more interested in it over the years in talking to other guys, my age or older, that have more of a political opinion, that have been following politics longer than I have. Just get pulled into discussions there.

Several others echoed Dylan's burgeoning interest in political life. Alan had been politically active prior to his incarceration for criminal sexual conduct. He described the change in his viewing habits, and increased attention to political news, while in prison:

> You know it's weird because before my crime I really . . . didn't follow the elections or anything that close. And since I've been in prison, I've been watching the way the Senate works on like channel 17. . . . I've been watching the political process a lot since I've been in here . . . 200 percent more at least. You know? 'Cause before I didn't even turn on the TV. You know I rarely watched the news or anything like that. Now I watch the city council meetings sometimes if they have them. Like [*city name*] has a local station that has their city council meetings on, and channel 17 has the Senate coverage and things like that.

Like most Americans, many of our interviewees closely followed the 2000 presidential election and its aftermath, although here it is hard to separate the entertainment value of that unique event from its substantive political meaning. We were, however, surprised to learn from Alan that inmates in several housing units or "cottages" organized their own mock elections:

> There was a lot of going back and forth on it [the 2000 election] . . . people were going around doing kind of a silent mock election just to see how people would vote even in our cottage. And, you know, the winner was, was Bush. But not by very much. It was, you know, out of 74 people in our cottage, I think it was pretty split down the middle, you know? . . . I know that was happening in other cottages.

## Rebuilding Ties

While disenfranchisement and other sanctions limit civic participation in important ways, many of the people we spoke with still conveyed a desire to participate in their communities. Paralleling the findings of Kathryn Edin and her colleagues, we were struck by the degree to which time in prison encourages reflection on civic duties and responsibilities.[15] Among the activities mentioned were volunteering, coaching youth sports, and public speaking about their experiences and mistakes. The motivation behind these plans, however, differed. Susan felt that her offending created a new responsibility, commenting: "You can't always undo what you've done, but you can try to promote harmony in another area."

Several people specifically linked civic participation with their desire to stay away from crime. Pamela discussed how her volunteer work helped her:

> I'm [making blankets] for kids I'll never see and they'll never
> see me. But that makes me feel so good that I'm doing some-
> thing here that's not about me. You know that's not selfish. . . .
> and that's just a small example of the same thing on the outside.
> If you start filling yourself up. It's the same principle of sponsor-
> ship in AA and NA. You start helping other people who have
> less time than you clean and sober, you stay well, too. Because
> there's a connection there and there's people relying on you.

Alex, who had killed a relative while drunk, felt that sharing his experiences with alcohol would help him become a sober and law-abiding citizen:

> When I leave [prison], I want to go, maybe [start] going around
> to juvenile detention centers. Speaking about alcoholism . . .
> from the first time I started drinking to my incarceration and
> what I went through in prison. And just sharing that with
> younger kids around the community . . . will keep me aware of
> what I want . . . it would just remind me of what could happen,
> what I could go back to.

Dylan outlined bold plans to do volunteer work and public speaking:

> Well, the first thing I'm going to do, even when I'm on work
> release someday, there's an extension of the [city] Youth Services
> Bureau. We work with them here where they bring in their re-

peat offenders, and we talk to them. But once I'm on work release, or even once I'm paroled, you can go to schools, you can
go to community centers, all kinds of places and talk to kids.
. . . I'm in here for murder, and I can't ever get that person's life
back. I can't return him to his family, I can't balance that scale
any way, but I can keep trying for the rest of my life. . . . We
have a Toastmasters Club here. And I've been involved with that
for the last two and a half years, so that's definitely helped my
communication skills of being able to articulate myself so I want
to be able to use that when I go out, too. Actually go give talks,
not—I watch the legislators talk sometimes on [channel] 17, and
I can see myself actually, as. . . . It seems probably unrealistic
right now. A friend of mine who got out, he was a doctor before came in. He's up in [*city name*] now and he's given a talk
to a criminology class. . . . So I'm like, "If you can do that . . ."
I mean I'd love to go to criminology classes or talk in front of
the legislators.

Though these plans seem "unrealistic right now," felons such as Dylan
express commitment to civic-minded role behavior:

I've done everything I could since I've been in here to try and
do that [contribute something]. I've started youth groups to try
to talk to youth, and tried to get as much of an education as I
could, get as many job skills as I can.

To be sure, not all respondents believed they "owed" something to
their communities. Henry disagreed with the idea of restitution or "earned
redemption":[16]

[Wanting to give back to the community is] something that
they were taught in treatment. They got a therapist that installs
that inside of their head. That if you take something or hurt
somebody around your neighborhood, which is your community, don't you think you should give back? 'Cause only a bad
person wouldn't. So they make a person think maybe they
should feel that way. They should give back if they took some-

thing or harmed somebody. . . . I don't feel I owe anyone anything. I owe myself something. I owe myself a better life, you
know? I owe myself a chance to do better. That's what I owe.

Scott affirmed that he wanted to become a law-abiding citizen, but resisted
the idea that he should somehow repay society with anything other than
law-abiding behavior:

I don't feel guilty, man, after spending five years in the joint.
I'm sorry, I just don't. . . . All the people that are smoking drugs
and do that, yeah, I did help them get high. I helped them hurt
their body, yes, I did. But when you're talking about my freedom, the price of my freedom? I already paid for it . . . what I
owe society is to not get in trouble no more. To be law-abiding.
I've got that brand already, you know. I fucked up.

The idea that such brands are permanent and that they will always be
labeled "felons" makes it difficult for many to see themselves as active
citizens.[17] Paul explicitly resented the idea of "giving back" to the community that cast him out:

I really get kind of peeved when people say "give back to the
community" because I'm not a part of the community anymore
as far as I can see . . . so when they [say], "What are you going
to give back to the community for this and for that?" I'm like
well, hey, community doesn't want a damn thing to do with
me, why should I go back and give anything to do with the
community?

Such frank comments show the barriers to civic reintegration and taking one's place as a citizen in good standing. Thomas highlighted the ability
to manage stigma:

What choice do you have? You either deal with this, or you go
back to prison. The second time I got out [of prison], I
changed myself, my surroundings, the people I was with . . . I
was gonna be persistent . . . I was gonna show that I can do,
more or less, the same that any man can do.

Even for felons willing to get involved, their conviction creates a multitude of barriers that prevent full participation. Whether it is the continued stigma of the "felon" label or the formal loss of citizenship rights, these restrictions send messages that lead many to question whether they truly belong. Even if they remain outsiders, however, almost all felons eventually rejoin our communities. As Susan put it, "not being able to vote kind of says you don't matter, and you're not really a part of this community. But then here I am, your next-door neighbor."

## Conclusion

Criminologists tend to use the term "citizen" narrowly and in opposition to criminal offenders. Criminals are placed on one side of the street, and law-abiding "citizens" on the other. But this juxtaposition is problematic. Our interviews show that people with felony convictions are often politically engaged, just like other people. They think of themselves as citizens, with sometimes strong political beliefs and varying levels of political participation. Like other citizens, many felons expressed both a desire for the rights of citizenship and a willingness to involve themselves in civic life. They clearly felt the sting of disenfranchisement and other collateral consequences of their convictions, which marked them as outsiders. Despite these feelings, however, they consistently defended their rights and embraced their responsibilities as citizens.

While the ideas and analysis in this chapter are exploratory rather than confirmatory, we can take from them both provisional support for the idea of civic reintegration through voting and confirmation of the skepticism voiced by some interview respondents. Though political participation likely plays a small role relative to pressing work and family needs, the right to vote remains the most powerful symbol of stake-holding in our democracy. To the extent that felons begin to vote and participate as citizens in their communities, there is some evidence that they will bring their behavior into line with the expectations of the citizen role, avoiding further contact with the criminal justice system.

# 7 The Impact of Disenfranchisement on Political Participation

While working on this book over the past few years, we have spoken about felon disenfranchisement to a wide range of audiences, including social scientists, journalists, policymakers, activists, and legal scholars. One question we hear repeatedly, articulated in different ways, goes something like this: Do you really think very many felons would vote, even if they could? Underlying this question is a series of widely held assumptions about criminal offenders: they have little respect for the law and government institutions, they are too busy committing crimes to worry about voting, they are so poorly educated that they would be unlikely to understand or care about elections and politics.

The survey and interview data in chapters 5 and 6 imply otherwise. But several scholarly studies have reached the conclusion that felon disenfranchisement has little impact on state differences in turnout.[1] For example, economist Thomas Miles found no significant differences in voter registration and turnout rates in states with strict felon disenfranchisement laws compared with states lacking such laws. Other analysts, however, have suggested that the growth of the disenfranchised felon population has now reached a magnitude such that it affects overall turnout rates and even election outcomes. For example, in his study of the history of the right to vote in the United States, historian Alexander Keyssar notes that "convicted felons constitute the largest single group of American citizens who are barred from participating in elections." He speculates that "although their participation rates in elections would likely be low, their numbers are certainly sufficient to affect the outcomes of elections in numerous states."[2]

These questions about participation are important in thinking about larger issues of political representation. If the empirical impact of disenfranchisement is negligible, the focus of the debate would likely shift from concerns about representational inequalities to legal and philosophical concerns about democracy and justice, such as those discussed in chapter 1. The fact that a sizeable proportion of the electorate is locked out of the voting process alone raises questions. But if that locking out is also changing the character of political participation in America, by keeping large numbers of citizens away from the ballot box who would otherwise participate, a different set of concerns are raised.

In chapters 5 and 6, we analyzed survey and interview data about offenders' political views and their attitudes toward political participation. These data afforded us insight into the population of felons in one state; it is time to turn to a broader attempt to estimate how many disenfranchised felons would participate nationally and how they would vote if they were eligible.

## Felon Disenfranchisement and Voter Turnout

It is well known that participation rates in elections at all levels in the United States are very low compared to other countries. In recent presidential elections, typically only slightly more than one-half of the voting age population (VAP) voted, and midterm congressional elections without a presidential contest have had turnout rates as low as one-third of the VAP.[3] One international survey of turnout rates in national legislative elections ranked the United States a shocking 138th among the 170 countries that held elections in the 1990s. Its rate of participation was substantially lower than all similar capitalist democracies, except for those of Switzerland (which ranked 137th), and even lower than those of many developing countries.[4] The reasons for this poor overall participation rate are many, and have been the subject of wide discussion and debate.[5] In the previous chapter, we noted that low levels of political interest and involvement among felons and ex-felons must be put into perspective: many Americans are apathetic about politics, do not think deeply about political issues, and are unlikely to spend much time discussing politics or being involved in political activity. An identical logic applies to voting. Expected low turnout rates among the disenfranchised must be put into the perspective of low turnout among all Americans. In other words, we need to frame the problem as one of *relative*, rather than absolute, participation.[6]

### What Explains Who Votes?

Why, exactly, would we expect felons to have lower turnout rates than other Americans? Answering this question requires a brief detour into the research on why, in general, some individuals are more (or less) likely to vote in any given election. In elections where turnout is far from universal, resource-rich groups tend to vote at higher rates than more disadvantaged groups. The most widely documented individual attribute predicting turnout is education. For example, in his study of voter turnout in Chicago during the 1924 presidential election, political scientist Harold Gosnell concluded that "the more schooling the individual has the more likely he is to register and vote in presidential elections."[7] Other early research found similar results, and this conclusion has remained a staple finding of turnout research since that time. The effects of education on turnout are often found to be mediated by other factors. For example, better educated people have more knowledge about the candidates and issues, they read newspapers to keep up on current events, they have a greater sense of political efficacy, and they are more concerned with election outcomes.[8]

Other social attributes of individual voters that influence turnout have also been widely documented. African Americans vote at lower rates than whites (although the gap has varied depending on electoral context and other factors), and turnout among Latinos is lower still. Regional differences in turnout are more pronounced than is often recognized; for example, in the 2000 presidential election, turnout ranged from a low of 40.5 percent in Hawaii to a high of 68.8 percent in Minnesota. On average, turnout is lower in the South than in other regions of the country, although that gap has narrowed significantly in recent years. Younger people vote at significantly lower rates than older people. People who are married, and those holding stable jobs, are more likely to vote than people who are unmarried or unemployed. Higher income people vote at higher rates than lower income people.[9] We focus on these particular social attributes of individuals in the American electorate because we know something about the same characteristics for the felon population as a whole. By contrast, we know far less about individual psychological attributes of the felon population, such as knowledge of current events, belief in the efficacy of voting, level of interest in election outcomes, and other such beliefs. Unfortunately, the latter are often even better predictors of political behavior than demographic attributes, but we can still make some educated predictions with the information that is available.

### Demographic Characteristics of Criminal Offenders

We gain some sense of the likely levels of participation among current and former felons by examining demographic information about them. The best available source of information about the social characteristics of convicted felons is found in the *Survey of State Prison Inmates* data series. This survey, first carried out in 1974, has subsequently been carried out at approximately five-year intervals.[10] The survey uses a nationally representative sample of state prison inmates to provide comprehensive data about the characteristics of this population. (We drew from this survey in chapter 3.)

A clear, if unsurprising, portrait emerges from this profile. Most prisoners are male, and slightly under half are African American, with a growing Hispanic presence. Most prison inmates have low levels of education; in all survey years, less than one-third had graduated from high school (compared to 82 percent of the adult male population in the United States).[11] At the time they were incarcerated, only about two-thirds had either part-time or full-time jobs, also far below the national average for men in their prime working years. Their (self-reported) incomes at the time of incarceration were also very low, with median incomes of $19,322 in 1974 and just $14,430 in 1997 (amounts in real 1999 dollars). Inmates have also gotten older, with the average age at release increasing from 31 to 34 from 1990 to 2000 alone, reflecting longer sentences and stricter parole eligibility criteria.[12] At the time of incarceration, few were currently married (23.7 percent in 1974 and 17.7 percent in 1997), but more than half reported having been married at some point in their lives.

The types of crimes for which felons are incarcerated have also changed, reflecting changing priorities in the criminal justice system. Violent and property crimes were far less central in the late 1990s than in the mid-1970s (falling from 86 percent to just 60 percent of the total), with corresponding growth in the proportion of inmates incarcerated for drug crimes or "other" offenses.

We can use this information about the characteristics of the felon population to estimate the proportion of felons who might have voted in recent elections if they had been granted the right to vote. It is important to note, however, one important limitation related to our use of inmate survey data. The averages just discussed reflect what we know about currently *incarcerated* felons. As we saw earlier, only about a quarter of currently disenfranchised felons are incarcerated. A significant proportion of the disenfranchised population consists of individuals who were sentenced to probation and thus never went to prison.

As discussed in chapter 3, probationers are somewhat better off than prisoners. Over one-half have attained at least a high school diploma or equivalency, over one-fourth are married, and less than one-fifth have been convicted of a violent offense such as assault. The most frequent offenses for felons on probation are drug trafficking, drug possession, larceny, and fraud. Although males and racial minorities are overrepresented in all correctional populations, a larger percentage of the probation population is composed of whites and females. Less information is available for probationers than for prisoners, but this group also appears to be more socially advantaged with regard to characteristics such as education than felons who go to prison.

In addition to prisoners and probationers, almost half of the disenfranchised population is made up of people who have completed their sentences or have been released on parole. These people may have made transitions in life that will make them more likely to vote than the characteristics of the current inmate population would suggest. For example, they are, on average, older, more likely to be married, and employed in a stable full-time job and possibly have acquired further education.

Using inmate characteristics to estimate the average turnout rate among felons results in conservative estimates because the social and demographic information described earlier suggests that the "average" disenfranchised felon would be more likely to vote than the average *incarcerated* felon observed in the inmate surveys. In other words, by using sociodemographic information obtained during incarceration, we obtain a lower-bound (rather than an upper-bound) estimate of what we might find if we had a more accurate sociodemographic profile for the group as a whole. This is important because we would prefer to err on the side of understating, rather than overstating, the impact of felon disenfranchisement on turnout.

## Estimating the Impact of Disenfranchisement on Participation

To test conjectures about the political consequences of felon disenfranchisement, we need to estimate several different kinds of impacts: on turnout, voting outcomes, and public policy. We must begin by estimating how many felons and ex-felons are actually prevented from voting, how those now-disenfranchised felons might have voted if they had been allowed to do so, whether those votes would have influenced any actual elections, and finally, whether any policy outcomes might have been altered as a consequence. Developing plausible estimates for each step is complicated, as we have already seen in our attempt to estimate the disenfranchised population in chapter 3. In this chapter and the next, we will provide further estimates of turnout and vote choice.

The known characteristics of those who make up the disenfranchised population permit some initial guesses about their hypothetical turnout and voting behavior. The social characteristics of felons and ex-felons—in particular their below-average levels of education and income, their lower rates of stable marriage or employment when out of prison, and the disproportionate share of the disenfranchised who are minorities—suggest that their turnout rates would be significantly lower than the rest of the population. We would also expect that, given these characteristics, more of them would vote for Democratic than Republican candidates if they could vote. But how much lower would their predicted turnout rate be? And how much stronger are their Democratic preferences likely to be?

A state-by-state canvass of which categories of felons are disenfranchised (a task we undertook in chapter 3) is the only way to begin to answer such questions. Trying to estimate the *impact* of disenfranchisement on turnout and electoral participation requires several further steps. In the appendix (see pages 267–72), we provide a more detailed discussion of why such an estimate is so difficult. The main problem is that there is simply no nationally representative survey or polling data that contains information about both the respondents' criminal records and their political participation and voting behavior. However, we can use information about the sociodemographic characteristics of the felon population and nationally representative election data from the Current Population Survey (CPS) to develop a regression analysis that allows us to estimate a counterfactual turnout rate among disenfranchised felons if they were permitted to vote.

Of the millions of people disenfranchised because of a felony conviction, how many would have voted, if they could? Figure 7.1 provides a graphical representation of the results of a regression analyses predicting hypothetical felon turnout in presidential elections between 1972 and 2000, and figure 7.2 shows the same trends for midterm congressional elections between 1974 and 2000.[13] They are adjusted for survey over-reporting of turnout.

In both figures, the top line represents the actual turnout rate for the entire electorate, while the bottom line is our estimated turnout rate for felons. As we would expect, turnout rates among disenfranchised felons would be significantly lower than among the general population. We estimate that an average of approximately 35 percent of disenfranchised felons would have voted in presidential elections in this period (compared to an average of 52 percent of the entire electorate), and an average of 24 percent

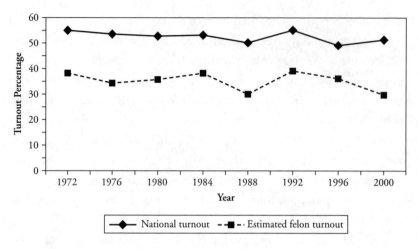

**Figure 7.1.**
Overall turnout rates and estimated turnout among disenfranchised felons, presidential elections 1972–2000.

**Figure 7.2.**
Overall turnout rates and estimated turnout among disenfranchised felons, congressional elections 1974–2000.

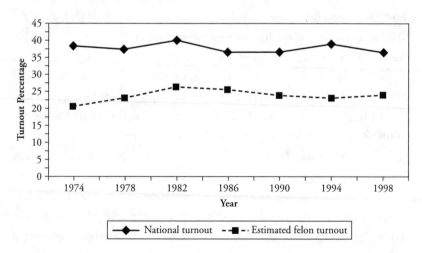

would have voted in midterm congressional elections (compared to an average of 38 percent of the entire electorate).

While these turnout estimates for the disenfranchised felon population are considerably below those of the actual electorate, they nevertheless suggest that a significant proportion of felons would have voted in any given election. Even taking the most conservative predictions about turnout rates in any of these elections (20.5 percent in 1974), and given the current number of more than 5 million disenfranchised felons today, we would expect that at least 1 million would turn out to vote in any federal election.

### Assessing the Validity of the Estimated Felon Turnout Rate

Our analysis suggests that while turnout among disenfranchised felons would be well below that of the rest of the electorate, it would nonetheless be far from negligible. At the same time, that analysis also contains a number of assumptions that might be challenged. On the one hand, it may be too conservative because it is based on sociodemographic characteristics at the time of incarceration. That is, it does not consider changes in age and personal circumstances (for example, greater residential stability, labor force attachment, and marriage) that are likely to increase turnout for the nonincarcerated population. During or after completion of a sentence, many felons (though certainly not all) will acquire greater education and more stable attachments to work, family, and their communities that will likely increase their probability of voting.[14] Moreover, as we suggested earlier, the *inmate* population is generally less educated, less likely to be married, and less likely to be employed than the *entire felon* population.

Other unmeasured characteristics of felons and ex-felons, beyond the demographic information available from the inmate surveys, could also have a significant effect on political participation among criminal offenders. In particular, felons may be less cognizant of, or less willing to accept, basic norms of citizenship and acceptable behavior than nonfelons with otherwise identical characteristics.[15] If so, they could be less likely to vote than a model based solely on social traits would predict. In other words, our counterfactual analysis hinges on the key assumption that the political behavior of disenfranchised felons would approximate that of non-felons matched to them in terms of age, race, gender, education, income, and marital status. It does not address the possibility that other characteristics of individual felons, such as low citizenship norms, might be influencing their propensity to both commit crime and participate in politics.

Exploring the issue of whether unmeasured characteristics are significant is not straightforward. Given the absence of national survey data with information about the political participation of felons and nonfelons, we cannot definitively test our assumptions. Nevertheless, we were able to address this issue using information gathered in the YDS. Though it is limited to an urban Minnesota population, the YDS includes a much wider range of information than the CPS data analyzed earlier. Its greatest asset for our purposes is that it includes both crime and voting data for each person surveyed. We used the YDS to test whether the correlation between criminal justice experiences and voting in these elections could be accounted for by the sociodemographic characteristics we used to match the felon population with nonfelons. (The full regression results are reported in other work[16].)

The YDS results shown in figure 7.3 give us considerable confidence in the turnout estimates reported earlier. As we would expect, the "unadjusted" comparison of arrestees and nonarrestees shows a statistically significant relationship between arrest and turnout in the 1996 presidential election. In the YDS, we find that the probability of (self-reported) turnout is about .72 for people who had never been arrested and .56 for people who had been arrested at least once. After adjusting for the effects of race, sex, education, income, employment, and marital status—the same characteristics we use to adjust our CPS analyses above—the difference in self-reported turnout is no longer statistically significant. Several of those factors help to explain the turnout differences between arrestees and nonarrestees. For example, education is a strong predictor of turnout, and arrestees have lower levels of education than nonarrestees.

Once we have controlled for the differences, we would predict that the probability of voting in 1996 was about .63 for arrestees and .69 for nonarrestees, a statistically insignificant difference.[17] Figure 7.3 also shows predicted probabilities for hypothetical individuals representing higher and

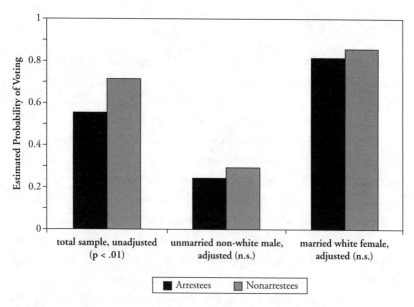

**Figure 7.3.**
The estimated probability of voting in 1996, arrestees versus nonarrestees, before and after statistically adjusting for sociodemographic characteristics. Predicted probabilities calculated for: (1) overall sample without adjustment for other variables; (2) nonwhite, unmarried male with 11 years of education and annual income of $19,000; and (3) married white female with college degree and annual income of $19,000.

lower turnout groups: an unmarried nonwhite man with 11 years of education and a married white woman with a college degree. Arrest reduces the probability of voting from .30 to .25 in the first case and from .86 to .82 in the second. In short, the sociodemographic characteristics appear to do a good job accounting for preexisting differences of offenders and nonoffenders that might affect both voting and crime. It is likely that at least part of the small remaining turnout gap is due to legal restrictions on voting for arrestees still under correctional supervision. In Minnesota, those convicted of felonies may not vote until they are "off paper," having completed probation or parole supervision in addition to any prison sentence. Unfortunately, we cannot determine from the YDS data whether individual arrestees were legally eligible to vote at the time of the election.[18]

*Some Cautions*

Given these confirmatory results from the Minnesota study, we believe our original counterfactual assumptions in matching characteristics of the felon population to national survey data are plausible. To be sure, these Minnesota data cannot conclusively validate national-level results, and we should be clear about the limitations of this test. Higher overall turnout rates (as in Minnesota) reduce between-group differences in participation, making higher turnout and lower turnout groups more similar. Minnesota is one of a handful of states with same-day voter registration, which makes voting easier. The state's unusual (social-democratic) political traditions and the political turmoil in the late 1990s associated with the Jesse Ventura election are also potentially significant. Moreover, the average felon nationally may differ from the average YDS arrestee in important ways that affect political participation. In a perfect world, we would have direct national survey data, or data from other states, to further test our assumptions. In a world of imperfect information, however, the best we can do is to rigorously assess the information that is available to us. On the basis of this confirmation, we conclude that our turnout estimates are reasonable.

*Felon Disenfranchisement and Turnout Decline*

There has been a contentious and vigorous debate over falling turnout in U.S. national elections since 1960. Between 1960 and 1988, official turnout figures in national elections fell from 62.8 percent to 50.3 percent, and they have hovered within a narrow band between 49 percent and 53 percent ever since (with a one-shot increase to 55 percent in 1992). Turnout in congressional elections is even lower, sliding from 45 percent in 1966 to just 33 percent in 1990 and fluctuating between 33 percent and 40 percent since. The implications of declining voter turnout in the United States, both in relation to recent downward trends and in comparison with other countries, have been the subject of a great deal of discussion and scholarly concern.[19] Turnout decline has also been viewed as something of a paradox, because steady increases in education and declining barriers to participation (principally in terms of registration laws) should have combined to increase turnout during the same period.[20]

Because the denominator used to calculate the "voting age population" (VAP) includes millions of ineligible felons, however, some of the fall in turnout is an *artifact* of the growing proportion of the adult population that cannot vote due to a felony conviction. From a simple accounting perspective, declining turnout is partially a byproduct of rising rates of criminal punishment. Immigration represents an additional source of error in calculating the turnout rate, since legal immigrants who cannot vote are also included in this denominator.

We are not the first to notice the importance of the difference between the official VAP number used in the denominator to calculate the overall turnout rate and the corrected figure once rising felon disenfranchisement and immigration status is taken into account. Political scientists Michael McDonald and Samuel Popkin have argued that, contrary to the conventional wisdom, the entire decline in turnout since 1972 is due to the rising proportion of ineligible individuals improperly included in the denominator of official turnout statistics or survey data.[21] Their estimated turnout among what they call the "voting eligible population" (VEP ) is essentially the same as the official measure of the voting age population in the 1950s and 1960s, when the proportion of ineligible felons and noncitizens was far lower than in more recent elections. The VEP and the VAP began to diverge in the 1970s, and by the 1990s there was a 3 to 7 percent gap in the turnout estimates based on the two different measures. The gap is potentially even greater than they estimate, however, because they do not include ex-felons in their estimate of the felon population (thus using a figure of 2.8 million in 2000 and 3.2 million in 2004 for prisoners, parolees, and felony probationers, rather than our more comprehensive estimate of 4.7 million in 2000, and 5.3 million in 2004).

Using the McDonald/Popkin approach, but using a corrected figure for felon disenfranchisement, the new VEP is even lower than they estimate (hence the corresponding "corrected" turnout figure is slightly higher than they estimate). It is worth noting, however, that the McDonald/Popkin analysis looks simply at the "accounting" impact of disenfranchisement on the VEP (by adjusting the denominator). If we do that, the overall national turnout rate is reduced by 2.65 percent due to felon disenfranchisement. A more realistic estimate, however, of the impact of felon disenfranchisement on actual turnout would also consider likely patterns of participation. Instead of removing all 5.3 million felons from the denominator, a better approach is to take into account the below average turnout rate among (prospective) felon voters.[22] Doing so would reduce the impact by about one-third.

### Is It Possible That There Is No Impact?
### Miles's Triple Difference Approach

One analyst has reported results significantly at odds with the conclusion drawn here. Economist Thomas Miles analyzed turnout data from 1986 to 2000, and concluded that "disenfranchisement has no impact on state-level rates of voter turnout."[23] In contrast to our counterfactual approach, Miles attempted to estimate the average effect of the laws using an econometric technique that compared turnout of African Americans and whites (the first difference) and of males and females (the second difference) in states with and without laws restricting ex-felon voting (the third difference). This type of design aims to isolate the treatment effect of ex-felon disenfranchisement among the target group most likely to experience a voting restriction: African American males. Using this "triple difference" technique, Miles finds no significant effects of disenfranchisement on turnout. In fact, his tables suggest that, if anything, ex-felon voting restrictions are *increasing* rather than decreasing voter turnout.

There are a number of practical and technical reasons for the disparity between our results and those of Miles.[24] Apart from these, Miles's research provides evidence about the statistical significance of the *average* effect of disenfranchisement and suggests that this average effect is likely to be small. Nevertheless, we think it safest to conclude that this study fails to find a significant effect only under a particular model specification, rather than to conclude that there is simply no effect. Further, in elections even small differences may have great practical importance. As we discuss in chapter 8, there were over 800,000 disenfranchised felons in Florida on Election Day in 2000, and we estimate that about 27 percent of them would have voted if given the opportunity. Yet even if only 10 percent—or even 1 percent—had voted that day, it could have meant the difference in a presidential election decided by a margin of 537 votes. Even if there is no statistically significant effect on overall turnout, a restriction can still matter in a practical sense. In our view, and in view of the analysis presented here, it is implausible to believe that *none* of the approximately 5 million felons, or 2 million ex-felons, would turn out to vote if so permitted.

It is also worth noting that, in our experience, former felons tend to overstate the severity of voting restrictions, often thinking they cannot vote when in fact they have regained their rights.[25] In the pure counterfactual scenario, however, there would be no information problem because the strictest laws (e.g., those in place until the 1970s) would never have existed. Thus, actual turnout among former felons today likely remains suppressed by the residue of these harsh laws and the information problems associated with them. We saw this in our interviews. We began the interviews by confirming that respondents have been convicted of a felony, and asking what they understood about their future voting rights. In Minnesota, felons are not permitted to vote until their entire sentence has been served. But there are no restrictions on voting once the sentence is complete. We were somewhat startled to discover that only a few of our respondents were aware of exactly how long they would remain disenfranchised; while all knew that they were not currently permitted to vote, many assumed they would continue to be disenfranchised for some period after the completion of their sentence. Respondents told us that they had learned about these restrictions from probation and parole officers, Department of Corrections officials, or other felons. It appears that either these sources of information were inaccurate or that there was a breakdown in communication. In either case, such misinformation will hinder participation among felon offenders until correct information is provided.

## Conclusion

We can now answer the question posed at the beginning of the chapter. A significant share of the disenfranchised felon population would vote if they were given the opportunity. To be sure, their turnout rates would fall far below those of the rest of the electorate. In presidential elections such as the 2000 or 2004 contests, we calculate that about one-third, or over 1.5 million currently disenfranchised citizens, would have participated if they had been eligible. In light of the conservative assumptions of our models, it seems more likely that this figure is too low than that it is too high. Under any circumstance, it represents the loss of a very large number of voices and votes. Whether those lost votes would have changed any particular election outcome is the subject of the next chapter.

# 8  A Threat to Democracy?

Kentucky Republican Mitch McConnell was first elected to the U.S. Senate in 1984. He has been a forceful and prominent conservative voice in the Senate, especially as both his seniority and Republican influence in Congress have grown. He is particularly known for his willingness to defend vigorously unpopular positions that others try to avoid. In recent years, for example, he has emerged as a vocal opponent of campaign finance reform. His articulate defense of such positions has made him a popular guest on political talk shows.

In February 2002, the U.S. Senate briefly debated an amendment to a bill offered by Nevada senator Harry Reid that sought to restore to ex-felons the right to vote in federal elections. During the debate, McConnell rose to deliver a characteristically blunt and critical response. He began by taking a classic states' rights position ("it is highly doubtful that Congress has constitutional authority to pass legislation preempting the states with regard to this issue") and then proceeded to offer a substantive defense of felon disenfranchisement:

States have a significant interest in reserving the vote for those who have abided by the social contract that forms the foundation of a representative democracy. We are talking about rapists, murderers, robbers, and even terrorists and spies. Do we want to see convicted terrorists who seek to destroy this country voting in elections? Do we want to see "jailhouse blocs" banding together to oust sheriffs and government officials who are tough on crime?[1]

The speech embodies several components of McConnell's rhetorical approach. On the one hand, he invokes classical philosophical considerations ("the social contract that forms the foundation of a representative democracy") and offers a vigorous defense of states' rights. On the other hand, he lays out some of the most extreme and least palatable aspects of restoring voting rights to ex-felons (the idea that antigovernment terrorists might use the ballot to "destroy this country") as the basis for opposing the entire bill.

There is no small irony to McConnell's high profile in the Senate debate over ex-felon voting rights: he may well owe much of his career in the Senate to the fact that his home state, Kentucky, disenfranchises ex-felons. In 1984, McConnell was a relatively unknown judge in Jefferson County, Kentucky, running against a two-term incumbent, Senator Walter Huddleston. McConnell benefited from the Republican presidential landslide of that year (Ronald Reagan trounced Walter Mondale by nearly 300,000 votes in Kentucky). His uphill campaign against Huddleston just managed to squeak by; he won by a narrow margin of 5,269 votes in an election with nearly 1.3 million ballots cast. As we will show later, it is quite possible that the disenfranchisement of ex-felons in Kentucky put McConnell over the top. Had he instead lost his 1984 campaign, it is quite likely—owing to the vicious competitive nature of the political field, in which losers rarely get a second chance—that McConnell never would have held a major elective office.

Such a counterfactual scenario is, of course, difficult to assess. It is certain, however, that the Democratic Party has lost some votes (in Kentucky and elsewhere) because of felon disenfranchisement. A disproportionate share of the disenfranchised felon population is African American. Many convicted felons come from poor or working-class urban districts, with low incomes, few job prospects, and low levels of formal education. The combination of these factors tends to push the "average" felon toward the Democratic Party in any given electoral contest. Whether those lost votes would have been sufficient to influence any election outcomes, however, is not clear. We cannot conclusively resolve that question, but we can at least offer an educated guess as to what that impact might be.

Although our analysis of partisan implications suggests that such possibilities are real, we stress that our investigation in this chapter is not simply about those interests. Although there is a long history in American politics of enfranchising and disenfranchising voters for partisan gain, the main question we are concerned with in this chapter—and indeed, the entire book—cannot simply be reduced to a partisan calculus. Disenfranchisement of any group of people carries with it important implications for the legitimacy of democratic elections in the United States as a whole. But if disenfranchisement further influences election outcomes to such an extent that members of groups overrepresented in the disenfranchised population suffer a measurable loss of representation, additional concerns are raised.

To examine these possibilities, we must begin with an overview of the implications of incomplete suffrage rights for democratic practice. It is particularly important to note that felon disenfranchisement constitutes an unusual issue in the post–Voting Rights Act era, in which the question of *group* impacts becomes a relevant consideration.

## Just Elections without Representational Equality?

Whether felon disenfranchisement in the United States poses a threat to electoral justice and democratic legitimacy is not a simple question.[2] It in fact contains two distinct questions, neither of which has received much attention in contemporary discussions of felon disenfranchisement. First, from the standpoint of overall representational equality, are the interests and preferences of some polity members systematically devalued because other citizens with similar preferences or attributes are excluded from participation? Second, are the preferences of some key groups in the electorate—in this case, minority voters—denied full representation because of the practice of disenfranchisement?

A simple but robust definition of a democratic political system in the modern world is that such a system would be one in which there are periodic peaceful transfers of power from an existing government to the political opposition, as a result of freely contested elections in which all adult citizens have an equal opportunity to participate. Such a model presupposes that election outcomes reflecting the will of the voters define legitimate democratic governance. Indeed, it has been the structuring of outcomes, rather than the mere existence of elections, that has provided the basis for the most contested discussions. This is true whether we are evaluating electoral processes in other countries or at home.

In democratic theory, the heart of the problem in assessing the fairness of elections is one of representation: How well do electoral systems aggregate the preferences of individual citizens? Do democratic institutions grant each citizen, and meaningful groups of citizens, equal opportunity for influence?[3] There are many models for administering elections around the world. It is rather trite to say that no electoral system has ever been devised—or indeed ever could be devised—that perfectly registers all citizen preferences. But that does not diminish the importance of the question.

In recent years, claims about the fairness of the electoral process in the United States have been posed most vigorously in terms of minority group representation. Since the passage of the Voting Rights Act of 1965 (and its 1982 amendments), state legislatures, courts, and a variety of interest groups and civil rights organizations have struggled over whether and how to ensure that racial minorities have fair opportunities to elect representatives of their choosing. In practice, this has often meant the opportunity to elect members of the same racial or ethnic group into political office. While there have been important cases of continuing individual disenfranchisement, the current controversies have, for the most part, centered not on the right to vote but rather the continuing disparity between the size of the African American or Latino population in the electorate as a whole and the election of black or Latino politicians to office. A brief discussion of these controversies provides a point of departure for our analysis.[4]

### The Problem of Equal Representation of Citizens and Groups

Are the voices of individual citizens, or significant groups of citizens, devalued when other members of the political community are denied the right to participate? This question goes right to the heart of why we value popular sovereignty and universal suffrage in the first place (an issue we took up briefly in chapter 1).

A useful example of this issue can be seen in the recent debate over the question of ensuring that the votes of military personnel be counted. Before the adoption of new federal legislation in the fall of 2002, overseas members of the military and their families frequently had a difficult time casting valid votes. These problems arose because of cumbersome and confusing absentee ballot procedures, which required successful execution of multiple steps (preregistering for an absentee ballot, receiving the ballot, and returning the ballot in time without any errors) in a timely fashion in order to meet the requirements of the individuals' home state. The 2000 Florida election fiasco revealed one of the many normally hidden aspects of the counting of ballots: the routine discarding of thousands of military ballots because of late arrival or other technical errors. The uproar over this practice prompted new federal legislation, which Congress eventually passed with broad bipartisan support.[5]

The idea that members of the armed forces abroad would not have their ballots counted seemed particularly unjust. At the very moment when they were performing an important (and often risky) type of citizenship duty, they were frequently denied in practice one of the main benefits of citizenship. But aside from the obvious injustice to the individual members of the armed forces, a deeper set of issues about representation swirled around the military ballots debate in the battle for Florida in the 2000 election.[6] On the assumption that a disproportionate share of the uncounted military ballots would have been Republican votes, George W. Bush's supporters took the position that not counting those ballots would deny full representation to *all* Republican voters in Florida. To be sure, there was inconsistency in their position: while the Bush camp argued that military ballots (many without postmarks) should be counted, they simultaneously argued that incompletely punched but otherwise properly cast ballots on Election Day should not be counted. But the logic of the argument for counting the military ballots is clear and has broader implications: when any group has its ballots rejected, all citizens with similar preferences suffer.

Similar questions arise in the case of disenfranchised felons. The question at one level appears starkly different: "good" and "bad" citizens (soldiers versus felons). But questions of representational equality arise even if the like-minded citizens denied the franchise are not "good" citizens. No democratic polity today allows "good" citizens more votes than everyone else.[7] The "good" members of a group whose "bad" members are denied the vote suffer a diminution of their franchise. And further, as we noted in chapter 1, a criminal conviction does not change the formal citizenship status. Citizens who commit crimes cannot be forced to leave the country or legally declared noncitizens.[8]

The broader philosophical debate around exclusion and representation in the context of American elections has been carefully examined and forcefully reconstructed in a remarkable line of Supreme Court rulings during the 1960s. We discussed some of these cases with respect to universal suffrage in chapter 1, but it is worth underscoring some of the other implications they raise here. In declaring that the right to vote is fundamental, in accepting the political logic of the VRA, in establishing "one person, one vote" rules, and in criticizing state laws that restricted participation in various ways (such as poll taxes, onerous registration requirements, and other devices to make voting difficult), the Court has both explicitly and implicitly held that democracy requires that all citizens have an equal opportunity to influence election outcomes. This line of cases further demands that recognizable groups have equal opportunities to seek representation.

Perhaps nowhere is this clearer than in the Supreme Court's decisions about the size of legislative districts. In a series of cases beginning with *Baker v. Carr* in 1962, the Court held that state legislative districts and U.S. House of Representatives districts must have equal populations. The logic was that each vote should have approximately equal weight in determining the overall composition of the legislature, and that voters, particularly those in urban districts, may be discriminated against when districts are not equipopulous.[9] Prior to *Baker*, there was wide variation in the size of legislative districts in virtually all states. In the extreme case of California, the county with the smallest population had some 400 times as much representation as the most populous county, Los Angeles County.[10]

The Supreme Court has continued to develop this logic in holding that legislative districting should focus on populations and be race neutral. Attempts to form "majority minority" districts in which a majority of voters would be of a minority race have frequently been invalidated, primarily because they reinforce stereotypes that all members of a group think alike.[11] Anyone seeking to challenge legislative districting bears the burden of showing that in drawing district boundaries, the legislature subordinated traditional race-neutral districting principles to racial considerations. The challenger must further show that there are alternatives to the existing district that would have resulted in a significantly greater racial balance.[12] Moreover, federal courts will not hear general challenges to legislative districting unless they are based on the equal protection clause or allegations of gerrymandering.[13]

These limitations aside, it is fair to say that the general principle of equal representation is by now well established in American law and political culture. We firmly reject the idea that electoral institutions should be constructed in ways that make it almost impossible for particular groups to have an opportunity to elect representatives of their choosing. For minorities within a society having deep-seated divisions along racial and ethnic lines, that usually means the election of roughly proportionate numbers of minority representatives. To be sure, implementation of this principle has proved extraordinarily complicated in practice, but the general idea has by now become widely accepted.

### Assessing Dilution Claims

Dilution arguments become robust if there is good reason to expect an electoral impact. If there is no evidence of an empirical impact on elections, legal claims under the VRA have unclear status. And the same principle holds true about disenfranchisement and dilution for the larger impact on the practical functioning of democracy. So is there is an impact of felon disenfranchisement on election outcomes? It is to this question that we now turn.

## Assessing the Electoral Impact of Disenfranchisement

Calculating the impact of a particular type of disenfranchisement law on election outcomes is not straightforward. Raw counts of the size of the disenfranchised felon population are inconclusive: knowing how many people have lost the right to vote, or even how many of them might vote if granted the opportunity, does not by itself prove anything. The disproportionate racial impact of felon disenfranchisement and the very strong support for the Democratic Party among African American voters are suggestive of an impact, but also not conclusive. It could still be the case that the disenfranchised population is too small, especially when accounting for below-average turnout, to have altered any elections. In such a scenario, our concern about felon disenfranchisement should focus on the criminal justice side of the equation, and the implications for the punishment and reintegration of offenders.

Yet there are reasons to believe that felon disenfranchisement has not had a neutral impact on the American political system. We have already estimated (in chapter 7) how many of the disenfranchised would have voted. We now ask how they would have voted and whether their choices would have influenced electoral outcomes.

### Assumptions of the Counterfactual Analysis

As in the previous chapter, our counterfactual approach rests upon certain key assumptions, and many of the same logic and caveats we discussed in chapter 7 apply here (and see this chapter's section in the appendix for further methodological details about the vote choice analysis at pages 272–

75). There is one important assumption about our electoral analysis that is worth highlighting: that nothing else about the candidates or elections would have changed if people with felony convictions were allowed to vote. The implications of this assumption for the distribution of votes are likely more substantial than for turnout. Whether and how the vote-getting strategies of electoral campaigns of any particular campaign would change if felons and ex-felons could participate, however, is impossible to know. We underscore the same point we made in the last chapter: the number of disenfranchised felon voters is relatively small compared to the entire voting-age population. It would seem highly implausible that an otherwise viable campaign strategy would be significantly altered because of the addition of a small group of previously excluded voters.[14]

Where the counterfactual assumption is most vulnerable in predicting voting behavior, however, is in its cumulative impact. If some election outcomes would have been different at one point in time were it not for felon disenfranchisement, *future* election campaigns could also be altered. In a counterfactual scenario in which the Democrats had controlled the U.S. Senate throughout the 1980s and 1990s, for example, the context of congressional elections, presidential campaigns, and discussions by pundits, party professionals, and campaign managers might have been different. Differences in policy might also produce "feedback" effects that change strategies or outcomes.

All of these cumulative effects on the context of elections and campaigns are, again, simply unknowable. We doubt that they are likely to be too substantial, unless it could be shown that a large number of election outcomes would have been affected. We do not think that is the case (as we will show later). At the same time, we suspect that the impact is not completely negligible, either. For these reasons, we consider our results suggestive but not conclusive. Only a real-world exercise in which some or all of the disenfranchised population could vote could provide a full-blown test of our assumptions.

## Estimating the Political Impact of Felon Disenfranchisement

We now turn to a statistical analysis of the electoral impact of felon disenfranchisement that builds upon the counterfactual assumptions spelled out in more detail in the appendix. Figures 8.1 and 8.2 transform the results of our statistical analysis of National Election Study (NES) data into simple figures, showing the estimated party preferences for disenfranchised felons by year since 1972 (dashed lines), compared to the entire electorate (straight lines). In both figures we see the converse of the picture provided by the chapter 7 figures on turnout. There, the line for felony offenders was below that of the electorate as a whole. In figures 8.1 and 8.2, by contrast, disenfranchised felons have a significantly higher expected level of Democratic support (the *y*-axis of the figure).

What does this mean for particular elections? Even comparatively unpopular Democratic candidates such as George McGovern in 1972 would have garnered around 70 percent of felons' votes, with Bill Clinton winning the highest percentage of votes in 1996. Democratic preferences are less pronounced, and somewhat less stable in senatorial elections. Democratic candidates would on average have received about 7 of every 10 votes cast

**Figure 8.1.**
Democratic preference overall and among felons, major party voters in Senate elections, 1972–2000.

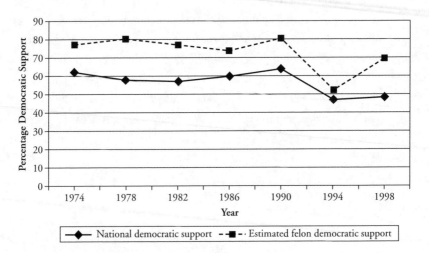

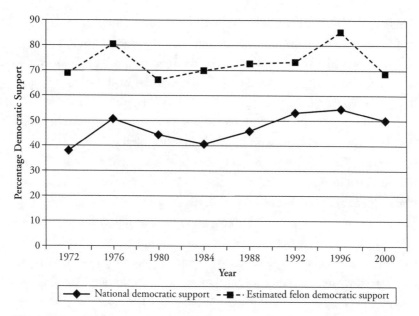

**Figure 8.2.**
Democratic preference overall and among felons, major party voters in presidential elections, 1972–2000.

by the felons and ex-felons, and substantial majorities in 14 of the last 15 U.S. Senate election years (excluding 1994, the year of the Republican sweep of Congress, when a much smaller majority—54 percent—of felon voters would have supported Democratic candidates). We can therefore conclude that felon disenfranchisement has provided a small but clear advantage to Republican candidates in every presidential and senatorial election from 1972 to 2000.

### Impact on Presidential Elections

Our big question, however, is not simply the overall distribution of the hypothetical felon vote. We also want to estimate the impact on actual elections. To assess the possible impact on any particular election, we have to combine our earlier estimates of both the size and location of the disenfranchised population with their prospective turnout and vote choice.

We start with the dramatic case of the closely fought 2000 presidential election. While Democratic candidate Al Gore won a plurality of the popular vote, defeating the Republican candidate George W. Bush by over 500,000 votes, he narrowly lost in the Electoral College. Had disenfranchised felons been permitted to vote, we estimate that Gore's national margin of victory in the popular vote would have surpassed 1 million votes (details in appendix table A8.1). Regardless of the popular vote outcome, however, the outcome in Florida determined the electoral college winner. If disenfranchised felons in that state had been permitted to vote, Al Gore would certainly have carried the state, and thus the election. There are more disenfranchised felons in Florida than in any other state (approximately 827,000 in 2000). Had they participated at our estimated rate of Florida turnout (27.2 percent) and national Democratic preference (68.9 percent), Gore would have carried the state by more than 80,000 votes. But even if we make drastically more conservative assumptions, Gore would still win. For example, if we halved the estimated turnout rate and consider only the impact of allowing *ex*-felons to vote, Gore's margin of victory still would have exceeded 30,000 votes, more than enough to overwhelm Bush's narrow victory margin (and to reverse the outcome in the Electoral College). The outcome of the 2000 presidential race thus hinged on the narrower question of *ex*-felon disenfranchisement rather than on the broader question of voting restrictions on felons currently under supervision.

What about earlier presidential elections? No previous presidential election outcome has been influenced by the prevailing rate of disenfranchisement at the time of the election. Since a greater share of the voting age population (VAP) is disenfranchised now than ever before, however, it is at least possible that some closely contested Democratic victories of the recent past might have gone to the Republicans had contemporary rates of disenfranchisement prevailed at the time. In particular, two close Democratic presidential victories in the last 40 years (in 1960 and in 1976) were decided by margins that might have been threatened if current levels of incarceration and disenfranchisement had existed back then.[15]

Democrat John F. Kennedy won the 1960 presidential election by a popular vote margin of 118,550 and a 303-to-219 margin in the Electoral College. Had contemporary rates of criminal punishment held at the time, however, Republican Richard M. Nixon likely would have won the popular vote. About 1.4 million felons were disenfranchised in 1960. If we apply the 2000 disenfranchisement rate (2.28 percent of the VAP) to 1960, however, about 2.5 million voters would have been disenfranchised (details available in appendix table A8.2). If 40 percent of this newly disenfranchised group had voted (in an election where the overall turnout rate reached a post–World War II peak of 62.8 percent), and 75 percent of this group selected the Democratic candidate—figures in line with our findings for other presidential elections—then Kennedy would have lost approximately 225,000 net votes. This estimate is almost twice the actual popular vote margin in the election. Even if the turnout rate of those with felony convictions had been only 20 percent, at current disenfranchisement levels Kennedy would have prevailed by only 6,000 votes.[16]

It is doubtful that applying contemporary disenfranchisement rates would have overturned the close Democratic victory in the 1976 presidential election, although Jimmy Carter's already slim margin of victory would have been even narrower. If current rates of disenfranchisement had existed in 1976, about 2.5 million additional citizens would have been denied the right to vote. Our estimates suggest that 34.3 percent of these would have voted and that 80.7 percent of this group would have voted for Carter. This would have accounted for about 525,000 votes, or almost one-third of Carter's final 1,682,970-vote victory margin.

## Impact on U.S. Senate Elections

We can apply a similar exercise to U.S. Senate elections, although the small sample size of the NES data does not permit us to directly estimate voting behavior at the state level (and thus we cannot take into the peculiarities of individual state elections). With that caveat in mind, we first identified a number of particularly close elections in which there was a possibility that felon disenfranchisement had influenced the outcome.[17] Because we already know that Republicans benefit from felon disenfranchisement, our practical task is to look at some very close elections carried by Republicans.

We began by identifying these elections, and then applied felon voting behavior estimates and state-level estimates of felon turnout to these close elections (taking advantage of the large sample size of the CPS to estimate turnout in those states). As with the presidential election, we determine the *net* number of Democratic votes lost to disenfranchisement by multiplying the number of disenfranchised felons by their estimated turnout rate (in each state), and the probability of selecting the Democratic candidate. Because some people would have voted for Republican candidates, we deducted from this figure the number of Republican votes lost to disenfranchisement, which we obtained in a similar manner, to calculate net votes lost. (See appendix table A8.3 for a display of these results.) We find that Democratic candidates would likely have prevailed in Texas (1978), Kentucky (1984 and 1992), Florida (1988 and 2004), and Georgia (1992).[18]

One of the most interesting implications of these elections concerns the role of ex-felon restrictions. Some analysts have asserted that ex-felon voting restrictions are "electorally insignificant."[19] In view of the much smaller numbers of disenfranchised *ex-felons* than all disenfranchised felons, it is a plausible claim. Our results, however, provide a different perspective on this issue. Recall that only 13 states disfranchise some or all people beyond completion of sentence. In only one instance (the late Paul Coverdell's election in Georgia in 1992), however, was a Senate election likely to have been overturned solely as a result of the disenfranchisement of those actively under correctional supervision.[20] Even in this case, however, the number of current prisoners (25,290) and convicted felony jail inmates (2,163) was too small to affect the election. Rather, it was the large number of nonincarcerated felony probationers (80,639, or a full 61 percent of the state's disenfranchised population) and parolees (23,819, or 18 percent of disenfranchised Georgians) that likely cost the Democrats the election. As this case illustrates, the political impact varies with the particular correctional populations that are disenfranchised. The other reversible cases all include net Democratic vote losses from *ex-felon* voters.

What if all nonincarcerated felons were enfranchised, as is the practice elsewhere in the world? Indeed, as we will show in chapter 9, public opinion and many of the current efforts for reform typically make a sharp distinction between voting rights for the *incarcerated* population versus the nonincarcerated population. We repeated our analyses for the (politically more realistic) scenario in which all nonincarcerated felons are permitted to vote, and repeated it again to consider restoration of voting rights just for ex-felons (see appendix table A8.4 for those results).

Even with these limitations on the "disenfranchised" population, we still find evidence of a significant electoral impact. If *all* nonincarcerated felons had been enfranchised, and employing the same assumptions as before, six of the seven elections identified earlier would remain potentially reversible with these assumptions. One election would not be reversed with all nonincarcerated felons voting in this scenario (the 1992 Senate election in Georgia, and by a very small margin). Even if we limit reenfranchisement to ex-felons, four of the seven Senate elections (Virginia in 1978, Kentucky in 1984 and 1998, and Florida in 2004) would remain potentially reversible.

### Impact on the Composition of the U.S. Senate

These results provide evidence of a national political impact of felon disenfranchisement. Have the (relative handful) of elections that have potentially been influenced by felon disenfranchisement had any larger implications for American politics? The answer is not obvious. Since 1978, there have been over 400 Senate elections, and we find evidence that as few as seven elections (or less than 2 percent of all Senate elections in that period) might have been reversed in the absence of felon disenfranchisement laws.

Yet even if these few elections had yielded different outcomes, it might have been enough to shift the balance of power in the U.S. Senate in some years. To assess this possibility, we recomputed the U.S. Senate composition after each election, taking into account elections that might have been reversed if some or all felons were allowed to vote (see appendix table 21 for our results). We considered both a "limited counterfactual scenario" (in which the Democratic winner of the reversed election holds the seat for a single term) and a "cumulated counterfactual scenario" (in which the Democratic winner of the reversed election holds the seat for as long as the actual winner did). We cannot know whether the Democrat would have held these seats in subsequent elections, although the well-known advantages of incumbency make this a plausible scenario.[21]

In the cumulated counterfactual scenario, since two Republican seats were overturned in the 1978 elections, the Democratic majority would have increased from 58:41 to 60:39 (see table A8.5 for details). We followed the beneficiaries of these closely contested elections to see how long their seats remained under Republican control. John Warner of Virginia remains in office today, and John Tower's Texas seat also remains in Republican hands (with Phil Gramm holding office until 2002, when John Cornyn took over the seat). In 1984, the Republicans held a narrow 53:47 Senate majority. Under the cumulated counterfactual scenario, Democrats would have achieved parity with the Republicans after the 1984 elections, which included the McConnell election. Were it not for felon disenfranchisement, the cumulative counterfactual suggests that Democrats might have controlled the Senate during much of the 1990s.

It is arguable that the *ceteris paribus* assumptions of the cumulative counterfactual are too strong to be plausible. While all incumbents have considerable electoral leverage, these advantages are lower for the Senate than for the House. Further, the specific Senate elections that we have identified—most of which are in Southern states that have been moving in an increasingly Republican direction over the past 30 years—are probably cases where it would have been difficult for the Democrats to hold the seat for as long as an incumbent holds the "average" seat.[22] Our limited counterfactual results capture the most conservative assumption, one that assumes the victor's party would hold the seat for only one term. The conservative assumptions of the limited counterfactual—that none of the Democratic victors would have held their seats for even one additional term—drastically reduce the political impact of felon disenfranchisement in the Senate. Even in this extreme scenario, however, the Democrats would potentially have had a filibuster-proof majority after the 1978 election.

If we limit these scenarios to reenfranchising only nonincarcerated felons, or only ex-felons, the impact on Senate composition would be reduced, but not entirely eliminated (see appendix table A8.6). A number of seats would change hands in each scenario, suggesting that restrictions on probationers, parolees, and ex-felons have a demonstrable potential impact.

The actual impact of possible Democratic victories would likely fall somewhere between the outcomes envisioned by the cumulated and limited counterfactual scenarios. In other words, some, but not all, of the new Democratic victors would have held their seats for more than one term, and those changes would have had some impact on partisan control of the Senate. Whether shifting partisan control of the Senate would have significantly altered policy outcomes is impossible to know. In general, because of procedural rules in that body, partisan control there is somewhat less significant than in the House (where committee chairs occupied by the dominant party, for example, are able to exert more leverage over the handling of legislation in their domains). Senate committee chairs, however, have some important powers in relation to agenda setting. Some chairs, most famously Jesse Helms as chair of the Senate Foreign Relations Committee, have used those powers. Partisan control of the Senate can also matter greatly for the appointment of federal judges, particularly in recent years when straight party votes on judicial appointments have become increasingly common.

## Gubernatorial and Other Elections

Because the NES does not ask respondents how they voted in specific gubernatorial (or other state) elections, we cannot estimate felon voting behavior in such elections in any meaningful way. We can, however, make some informed guesses. If we apply the mean rate of turnout (24 percent) and Democratic preference (73 percent) in Senate elections to these races, it is possible that at least four Republican gubernatorial victories would have been overturned: two elections in Alabama (with James Folsom [D] defeating James Forrest [R] in 1994, and Don Siegelman [D] defeating Bob Riley [R] in 2002), New Jersey (James Florio [D] defeating Thomas Kean [R] in 1981), and one in Texas (John Hill [D] defeating William Clements [R] in 1978).

Felon disenfranchisement would be almost certain to have a more dramatic electoral impact in the urban legislative districts from which the largest share of the felon population is drawn. Unfortunately, we do not have reliable data regarding the exact locations and legislative districts in which the largest concentrations of votes are lost. We also lack, for the most part, good survey data on voting behavior below state-level elections, thus making any attempt to estimate such impact doubly speculative. Given the demonstrable electoral impact at the state level, however, disenfranchisement surely plays a role in the election of mayors, city councils, state representatives, and other officials.

## Challenging Our Results

As in chapter 7, our counterfactual scenarios matching characteristics of the disenfranchised felon population to the rest of the population produce some intriguing results, but they are vulnerable to the same challenges as our results on turnout. Based purely on social characteristics of individual offenders at the time of incarceration, they may simply not have captured some important factors that shape partisan preferences.

Our main concern in the voting analysis is whether we have overstated the likelihood of Democratic political alignment. It is harder to guess than it was with turnout whether unmeasured factors would push the disenfranchised toward higher or lower levels of Democratic loyalty than we would predict from the sociodemographic information we have at our disposal.

As in the previous chapter, however, we can use data from the YDS to test the key assumption that the voting behavior of disenfranchised felons would approximate that of nonfelons matched to them in terms of age, race, sex, education, income, and marital status. We used those data to analyze the effects of arrest on party preference in the 1996 presidential and 1998 Minnesota gubernatorial elections.

Unlike the confirming YDS turnout analyses in chapter 7, we find some minor evidence that criminal justice sanctions remain associated with party preferences even after controlling for other factors. In particular, those arrested for drug- or alcohol-related offenses were significantly *more* likely than the national data suggest to favor the Democratic presidential candidate Bill Clinton in 1996 and the Independent Party gubernatorial candidate Jesse Ventura in 1998 (see appendix table A8.7). Since our major concern is that we might overstate Democratic partisanship, the YDS results provide some comfort. If anything, they suggest we may be *underes-*

*timating* Democratic partisanship among offenders. It is harder to account for the greater support for Ventura, but the finding is consistent with our in-depth interviews with former offenders discussed in chapter 6. Because independent and third-party candidates are so rarely significant in American politics, that particular anomalous result is unlikely to affect most elections dominated by the two major parties.

### What about Illegal Felon Voting?

Our analyses to this point have assumed that felon disenfranchisement laws are well enforced, and that there are no attempts to vote in disregard of these laws. Widespread fraudulent voting by felons would significantly diminish the projected impact we have outlined here. On the other hand, there is also some evidence that state authorities have improperly purged ex-felons from the rolls, thereby offsetting or even eclipsing the number of votes cast fraudulently. The most famously documented case is that of Florida in the 2000 election. Prior to the election, tens of thousands of people who had been convicted of a felony but had had their voting rights restored, or had an identical name to an ineligible convicted felon, were improperly purged from voting registries and thus unable to vote. Similar problems surfaced before the 2004 election, and only the threat of litigation prompted the state to halt all use of problematic "purge" lists.[23]

We know relatively little about the purging practices of other states, but the possibility of errors arising from politically motivated purges will continue as long as disenfranchisement is practiced. Investigations of improper voting by felons and ex-felons often do, in fact, produce evidence that a handful of felons have voted. Indeed, follow-up canvasses of hotly contested elections with recounts, including in Florida after the 2000 presidential elections, returned evidence that a handful of these individuals (a few hundred out of over 800,000 in Florida) may have managed to register and vote.[24] Investigations in other states yield similarly small numbers. For example, 361 ineligible felons were alleged to have voted in Wisconsin in 2000. A vigorous and months-long search for illegal felon voters in the Washington 2004 gubernatorial election turned up 1,740 names (out of 2.8 million cast), and a follow-up examination by the *Seattle Times* reported that at least 11 percent of those names were incorrect.[25] We simply do not believe that such cases are likely to be of such a magnitude as to significantly reduce the overall size of the disenfranchised felon population. Motivated journalists, partisan activists, and other investigators have not yet uncovered or produced such evidence. On the basis of what has been rigorously documented so far, it appears that the national impact of illegal felon voting is negligible.[26]

Further, and likely offsetting any possible impact from illegal felon votes, are two additional aspects of felon disenfranchisement that keep individuals who *are* eligible to vote from voting. First, there is a considerable amount of misinformation among election officials, criminal justice system officials, and former offenders about who is eligible to register to vote. Anecdotal reports from voter registration campaigns around the country during the 2004 election confirm this confusion. For example, Reginald Dorsett, a Berkeley, California, resident who spent two years in a state prison for a drug conviction in 1989 but had been off parole for 10 years by 2004, told a newspaper reporter "I've always wanted to vote . . . [but] it has always been told to me that if you were convicted of a felony, you can't vote."[27] During our in-depth interviews with offenders in Minnesota, we discovered that the majority incorrectly believed that they were disenfranchised for life or for a lengthy waiting period after they complete their sentences. Alec Ewald's recent investigation of state administrative practices reveals significant misunderstandings on the part of election officials who may in turn provide incorrect information to eligible former felons.[28]

Second, as we noted in chapter 3, our decision to exclude unconvicted detainees in jails awaiting trial at the time of the election understates the full impact of felon disenfranchisement. These are individuals who, in most states, would have very limited practical or even legal access to the ballot. If we add in people convicted of misdemeanors, the impact is magnified further. Thus, using the convicted felon population understates the de facto impact of the criminal justice system on the right to vote and participate.

The numbers are far from trivial. According to the Bureau of Justice Statistics, there were 275,500 jail inmates serving sentences for misdemeanor offenses, and approximately 419,000 unconvicted pretrial detainees held in jail in 2003.[29] Both of these groups are practically, if not legally, disenfranchised in most states. In other words, more than 600,000 individuals who are *not* included in our national estimates would likely have been unable to vote on Election Day.

In light of all of these factors, we conclude that our estimates are appropriately conservative. On balance, there are likely *far more* eligible ex-felons and unconvicted jail inmates who are denied the vote despite their legal right to vote because of felon disenfranchisement rules.

### Still Broader Political Impacts? Prisoner Enumeration in the Census

The rising number of felons described in chapter 3, the discussion of political attitudes and partisanship in chapters 5 and 6, and the effects of disenfranchisement on turnout described in chapter 7 are all closely linked to the bottom-line question of impact. We have provided evidence in this chapter suggesting that disenfranchised felons would likely have made a decisive difference in a small number of national elections. Nevertheless, we believe the question of political impact is far broader than the results of individual elections discussed in this chapter.

As noted in chapter 6, some felons hesitate to participate in demonstrations for fear of being arrested and returned to prison. Far more avoid political conversations with friends and family members, either out of embarrassment or because they feel shut out of the process. Such reticence may have a lingering impact upon the political participation of their children and their communities. Felon voting restrictions leave over 5 million mostly poor, disproportionately black citizens out of the political conversation. If neither Republicans nor Democrats need attend to their concerns, the terms of debate are likely to shift on many issues, from education to health care, to social security, to defense, to welfare reform.

A final potential and less speculative impact of disenfranchisement concerns the way the U.S. Census Bureau counts prisoners. Article 1, section 2 of the U.S. Constitution requires an "actual Enumeration" to be taken every 10 years for purposes of apportioning voting representation, redrawing political boundaries, and allocating funding to state and local governments.

Although prisoners are disenfranchised in 48 states, they are counted for enumeration purposes as residing in the jurisdictions in which they are incarcerated rather than in their home communities.[30]

Because prisons tend to be sited in rural communities while prisoners are drawn from urban areas, this practice results in a small but measurable transfer of political power and money from urban centers to rural towns. Some extreme examples have been noted: 60 percent of Illinois's prisoners are from Cook County, but only 1 percent are incarcerated in the county; Los Angeles County supplies 34 percent of California's felon population, but only 3 percent are housed in that county.[31] Moreover, such transfers are closely bound up with the racial disproportionality in incarceration detailed in chapter 3. When prisoners removed from African American communities are counted as residing in white communities, the home districts to which they will return are underrepresented. Such districts are also impoverished, as state and federal aid for many programs is distributed in rough proportion to the loss of population. These examples only hint at the full political consequences of felon disenfranchisement, though it is clear that the impact of felon voting restrictions extends far beyond the individual elections scrutinized in this chapter.

## Summing Up

We take for granted today that a democratic political system requires that both individual citizens and key protected groups should have an equal opportunity to influence the government that rules over them. Democratic equality rests on the simple notion that elections should reflect equal inputs from all citizens. This point is so thoroughly taken for granted that it is often not even argued. As political theorist Charles Beitz puts it, "political equality represents a persistent conviction among contemporary democratic theorists; indeed, it has become a kind of philosophical orthodoxy, perhaps because it has seemed to express so obvious a truth as not to require systematic defense."[32] Challenges to the legitimacy of democratic equality are primarily matters of historical concern.

But felon disenfranchisement, and its implications for elections, challenges this view. The results of this chapter suggest that felon disenfranchisement poses a threat to political equality. We do recognize a number of important caveats about these findings. Our counterfactual examples rely upon a *ceteris paribus* assumption—that nothing else about the candidates or elections would change save the voting rights of felons and ex-felons. Had these laws changed, other forces might have arisen to negate the political influence of felons and ex-felons. Second, although the Democrats lose votes to felon disenfranchisement, it is possible that adopting a punitive crime control agenda in recent years has gained them votes as well.[33] Third, we lack the individual-level data that would permit us to directly measure the political behavior of felons and ex-felons.

Despite these caveats, we find considerable evidence that felon voting restrictions have had a demonstrable impact on national elections. In this sense, rising levels of felon disenfranchisement constitute a reversal of the universalization of the right to vote. Further, our focus on national and state-level elections is likely to understate the full impact of felon disenfranchisement, which may be even more pronounced in local or district-level elections, such as U.S. House, state legislative, and mayoral races.[34] So long as felon disenfranchisement laws persist, the political consequences will continue unabated.

# 9 Public Opinion and Felon Disenfranchisement
## with Clem Brooks

The relationship between democracy and felon disenfranchisement has been a central theme of this book. Piece by piece, we have found good reasons to be concerned about current practices, and their implications for democratic governance. But what about the views of the mass public? If the political exclusion of citizens with felony convictions from the polity is preferred by most citizens, if public support for "tough on crime" policies extends to voting restrictions, then felon disenfranchisement laws may themselves reflect majority opinion. The case for reenfranchisement, however strong on other grounds, might thus be undermined.

In this chapter, we examine public attitudes toward disenfranchisement. There is very little existing survey data on the question, but we are able to draw upon a national telephone survey we conducted in July 2002.[1] Our survey included a series of question-wording experiments that allow us to assess public support or opposition to voting rights for different types of felons. We begin our discussion by first examining the complicated relationship between crime and democracy in public opinion.

## Public Opinion on Criminal Justice

Public attitudes toward felon disenfranchisement reflect an enduring tension in twentieth-century American political life: the clash between the desire to maintain social and political order on the one hand and the desire to extend civil rights and liberties to all citizens on the other. We have already described both the growth of mass punishment and the mystery of how such an extreme set of public policies has evolved and persisted, especially in view of falling crime rates. The most parsimonious explanation for this development, as a number of analysts have suggested, is simply that the public wanted it. Political scientist John DiIulio, for example, argues that "with respect to crime control, all that Americans have ever demanded from government, and all that they have been demanding since the mid-1960s, are commonsense policies . . . that do not return persons who assault, rape, rob, burglarize, deal drugs, and murder to the streets without regard to public safety."[2]

The main evidence of strong public support for punitive policies comes from repeated survey items asked since the 1960s and 1970s. Three items have been tracked the most consistently—and have been the most widely cited—in support of the view that the public has become more punitive: (1) support for the death penalty; (2) beliefs that courts do not treat criminals harshly enough; and (3) beliefs that the government spends too little on crime. Figure 9.1 charts the trends on these three items.

Overall, support for these items follows a common trend. Public punitiveness steadily increased from the 1960s through 1980, fluctuated at high levels through the 1980s, but has declined since the early 1990s. The increase in the 1970s parallels the beginnings of the incarceration boom, but what is striking is that ever-higher levels of punishment from the mid-1970s to the 1990s did not lead the public to withdraw support for more punitive measures. It was not until the 1990s that support began to fall. To account for this anomaly, one public opinion researcher has suggested the metaphor of a "broken thermostat": public support for harsh punishment failed to decline even though policymakers repeatedly delivered such policies.[3]

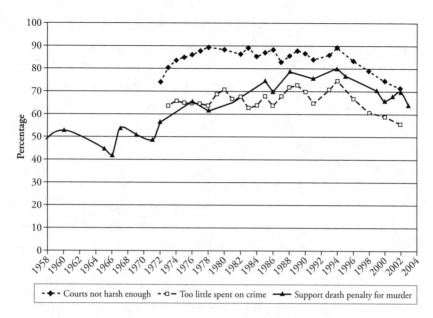

**Figure 9.1.**
Public support for punitive crime control measures.

The master trends represented in figure 9.1 have framed the debate over criminal justice policy. The predominant interpretation of public opinion in these debates has typically been that the public wants even more and stricter punishment. But there are at least two reasons to be cautious about such an interpretation. First, and most obviously, since the mid-1990s public support for two of the three measures (harshness and spending) has declined to levels not seen since the early 1970s (with support for the death penalty declining as well, but not nearly as far). The "broken thermostat" metaphor was therefore more appropriate a decade ago than it is today.

Second, the most plausible interpretation of the source of these trends is that political elites have shaped public attitudes, rather than the other way around.[4] In chapter 4, we noted that beginning in the mid-1960s political conservatives actively promoted the need for a crackdown on criminals, with the Barry Goldwater and Richard Nixon presidential campaigns and Governor Nelson Rockefeller's war on drugs in New York being signature moments. As these campaigns gained political traction, media coverage of crime became a staple of nightly news coverage. Eventually Democratic Party leaders also sought to show their toughness on crime, leading, in the most extreme case, to the bipartisan 1994 crime bill promoted and signed into law by Bill Clinton. By the mid-1990s, the era of mass incarceration had come to full flower, driven by a bipartisan consensus in favor of harsh criminal justice policies.

The mere fact that the public responded to the anti-crime agenda with support for tougher sanctions is in itself significant. Trends in public opinion gain meaning when political elites "read" them as reflecting a desire for some policy direction, in this case greater punishment. Yet the widely shared view of public support for harsh criminal justice policies may be a product of narrow opinion measures that fail to capture the complexity of public attitudes in this area. For example, what happens when survey respondents are given more choices, or are allowed to express more than one preference? A variety of experiment-based survey research suggests that the views of the public on criminal justice are much more complex, and less one-dimensional, than is suggested by the narrow range of items in figure 9.1.

Consider attitudes about the death penalty. While most Americans support the death penalty, this support drops drastically when respondents are presented with the alternative of life in prison without the possibility of parole.[5] Similarly, support for long prison terms is reduced when community-based alternatives are presented as a sentencing option, especially for nonviolent offenders.[6] And when given the opportunity to express multidimensional preferences, many survey respondents report wanting *both* to incapacitate offenders and to rehabilitate them.[7] None of this means that punitive views are not strongly held in the mass public, but experimental survey designs reveal a far more complex portrait than is commonly supposed. Rather than a clear consensus in favor of harshness, public opinion in the area of criminal justice is better characterized as multidimensional and subject to issue-framing effects.

*Civil Rights Liberalism*

If public opinion on criminal justice is sometimes contradictory, compelling evidence suggests that support for civil liberties and civil rights has risen substantially in the past 40 years.[8] Well-measured items over a long historical period show that the public has become significantly more supportive of democratic rights, including freedom of speech.[9] Liberalizing trends with respect to *overt* racism and the political participation of racial and ethnic minorities represent an important related piece of evidence.[10] Similarly, more egalitarian views on gender roles and the rights of women to participate in the public sphere are also important markers of the spread of civil rights liberalism.[11]

Support for democracy—and the right to vote—is the most critical type of civil rights issue that we investigate in this chapter. Unfortunately, however, we lack data on general attitudes toward the right to vote with which to develop comparisons. This is because in large part, voting rights have been assumed to be so universally supported that survey researchers have not bothered to field relevant items.

But the persisting power of democracy as a political ideal can be seen in a variety of ways. One example lies in the bipartisan appeal of democratizing policy measures, such as legislation making it easier for individuals to vote. In 1993, the so-called Motor Voter law required states to ease voter registration by presenting the necessary forms to individuals at departments of motor vehicles at the time they obtain or renew their driver's license. In the aftermath of the 2000 presidential election, Congress passed the Help America Vote Act, which sought to address a variety of voting problems, including those of the uncounted ballots raised so sharply in the Bush-Gore election. The difficulties faced by disabled citizens attempting to vote have also been addressed in a variety of ways in recent years. Finally, the Department of Justice pursues—though less vigorously than some democratic theorists and activists would like—cases of voter harassment and other incidents of disenfranchisement by officials at the county or precinct level. These measures all have fairly significant bipartisan support, and are largely noncontroversial.

The extent to which the public favors harsh punishment and anti-crime policies versus support for civil liberties and rights, rehabilitation, and second chances for offenders represents an important tension. Felon disenfranchisement epitomizes this tension. On the one hand, the desire to punish offenders sharply might include restricting their right to vote. On the other hand, support for universal suffrage and civil rights for all citizens could override punitive attitudes.

The existing research on this relationship presents a decidedly mixed portrait. The relationship between civil liberties and civil rights has been most widely studied as it relates to police practices and criminal courts. A classical example would be whether the police should be allowed to search a criminal suspect without a court-issued warrant. Such questions are, of course, related to the larger question of whether potential criminals should lose rights that Americans routinely endorse in other contexts. Among the mass public, survey respondents tend to both simultaneously endorse civil liberties *and* grant police the capacity to arrest suspected criminals.[12] Low levels of information about the scope of constitutional rights clearly contribute to some of the willingness of survey respondents to sacrifice civil liberties in favor of anti-crime measures.[13]

The debate over felon disenfranchisement similarly engages the tension between punitiveness and civil liberties. The right to vote is usually thought of as a simple right of citizenship, not something to be traded off against other rights. Yet "cracking down on crime" and criminals may dispose citizens to support the suspension of democratic rights for criminal offenders. As key building blocks of democracy, civil rights and civil liberties are thus directly threatened by conflicting preferences for reducing crime.

We do not have a large body of scholarship with which to predict how the public may resolve or express these tensions. The emerging national debate over disenfranchisement raises questions rarely asked in recent decades. Since the passage of the Voting Rights Act (VRA), policy debates around suffrage in the United States have largely shifted from questions about formal individual rights to participation to questions about fairness in the practical implementation of those rights. Prior to the VRA, the disenfranchisement of African American voters provided a vivid example of persistent suffrage inequities in the American political system. Its passage was, therefore, a landmark development in struggles to extend the franchise to all citizens. Broad public debates over democracy and freedom in the civil rights era of the 1950s and 1960s put suffrage into play in a way not seen since the fight over the enfranchisement of women in the early twentieth century. Following passage of the VRA, however, concern over voting rights faded rapidly.

In short, in view of both contradictory pressures on public opinion and the lack of existing survey data on attitudes toward democratic rights for less-than-perfect citizens, it is simply not clear how the public feels about voting rights for felons. We therefore now turn to investigate that question.

## Measuring Public Support for Felon Disenfranchisement

In July 2002, we placed a series of questions on a Harris Interactive telephone survey using a nationally representative sample of 1,000 adults aged 18 years or older.[14] Respondents were asked about their attitudes toward crime, punishment, and the civil liberties of criminals and ex-offenders.

Some technical details of the telephone survey are worth mentioning at the outset. To maximize the representation of all persons within the 48 continental United States and the District of Columbia, telephone numbers were generated using a random-digit-dial (RDD) selection procedure. The national sample was stratified by geographic region and by metropolitan versus nonmetropolitan residence.[15] The response rate was 39 percent.[16]

### Are These Responses Non-attitudes?

A sophisticated public opinion literature has criticized the view that policy preferences of most citizens are measurable in meaningful ways by opinion polls and surveys. According to this argument, people have notably low levels of information about policy issues, leading them to guess in response to survey research questions. Such responses are thus characterized as "non-attitudes," in the famous formulation of political scientist Philip Converse.[17]

The existence of non- or weakly held attitudes may be precisely the aspect of public opinion that permits easy manipulation by elites. In this view, "public opinion surveys present only a rough idea of what people generally think because the results are highly sensitive to a number of factors. . . . Polls may even create the impression of public opinion on questions in which none actually exists."[18]

But a countermovement in public opinion research has challenged these conclusions. One response is that it is the ambiguities of the questions, or the complexities of the issues, rather than non-attitudes, that produce respondent instability.[19] Political scientist John Zaller's powerful theoretical model of survey response claims that people sample among the different possible answers they have in their heads in responding to surveys. The likelihood of any particular response is based on the relative strength of the different possible answers known to the respondent. This explains response inconsistency, but also implies that polls convey meaningful information, where the latter is accordingly subject to the framing of questions and to the contingent nature of individuals' short-term memory and information level.[20] The second, increasingly influential individual-level response has been to show how citizens are capable of reasoning through cues and heuristics of various sorts, *even* in the absence of detailed information or policy understandings.[21] The introduction of cognitive psychology into survey research has produced a massive literature showing how survey respondents can—at least sometimes—provide meaningful answers even when they have to guess. Finally, at the macro level, political scientists Benjamin Page and Robert Shapiro argue that even if some individuals guess in response to survey questions, examination of *aggregate* responses provides a systematic means of filtering out response instability and non-attitudes.[22]

It is important to consider at the outset the possibility that surveys may be measuring non-attitudes in the case of felon disenfranchisement. Most survey respondents will know very little about felon voting rights. In responding to survey questions, they may thus be doing exactly what Converse suggested: guessing. On the other hand, since questions about felon disenfranchisement tap sentiments concerning issues of democracy and crime, survey responses may instead reflect considerations about which most respondents do have real opinions. Felon disenfranchisement questions may thus provide, particularly in the aggregate, a plausible portrait of Americans' reasoning and policy evaluations of this issue.

We test for this possibility by embedding a little experiment within our question-wording design. The experiment involves two items that refer to probationers in identical ways, except that one invites respondents to choose the option "I haven't thought much about this." The inclusion of this option gives respondents the opportunity to comfortably avoid answering the question. The item does result in a somewhat lower proportion of respondents selecting the primary "yes" or "no" response categories: an additional 8 percent of those given the additional prompt volunteered "not sure/don't know." But even when encouraged not to respond, most survey respondents felt comfortable enough with the underlying issue to offer a response. While not an air-tight test of the nonattitudes problem, this at least provides some measure of confidence that respondents are able to answer these items meaningfully.

### Survey Experiments

Our measurement of attitudes about felon voting restrictions varied across two important dimensions: the status of convicted criminals as prisoners, probationers, parolees, or ex-felons; and the nature of the crime. We measured how this variation affects public attitudes using a series of question-wording experiments. Small changes in question-wording can sometimes have a significant impact on respondents' answers. Different kinds of question-wordings, or "framings," elicit different ideas or invoke different values on the part of respondents.[23] While this fact greatly frustrates simple-minded polling, it enables us to test systematically various kinds of wordings to see where survey respondents draw the line, so to speak, on a particular policy question.

We designed our experiments to tell us whether different arguments employed in the public debate over disenfranchisement actually command popular support. To accomplish this, we varied references to target groups (such as violent versus white-collar offenders) and examined several different types of political rights (such as free speech as well as the right to vote).

As we have shown already, state laws distinguish between criminal offenders at different stages of punishment. Our first set of experiments, therefore, focused on the status of a (prospective) felon voter in the criminal justice system. We asked respondents whether they support voting rights for three types of current felons: probationers, parolees, and current inmates. Approximately one-quarter of the sample were asked each item.

The second experiment considered different types of ex-felons. By varying the specific crime committed by the hypothetical ex-felon, we learn whether support is significantly lower for violent criminals or sex offenders in comparison to white-collar criminals or a "generic" ex-felon whose crime is not mentioned. The third set of experiments examined respondents' attitudes toward extending basic free speech rights to ex-felons. (Further details about the experiments are available in the appendix section for chapter 9, at pages 283–84; see also table A9.1.)

## Results

Do Americans support the enfranchisement of people convicted of a crime, and does the level of public support vary depending upon the level of supervision or the nature of the crime? Figure 9.2 shows the results of our analysis for the first set of enfranchisement items, which ask about voting rights for probationers (both with and without the "haven't thought much about this" attachment), parolees, and current inmates.

A majority of respondents support allowing probationers and parolees to vote. Differences in question wording for the two probationer items initially suggest varying levels of support, but the 8 percent difference is not statistically significant (nor is the 8 percent difference between the probationer and parolee items).[24] The final item in figure 9.2, however, reveals quite different attitudes toward prisoners, with only 31 percent of those respondents who received the inmate item supporting their enfranchisement. Americans appear to draw a clear distinction between impris-

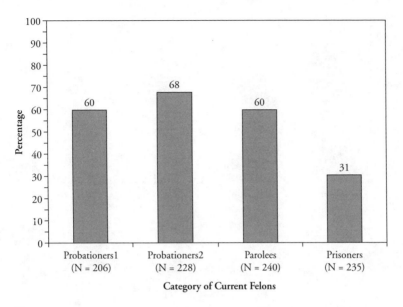

**Figure 9.2.**
Support for reenfranchisement by correctional population. (See appendix table A9.1 for wording.)

oned offenders and those who are living in the community (regardless of whether the latter have completed their sentences).

Figure 9.3 shows the results of our second experiment concerning the level of public support for ex-felon voting rights by the category of offender.[25] While 80 percent support enfranchisement for ex-felons when no crime is mentioned, specific types of criminal conviction results in lower levels of support: 63 percent for white-collar ex-felons, and 66 percent for ex-felons convicted of a violent offense (the 3 percent difference is not statistically significant, but the larger differences between these items and support for the generic ex-felon is). This suggests that the willingness of Americans to grant voting rights is shaped in part by whether a policy question is framed abstractly versus by reference to a specific criminal offense. Moreover, particularly high levels of support for the enfranchisement of generically described ex-felons appear to overestimate support under the more realistic conditions in which political elites or media coverage refer to particular types of crimes or criminals. Support for enfranchising white-

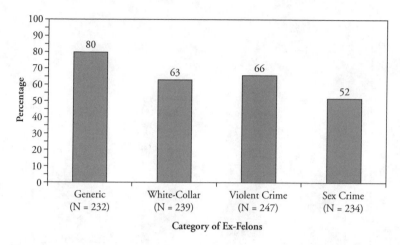

**Figure 9.3.**
Support for reenfranchisement among different categories of ex-felons. (See appendix table A9.1 for wording.)

collar and violent ex-felons mentioned earlier is very similar to the corresponding levels found earlier for probationers and parolees, providing evidence that most Americans favor extending voting rights across a wide variety of criminal statuses and felony convictions.

The fourth item, referencing a "sex offense," elicits the lowest level of support (52 percent). This contrasts significantly with the greater (66 percent) support for ex-felons convicted of a violent crime, attesting to the extreme stigma that attaches to sex crimes and those convicted of them.[26] While it would be informative to know whether even greater specificity in the framing or description of sex offenses (or other offenders) might mediate support for extending the franchise to this category of offenders, we would also note that sex offenders constitute a small proportion of current prisoners and ex-felons.[27] Taken together, these considerations imply that the main avenue through which defenders of felon disenfranchisement might influence public opinion would be to target the most stigmatized categories of criminal offenders (a point we discuss further in chapter 10).

With almost all categories of criminal offenders receiving majority support for voting rights, an important further question is whether Americans reason about voting rights differently from other civil liberties. For instance, comparably high levels of support for the civil liberties of criminal offenders within domains other than voting would suggest that a principled form of reasoning undergirds Americans' attitudes.

Figure 9.4 shows the results of our analysis of attitudes toward civil liberties—as measured by the right to speak in general and on two specific topics (against prisons and in favor of drug legalization)—for felons versus non-felons (see table A9.1 for question wording). The first item is a standard baseline civil liberties item asked of the entire sample, whereas the other three items were randomly assigned to approximately one-third of respondents. Civil liberties support is high using the baseline item (82 percent), but the ex-felon item yields a similar level of support (85 percent). Comparing the sample proportions of the ex-felon versus ex-felon/legalization activist items is instructive, because the latter further specifies a particular type of criminal offense ("selling drugs") and the specific type of

**Figure 9.4.**
Support for civil liberties for felons versus non-felons (see appendix table A9.1 for wording).

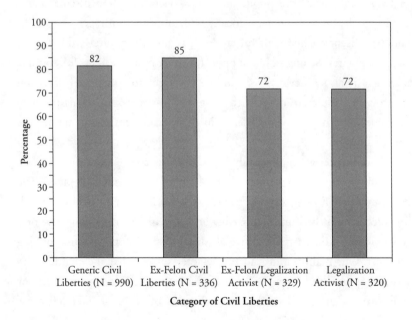

speech involved ("legalizing drugs"). Given negative views of drug dealers as well as expectations of threats stemming from drug-related activities, the 72 percent endorsement of the pro-civil liberties position on this item provides surprisingly strong evidence of Americans' willingness to extend civil liberties to criminal offenders.

The identical averages for the third and fourth items (72 percent) suggest that these slightly lower levels of support for civil liberties are linked to the controversial or threatening aspects of speech, rather than to the criminal status of the speaker. Although civil liberties reasoning among the American public is likely to involve some evaluation of the legitimacy or expected effects of speech itself, these processes thus appear to operate against a background of substantial support for civil liberties.

## The Myth of Public Support for Disenfranchisement

Our assessment of public attitudes toward felon disenfranchisement in the United States leads to us to a firm and far-reaching conclusion: there is little public support for stripping the right to vote from all people convicted of felonies. Instead, the public appears to view disenfranchisement as a harsh penalty in a democratic society with universal suffrage. The public endorses disenfranchisement for current prisoners, but "draws the line" at the prison gates. Strong public support for other political rights for criminal offenders is also noteworthy, including the right to speak freely even on controversial topics relating to the criminal justice system. This provides evidence for a degree of real depth in democratic sentiments among the American public.

Before undertaking this analysis, we were uncertain about the direction of public sentiments regarding political rights for criminal offenders. We could envision finding support for either a "civil death" model (in which offenders should be punished harshly and perhaps even permanently) or a "civil rights" model (in which we all should have rights by virtue of citizenship). Our main findings in this chapter suggest that the civil liberties view, tempered by knowledge of the offender's crime, trumps support for civil death with regard to the political rights of criminal offenders. It is well known that Americans have gradually become more willing to endorse the civil liberties of such generally disliked groups as Communists and atheists; it now seems they are willing to do so for ex-felons as well.

When, how, and to what extent policy change is informed by public opinion is a widely debated question among scholars. Of course, public opinion can only influence policy debates when it is knowable. On most issues before Congress, for example, little or no survey data about public preferences exist.[28] In the case of felon disenfranchisement, the results presented here suggest an important degree of coherence and policy direction. Moreover, they appear to be particularly timely with respect to the formation of future policies regarding the franchise.

# 10 Unlocking the Vote

Consider an illiterate, homeless, propertyless, African American woman who is on government assistance, has unpaid debts, and just moved to a new state three months ago. As political scientist Alec Ewald has pointed out, *each* of those attributes would once have been sufficient to deny her the right to vote in one or more states.[1] Times have changed, however. Over the past 200 years, virtually all restrictions on the right to vote have melted away. No state would be legally entitled, or normatively justified, in using any of those criteria to deny the right to vote. Only felon status remains as a legal means to bar participation.

The logic of disenfranchising ex-felons and current but nonincarcerated felons appears to be slowly giving way to modern democratic norms. Over the past 40 years, voting rights for felons have been steadily and significantly liberalized. But there is still a long way to go. Over 5 million felons and ex-felons remain disenfranchised. It is time to change America's felon disenfranchisement laws, once and for all.

## The Political Moment

### Felon Disenfranchisement Laws during the "Second" Reconstruction

Taking the long view, it is clear that the tide has begun to turn against felon disenfranchisement. Over the past four decades, restrictions on the voting rights of disenfranchised felons have loosened quite a bit. As we showed in chapter 2, a major wave of liberalizing changes began in the early 1960s and stretched through the mid-1970s. Although momentum for civil rights legislation has eroded since the mid-1970s, the pattern of liberalization in the states has continued, albeit at a slower pace.

Appendix table A10.1 lists the changes to felon disenfranchisement law in the past three decades. While a handful of states have adopted more conservative laws, far more have amended their laws to expand voting rights for felons. For example, in 2001 Connecticut, New Mexico, and Nevada all liberalized their felon voting laws. Connecticut changed its law to allow probationers to vote, New Mexico restored voting rights for all ex-felons upon completion of their sentences, and Nevada eliminated its five-year waiting period for ex-felons to apply for voting rights. In 2002, Maryland automatically restored voting rights for first-time ex-felons (and for non-violent recidivists after a three-year waiting period), and Nebraska automatically restored voting rights for all ex-felons after a two-year waiting period in 2005. Finally, in July 2005, Iowa governor Tom Vilsack signed an executive order granting immediate clemency to all ex-felons who had completed their sentences.[2]

One way of understanding the cumulative impact of these changes is illustrated in figure 10.1. Here we compare rates of felon disenfranchisement from 1960 to 2000 under two different scenarios, one counterfactual and the other the actual trend. The counterfactual case asks what would have happened if none of the liberalizing changes since the 1960s had occurred. We estimate that if the laws were frozen in their 1960 state, the rate of felon disenfranchisement would have doubled from 1.8 percent in 1976 to 3.6 percent by 1992, and risen to almost 5 percent of the electorate by 2000 (corresponding to approximately 10 million people). In other words, legal liberalization has reduced the number of disenfranchised by about half. We

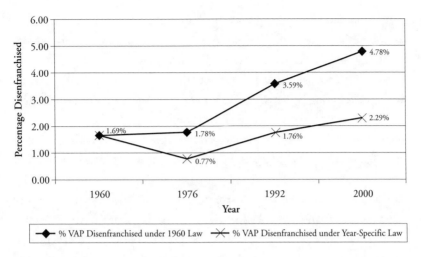

**Figure 10.1.**
Estimated disenfranchised felon population, 1960–2000, if 1960 laws remained in place.

have already shown the marked political consequences of felon disenfranchisement based on the actual rates in the bottom of figure 10.1. Imagine how much greater such consequences would be at disenfranchisement rates approximately double those of today.

### The Campaign against Felon Disenfranchisement

Reenfranchisement initiatives have gathered steam at the national level as well as in various states. A measure banning the states from placing any restrictions on the voting rights of ex-felons reached the floor of the Senate in February 2002, where it was defeated 63 to 31. In March 2005, Hillary Clinton and Barbara Boxer introduced election reform legislation that would restore ex-felon voting rights in national elections, renewing national discussion of the issue. A national civil rights campaign on behalf of disenfranchised felons is also under way, spearheaded by a coalition of policy organizations (notably the Sentencing Project in Washington, D.C.), foundations with interests in criminal justice issues or democracy (such as the Open Society Institute, the Ford Foundation, and Demos), and a variety of religious and civil rights groups (including the ACLU and NAACP).[3] A coalition called the National Right to Vote Campaign provides a focal point for state campaigns, giving expert advice on framing issues, launching a media campaign, getting different state-level organizations behind initiatives, and offering a "legal clearinghouse" to provide background information for campaigns challenging state laws.[4]

At the center of the national network has been a small but vibrant Washington D.C. policy advocacy organization, the Sentencing Project, under the leadership of Marc Mauer.[5] The first wave of media publicity surrounding the issue of felon disenfranchisement came from a report prepared by Mauer and Jamie Fellner in 1998, which we described in chapter 3. Mauer and the Sentencing Project have since played a crucial role in coordinating the various parts of the broader movement, sparking growing interest among social scientists, journalists, and civil libertarians.[6] The conflation of voting rights and criminal justice issues, and their ties to racial discrimination past and present, make felon disenfranchisement a front-burner issue in the African American community. Of special note has been the participation of African American religious organizations and ministers, as well as African American political leaders.

The primary effort of these campaigns has been in individual states, especially those states with ex-felon restrictions.[7] Although the dynamics are different in each state, the goals are the same: to force state legislatures to confront the issue in open debate. Friendly legislators have willingly introduced legislation to restore voting rights to ex- and nonincarcerated felons. An increasingly partisan environment in many states has meant that reform efforts usually move furthest where Democrats have power.[8] But the issues raised by disenfranchisement have, at their core, questions of citizenship and democracy that often find receptive audiences across normal political divides. (See the chapter appendix at pages 285–88 for more details of recent state campaigns.)

In addition to their legislative reform efforts, the national campaign and its state and local allies have focused considerable energy on jail-based get-out-the-vote campaigns.[9] As we noted in chapter 3, there were approximately 600,000 individuals held in jail on Election Day. Activists attempt to gain access to jails to conduct voter registration drives. In some jails, officials are supportive and willing to aid these efforts, although such responses are by no means universal. In some cases, inmates are recruited and trained to register other inmates. In others, the jail chaplain's office has proven a helpful ally. Jail inmates vote via absentee ballots, which frequently must be requested well in advance of the election (in some cases after registration is approved). Such technical complications have made jail-based campaigns difficult, but the biggest problem is that voluntary efforts at a few jails around the country cannot possibly make ballot access a reality for otherwise eligible jail inmates.

Another important effort has gone into informational campaigns targeted at helping eligible former felons registered to vote. We noted earlier that felons, including our own Minnesota respondents, often lack accurate information about when their right to vote will be restored. Accounts from around the country confirm the impression that many newly eligible former offenders or former inmates simply do not know that they may now register to vote.[10] The problem is magnified by fears that registering improperly will constitute a further criminal act, possibly resulting in incarceration. Civil rights organizations and other groups have launched campaigns to make such individuals aware of their rights. While voluntary efforts are important, however, they can only reach a limited number of people in a pool of millions who may not understand their rights.

## Is There a Legal Road to Reenfranchisement?

Felon disenfranchisement has been as much a legal controversy as a political one, especially in the post-1960s era. Fully one-third of the states have been subject to a legal challenge at some point.[11] With few exceptions, the states have prevailed in these battles. A recent outpouring of legal scholarship and challenges, however, has launched a new struggle over disenfranchisement in the courts. While the Supreme Court's ruling in *Richardson v. Ramirez* in 1974 presents a formidable roadblock to litigation, the recent round of challenges advances new legal theories and empirical facts.

The current wave of legal challenges emerged in the late 1990s. Although these challenges have offered numerous constitutional arguments, few have been successful.[12] For claims under the Fourteenth Amendment, courts continue to rely on the *Ramirez* decision and consider the issue settled. But as new evidence has become increasingly available—and the racial impact of these laws becomes better understood—lawsuits have argued that felon disenfranchisement violates the Voting Rights Act of 1965 (VRA), as amended in 1982. The VRA uses a "result-based" test that bans any electoral practice that has the effect of denying the right to vote based on race.[13] Thus, challenges to felon disenfranchisement under the VRA root themselves in the racial impact of the laws, based on theories of vote dilution.

The reception of challenges under the VRA has been more varied than that of those under the Fourteenth Amendment. Federal courts have differed on whether, and how, the VRA applies to felon disenfranchisement. The Ninth and Sixth Circuit Courts have held that the act applies, while the Second and Eleventh Circuits have recently held that it does not. Although splits among federal appellate courts provide a strong context for the Supreme Court to step in and settle the issue, it has thus far declined to do so.

For those courts that have applied the VRA, the debate focuses on the meaning of the racial disparity that results from disenfranchisement. For example, the Sixth Circuit held that the disparity did not "result from the state's qualification."[14] In 2003, the Ninth Circuit provided a different perspective on how the act should apply. In *Farrakhan v. Washington,* the plaintiffs argued that racial disparities within the state's criminal justice system meant that its failure to restore voting rights upon completion of sentence violated the VRA.[15] The district court recognized evidence of racial bias, but found no violation of the act, noting that the law applied equally to all convicted of a felony without regard to race. By itself, the law was not discriminatory.[16] On appeal, the Ninth Circuit reversed, finding that proper application of the VRA requires consideration of "how a challenged voting practice interacts with external factors such as 'social and historical conditions' to result in denial of the right to vote on account of race or color."[17]

Whether a conservative Supreme Court will one day overturn the practice of felon, or ex-felon, disenfranchisement remains unclear. Given the failure of the numerous legal challenges and the uncertainty of theories based on the VRA, however, proponents of reenfranchisement have had far less success in the courts than they have had in state legislatures. Yet electoral law is clearly not isolated from politics, and legal challenges can have other important consequences. For example, states such as Florida and Alabama have revised some of their restoration procedures in the face of litigation (both actual and threatened). When plaintiffs in Florida litigation showed that African American ex-felons were far more likely to have a restoration claim rejected for failure to pay outstanding financial obligations, the state relaxed the rules regarding outstanding court costs (though not for victim restitution or pecuniary penalties or liabilities exceeding $1,000).[18] Legal challenges also keep the issue before the public, obliging defenders of disenfranchisement laws to articulate justifications in open legal proceedings. While these outcomes of litigation strategy are far from negligible, we suspect that, ultimately, a political strategy is likely to be most fruitful for proponents of reform.

## Thinking about Policy Change

In closing our examination of felon disenfranchisement, we see legislative change as the most likely source of policy change in the forseeable future. As policymakers think about disenfranchisement, both short-term and long-term policy changes can be considered in response to the issues we have raised. In the short term, we would urge legislation—which might be called the Civic Reintegration Act—that would require states to make eligibility rules clear and transparent to former felons, and to encourage them to register to vote. Informational problems relating to voting eligibility are widespread, but entirely fixable. Evidence of misinformation—on the part of state, county, and local voting officials, current and former inmates, and criminal justice officials—is so widespread at present that clear communication about voting eligibility and the mechanisms for restoration is of fundamental importance.

The best way to ensure clear communication is to require state governments to provide all parties with accurate information about when individuals regain the right to vote. Fortunately, requirements are already in place to facilitate the necessary recordkeeping. The recent federal election reform legislation (the Help America Vote Act) requires the states to maintain accurate lists of ineligible felons beginning in 2006.[19] A Civic Reintegration Act would merely add a formal notification step, requiring states to inform formerly disenfranchised felons of their eligibility as soon as their right to vote is restored.

Beyond that, however, we would also suggest that a Civic Reintegration Act include the requirement that states also assist newly eligible individual felons in registering to vote. This can best be accomplished by supplying them with registration materials at the same time they receive written documentation of their eligibility to vote. A single mailing could include both an official confirmation of voting eligibility, and a voter registration pamphlet (at least in those states where mail-in registration is allowed). For those states that do not provide mail-based registration, clear instructions as to what the potential registrant needs to do in order to register might be substituted.

Including voter registration materials or instructions alongside official notice of eligibility would not require formerly ineligible felons to register to vote. Rather, it would merely alert them of their eligibility and offer them the forms or advice that would help them do so. The bundling of these two requirements—timely and accurate notification and distribution of voter registration materials—would immediately improve felons' knowledge of their voting rights and their capacity to exercise them.

*Restoring Voting Rights*

The key longer-term reforms, however, require reconsideration of all voting restrictions on disenfranchised felons. We can break the issue into three separate questions: (1) restoring voting rights for people who have completed their entire sentence (ex-felons); (2) restoring voting rights for people who remain under supervision of the criminal justice system on probation or parole, but live in their communities (nonincarcerated felons); and (3) restoring voting rights for currently incarcerated felons. The distinctions between the three categories of punishment are significant, although it is possible to overstate them as well. While ex-felons present the most difficult case for supporters of disenfranchisement to defend, current inmates present the most difficult case for supporters of reenfranchisement.

We begin with the case of ex-felons. It was once true that permanent ex-felon disenfranchisement—lifetime bans on the right to vote for criminal offenders—was standard practice in most states. As we have shown, over the past 40 years many states have done away with their ex-felon bans. Nevertheless, 13 states disenfranchise some or all ex-felons, and no other country in the world disenfranchises ex-felons to the extent that the United States does today. Campaigns to eliminate ex-felon restrictions in the remaining states have become increasingly active and sometimes successful. Supporters of ex-felons' restrictions are clearly on the defensive. They must make arguments with very strong assumptions about the incorrigibility of ex-offenders to even begin to build a plausible case. Either ex-felons must have the capacity to corrupt or taint the political system, restoration procedures must be easily available and costless to those ex-felons who should have their rights restored, or permanent denial of voting rights must serve one of the established purposes of criminal punishment. As we have shown, none of these conditions hold true.

Procedures requiring application for restoration of ex-felon voting rights in states with lengthy or permanent disqualifications are especially problematic and hard to justify. Testing the worthiness of voters has no logic place in a modern polity. For example, we allow drunkards and people with psychological problems to vote—and indeed, it is impossible to imagine not allowing them to vote because of those behaviors. Yet when the governor of a major state asks applicants for restoration whether they have been drinking or dealing with their anger management issues (as we showed in chapter 3), we are moving dangerously close to making virtue a condition of participation.

While states have legitimate reasons to compel felons to make restitution to their victims, and to punish recidivists or violent offenders more harshly than others, there are no logical reasons for imposing disenfranchisement in such cases. Requiring payment of financial obligations as a prerequisite to voting imposes a kind of poll tax on ex-felons. Such penalties can be enforced in other ways. Some states impose ex-felon disenfranchisement for only some types of criminal convictions, such as violent offenses. Yet singling out violent ex-offenders who have completed their sentences is illogical, as they are no more likely to commit electoral fraud or use the ballot improperly than any other category of offender. Moreover, the greater severity of their crimes is already addressed in the length of their sentences. The same point applies to multiple offenders: they are already punished more severely by the criminal court for their repeat offenses. Restricting their voting rights after their sentence has no compelling justification for the same reason. Finally, the logic of imposing a waiting period is also puzzling. In most states with waiting periods, restoration is automatic after that period unless a further offense is committed. The logic of requiring a waiting period in order to learn whether former felons "go straight" results merely in the removal of a large group of citizens from the electorate.

The case for restoring voting rights to nonincarcerated felons occupies the middle ground between ex-felon disenfranchisement and the disenfranchisement of current inmates. Nonincarcerated felons are like inmates, in that they are still serving a felony conviction and remain subject to certain conditions of probation or parole. But they are also like ex-felons, in that both groups are encouraged to work, pay taxes, raise families, and assume other responsibilities of citizenship. Just as ex-felons, they are free to make choices that inmates cannot make and are generally subject to the same laws as nonfelons. The two groups are also similar in that there are virtually no foreign examples of disenfranchisement of either former offenders or current, but not incarcerated, offenders.

Nonincarcerated felons are living in their communities so that they may retain (in the case of probationers) or rebuild (in the case of parolees) their ties to their families, employers, and their communities. If they are politically disenfranchised, nonincarcerated felons are denied participation in the political process that governs them in their daily lives. Allowing them to reestablish ties as stakeholders in political life provides an analogous and important reintegrative purpose, as suggested by the evidence in chapters 5 and 6. We therefore favor reenfranchising probationers and parolees.

The strongest case for continuing disenfranchisement is for currently incarcerated inmates, who cannot vote in 48 states. These restrictions are the least anomalous in the international context, as many other nations disenfranchise prison inmates. Current public opinion clearly supports the continuing disenfranchisement of prison inmates. The wave of democratization since the 1960s has swept past inmates, without so much as a single state expanding their voting rights. Should this group remain locked out?

There are a number of reasons why even the disenfranchisement of current inmates is problematic. To be sure, prisoners are denied many freedoms. Inmates are not free to choose whom they want to work for, to travel, to have their choice of goods and services, and so forth. But these restrictions arise simply because of their incapacitation in prison. In other words, they do not *lose* these rights as part of their criminal sentence under state or federal law, but they are *deprived* of these things by virtue of their confinement and the necessary limitations on freedom of movement it imposes.

Prison administrators have a responsibility to maintain a safe and orderly environment in prison, and they have great discretion in determining which individual deprivations are necessary to meet these goals. But a long series of court rulings has established that restrictions on fundamental rights must be justified, rather than imposed arbitrarily on inmates. For example, in *Cutter v. Wilkinson* (2005) the Supreme Court unanimously upheld the constitutionality of a federal law requiring states to allow prisoners to practice their religious beliefs, unless prison officials can show that such accommodation would be disruptive.[20] Similarly, the First Amendment protects the right of prisoners to send and receive mail, although officials may censor letters or withhold delivery for rational security reasons.[21] Courts thus strike a balance between prisoners' rights and the objectives of security, order, and rehabilitation. Where rights such as access to the courts or to free expression are not clearly part of the punishment or necessary for prison administration, they are generally retained by inmates.

The right to vote is potentially one such right. Limited information about prisoner voting (by absentee ballot) in Maine and Vermont, and in many other countries around the world, provides no evidence that it would create significant problems for prison officials.[22] Voting by inmates in other countries, sometimes even facilitated by the use of polling booths in prison, does not appear to have created security or other problems.[23] Because voting presents few security concerns and could be facilitated by either absentee ballots or polling places inside prisons, the question of restoring voting rights to inmates becomes a matter of choice, not necessity. From there, it is not a leap to suggest that the same logic in favor of voting rights for ex-felons and nonincarcerated felons might be extended to current inmates as well. Allowing voting provides a costless way of allowing them to practice citizenship.

It is noteworthy that supreme courts in Israel, Canada, and South Africa have all recently restored inmate voting, as has the European Court of Human Rights. In each case, and despite invoking different legal and political traditions, all three national courts noted that the right to vote is fundamental to democracy, outweighing other considerations.[24] In Israel, the Supreme Court, remarkably, restored the voting rights of Yigal Amir, the assassin of Yitzhak Rabin. It declared that "we must separate contempt for his act from respect for his right," and that if the right to vote was denied, "the base of all fundamental rights is shaken."[25] In striking down the disenfranchisement of prisoners, the Supreme Court of Canada similarly noted that the practice has "no place in a democracy built upon the principles of inclusiveness, equality, and citizen participation."[26]

The South African Constitutional Court applied similar logic to the Canadian and Israeli courts, but offered an especially elegant and forceful ruling that is worth quoting at length:

> The universality of the franchise is important not only for nationhood and democracy. The vote of each and every citizen is a badge of dignity. Quite literally, it says that everybody counts.
> In a country of great disparities of wealth and power, exalted or disgraced, we all belong to the same democratic South African nation; that our destinies are intertwined in a single interactive polity. Right may not be limited without justification and legislation dealing with the franchise must be interpreted in favor of enfranchisement rather than disenfranchisement.[27]

Following this ruling, there have been several twists and turns, as the South African government formally adopted new legislation disenfranchising felons in 2000, but another ruling in 2004 once again restored inmate voting rights.[28]

The irony of the South African case is striking. The high court in a new democracy, throwing off the yoke of undemocratic apartheid rule, concludes that voting is a fundamental right of all citizens, and one in which "our destinies are intertwined in a single interactive polity." No clearer statement of the argument of this book can be found. Democracy rests on universal participation, even among those citizens who have committed criminal offenses. Their exclusion affects everyone and diminishes the democratic polity as a consequence.

# Appendix

*Chapter 1: Foundations*

Table A1.1
International Disenfranchisement Laws on the Voting Rights of Prisoners

- **No restrictions:** Bosnia, Canada, Croatia, Czech Republic, Denmark, Finland, Iceland, Ireland, Israel, Latvia, Lithuania, Macedonia, Poland, Serbia, Slovenia, Spain, South Africa, Sweden, Switzerland, Ukraine

- **Selective restrictions:** Australia, Austria, Belgium, France, Germany, Greece, Italy, Malta, New Zealand, Norway, San Marino

- **Complete ban on inmate voting:** Argentina, Brazil, Bulgaria, Estonia, Hungary, India, Luxembourg, Portugal, Romania, Russia, United Kingdom

- **Postrelease restrictions:** Armenia, Belgium (sentences over seven years), Chile, Finland (for up to seven years after imprisonment), Germany (court-imposed only in rare cases)

*Source:* Brandon Rottinghaus, *Incarceration and Enfranchisement: International Practices, Impact, and Recommendations for Reform* (Washington, D.C.: International Foundation for Election Systems, 2003); and authors' updates

## Chapter 2: The Racial Origins of Felon Disenfranchisement

### Methods and Data Used in Historical Analyses

We employ event history analysis in chapter 2. These statistical methods are useful for studying the occurrence and timing of events, or discrete changes from one condition (e.g., the absence of a restrictive felon disenfranchisement law) to another (e.g., passage of such a law). For this sort of analysis, two key pieces of information are required: *whether* a state has a particular type of law in place and *when* any changes in the law occurred. An excellent hands-on introduction to these models is found in Paul Allison's *Survival Analysis Using the SAS System: A Practical Guide* (Cary, N.C.: SAS Institute, 1995) and Kazuo Yamaguchi's *Event History Analysis* (Newbury Park, Calif.: Sage, 1991).

We use event history methods to statistically model passage of felon disenfranchisement laws because this approach treats "censored" cases appropriately and because it allows us to estimate the effects of "time-varying" as well as fixed predictors. Correctly modeling censored cases is necessary so that states are included in the analysis only when they are at risk of changing their felon disenfranchisement regime. For example, Alaska and Hawaii were not at risk of passing a restrictive law until they attained statehood in 1959. If a state was not at risk of adopting a more restrictive law because it already had the most severe voting ban in place—disenfranchising ex-felons—that state was treated as censored until it repealed its ex-felon disenfranchisement law. Time-varying independent variables are important for this study because it would be extremely unrealistic to assume stability over 150 years in key predictors such as imprisonment and racial composition.

We estimate the effects of racial threat and other factors using the following discrete-time logistic regression model.

$$\log (P_{st}/(1-P_{st})) = \alpha_t + \beta_1 X_{st1} + \ldots + \beta_k X_{stk},$$

where $P_{st}$ represents the conditional probability that state $s$ passes a law at time $t$, given that the state has not already passed such a law. Here, $s$ denotes individual states, $t$ represents time or decade, $\beta$ signifies the effect of independent variables, X denotes time-varying explanatory variables, and $\alpha_t$ represents a set of constants corresponding to each decade or discrete-time unit. While we have complete information on disenfranchisement law changes spanning from 1788 to 2002, the time-varying explanatory variables are limited to the period from 1850 to 2002. Four states are "left censored" because they passed restrictive laws prior to 1840, when data on key independent variables are unavailable. Seven states passed a first restrictive law between 1841 and 1849. As a check on our results, we estimated models that applied 1850 data to the 1840 period (assuming stability on the values of independent variables, except gubernatorial partisanship) as well as models that treated these states as censored, obtaining very similar results to those presented in the chapter.

We gathered information about the adoption and amendment of these laws by examining the elector qualifications and consequences of felony convictions as specified in state constitutions and statutes. We located the information by first examining the state constitutions and legislative histories reported by those states that incorporate such information into their statutory codebooks. For other states, we consulted earlier codebooks that referred specifically to voting laws, all of which are archived at several university law libraries. Our analysis, undertaken independently from that of historian Alexander Keyssar, contains some slight differences from his analysis (compare Keyssar, *The Right to Vote: The Contested History of Democracy in the United States* [New York: Basic Books, 2000], pp. 376–86). As with any textual evidence, interpretation is key when reading historical legal provisions, and in some cases it was difficult to identify precisely when a state passed or implemented a broad disenfranchisement provision for felony-level crimes. For example, the Alabama legislature enacted a provision in 1819 that mandated that "any person who may be convicted of bribery, forgery, perjury, or any other high crime or misdemeanor, shall be disqualified from holding or exercising any office under the authority of this State, from serving in any case as a juror, and from voting at any election" (see Acts of the General Assembly of the State of Alabama, *An Act Excluding from Suffrage, Serving as Jurors, and Holding Offices, such Persons as may be Convicted of Bribery, Forgery, Perjury, and other High Crimes and Misdemeanors* (Huntsville, Ala.: John Boardman, 1820). Relying on the principle of *ejusdem generis*, we interpret "other high crime or misdemeanor" as those crimes akin to bribery, forgery, and perjury. While Alabama's statute uses "high crime" (which appears to take a different historical meaning than "infamous crime"), we followed the same principle when reading statutes that enumerated a narrow class of offenses (usually bribery and perjury) followed by "or other infamous crime."

Table A2.1
State-Level Changes to Felon Disenfranchisement Laws.[1]

| State | Year of Statehood | Year of First Felon Disenfranchisement Law[2,3] | Major Amendments[3,4] |
|---|---|---|---|
| Alabama | 1819 | 1867^ | |
| Alaska | 1959 | 1959* | 1994 |
| Arizona | 1912 | 1912* | 1978 |
| Arkansas | 1836 | 1868 | 1964 |
| California | 1849 | 1849* | 1972 |
| Colorado | 1876 | 1876* | 1993, 1997 |
| Connecticut | 1788 | 1818 | 1975, 2001 |
| Delaware | 1787 | 1831 | 2000 |
| Florida | 1845 | 1868^ | 1885 |
| Georgia | 1788 | 1868 | 1983 |
| Hawaii | 1959 | 1959* | 1968 |
| Idaho | 1890 | 1890* | 1972 |
| Illinois | 1818 | 1870^ | 1970, 1973 |
| Indiana | 1816 | 1852^ | 1881 |
| Iowa | 1846 | 1846* | 2005 |
| Kansas | 1861 | 1859* | 1969, 2002 |
| Kentucky | 1792 | 1851^ | |
| Louisiana | 1812 | 1845^ | 1975 |
| Maine | 1820 | | |
| Maryland | 1788 | 1851 | 1957, 2002 |
| Massachusetts | 1788 | 2000 | |
| Michigan | 1837 | 1963 | |
| Minnesota | 1858 | 1857* | |
| Mississippi | 1817 | 1868 | |
| Missouri | 1821 | 1875^ | 1962 |

*(continued)*

| State | Year of Statehood | Year of First Felon Disenfranchisement Law[2,3] | Major Amendments[3,4] |
|---|---|---|---|
| Montana | 1889 | 1909 | 1969 |
| Nebraska | 1867 | 1875 | 2005 |
| Nevada | 1864 | 1864* | 2003 |
| New Hampshire | 1788 | 1967 | |
| New Jersey | 1787 | 1844 | 1948 |
| New Mexico | 1912 | 1911* | 2001 |
| New York | 1788 | 1847 | 1976 |
| North Carolina | 1789 | 1876 | 1970, 1971, 1973 |
| North Dakota | 1889 | 1889* | 1973, 1979 |
| Ohio | 1803 | 1835^ | 1974 |
| Oklahoma | 1907 | 1907* | |
| Oregon | 1859 | 1859* | 1961, 1975, 1999 |
| Pennsylvania | 1787 | 1860 | 1968, 1995, 2000 |
| Rhode Island | 1790 | 1841 | 1973 |
| South Carolina | 1788 | 1868 | 1895, 1981 |
| South Dakota | 1889 | 1889* | 1967 |
| Tennessee | 1796 | 1871 | 1986 |
| Texas | 1845 | 1869^ | 1876, 1983, 1997 |
| Utah | 1896 | 1998 | |
| Vermont | 1791 | | |
| Virginia | 1788 | 1830^ | |
| Washington | 1889 | 1889* | 1984 |
| West Virginia | 1863 | 1863* | |
| Wisconsin | 1848 | 1848* | 1947 |
| Wyoming | 1890 | 1890* | |

* Disenfranchised felons at statehood

^ First state constitution gave legislature power to restrict suffrage

1. Based on authors' canvass of state constitutional and statutory histories; full details available upon request.

2. Many states disenfranchised for specific crimes before amending laws to disenfranchise for all felony convictions.

3. Years listed are according to the year of legal change, rather than year the change became effective.

4. "Major" amendments are those that have changed which groups of felons are disenfranchised. Most states have changed the wording of disenfranchisement laws in ways that generally do not affect who is disenfranchised.

Table A2.2

Comparison of Adoption of Universal White Suffrage and First Felon
Disenfranchisement Provision, 1840–1865

| State | Universal White Male Suffrage[1] | First Felon Disenfranchisement Provision |
|---|---|---|
| California | 1849[2] | 1849 |
| Indiana | 1816[2] | 1852 |
| Iowa | 1846[2] | 1846 |
| Kansas | 1861[2] | 1861 |
| Kentucky | 1792[2] | 1851 |
| Louisiana | 1845 | 1845 |
| Maryland | 1801 | 1851 |
| Minnesota | 1858[2] | 1858 |
| Nevada | 1864[2] | 1864 |
| New Jersey | 1844 | 1844 |
| New York | 1821 | 1847 |
| Oregon | 1859[2] | 1859 |
| Pennsylvania | 1931 | 1860 |
| Rhode Island | 1928 | 1841 |
| West Virginia | 1863[2] | 1863 |
| Wisconsin | 1848[2] | 1848 |

1. Considered as the year in which the state no longer required property ownership or taxpaying as a condition to vote.

2. At time of statehood, state had neither a property nor a taxpaying requirement (year reflects year of statehood).

Sources: Alex Keyssar, The Right to Vote (New York: Basic Books, 2000), table A.2; Chilton Williamson, American Suffrage: From Property to Democracy, 1760–1860 (Princeton: Princeton University Press, 1960), 136, 268.

**Table A2.3**

**Summary of Variables, 1850–2002**

| Variable | Description | Coding | Mean |
|---|---|---|---|
| *Disenfranchisement Law* | | | |
| First law | Passage of first felon disenfranchisement law | 0 = no <br> 1 = yes | |
| Ex-felon law | Passage of first ex-felon disenfranchisement law | 0 = no <br> 1 = yes | |
| *Racial threat* | | | |
| Nonwhite prison | Percent of prison population that is nonwhite | Percentage | 30.2% |
| Nonwhite males | Percent of male population that is nonwhite | Percentage | 6.8% |
| Nonwhite population | Percent of total population that is nonwhite | Percentage | 13.6% |
| Black population | Total African American population | 100,000s | 3.1 <br> (4.7) |
| Nonblack population | Total non–African American population | 100,000s | 24.4 <br> (32.6) |
| *Economic competition* | | | |
| Idle white males | Percent of white males, ages 15–39, unemployed or both not in the labor force and not in school | Percentage | 7.4% |
| National recession | Proportion of decade in business contraction | Proportion | .33 |
| *Region* | | | |
| Northeast | Dichotomous northeastern state indicator (Connecticut, Maine, Massachusetts, New Hampshire, New Jersey, New York, Pennsylvania, Rhode Island, Vermont) | 0 = no <br> 1 = yes | 19.6% |
| Midwest | Dichotomous midwestern state indicator (Illinois, Indiana, Iowa, Kansas, Michigan, Minnesota, Missouri, Nebraska, North Dakota, Ohio, South Dakota, Wisconsin) | 0 = no <br> 1 = yes | 25.1% |

(*continued*)

**Table A2.3** (*continued*)

| Variable | Description | Coding | Mean |
|---|---|---|---|
| South | Dichotomous southern state indicator (Alabama, Arkansas, Delaware, Florida, Georgia, Kentucky, Louisiana, Maryland, Mississippi, North Carolina, Oklahoma, South Carolina, Tennessee, Texas, Virginia, West Virginia). | 0 = no 1 = yes | 34.1% |
| West | Dichotomous western state indicator (Alaska, Arizona, California, Colorado, Hawaii, Idaho, Montana, Nevada, New Mexico, Oregon, Utah, Washington, Wyoming). | 0 = no 1 = yes | 21.1% |
| *State punitiveness* | | | |
| Incarceration rate | State incarceration rate per 100,000 population. | Per 100,000 | 134.3 (114.4) |
| *Political power* | | | |
| Pre-1870 Democrat | Dichotomous Democratic governor indicator, pre-1870. | 0 = no 1 = yes | 5.7% |
| 1870–1959 Democrat | Dichotomous Democratic governor indicator, 1870–1959. | 0 = no 1 = yes | 26.9% |
| 1960–2002 Democrat | Dichotomous Democratic governor indicator, post-1959. | 0 = no 1 = yes | 17.2% |
| *Timing* | | | |
| Time since statehood | Number of years since statehood | Years | 103.9 (56.4) |
| *Time* | | | |
| Year | Individual decade indicator variables (1850–59, 1860–69, etc.) | 0 = no 1 = yes | |
| Total state-years | | | 733 |

**Table A2.4**
Statistically Significant Predictors of First Felon Disenfranchisement Law, 1850–2002, with and without Statistical Controls

| | Bivariate (separate models) | Multivariate (full model) |
|---|---|---|
| *Racial threat* | | |
| Percent nonwhite prison | (+) | (+) |
| Black population (100,000s) | (ns) | (ns) |
| Nonblack population (100,000s) | (ns) | (ns) |
| *Region (v. Northeast)* | | |
| South | (+) | (ns) |
| Midwest | (ns) | (ns) |
| West | (+) | (ns) |
| *State punitiveness* | | |
| Incarceration rate/100,000 | (ns) | (ns) |
| *Economic competition* | | |
| Idle/unemployed white males 15–39 | (ns) | (ns) |
| National recession | (ns) | (ns) |
| *Political power* | | |
| Democratic governor | (ns) | (−) |
| *Timing* | | |
| Time since statehood | (−) | (−) |
| *Time (v. 1850)*[1] | | |
| 1860s | (+) | (ns) |
| 1870s | (+) | (ns) |
| 1880s | (+) | (ns) |
| 1890s | (ns) | (ns) |
| 1900s | (ns) | (ns) |
| 1910–1949 | (ns) | (ns) |
| 1950–2002 | (ns) | (ns) |
| −2 log likelihood | − | 101.5 |
| Chi-square (df) | − | 77.4 (18) |
| Events | 42–48 | 40 |
| N | 159–277 | 158 |

*Note:* Bivariate results are based on 26 separate discrete-time event history models predicting the timing of passage of the first felon disenfranchisement law. Region and timing models span the period from 1780 to 2002 rather than 1850 to 2002. Coefficients and standard errors are available in Angela Behrens, Christopher Uggen, and Jeff Manza, "Ballot Manipulation and the Menace of Negro Domination: Racial Threat and Felon Disenfranchisement in the United States, 1850–2002," *American Journal of Sociology* 109 (November 2003): 584–87.

## Table A2.5
### Racial and Economic Threat Predictors of First Felon Disenfranchisement Law

| Statistically Significant Predictors | | Nonsignificant Predictors |
|---|---|---|
| *Panel A. Pre-1870* | | |
| % nonwhite prison | (+) | % nonwhite population |
| | | % nonwhite males |
| | | % idle/unemployed males |
| *Panel B. 1870–2002* | | |
| % nonwhite population | (+) | % idle/unemployed white males |
| % nonwhite males | (+) | |
| % nonwhite prison | (+) | |

*Note:* Models additionally control for region, Democrat governor, idle or unemployed white males, state population, incarceration rate, and time since statehood.

Table A3.1
Characteristics of Prison Inmates, Parolees, and Felony Probationers

| | Prison Inmates | | | Parole | Felony Probation | U.S. Males 25–34 |
|---|---|---|---|---|---|---|
| | 1974 | 1986 | 1997 | 1999 | 1995 | 1997 |
| *Education* | | | | | | |
| Years of education | 9.9 | 10.9 | 10.7 | | | |
| % with HS diploma/GED | 21.1 | 31.9 | 30.6 | 49.2 | 54.4 | 87.3 |
| *Employment* | | | | | | |
| % FT employed | 61.6 | 57.3 | 56.0 | | | 77.0 |
| % PT/occasional employed | 7.3 | 11.6 | 12.5 | | | 12.1 |
| % looking for employment | 12.5 | 18.0 | 13.7 | | | 3.9 |
| % not employed and not Looking for work | 18.5 | 13.0 | 17.8 | | | 7.0 |
| Sex (percent male) | 96.7 | 95.6 | 93.7 | 90.1 | 79.1 | 100 |
| Current age | 29.6 (10.0) | 30.6 (9.0) | 34.8 (10.0) | 34 | 31.9 | 29.7 |
| Age at admission to prison | 26.5 (9.3) | 27.6 (8.7) | 32.5 (10.4) | | | |
| *Race* | | | | | | |
| % black, non-Hispanic | 49 | 45 | 47 | 47.3 | 31 | 12.8 |
| % white, non-Hispanic | 39 | 40 | 33 | 35.4 | 55 | 68.9 |

*(continued)*

Table A3.1 (continued)

| | Prison Inmates | | | Parole | Felony Probation | | U.S. Males 25–34 |
| | 1974 | 1986 | 1997 | 1999 | 1995 | | 1997 |
|---|---|---|---|---|---|---|---|
| % Hispanic | 10 | 13 | 17 | 16.1 | 11 | | 13.2 |
| % other | 2 | 3 | 3 | 1.2 | 3 | | 5.0 |
| *Family status* | | | | | | | |
| % never married | 47.9 | 53.7 | 55.9 | | 50.8 | | 40.4 |
| % married | 23.7 | 20.3 | 17.7 | | 26.8 | | 53.0 |
| % with children | 60.2 | 60.4 | 56.0 | | | | |
| Number of children | 1.7 | 2.3 | 2.5 | | | | |
| | (2.0) | (1.7) | (1.9) | | | | |
| **Conviction offense** | | | | | | | |
| % violent offense | 52.5 | 64.2 | 46.4 | 24.4 | 19.5 | | |
| % property offense | 33.3 | 22.9 | 14.0 | 30.8 | 36.6 | | |
| % drug offense | 10.4 | 8.8 | 26.9 | 35.3 | 30.7 | | |
| % public order offense | 1.9 | 3.3 | 8.9 | 9.0 | 12.1 | | |
| % other offense | 2.0 | 0.9 | 3.7 | 0.5 | 1.0 | | |

*Note:* Standard deviations for continuous variables in parentheses.

*Sources: Survey of Inmates in State and Federal Correctional Facilities, Trends in State Parole 1990–1999,* and *Characteristics of Adults on Probation, 1995* and *Statistical Abstract, 1998* (Washington, D.C.: U.S. Government Printing Office).

## Table A3.2
## Summary of State Felon Disfranchisement Restrictions

| No Restriction (2) | Inmates Only (13) | Inmates and Parolees (4) | Inmates, Parolees, and Probationers (17) | Inmates, Parolees, Probationers, and Some or All Ex-felons (14) |
|---|---|---|---|---|
| Maine | Hawaii | California | Alaska | Alabama |
| Vermont | Illinois | Colorado | Arkansas | Arizona[1] |
| | Indiana | Connecticut* | Georgia | Delaware*,[2] |
| | Massachusetts* | New York | Idaho | Florida |
| | Michigan | | Kansas* | Iowa |
| | Montana | | Louisiana | Kentucky |
| | New Hampshire | | Minnesota | Maryland[3] |
| | North Dakota | | Missouri | Mississippi |
| | Ohio | | New Jersey | Nebraska*,[4] |
| | Oregon | | New Mexico* | Nevada[5] |
| | Pennsylvania | | North Carolina | Tennessee[6] |
| | South Dakota | | Oklahoma | Virginia |
| | Utah | | Rhode Island | Washington[6] |
| | | | South Carolina | Wyoming |
| | | | Texas | |
| | | | West Virginia | |
| | | | Wisconsin | |

* Indicates a recent change since 2000.

1. State disfranchises recidivists.

2. State requires a five-year waiting period.

3. State disfranchises recidivists convicted of violent crimes; all other recidivists must wait three years after completion of sentence.

4. Nebraska reduced its indefinite ban on ex-felon voting to a two-year waiting period in 2005.

5. State disfranchises recidivists and those convicted of violent felonies.

6. State disfranchises those convicted prior to repeal of ex-felon disfranchisement law.

7. The Iowa governor issued an executive order in 2005 restoring the voting rights of all ex-felons.

**Table A3.3**

Estimates of Disenfranchised Felons by State, December 31, 2004

| State | Prisoners | Parolees | Felony Probation | Jail Inmates | Estimated Ex-felons | Total | Voting Age Population | Disenfranchisement Rate |
|---|---|---|---|---|---|---|---|---|
| Alabama | 30,628 | 9,098 | 30,387 | 1,418 | 178,516 | 250,046 | 3,392,779 | 7.37% |
| Alaska | 4,658 | 927 | 5,083 | 463 | | 11,132 | 459,529 | 2.42% |
| Arizona | 33,103 | 9,291 | 55,259 | 1,315 | 77,136 | 176,103 | 4,061,499 | 4.34% |
| Arkansas | 13,699 | 15,461 | 28,532 | | | 57,691 | 2,043,701 | 2.82% |
| California | 167,612 | 107,580 | | 7,932 | | 283,124 | 26,064,483 | 1.09% |
| Colorado | 20,537 | 6,920 | | 1,180 | | 28,636 | 3,397,937 | 0.84% |
| Connecticut | 19,012 | 3,090 | | 752 | | 22,854 | 2,647,997 | 0.86% |
| Delaware | 6,808 | 508 | 10,818 | 516 | 28,028 | 46,677 | 618,649 | 7.54% |
| District of Columbia* | 374 | | | 356 | | 730 | 454,981 | 0.16% |
| Florida | 84,210 | 4,694 | 127,794 | 5,565 | 957,423 | 1,179,687 | 13,094,945 | 9.01% |
| Georgia | 46,972 | 23,530 | 209,442 | 3,664 | | 283,607 | 6,387,956 | 4.44% |
| Hawaii | 6,265 | | | 264 | | 6,530 | 960,466 | 0.68% |
| Idaho | 6,034 | 2,767 | 8,265 | 350 | | 17,416 | 994,305 | 1.75% |
| Illinois | 44,156 | | | 1,669 | | 45,825 | 9,422,938 | 0.49% |
| Indiana | 24,615 | | | 1,630 | | 26,245 | 4,591,742 | 0.57% |
| Iowa | 8,700 | 3,446 | 10,632 | 330 | 98,311 | 121,418 | 2,250,634 | 5.39% |

| State | | | | | | | | |
|---|---|---|---|---|---|---|---|---|
| Kansas | 9,333 | 4,146 | 13,907 | 477 | | 27,863 | 2,028,426 | 1.37% |
| Kentucky | 17,470 | 9,609 | 29,311 | 1,183 | 128,775 | 186,348 | 3,123,645 | 5.97% |
| Louisiana | 36,047 | 25,065 | 34,366 | 2,712 | | 98,190 | 3,318,779 | 2.96% |
| Maine | | | | | | — | 1,018,982 | 0.00% |
| Maryland | 23,434 | 14,223 | 20,482 | 1,111 | 52,272 | 111,521 | 4,130,817 | 2.70% |
| Mass. | 10,140 | | | | | 10,140 | 4,946,304 | 0.20% |
| Michigan | 48,173 | | | 1,615 | | 49,788 | 7,541,065 | 0.66% |
| Minnesota | 8,675 | 3,614 | 25,768 | 727 | | 38,784 | 3,810,605 | 1.02% |
| Mississippi | 23,669 | 1,816 | 21,967 | 1,153 | 97,550 | 146,155 | 2,120,013 | 6.89% |
| Missouri | 30,515 | 17,123 | 45,305 | 810 | | 93,752 | 4,297,142 | 2.18% |
| Montana | 3,942 | | | 203 | | 4,145 | 701,847 | 0.59% |
| Nebraska | 4,024 | 736 | 5,385 | 239 | 51,612 | 61,996 | 1,298,451 | 4.77% |
| Nevada | 10,606 | 4,287 | 6,987 | 547 | 21,166 | 43,594 | 1,659,757 | 2.63% |
| New Hamp. | 2,417 | | | 170 | | 2,587 | 981,456 | 0.26% |
| New Jersey | 26,619 | 13,950 | 85,186 | 1,423 | | 127,178 | 6,506,779 | 1.95% |
| New Mexico | 6,466 | 2,953 | 8,002 | 658 | | 18,080 | 1,372,580 | 1.32% |
| New York | 63,372 | 55,741 | | 2,904 | | 122,018 | 14,657,367 | 0.83% |
| North Carolina | 34,298 | 216 | 37,136 | 1,463 | | 73,113 | 6,319,805 | 1.16% |
| North Dakota | 1,380 | | | 86 | | 1,466 | 487,010 | 0.30% |
| Ohio | 43,927 | | | 1,560 | | 45,487 | 8,620,509 | 0.53% |
| Oklahoma | 22,844 | 4,047 | 21,962 | 688 | | 49,541 | 2,633,289 | 1.88% |

*(continued)*

Table A3.3 (continued)

| State | Prisoners | Parolees | Felony Probation | Jail Inmates | Estimated Ex-felons | Total | Voting Age Population | Disenfranchisement Rate |
|---|---|---|---|---|---|---|---|---|
| Oregon | 13,376 | | | 852 | | 14,228 | 2,710,424 | 0.52% |
| Pennsylvania | 41,626 | | | | | 41,626 | 9,534,761 | 0.44% |
| Rhode Island | 3,534 | 400 | 16,622 | 237 | | 20,793 | 832,115 | 2.50% |
| So. Carolina | 23,719 | 2,953 | 20,904 | 946 | | 48,523 | 3,123,648 | 1.55% |
| South Dakota | 3,138 | | | 133 | | 3,271 | 568,883 | 0.58% |
| Tennessee | 25,835 | 7,983 | 32,288 | 2,254 | 25,899 | 94,258 | 4,447,269 | 2.12% |
| Texas | 171,918 | 101,453 | 243,413 | 6,103 | | 522,887 | 15,878,347 | 3.29% |
| Utah | 5,970 | | | | | 5,970 | 1,608,540 | 0.37% |
| Vermont | | | | | | — | 481,661 | 0.00% |
| Virginia | 35,172 | 5,158 | 37,463 | 2,153 | 297,901 | 377,847 | 5,587,563 | 6.76% |
| Washington | 16,229 | 116 | 120,014 | 1,173 | 29,785 | 167,316 | 4,634,864 | 3.61% |
| West Virginia | 4,982 | 1,308 | 4,159 | 352 | | 10,800 | 1,419,453 | 0.76% |
| Wisconsin | 23,134 | 12,911 | 24,873 | 1,423 | | 62,342 | 4,139,405 | 1.51% |
| Wyoming | 2,018 | 586 | 3,171 | 118 | 14,304 | 20,198 | 380,169 | 5.31% |
| **Total** | **1,315,387** | **477,704** | **1,344,883** | **62,878** | **2,058,678** | **5,259,530** | **217,766,271** | **2.42%** |

Note: 6,677 District of Columbia prisoners were under the jurisdiction of the Federal Bureau of Prisons.

Table A3.4
Estimates of Disenfranchised African American Felons by State, December 31, 2004.

| State | Black Prison | Black Parole | Black Probation | Black Jail | Est. Black Ex-felons | Total | Voting Age Population | Disenfranchisement Rate |
|---|---|---|---|---|---|---|---|---|
| Alabama | 20,123 | 4,429 | 13,033 | 784 | 86,030 | 124,398 | 813,208 | 15.30% |
| Alaska | 695 | 97 | 655 | 23 | | 1,469 | 19,212 | 7.64% |
| Arizona | 5,015 | 1,453 | 4,719 | 179 | 12,815 | 24,181 | 114,708 | 21.08% |
| Arkansas | 7,583 | 7,712 | 10,191 | — | | 25,486 | 284,210 | 8.97% |
| California | 82,767 | 28,765 | — | 2,773 | | 114,305 | 1,504,362 | 7.60% |
| Colorado | 5,154 | 2,062 | — | 243 | | 7,459 | 137,783 | 5.41% |
| Connecticut | 11,999 | 1,944 | — | 362 | | 14,304 | 212,894 | 6.72% |
| Delaware | 4,364 | 266 | 5,074 | — | 11,159 | 20,862 | 106,283 | 19.63% |
| District of Columbia | 371 | — | — | 327 | | 697 | 224,361 | 0.31% |
| Florida | 39,427 | 2,696 | 43,305 | 2,774 | 205,342 | 293,545 | 1,559,354 | 18.82% |
| Georgia | 31,415 | 15,574 | 111,661 | 2,256 | | 160,905 | 1,681,040 | 9.57% |
| Hawaii | 355 | — | — | 11 | | 366 | 21,442 | 1.71% |
| Idaho | 115 | 54 | 132 | 6 | | 308 | 5,110 | 6.03% |
| Illinois | 31,965 | — | — | 1,088 | | 33,053 | 1,230,967 | 2.69% |
| Indiana | 10,596 | — | — | 775 | | 11,371 | 354,616 | 3.21% |
| Iowa | 2,218 | 513 | 1,162 | 62 | 10,750 | 14,705 | 43,275 | 33.98% |
| Kansas | 3,600 | 1,471 | 3,548 | 130 | | 8,750 | 118,799 | 7.37% |

(continued)

Table A3.4 *(continued)*

| State | Black Prison | Black Parole | Black Probation | Black Jail | Est. Black Ex-felons | Total | Voting Age Population | Disenfranchisement Rate |
|---|---|---|---|---|---|---|---|---|
| Kentucky | 6,695 | 2,695 | 6,572 | 365 | 32,965 | 49,293 | 207,961 | 23.70% |
| Louisiana | 27,585 | 18,312 | 20,030 | 1,923 | — | 67,850 | 1,000,499 | 6.78% |
| Maine | — | — | — | — | — | — | 3,466 | 0.00% |
| Maryland | 18,148 | 10,722 | 11,897 | 733 | 22,903 | 64,403 | 1,111,217 | 5.80% |
| Mass. | 3,804 | — | — | — | — | 3,804 | 236,703 | 1.61% |
| Michigan | 27,490 | — | — | 578 | — | 28,067 | 985,837 | 2.85% |
| Minnesota | 2,309 | 1,841 | 4,587 | 128 | — | 8,865 | 111,714 | 7.94% |
| Mississippi | 17,710 | 1,286 | 13,221 | 816 | 59,200 | 92,232 | 696,831 | 13.24% |
| Missouri | 13,948 | 6,879 | 13,524 | 335 | — | 34,685 | 435,218 | 7.97% |
| Montana | 56 | — | — | 6 | — | 61 | 2,783 | 2.21% |
| Nebraska | 1,194 | 181 | 846 | 48 | 9,135 | 11,403 | 50,230 | 22.70% |
| Nevada | 3,303 | 1,406 | 1,540 | 163 | 6,219 | 12,632 | 101,951 | 12.39% |
| New Hamp. | 134 | — | — | 13 | — | 148 | 5,497 | 2.68% |
| New Jersey | 19,038 | 8,406 | 41,934 | 872 | — | 70,249 | 808,463 | 8.69% |
| New Mexico | 752 | 352 | 566 | 52 | — | 1,722 | 25,680 | 6.71% |
| New York | 35,072 | 42,041 | — | 1,579 | — | 78,692 | 1,868,249 | 4.21% |
| North Carolina | 22,466 | 136 | 18,672 | 952 | — | 42,227 | 1,277,505 | 3.31% |

| State | | | | | | | |
|---|---|---|---|---|---|---|---|
| North Dakota | 35 | — | — | 2 | | 37 | 3,732 | 0.99% |
| Ohio | 23,797 | — | — | 690 | | 24,487 | 928,659 | 2.64% |
| Oklahoma | 8,215 | 1,362 | 5,084 | 222 | | 14,882 | 202,628 | 7.34% |
| Oregon | 1,895 | — | — | 93 | | 1,988 | 45,588 | 4.36% |
| Pennsylvania | 26,101 | — | — | — | | 26,101 | 829,353 | 3.15% |
| Rhode Island | 1,232 | 113 | 3,775 | 63 | | 5,183 | 27,489 | 18.86% |
| So. Carolina | 16,622 | 2,054 | 11,515 | 649 | | 30,840 | 830,653 | 3.71% |
| South Dakota | 139 | — | — | 4 | | 142 | 3,830 | 3.71% |
| Tennessee | 13,143 | 4,542 | 13,675 | 1,311 | 10,526 | 43,198 | 672,913 | 6.42% |
| Texas | 78,251 | 40,213 | 45,203 | 2,318 | | 165,985 | 1,785,595 | 9.30% |
| Utah | 459 | — | — | — | | 459 | 13,385 | 3.43% |
| Vermont | — | — | — | — | | — | 2,126 | 0.00% |
| Virginia | 23,591 | 3,329 | 19,096 | 1,375 | 160,952 | 208,343 | 1,054,523 | 19.76% |
| Washington | 3,674 | 17 | 15,987 | 223 | 3,464 | 23,364 | 135,689 | 17.22% |
| West Virginia | 794 | 256 | 362 | 50 | | 1,462 | 42,499 | 3.44% |
| Wisconsin | 11,156 | 6,129 | 6,483 | 526 | | 24,293 | 218,943 | 11.10% |
| Wyoming | 121 | 25 | 98 | 2 | 439 | 685 | 3,420 | 20.03% |
| **Total** | **666,687** | **219,329** | **448,146** | **27,887** | **631,898** | **1,993,947** | **24,162,453** | **8.25%** |

*Note:* 6,343 African American District of Columbia prisoners were under Federal Bureau of Prisons jurisdiction.

## Table A3.5
## Restoration of Voting Rights in States That Disenfranchise
## beyond Completion of Sentence

| State | Disenfranchised Ex-felons (2004) | Restorations | Period of Restoration Estimates | Percentage of Total Ex-felons | Felons Released in Period[3] | Percentage Restored |
|---|---|---|---|---|---|---|
| Alabama | 189,899 | 1,697 | 2004 | 0.89% | 26,719 | 6.35% |
| Arizona | 76,112 | N/A[1] | — | — | — | — |
| Delaware | 19,134 | 800 | 2000 | 4.18% | 4,746 | 16.86% |
| Florida | 957,423 | 48,000 | 1998–2004 | 5.01% | 1,430,105 | 3.36% |
| Iowa | 90,729 | 2,210 | 1999–2004 | 2.44% | 72,471 | 3.05% |
| Kentucky | 121,973 | 1,320 | 2002–2004 | 1.08% | 65,514 | 2.01% |
| Maryland | 44,605 | 147 | 1996–2003 | 0.33% | 61,999 | 0.24% |
| Mississippi | 99,855 | 107 | 1992–2004 | 0.11% | 155,127 | 0.07% |
| Nebraska | 50,203 | 343 | 1993–2004 | 0.68% | 62,071 | 0.55% |
| Nevada | 20,067 | 50 | 2004 | 0.25% | 9,476 | 0.53% |
| Tennessee | 25,899 | 393 | 2001–2004 | 1.52% | N/A[2] | 1.52% |
| Virginia | 303,743 | 5,043 | 1982–2004 | 1.66% | 637,350 | 0.79% |
| Washington | 29,785 | 53 | 1996–2004 | 0.18% | 57,144 | 0.09% |
| Wyoming | 14,254 | 17 | 1995–2002 | 0.12% | 17,493 | 0.10% |

1. In Arizona, voting rights are restored on a county-level basis and no statewide records are kept. Mauer and Kansal, *Barred for Life*, 8.

2. In Tennessee, disenfranchisement procedures vary dramatically, depending on the date of conviction and type of crime.

3. Release information compiled from annual Bureau of Justice Statistics sources (without reduction for recidivism or mortality).

*Source:* Adapted from Marc Mauer and Tushar Kansal, *Barred for Life: Voting Rights Restoration in Permanent Disenfranchisement States* (Washington, D.C.: Sentencing Project, 2005).

# Chapter 4: The Contemporary Disenfranchisement Regime

**Table A4.1**

**Variation in 2003 State Prison Incarceration Rates
(Per 100,000 Population)**

| 10 Highest Prison Incarceration Rate States | Rate[1] |
|---|---|
| *State* | |
| Louisiana | 801 |
| Mississippi | 768 |
| Texas | 702 |
| Oklahoma | 636 |
| Alabama | 635 |
| South Carolina | 551 |
| Georgia | 539 |
| Missouri | 529 |
| Arizona | 525 |
| Delaware | 501 |

| 10 Lowest Prison Incarceration Rate States | |
|---|---|
| *State* | |
| Maine | 149 |
| Minnesota | 155 |
| North Dakota | 181 |
| Rhode Island | 184 |
| New Hampshire | 188 |
| Vermont | 226 |
| Nebraska | 228 |
| Massachusetts | 233 |
| Utah | 240 |
| Washington & West Virginia | 260 |

1. The number of prisoners with a sentence of more than one year
per 100,000 residents in the state population. The Federal Bureau
of Prisons and the District of Columbia are excluded.

*Source: Prisoners in 2003* (Washington, D.C.: Government Printing
Office, 2004).

## Chapter 5: Political Attitudes, Voting, and Criminal Behavior

### The Youth Development Study: A Description

The Youth Development Study (YDS) is an ongoing longitudinal study of a cohort of St. Paul, Minnesota, students that began in 1987–88 with the purpose of investigating youth work experiences.[1] At that time, the students were in ninth grade and most were 14–15 years old. The cohort was drawn from a random sample of ninth-graders in the St. Paul public school district. Of the 1,779 randomly drawn cases, 1,010 consented to participate in the first wave. In this original sample, 74 percent were white, 10 percent were African American, 5 percent were Hispanic, and 4 percent were Asian. The median household income was between $30,000 and $39,999, and 27 percent of fathers and 19 percent of mothers were college graduates, while 59 percent of fathers and 61 percent of mothers had not attained more than a high school education. Since 1998, the survey has included new modules on a wide range of topics. Our module on political participation was included in the 2000 YDS.

Surveys were administered in classrooms for each year of high school. Parents also completed surveys by mail during Wave 1 and Wave 4, when the students were freshmen and seniors, respectively. These surveys provided information about family background and context, with 96 percent of parents responding at Wave 1. After high school, the respondents were surveyed by mail, with telephone follow-ups being used to provide clarifications of inconsistent information when necessary. During the high school period, panel retention remained high, with 93 percent responding in the fourth year. After high school, attrition increased, with a retention rate of 76 percent in 2000.

**Table A5.1**

**YDS Question Wording: Political Module (2000)**

| Question | Coding |
|---|---|
| *Voting* | |
| In 1996 Bill Clinton ran on the Democratic ticket against Bob Dole for the Republicans, and Ross Perot as an independent candidate. Do you remember for sure whether or not you voted in that election? | 0 = No, 1 = Yes |
| Which candidate did you vote for? | |
|     Bill Clinton | 0 = Other, 1 = Clinton |
|     Bob Dole | 0 = Other, 1 = Dole |
|     Ross Perot | 0 = Other, 1 = Perot |
| In 1998, Hubert Humphrey ran for governor of Minnesota on the Democratic ticket, Norm Coleman ran for the Republicans, and Jesse Ventura for the Reform Party. Did you vote in that election? | 0 = no, 1 = yes |
| Which candidate did you vote for? | |
|     Hubert Humphrey | 0 = other; 1 = Humphrey |
|     Norm Coleman | 0 = other; 1 = Coleman |
|     Jesse Ventura | 0 = other; 1 = Ventura |
| So far as you know now, do you expect to vote in the national elections this coming November or not? | 0 = no; 1 = yes |
| *Political Views* | |
| Do you think of yourself as closer to the Republican Party or the Democratic Party? | |
|     Republican Party | 0 = other; 1 = Republican |
|     Democratic Party | 0 = other; 1 = Democratic |
|     Do not lean towards either | 0 = no; 1 = yes |
| Would you identify yourself as part of the Christian right? | 0 = no; 1 = yes |
| If you had to choose, would you consider yourself a liberal, a moderate, or a conservative? | 1 = extremely liberal<br>2 = liberal<br>3 = moderate<br>4 = conservative<br>5 = extremely conservative |

(*continued*)

**Table A5.1** (*continued*)

| Question | Coding |
|---|---|
| *How much would you agree with the following statements?* | |
| | 1 = strongly disagree |
| | 2 = disagree |
| The government can be trusted to do what is best for the country. | 3 = agree |
| | 4 = strongly agree |
| People like me do not have any say about what the government does. | 1 = strongly disagree |
| | 4 = strongly agree |
| The average person can get nowhere by talking to public officials. | 1 = strongly disagree |
| | 4 = strongly agree |
| Elections are a good way of making the government pay attention to what people think. | 1 = strongly disagree |
| | 4 = strongly agree |
| Quite a few people running the government are crooked. | 1 = strongly disagree |
| | 4 = strongly agree |
| I have a great deal of confidence in the criminal justice system. | 1 = strongly disagree |
| | 4 = strongly agree |
| *Other Variables* | |
| Self-identified sex | 0 = Female, 1 = Male |
| Self-identified race | 0 = Other, 1 = White |
| Self-identified marital status | 0 = Not married, 1 = Married |
| Number of children | |
| Self-identified years of education completed | |
| Self-identified annual income | 0 = Part-time, 1 = Full-time |
| Full-time employment | |
| Which of the following have you been arrested for? | |
| For crimes involving money, such as shoplifting, burglary, forgery, robbery, or selling illegal drugs | 0 = No, 1 = Yes |
| For drug and alcohol crimes that did not involve money, such as drunkenness, driving under the influence (DUI), or possession of illegal drugs. | 0 = No, 1 = Yes |
| For personal or violent crimes that did not involve money, such as assault or attempted assault. | 0 = No, 1 = Yes |
| For some other crime that did not involve money, such as disturbing the peace, vandalism, violation of weapon laws, or any other offense. | 0 = No, 1 = Yes |

## Table A5.2
## Variable Descriptions and Descriptive Statistics for YDS

| Variable | Description | Percentage/ Mean |
|---|---|---|
| *Voting* | | |
| 1996 voting | Percentage reporting voting in the 1996 presidential election. | 65.2 |
| *Background* | | |
| Female | Percentage female | 56.5 |
| White | Percentage reporting white race | 76.7 |
| Years education in 1995 | Number of years of education | 13.6 |
| Marriage in 1995 | Percentage married | 11.6 |
| Employed in 1995 | Percentage employed | 82.3 |
| *Subsequent crime* | | |
| Arrested 1997–2000 | Percentage reporting arrest in 1997, 1998, 1999, or 2000 | 8.8 |
| Incarcerated 1997–2000 | Percentage reporting incarceration in jail or prison in 1997, 1998, 1999, or 2000 | 7.4 |
| Violent crime 1997–1998 | Percentage reporting hitting or threatening to hit someone, fighting, or robbing someone | 32.3 |
| Property crime 1997–1998 | Percentage reporting shoplifting, theft, check forgery, or burglary | 13.4 |
| Any crime 1997–1998 | Percentage reporting at least one property or violent offense in 1998 or 1999 | 38.3 |
| *Prior deviance* | | |
| Arrest prior to 1996 | Percentage arrested prior to 1996 | 18.7 |
| Prior drunk driving | Percentage reporting driving after having too much to drink during high school (1988–91) | 28.4 |
| Prior shoplifting | Percentage reporting shoplifting during high school during high school (1988–91) | 38.0 |
| Prior violence | Percentage reporting hitting or threatening to hit someone during high school (1988–91) | 41.4 |

**Table A5.3**

**Relationship between Criminal Sanctions and Political Attitudes and Experiences**

| Characteristic | Never Arrested | Arrested but Not Incarcerated | Incarcerated |
|---|---|---|---|
| Political Orientation | | | |
| % Republican | 15.4 | 14.3 | 7.9 |
| % Democrat | 48.3 | 37.8 | 38.2 |
| % neither party* | 36.3 | 48.0 | 54.0 |
| Ideological self-identification (1 = extreme liberal; 5 = extreme conservative) | 2.75 | 2.86 | 2.96 |
| % Christian right | 13.2 | 12.8 | 14.1 |
| Political Attitudes (1 = strongly disagree; 4 = strongly agree) | | | |
| *Trust in government* | | | |
| Government cannot be trusted* | 2.53 | 2.79 | 2.82 |
| People running government are crooked* | 2.78 | 2.94 | 3.08 |
| No confidence in criminal justice system* | 2.75 | 3.07 | 3.09 |
| *Political efficacy* | | | |
| People like me have no say* | 2.31 | 2.49 | 2.70 |
| Get nowhere talking to public officials* | 2.29 | 2.44 | 2.69 |
| *Political engagement* | | | |
| % talk with spouse/partner, 2000* | 49.2 | 29.9 | 35.9 |
| % talk with friends, 2000 | 40.0 | 40.2 | 28.2 |
| % talk with relatives, 2000* | 44.3 | 33.0 | 30.8 |

* The significance of the differences across the nonarrest, arrest, and incarceration groups was tested by analysis of variance (ANOVA). To obtain direct comparisons (arrested versus nonarrested and incarcerated versus nonincarcerated), we also conducted a supplementary set of *t*-tests (tables available from authors). An asterisk indicates that the *F*-test is statistically significant at $p < .05$ and that we can reject the null hypothesis that the three groups are equivalent on the characteristic.

## Chapter 6: Disenfranchisement and Civic Reintegration: Felons Speak Out

*Interview Procedures Used in the Exploratory Study of Voting and Citizenship among Convicted Felons*

The interviews discussed in chapter 6 generally ran from 45 to 90 minutes, and (with the permission of the interviewees) were recorded and later transcribed. To protect the participants' confidentiality throughout the book, we use pseudonyms when quoting from the transcripts. All major offense categories were represented among the interviewees, and almost all had been convicted of at least one of the serious "index" offenses reported in the FBI's Uniform Crime Reports. A detailed profile of each interviewee, with identifying information removed, is available online at www.soc.umn.edu/~uggen/profiles.pdf.

Prison respondents were recruited by including an invitation to participate in "a study about voting and politics" in the daily announcements at each facility. Prisoners then sent a response (or "kite form") to a staff contact person to schedule interviews. Probation and parole participants were recruited by (1) office staff mentioning the study at the conclusion of their daily interviews, and (2) a posted invitation (again inviting participation in "a study about voting and politics") outside the door to the interview room. Probationers and parolees were paid $10 upon completion of the interview. Unfortunately, prisoners could not be similarly compensated. There were two reasons for this: (1) prison staff suggested that such payments were likely to create a surplus of respondents that would introduce potential inequities among volunteers not selected to participate, and (2) we also encountered logistical difficulties in setting up a payment transfer system to credit inmates' institutional accounts.

*Interview Guide*

*Introduction*

Thanks for agreeing to be interviewed. We appreciate your helping us with this study. My name is Chris Uggen. I'm a professor who studies law and crime and I'm working with another professor who studies politics and voting. For about two years, we have been studying laws that stop people from voting after they have been convicted of certain crimes. Now we are doing interviews to hear how they really affect people. So, we'll ask you to describe your own experiences with voting and involvement in politics and your community. We are not interested in particular crimes, but want to learn all that we can about how these laws affect people.

*Informed Consent Procedure*

[Go through informed consent form and obtain signatures]

*Current Status*

1. To start with, I'd like to get some basic information down. Could you tell me a little about yourself—your hometown, age, marital status, etc.?

2. Because these laws only apply to people who have been in trouble with the law, I will ask a couple questions about criminal convictions. Have you ever been convicted of a felony? Was this in Minnesota or another state? What year was the first and last conviction?

3. What is your current legal status? When do you expect to be released?

*Political Involvement and Engagement*

4. Have you ever voted in an election? When was that? Could you name some of the candidates you voted for?

5. Did you ever lose your right to vote because of a felony conviction? How did you find out about this? Have you voted since then? Why or why not? What do you understand your voting rights to be?

6. Were you able to vote in the last presidential election? Do you think you would have voted if you had the legal right to vote? Why or why not? What about in the future? Do you think you will ever vote in an election?

7. Who would you have voted for? Which issues are important to you in deciding between candidates?
8. Did you care who won the presidential election? Did you watch stories about the election on TV or read about it in newspapers or magazines?

### Partisanship, Efficacy, and Trust

9. If you had to choose would you generally consider yourself a liberal, a moderate, or a conservative? *What do these words mean to you?* Do you think of yourself as closer to the Republicans or to the Democrats?
10. Do you think elections are a good way to make the government pay attention to what people think? Do you think that people like you have a say about what the government does?
11. Do you think the government can be trusted to do what is best for the country? Or, do you think most of the people running the government cannot be trusted?
12. The word "politics" means different things to different people. What do you think of when you hear the word "politics"?

### Community Involvement Generally

13. Just like "politics," the word "community" has a lot of different meanings. A lot of people that I've talked to in prison mention the word "community"—saying things like "I want to give back to my community." What do you think of when you hear the word "community"?
14. How can people who have been in trouble with the law help out their communities? Is there anything that you have done to help out your community [PROBE: volunteering, community center, etc.]?
15. Do you think that former prisoners who help out (or get involved) in their communities are less likely to go back to jail or prison? Can you think of any people or examples of how this might work? [PROBE: restorative justice involvement]

*Voting and Reintegration*

16. Some states have laws that let people in prison, or on parole and probation vote and others have laws that take away voting rights for life. Do you think that people should lose the right to vote when they are in prison? What about when they are out on parole? On probation?

17. How does losing the right to vote affect a person's ideas about being a part of their community? About their government?

18. Have you lost other rights because of a criminal conviction? Which ones are most important to you? Do you feel like you are less of a citizen because you have lost these rights?

19. Do you think of voting as a right or a privilege?

20. Aside from voting and politics, I'm interested in how people who've been in the criminal justice system eventually move away from crime. Could you describe things in your life that have moved you away from crime—or pulled you into crime? Can you name any turning points in your life?

    ___ *Work:* Have any jobs or work experiences influenced you? How?

    ___ *Family:* Have any family members been especially helpful or harmful? Friends?

    ___ *Community:* Is there anything about your community or neighborhood that has made it tougher or easier to move away from crime?

    ___ *Time:* How long would you say it has been since you've done any crime? Serious crimes or smaller crimes?

21. To tie this back to politics, do you think that losing the right to vote makes it tougher to stay clean or out of trouble with the law? Or is it a really small factor compared to other issues? How?

*Wrap-up*

We've been talking about a lot of issues and I wanted to give you the chance to add anything to any of the topics we've covered. In thinking back over the last hour are there any other thoughts or experiences you'd like to mention which are relevant to the things we've been discussing?

And finally are there any questions you'd like to ask me?

*Probing Themes*

*Civic participation*

- Feeling a part of a larger community, or apart from the larger community
- Personal understanding of politics
- Personal understanding of community

*Political engagement*

- Experiences with and understanding of disenfranchisement

*Reintegration*

- Civic participation and reintegration
- Other achievements, social supports, experiences promoting reintegration

Table A6.1
Characteristics of Felon Interviewees (n = 33)

| Characteristic | Frequency | Percentage |
|---|---|---|
| Race | | |
| White | 22 | 67% |
| Black | 6 | 18% |
| Native | 5 | 15% |
| Sex | | |
| Male | 23 | 70% |
| Female | 10 | 30% |
| Age | | |
| Age 20–29 | 15 | 45% |
| Age 30–39 | 11 | 33% |
| Age 40 and over | 7 | 21% |
| | | *(continued)* |

**Table A6.1** (*continued*)

| Characteristic | Frequency | Percentage |
|---|---|---|
| Party | | |
| Democrat | 18 | 55% |
| Republican | 9 | 27% |
| Independent | 2 | 6% |
| Don't know/unknown | 4 | 12% |
| Political label | | |
| Conservative | 9 | 27% |
| Liberal | 7 | 21% |
| Moderate | 2 | 6% |
| Conservative or moderate liberal | 3 | 9% |
| "Independent" | 1 | 3% |
| "Everything" | 1 | 3% |
| Don't know/unknown | 10 | 30% |
| Correctional status | | |
| Prison | 23 | 70% |
| Probation | 7 | 21% |
| Parole | 3 | 9% |
| Ever voted? | | |
| Yes | 22 | 67% |
| No | 11 | 33% |
| Plan to vote in future? | | |
| Yes | 24 | 73% |
| No | 1 | 3% |
| Unknown | 8 | 24% |
| 2000 Presidential choice | | |
| Gore | 16 | 48% |
| Bush | 8 | 24% |
| Nader | 3 | 9% |
| No preference/unknown | 6 | 18% |

## Chapter 7: The Impact of Disenfranchisement on Political Participation

### Methodological Issues in Estimating the Impact of Disenfranchisement on Turnout

We face a number of methodological difficulties in undertaking the turnout analysis (chapter 7) and the vote choice analysis (chapter 8) that warrant further discussion.

#### How Many Disenfranchised Felons Are There?

Before undertaking the investigation of chapter 7, we had already developed an answer to the question of how many disenfranchised felons were in each state. To reiterate our main findings, at the time of the 2004 presidential election there were some 5.3 million disenfranchised felons and ex-felons. Approximately 26 percent of this group were inmates, about 25 percent were probationers, 9 percent were parolees, and 39 percent were former felons who have completed their sentences. This population was largely concentrated in states with more restrictive disenfranchisement laws, such as Florida and Alabama, which restrict voting rights of former felons as well as those currently serving sentences.

#### A Counterfactual Approach

The nature of our question in chapter 7—how many felons would have voted if they had been able—is by definition a counterfactual question. In chapter 8, we extend this counterfactual to ask *how* they might have voted, and whether their votes might have influenced who won some close electoral contests.

Our analysis of these questions starts with some important advantages. We are fortunate to have much more information at our disposal than most standard statistical analyses in the social sciences. In particular, we have access to population data rather than sample data. We know the precise number of votes cast in each election, and for which candidates, and their plurality or margin of victory in each election. We also know precisely the number of prisoners, probationers, and parolees in each state who cannot vote, along with a reasonable estimate of the number of ex-felons in states that restrict their voting rights. The uncertainty lies in estimating how many of them would have turned out to vote, and which candidate they would have selected.

To be sure, estimating these two pieces of information is tricky. The use of a counterfactual design reflects a larger debate in the social sciences: how can researchers establish a causal relationship when the potential cause cannot be randomly assigned in an experiment?[2] The key problem is that our counterfactual approach implicitly assumes that nothing else in the world would have changed except for the condition we want to test, in this case, allowing felons to vote. In many counterfactual scenarios, this is deeply problematic. Consider the following example. Assume we wanted to know how much the rise in incarceration rates in the United States has (artificially) reduced unemployment, a figure that a number of analysts have tried to estimate.[3] The typical approach in this literature has been to develop a corrected measure of unemployment in which those who are incarcerated are not included in the denominator used to calculate the unemployment rate, or to include information about employment rates of inmates prior to imprisonment to adjust the overall rate of unemployment. While almost all of these studies find evidence that the official unemployment rate would be higher if incarceration had not grown, there are many important types of macroeconomic effects of incarceration that the existing literature is unable to incorporate into its analyses: the economic benefits of public sector spending on prison construction, the multiplier effects of new, usually decent-paying, jobs created in often economically depressed areas, and so forth.[4]

Similar issues can be raised in the case of felon disenfranchisement and attempts to estimate the impact of disenfranchisement on overall turnout rates. It is certainly possible that if 5.3 million felons and ex-felons were allowed to vote in a national election, the major parties might emphasize different themes or alter their appeals in ways that could influence turnout rates, or even election outcomes. For example, the Democratic Party candidates might expand their appeals to groups with high felon populations. Changes in these appeals could motivate higher turnout levels and perhaps influence election outcomes by changing the relative appeal of Democratic versus Republican candidates in some elections.

For all of these reasons, it is important to be cautious when evaluating results that cannot (by definition) take into account the strategies of parties or candidates in an altered political environment. In practice, however, the impact of adding disenfranchised felons to the voting rolls would have been unlikely to produce significant changes in other aspects of recent American elections. It is certainly hard to imagine that either major party would have fundamentally altered its appeals to voters in response to an increase in the size of the electorate by 2.5 percent (although in some states, the proportion eligible in the counterfactual case would be much higher, suggesting greater possibility of an impact in those regions).

In general, a campaign strategy that made sense with an electorate that included 98 percent of the voters in the (hypothetically expanded) electorate would still make sense.[5] In even the most extreme case—Florida, which would see a 9 percent expansion of the electorate if felons were included—there is no proof that party strategies would necessarily or rationally change in response. It is possible that different election outcomes at one point in time would influence future campaigns, either by changing the balance of control in Congress (a possibility we suggest in chapter 8) or through the feedback effects of policy change. It is impossible, however, to measure such impacts with certainty. Our default assumption—that hypothetical recent elections with the expanded electorate would closely resemble those actual contests excluding felons and ex-felons—is the most reasonable assumption to make.

### Estimating the Counterfactual Turnout Rate for Disenfranchised Felons

Even if we accept the implicit assumption that nothing about the campaigns would change if disenfranchised felons were included in the electorate, we face further problems when trying to estimate turnout rates for those (hypothetical) voters. Our task would be simplified if we could assume what statisticians refer to as "unit homogeneity": that disenfranchised felons (the individual "units" in the analysis) would have voted in the same numbers and with the same preferences as nonfelons. Then we could simply count the disenfranchised felons and apply national turnout and party preference averages to estimate how many would have voted and the candidates for whom they would have voted. Because felons differ from nonfelons in ways that are likely to affect political behavior, however, this sort of blanket assumption is untenable. But we lack survey data that would allow us to estimate turnout and party preferences among felons and ex-felons in those states where they are allowed to vote.

Our solution to this problem is to "match," as closely as we can, the characteristics of the felon and ex-felon population to the rest of the electorate using existing representative national election survey data. This procedure essentially identifies two groups of otherwise similar individuals (on the basis of the social characteristics for which we have information about the felon population): one group is able to vote, the other is not.[6] The historical underpinnings of this approach are relevant, as we consider changes in punishment and disenfranchisement as a natural experiment. Far more individuals today are receiving felony convictions than in the period before 1972. If the punishment practices of the period from 1920 to 1972 existed today, many of those currently disenfranchised would be able to vote. In other words, many disenfranchised felons have received a "treatment" that puts them in a different category than the identical individual in, say, 1970.

Taking what we know about the felon population from the inmate surveys discussed earlier, we can develop an estimate of whether and how the disenfranchised might have voted. This exercise can tell us whether the U.S. political landscape might change if our disenfranchisement laws looked more like those in the rest of the world—where all felons, or at least all nonincarcerated felons, can vote. In sum, we estimate how many in the disenfranchised population *would have* voted and *how* they would have voted, on the basis of the voting patterns observed in very similar segments of the eligible population.

### Data and Methods

Our analyses of turnout (and voter choice in chapter 8) utilize standard election data sources. To derive turnout estimates for the disenfranchised population, we analyze data from the Voter Supplement File of the Current Population Survey (CPS). The CPS is a monthly survey of individuals conducted by the Census Bureau. Since 1964, in each November of even-numbered (national election) years, the survey includes questions about political participation. All sampled households are asked: "In any election some people are not able to vote because they are sick or busy or have some other reason, and others do not want to vote. Did [you/another household member] vote in the election on November ?" Because of its very large sample size (approximately 110,000 persons) and durable reputation for accurate measurement, the CPS has many desirable properties for our analysis.

Questions like those asked by the CPS produce slightly inflated estimates of turnout (although far lower than in alternative data series such as the National Election Study). The inflation factor in the CPS series ranges from a low of 7.5 percent (1968) to a high of 11.1 percent (1988) in presidential elections between 1964 and 2000. Accordingly, after obtaining estimated turnout percentages for the felon population, we reduce them by a CPS inflation factor, multiplying predicted turnout rates by the ratio of actual to reported turnout for each election.[7] Because turnout is most overreported among better educated citizens, inflated reporting is likely to be lower among disenfranchised felons than among nonfelons.[8] So our approach again tends to err on the side of producing more conservative estimates.

To estimate the expected turnout rates of disenfranchised felons, we match the felon population to the rest of the voting age population, using information on a series of sociodemographic attributes available from the inmate surveys discussed earlier. These characteristics include the following: age (measured in years), education (measured in years), income (measured in constant dollars), labor force status (working or not), marital status (married or not married), gender (male or female), race (white or nonwhite).

We use similar measures to estimate both turnout (using CPS data) and voter choice (presented in chapter 8 using National Election Study data). We first estimate levels of political participation and party preference as a function of the sociodemographic attributes of the general population. We then insert the mean characteristics of disenfranchised felons into these equations to obtain the predicted rates of turnout for this group. As part of our equation predicting the probability that felons would participate in each election, for example, we multiply the mean years of education for felons by the estimated effect of education on turnout in the general population. Because both the turnout and voting outcomes are dichotomous, we estimated logistic regression models of the probability of participation for each election.[9]

## Chapter 8: A Threat to Democracy?

### Data and Methods Used to Estimate the Electoral Impact of Disenfranchisement

Our approach here is the same as that adopted in estimating the impact of disenfranchisement on turnout (chapter 7). We take state-by-state calculations of the number of felons and ex-felons presented in chapter 7 and their expected turnout rate. Next, we estimate their hypothetical vote choices, again on the basis of their known demographic characteristics. Using information about size, turnout, and vote choice, we can then estimate the number of votes lost to candidates. To assess the political consequences of disenfranchisement, we then compare the actual margin of victory with counterfactual results that take into account the likely political behavior of the disenfranchised population.

Our focus is on national elections, and more specifically, elections to the U.S. Senate and the presidency. Data restrictions make it extremely difficult to estimate the loss of voters (and the distribution of votes) below the state level. For the most part, we simply do not have enough information to know exactly in which House or state legislative district currently disenfranchised felons might have voted if they were eligible and chose to participate. Because the great bulk of the criminal justice system is administered at the state level, however, we can reasonably estimate the impact at state-level elections.

In analyzing the expected turnout and vote choice of disenfranchised felons we also do not have any survey data that ask members of this group how they would have voted (with the exception of the YDS data which we use later in the chapter to confirm our results). Our analytical approach is similar to that of chapter 7. We match known characteristics of the felon population to the rest of the voting-age population to estimate their expected vote choice in a given election. Our estimates of voting behavior are thus able to account for the same individual and group attributes as the Justice Department's periodic inmate survey used to estimate turnout:

sex, race, age, income, labor force status, marital status, and education. As before, we analyze age and education in years as continuous variables. Income is a continuous variable measured in constant dollars. Labor force status, marital status, sex, and race are dichotomous variables. We use similar measures for both the turnout analyses and vote choice analyses. Once we have estimated political participation and party preference equations on the general population, we then simply insert the mean characteristics of disenfranchised felons into these equations to obtain their predicted rates of turnout and Democratic Party preference.[10]

In chapter 7, we used data from the CPS's Voter Supplement module to estimate turnout. Unfortunately, however, the CPS does not ask respondents how they voted, only whether they voted. To generate estimates of how the disenfranchised would have voted, we rely on data from the National Election Study (NES), a biennial survey of the American electorate conducted by the Survey Research Center and its Center for Political Studies at the University of Michigan. This survey is an extraordinary record of American society and politics, spanning more than four decades. These data are unique in containing a full battery of questions about each respondents' sociodemographic characteristics and measures of attitudes on policy issues and political conflicts, as well as a precise battery of questions about voting, turnout, and party identification.[11] Fielded in two parts (the first wave is carried out right before a national election, while the second wave is fielded immediately after the election), the NES contains the most reliable data on the main dependent variable of interest to us in this study: how a respondent actually voted. As a survey instrument that has been widely used by political scientists and political sociologists, it has served a range of research purposes over the years and has become the standard source of historical election data.[12]

Despite the advantages of the NES as a data source, however, there are also certain limitations that lead us to urge some caution in interpreting the results. First, the small sample size does not permit us to directly estimate voting behavior at the state level. All respondents in states with U.S. Senate elections are asked how they voted in that election, but in view of the small sample size for any particular state, analysts of Senate elections have typically focused on the overall national partisan Senate vote. In asking about specific election outcomes, we apply those national averages to specific state contests. This procedure clearly introduces some errors, because the demography of the states varies, and any particular Senate candidate could have more or less appeal to the disenfranchised population. Our data limitations do not push us toward knowing (in the absence of suitable state-level data) whether the level of Democratic partisanship would be enhanced or reduced. In practice, the impact is likely not great, because the state elections we zero in on are ones that are extremely close and thus mirror the fairly even overall national distribution closely (where in recent elections the Democratic and Republican candidates have overall received roughly equal vote shares).

Ideally, to develop more precise estimates of vote choice, we would also have information about the party and ideological identifications, and the policy preferences, of the "average" disenfranchised felon. A long line of research has shown that such partisan identities are more predictive of actual voting behavior than sociodemographic correlates.[13] However, the inmate survey does not ask any questions about the political orientations of offenders that would permit us to include that information in estimating the voting behavior of hypothetical felon voters.[14]

Finally, some technical details. We consider only major party voters in this analysis. In Senate elections very few third-party or independent candidates have come close to winning office. In the period under consideration, the only independent candidate to win a Senate seat since 1972 was Harry F. Byrd, Jr., of Virginia in 1976. Since the dependent variable in the voting analyses is dichotomous—major party votes—we estimate logistic regression models of the probabilities of participation and Democratic vote choice, respectively.[15] In the voting equations, the outcome is coded "1" for Democratic and "0" for Republican choice. We have reported the coefficients from these regressions elsewhere, as well as estimates of the raw percentage of the proportion of Democratic Senate and presidential election voters.[16]

The results of our analysis of presidential elections are shown in appendix tables A8.1 (the 2000 election) and A8.2 (the 1960 election), and the handful of Senate elections between 1978 and 2004 that potentially would have reversed are shown in appendix table A8.3. Some explanation of the latter may be useful. For the 1978 Virginia election detailed in the top row of appendix table A8.3, for example, we estimate from CPS data for that state election that 15,343 of the state's 93,564 disenfranchised felons would have voted if they were eligible (16.4 percent). We further estimate that 12,305 of these voters would have selected Andrew Miller, the Democratic candidate (80.2 percent of 15,343), and that the remaining 19.8 percent (or 3,038) would have chosen John Warner, the Republican candidate. This results in a net total of 9,268 Democratic votes lost to disenfranchisement in the 1978 U.S. Senate race in Virginia, almost double the actual Republican victory margin of 4,721 votes. We use the same approach for the other cases.

These results are highly suggestive of the possibility of an electoral impact, but also sensitive to a number of assumptions. Moreover, while the NES is a nationally representative sample, it is not representative within any one state. We therefore urge caution in interpreting these findings.

Table A8.1

Applying Contemporary Disenfranchisement Rates to the 2000 Presidential Election

| Unit | Actual (R) Margin | Total Disenfran- chised | Est. Turnout Rate | Est. Percent Democrat | Net Democrat Votes Lost | Counter- factual (D) Margin |
|---|---|---|---|---|---|---|
| U.S. total | −539,947 | 4,695,729 | 29.7% | 68.9% | 527,171 | 1,067,118 |
| Florida | 537 | 827,207 | 27.2% | 68.9% | 85,050 | 84,513 |
| 50% lower turnout | | | 13.6% | 68.9% | 42,525 | 41,988 |
| Florida Ex-felons only | | 613,514 | 27.2% | 68.9% | 63,079 | 62,542 |
| 50% lower turnout | | | 13.6% | 68.9% | 31,540 | 31,003 |

Table A8.2

What If Felons Were Disenfranchised in 1960 at 2000 Rates?

| Unit | Actual (D) Margin | Actual Disenfran- chised | Counter- factual Disenfran- chised | Est. Turnout Rate | Est. Percent Dem. | Net Democrat Votes Lost | Counter- factual (R) Margin |
|---|---|---|---|---|---|---|---|
| U.S. Total | 118,550 | 1,378,156 | 2,502,211 | 40% | 75% | 224,811 | 106,261 |
| 50% lower turnout | | | | 20% | 75% | 112,405 | (6,145) |

Table A8.3
The Impact of Felon Disenfranchisement on U.S. Senate Elections, 1978–2004

| Year | State[1] | Disenfranchised Population | | | Estimated Voting Behavior | | | Republican Victory Margin | | |
|---|---|---|---|---|---|---|---|---|---|---|
| | | Current Felons | Ex-felons | Total | Turnout Rate | Percent Dem. | Net Dem. Votes Lost | Actual Margin | Counterfactual Margin | Rep. Held Seat through |
| 1978 | Virginia[2] | 21,776 | 71,788 | 93,564 | 16.4% | 80.2% | 9,268 | 4,721 | −4,547 | 2008+ |
| 1978 | Texas[3] | 100,707 | 89,662 | 190,369 | 13.4% | 80.2% | 15,408 | 12,227 | −3,181 | 2008+ |
| 1980 | unchanged | | | | | | | | | |
| 1982 | unchanged | | | | | | | | | |
| 1984 | Kentucky[4] | 20,583 | 54,481 | 75,064 | 38.5% | 68.9% | 10,925 | 5,269 | −5,655 | 2008+ |
| 1986 | unchanged | | | | | | | | | |
| 1988 | Florida[5] | 87,264 | 206,247 | 293,512 | 26.5% | 79.4% | 45,735 | 34,518 | −11,217 | 2000 |
| 1990 | unchanged | | | | | | | | | |
| 1992 | Georgia[6] | 131,911 | 0 | 131,911 | 29.6% | 74.7% | 19,289 | 16,237 | −3,052 | 2000 |
| 1994 | unchanged | | | | | | | | | |
| 1996 | unchanged | | | | | | | | | |
| 1998 | Kentucky[7] | 31,456 | 94,584 | 126,040 | 25.4% | 69.7% | 12,614 | 6,766 | −5,848 | 2010+ |

| | | | | | | | | | 2010+ |
|---|---|---|---|---|---|---|---|---|---|
| 2000 | *unchanged* | | | | | | | | |
| 2002 | *unchanged* | | | | | | | | |
| 2004 | Florida[8] | 302,022 | 957,423 | 1,259,445 | 30.0% | 70.0% | 151,133 | 83,345 | −67,788 |

1. Data on actual senate composition taken from *Senate Statistics: Majority and Minority Parties.*

2. In Virginia, Warner (R) defeated Miller (D) in 1978, Harrison in 1984, Spannaus in 1990, M. Warner in 1996, and independents Spannaus and Hornberger in 2002.

3. In Texas, Tower (R) defeated Krueger (D) in 1978; Gramm (R) defeated Doggett in 1984, Parmer in 1990, and Morales in 1996. In 2002, Cornyn (R) defeated Kirk (D).

4. In Kentucky, McConnell (R) defeated Huddleston (D) in 1984, Sloane in 1990, Beshear in 1996, and Weinberg in 2002 (class 2 election).

5. In Florida, Mack (R) defeated MacKay (D) in 1988, and Rodham in 1994; McCollum (R) defeated Nelson (D) in 2000.

6. In Georgia, Coverdell (R) defeated Fowler (D) in 1992, and Coles in 1998. After Coverdell's death in 2000, he was succeeded by Miller (D).

7. In Kentucky, Bunning (R) defeated Baesler (D) in 1998 and Mongiardo (D) in 2004 (class 3 election).

8. In Florida, Martinez (R) defeated Castor (D) in 2004.

Table A8.4

Impact of the Disfranchisement of Nonincarcerated Felons on U.S. Senate Elections, 1978–2004

*A. What if prisoners remained disfranchised, but other felons (probationers, parolees, and ex-felons) had been allowed to vote?*

| | | Disfranchised Population | | | Estimated Voting Behavior | | | Republican Victory Margin | | |
|---|---|---|---|---|---|---|---|---|---|---|
| Year | State* | Probationers and Parolees | Ex-felons | Total | Turnout Rate | Percent Dem. | Net Dem. Votes Lost | Actual Margin | Counterfactual Margin | Rep. Held Seat through |
| 1978 | Virginia[1] | 13,432 | 71,788 | 85,220 | 16.4% | 80.2% | 8,442 | 4,721 | −3,721 | 2008+ |
| 1978 | Texas[2] | 76,132 | 89,662 | 165,794 | 13.4% | 80.2% | 13,419 | 12,227 | −1,192 | 2008+ |
| 1984 | Kentucky[3] | 15,763 | 54,481 | 70,244 | 38.5% | 68.9% | 10,223 | 5,269 | −4,954 | 2008+ |
| 1988 | Florida[4] | 52,532 | 206,247 | 258,779 | 26.5% | 79.4% | 40,323 | 34,518 | −5,805 | 2000 |
| 1998 | Kentucky[5] | 16,469 | 94,584 | 111,053 | 25.4% | 69.7% | 11,114 | 6,766 | −4,348 | 2010+ |
| 2004 | Florida[6] | 109,080 | 957,423 | 1,066,503 | 30% (est.) | 70% (est.) | 127,980 | 83,345 | −44,635 | 2010+ |

**B. What if all current felons remained disenfranchised, but ex-felons had been allowed to vote?**

| Year | State* | Disfranchised Population | | Estimated Voting Behavior | | Republican Victory Margin | | |
|---|---|---|---|---|---|---|---|---|
| | | Ex-felons | Turnout Rate | Percent Dem. | Net Dem. Votes Lost | Actual Margin | Counterfactual Margin | Repub. Held Seat through |
| 1978 | Virginia[1] | 71,788 | 16.4% | 80.2% | 7,111 | 4,721 | −2,390 | 2008+ |
| 1984 | Kentucky[3] | 54,481 | 38.5% | 68.9% | 7,929 | 5,269 | −2,660 | 2008+ |
| 1998 | Kentucky[5] | 94,584 | 25.4% | 69.7% | 9,446 | 6,766 | −2,700 | 2010+ |
| 2004 | Florida[6] | 957,423 | 30% (est.) | 70% (est.) | 114,891 | 83,345 | −31,546 | 2010+ |

* Data on actual senate composition taken from *Senate Statistics: Majority and Minority Parties*

1. In Virginia, Warner (R) defeated Miller (D) in 1978, Harrison in 1984, Spannaus in 1990, M. Warner in 1996, and independents Spannaus and Hornberger in 2002.

2. In Texas, Tower (R) defeated Krueger (D) in 1978; Gramm (R) defeated Doggett in 1984, Parmer in 1990, and Morales in 1996. In 2002, Cornyn (R) defeated Kirk (D).

3. In Kentucky, McConnell (R) defeated Huddleston (D) in 1984, Sloane in 1990, Beshear in 1996, and Weinberg in 2002 (class 2 election).

4. In Florida, Mack (R) defeated MacKay (D) in 1988, and Rodham in 1994; McCollum (R) defeated Nelson (D) in 2000.

5. In Kentucky, Bunning (R) defeated Baesler (D) in 1998 and Mongiardo (D) in 2004 (class 3 election).

6. In Florida, Martinez (R) defeated Castor (D) in 2004.

## Table A8.5
## Estimated Impact of Felon Disenfranchisement on U.S. Senate Composition, 1978–2004

| | | | Senate Composition | |
| --- | --- | --- | --- | --- |
| Year | State | Actual[1] | Limited Counterfactual | Cumulated Counterfactual |
| 1978 | Virginia[2] | 58:41-D | 60:39-D | 60:39-D |
| 1978 | Texas[3] | 58:41-D | 60:39-D | 60:39-D |
| 1980 | unchanged | 53:46-R | 51:48-R | 51:48-R |
| 1982 | unchanged | 54:46-R | 52:48-R | 52:48-R |
| 1984 | Kentucky[4] | 53:47-R | 52:48-R | 50:50— |
| 1986 | unchanged | 55:45-D | 56:44-D | 58:42-D |
| 1988 | Florida[5] | 55:45-D | 57:43-D | 58:42-D |
| 1990 | unchanged | 56:44-D | 57:43-D | 60:40-D |
| 1992 | Georgia[6] | 57:43-D | 59:41-D | 62:38-D |
| 1994 | unchanged | 52:48-R | 50:50- | 53:47-D |
| 1996 | unchanged | 55:45-R | 55:45-R | 50:50- |
| 1998 | Kentucky[7] | 55:45-R | 55:45-R | 51:49-R |
| 2000 | unchanged | 50:50— | 51:49-D | 54:46-D |
| 2002 | unchanged | 52:48-R | 52:48-R | 54:46-D |
| 2004 | Florida[8] | 55:44-R | 54:45-R | 50:49-D |

1. Data on actual senate composition taken from *Senate Statistics: Majority and Minority Parties*

2. In Virginia, Warner (R) defeated Miller (D) in 1978, Harrison in 1984, Spannaus in 1990, M. Warner in 1996, and independents Spannaus and Hornberger in 2002.

3. In Texas, Tower (R) defeated Krueger (D) in 1978; Gramm (R) defeated Doggett in 1984, Parmer in 1990, and Morales in 1996. In 2002, Cornyn (R) defeated Kirk (D).

4. In Kentucky, McConnell (R) defeated Huddleston (D) in 1984, Sloane in 1990, Beshear in 1996, and Weinberg in 2002 (class 2 election).

5. In Florida, Mack (R) defeated MacKay (D) in 1988, and Rodham in 1994; McCollum (R) defeated Nelson (D) in 2000.

6. In Georgia, Coverdell (R) defeated Fowler (D) in 1992, and Coles in 1998. After Coverdell's death in 2000, he was succeeded by Miller (D).

7. In Kentucky, Bunning (R) defeated Baesler (D) in 1998 and Mongiardo (D) in 2004 (class 3 election).

8. In Florida, Martinez (R) defeated Castor (D) in 2004.

Table A8.6

Estimated Impact of the Disenfranchisement of Nonincarcerated Felons on U.S. Senate Composition, 1978–2004

| Year | State | | Senate Composition | |
|------|-------|--------|-------------------------|-------------------------|
| | | Actual | Limited Counterfactual | Cumulated Counterfactual |

**A. What if prisoners remained disenfranchised, but other felons (probationers, parolees, and ex-felons) had been allowed to vote?**

| Year | State | Actual | Limited Counterfactual | Cumulated Counterfactual |
|------|-------|--------|-----------------------|--------------------------|
| 1978 | Virginia[1] | 58:41-D | 60:39-D | 60:39-D |
| 1978 | Texas[2] | 58:41-D | 60:39-D | 60:39-D |
| 1984 | Kentucky[3] | 53:47-R | 52:48-R | 50:50— |
| 1988 | Florida[4] | 55:45-D | 57:43-D | 59:41-D |
| 1998 | Kentucky[5] | 55:45-R | 54:46-R | 50:50— |
| 2004 | Florida[6] | 55:44-R | 54:45-R | 50:49-R |

**B. What if all current felons remained disenfranchised, but ex-felons had been allowed to vote?**

| Year | State | Actual | Limited Counterfactual | Cumulated Counterfactual |
|------|-------|--------|-----------------------|--------------------------|
| 1978 | Virginia[1] | 58:41-D | 59:40-D | 59:40-D |
| 1984 | Kentucky[3] | 53:47-R | 52:48-R | 51:49-D |
| 1998 | Kentucky[3] | 55:45-R | 54:46-R | 52:48-R |
| 2004 | Florida[6] | 55:44-R | 54:45-R | 51:48-R |

\* Data on actual senate composition taken from *Senate Statistics: Majority and Minority Parties*

1. In Virginia, Warner (R) defeated Miller (D) in 1978, Harrison in 1984, Spannaus in 1990, M. Warner in 1996, and independents Spannaus and Hornberger in 2002.

2. In Texas, Tower (R) defeated Krueger (D) in 1978; Gramm (R) defeated Doggett in 1984, Parmer in 1990, and Morales in 1996. In 2002, Cornyn (R) defeated Kirk (D).

3. In Kentucky, McConnell (R) defeated Huddleston (D) in 1984, Sloane in 1990, Beshear in 1996, and Weinberg in 2002 (Class 2 election).

4. In Florida, Mack (R) defeated MacKay (D) in 1988, and Rodham in 1994; McCollum (R) defeated Nelson (D) in 2000.

5. In Kentucky, Bunning (R) defeated Baesler (D) in 1998 and Mongiardo (D) in 2004 (class 3 election).

6. In Florida, Martinez (R) defeated Castor (D) in 2004.

Table A8.7
Effects of Arrest Type on 1996 and 1998 Party Preference

| Arrest Type | 1996 Clinton (D) | 1998 Ventura (I) |
|---|---|---|
| Property crime arrest | (ns) | (ns) |
| Drug/alcohol crime arrest | (+) | (+) |
| Violent crime arrest | (ns) | (ns) |
| Other crime arrest | (ns) | (ns) |

*Note:* A positive sign indicates a statistically significant (p < .05) positive coefficient, a negative sign indicates a statistically significant (p < .05) negative coefficient, and *ns* indicates a nonsignificant coefficient.

*Source:* Adapted from Christopher Uggen and Jeff Manza, "Democratic Contraction? The Political Consequences of Felon Disenfranchisement in the United States," *American Sociological Review* 67 (2002): 791.


*Chapter 9: Public Opinion and Felon Disenfranchisement*

*Details of Survey Experiments*

To probe attitudes toward felon disenfranchisement, we developed four parallel survey items that employ identical question-wording. As summarized in appendix table A9.1, these items ask respondents their level of support for enfranchising probationers, parolees, and prisoners. The first two items vary according to the degree of specificity regarding the nature of probation, with the *probationer₂* item explicitly clarifying that the probationer has *not* been sentenced to prison, and the *probationer₁* item leaving this implicit. The third and fourth items use the initial item wording but refer, respectively, to *parolees* (who at been released from prison) and *prisoners* (who are still serving their prison sentences). These items were assigned to survey respondents randomly, so that approximately one-fourth of the total sample was asked each item. This randomization facilitates comparisons by ensuring that any observed differences in measured opinion are a product of the group invoked in the question wording.

The second set of experiments on ex-felons examines how the types of crimes committed might influence the right to vote. We again do this by way of question-wording experiment. Whereas the *Baseline Ex-felon* item makes no specific references to the crime committed, the *White-Collar Ex-felon* item specifies the "illegal trading of stocks," the *Violent Crime Ex-felon* item refers to a "violent crime," and the *Sex Crime Ex-felon* item refers to "people convicted of a sex offense."

The third set of experiments examines attitudes toward civil rights for ex-felons. Our *Baseline Civil Liberties* measure, asked of all respondents, is one of the items fielded initially by Samuel Stouffer in his famous 1950s study of tolerance, and subsequently incorporated into the widely used General Social Survey (an annual or biennial in-person survey of Americans conducted by the National Opinion Research Corporation). The next three items vary the reference to either the target group or content of speech involved in the expression of civil liberties. The *Ex-felon Civil Liberties* item refers to someone whose prison sentence has been completed (without specifying the content of their speech). The *Ex-felon/Legalization Activist* item refers to someone who has completed a sentence for drug dealing, further specifying "legalizing drugs" as the content of the speech in question. The *Legalization Activist* item also refers to a speech in favor of legalizing drugs, but makes no reference to the status of the speaker. These three items were randomly assigned to one-third of the sample, and they enable us to observe differences in support for civil liberties across the four sets of conditions.

The various question wordings we employed are listed in appendix table A9.1.

**Table A9.1**

**Question Wording and Variables in the Analysis**

| Items | Question Wording (coding) |
|---|---|
| *Enfranchisement Items—Target Group Dimension 1* | |
| Probationers$_1$ | There has been some discussion recently about the right to vote in this country. Some feel that people convicted of a crime who are sentenced to probation and are living in the community should have the right to vote. Others feel that they should not have the right to vote. What about you? Do you think people on probation should have the right to vote? Or haven't you thought much about this? (0. no; 1. yes) |
| Probationers$_2$ | There has been some discussion recently about the right to vote in this country. Some feel that people convicted of a crime who are sentenced to probation, but not prison, and are living in the community should have the right to vote. Others feel that they should not have the right to vote. What about you? Do you think people on probation should have the right to vote? (0. no; 1. yes) |
| Parolee | There has been some discussion recently about the right to vote in this country. Some feel that people convicted of a crime who have been released from prison on parole and are living in the community should have the right to vote. Others feel that they should not have the right to vote. What about you? Do you think people on parole should have the right to vote? (0. no; 1. yes) |
| Prisoner | There has been some discussion recently about the right to vote in this country. Some feel that people convicted of a crime who are in prison should have the right to vote. Others feel that they should not have the right to vote. What about you? Do you think people in prison should have the right to vote? (0. no; 1. yes) |
| *Enfranchisement Items—Target Group Dimension 2* | |
| Baseline ex-felon | Now how about people convicted of a crime who have served their entire sentence, and are now living in the community. Do you think they should have the right to vote? (0. no; 1. yes) |
| White-collar ex-felon | Now how about people convicted of the illegal trading of stocks, who have served their entire sentence, and are now living in at the community. Do you think they should have the right to vote? (0. no; 1. yes) |
| Violent crime ex-felon | Now how about people convicted of a violent crime, who have served their entire sentence, and are now living in the community. Do you think they should have the right to vote? (0. no; 1. yes) |

*(continued)*

| Items | Question Wording (coding) |
|---|---|
| Sex crime ex-felon | Now how about people convicted of a sex offense, who have served their entire sentence, and are now living in the community. Do you think they should have the right to vote? (0. no; 1. yes) |
| *Other items* | |
| Attitude toward criminal justice | Once people who commit crimes are in prison, which one of the following goals do you think should be the most important goal of prison? Rehabilitation of criminals so they do not commit future crimes; punishment for their crime; deter them from and others from committing similar crimes? (categorical: reference = rehabilitation) |
| Baseline civil liberties | There are always some people whose ideas are considered bad more dangerous by other people. For instance, somebody who is against all churches and religion. If such a person wanted to make a speech in your city or town against churches and religion, should that person be allowed to speak or not? (0. no; 1. yes) |
| Ex-felon civil liberties | How about someone who served a prison sentence, and is now living in the community. If such a person wanted to make a speech in your city or town against prisons, should that person be allowed to speak or not? (0. no; 1. yes) |
| Ex-felon/legalization activist civil liberties | How about somebody who served a prison sentence for selling drugs and is now living in the community. If such a person wanted to make a speech in your city or town in favor of legalizing drugs, should that person be allowed to speak or not? (0. no; 1. yes) |
| Legalization activist civil liberties | How about somebody who wanted to make a speech in your city or town in favor of legalizing drugs. Should that person be allowed to speak or not? (0.no; 1. yes) |

*Source:* Data are from the Harris Interactive Omnibus Telephone Poll, July 18–22, 2002.

## Chapter 10: Unlocking the Vote

### Recent State Legislative Activity

In this section we provide some more details of some significant recent state-level changes that we describe in chapter 10. Appendix table A10.1

**Table A10.1**

**Summary of Major State Disenfranchisement Law Changes since 1975**

| Expanded Voting Rights | Restricted Voting Rights |
|---|---|
| 1975 Connecticut (restoration upon completion of sentence) | |
| 1975 Oregon (voting rights restored to probationers and parolees) | |
| 1976 New York (restoration upon completion of sentence) | |
| 1978 Arizona (restoration upon completion of sentence for first-time offenders) | |
| 1981 South Carolina (restoration upon completion of sentence) | 1981 Tennessee (disenfranchised until pardoned)* |
| 1983 Georgia (restoration upon completion of sentence) | |
| Texas (restoration two years after completion of sentence) | |
| 1984 Washington (restoration upon completion of sentence for those convicted after 1984) | |
| 1986 Tennessee (restoration upon completion of sentence for those convicted after 1986) | |
| | 1993 Colorado (disenfranchised parolees) |
| | 1995 Pennsylvania (five-year post-prison voting ban enacted)* |
| 1997 Texas (restoration upon completion of sentence) | |
| | 1998 Utah (disenfranchised inmates) |
| 2000 Delaware (voting rights restored five years after completion of sentence) | 2000 Massachusetts (disenfranchised inmates) |
| 2000 Pennsylvania (five-year postprison waiting period eliminated for nonregistered voters) | |
| 2001 New Mexico (restoration upon completion of sentence) | |
| 2001 Connecticut (restoration for probationers) | |

*(continued)*

| Expanded Voting Rights | Restricted Voting Rights |
|---|---|
| 2001 Nevada (eliminated five-year waiting period to apply for voting rights) | |
| 2002 Maryland (restoration three years after completion of sentence for nonviolent recidivists) | 2002 Kansas (disenfranchised probationers) |
| 2003 Nevada (restoration upon completion of sentence for first-time nonviolent offenders) | |
| 2005 Nebraska (restoration two years after completion of sentence) | |
| 2005 Iowa (executive order by governor restoring voting rights to all ex-felons) | |

* Tennessee and Pennsylvania undid these changes shortly after adopting them.

lists all changes in state disenfranchisement laws since 1975. Some otherwise conservative states have liberalized their laws. Texas, for example, removed its two-year waiting period for the restoration of voting rights for all people convicted of a felony, a measure signed into law by then governor George W. Bush in 1997. The new law makes restoration automatic upon completion of the sentence. In New Mexico, the state legislature repealed the state's lifetime ban for ex-felons, eliminating the requirement in 2001.[17] Instead, voting rights are automatically restored once the person "has satisfactorily completed the terms of a suspended or deferred sentence" or is "unconditionally discharged." Professor Timothy Canova of the University of New Mexico was one of the leaders of this campaign, and his report on the legislative hearings is revealing:

> We managed to produce fine witnesses at hearings of the Senate
> Rules and Senate Judiciary Committee, and then the House
> Voters and Elections Committee. The witnesses were people
> convicted of felonies years ago, and now are working hard, pay-
> ing taxes, raising families, and would like to vote. Whether it

was a recognition that this was the right thing to do, or a recognition that they had been helping to disenfranchise their own constituents, the Democrats pushed the bill through both houses—the Senate by a vote of 25 to 17 (nearly a straight party line vote), the House by a vote of 39 to 20 (with the support of several Republicans and virtually all Democrats). . . . We also worked the Republican Governor [Gary Johnson]. When the bill passed the House, it was reported that it would affect 7,000 people in New Mexico. I knew this was a gross undercount. But instead of talking about the political impact, we attempted to link the issue to the Governor's drug war agenda. And he was quite sympathetic to the arguments. He said in private that if people have done their time, they should be permitted to vote.[18]

The chairman of the state Republican Party acknowledged the partisan implications of enfranchising people convicted of felonies, but still supported the bill because "Fair is fair. When people have served their time, all of it, it's very hard for me intellectually to say that person should not be restored to full citizenship."[19]

Also in 2001, Connecticut became one of the few states in recent years to eliminate disenfranchisement for probationers.[20] The bill was supported by several Republican leaders and ultimately signed by then governor John Rowland, also a Republican. The new law was moved along by the lobbying efforts of a voting rights coalition made up of several civil rights groups, as well as some governmental agencies, such as the Department of Corrections and Department of Adult Probation.

Maryland provides perhaps the best example of a state liberalizing its law but drawing detailed lines to determine who will be enfranchised and when. That state had previously required all recidivists to seek a pardon while first-time offenders regained rights upon completion of sentence. In 2002, however, Maryland revised the law to restore voting rights to nonviolent recidivists three years after the completion of their sentence.[21]

In 2003, three states revised their disenfranchisement policies. Nevada amended its law to automatically reenfranchise first-time, nonviolent offenders upon completion of their sentence.[22] Wyoming passed a law allowing first-time nonviolent offenders to apply for restoration five years after the completion of their sentence.[23] Finally, Alabama implemented a new law to streamline the restoration process for people convicted of nonviolent felonies.[24] Those eligible can apply for a certificate of eligibility to register to vote from the Board of Pardons and Paroles immediately upon completion of sentence. The Board is obligated to restore rights within 45 days of determining that all obligations have been satisfied, although at this writing it appears to have difficulty meeting this deadline due to staffing shortages.[25]

Most recently, in the spring of 2005, Nebraska adopted legislation that reduced an indefinite ban on ex-felon voting to automatic restoration after a two-year waiting period. Although Governor Dave Heineman vetoed the voting rights bill, the state legislature decisively overrode the veto the next day on a 36-to-11 vote.[26] Finally, on July 4, 2005, Iowa governor Tom Vilsack issued an executive order that restored voting rights to all ex-felons in the state.

# Notes

*Introduction*

1. "The Trial of Susan B. Anthony," in George Klosko and Margaret G. Klosko, eds., *The Struggle for Women's Rights: Theoretical and Historical Sources* (Upper Saddle River, N.J.: Prentice-Hall, 1999), 133.
2. Frederick Douglass, "What Negroes Want," in *The Life and Writings of Frederick Douglass*, vol. 4, ed. Philip S. Foner (New York: International, 1955), 159–60, quoted in Judith Shklar, *American Citizenship* (Cambridge: Harvard University Press, 1991), 55–56.
3. John Cassidy, "Yankee Imperialist," *New Yorker*, July 8, 2002, 45.
4. *Reynolds v. Sims*, 377 U.S. 533 (1964), 555 (quotation); Frances Fox Piven and Richard A. Cloward, *Why Americans Don't Vote* (Boston: Beacon Press, 2002), 2 (quotation).
5. We provide details and analysis of the composition of the disenfranchised felon population in chapter 3.
6. In the state of Maryland, for example, the loss of voting rights is triggered by murder and rape, but also by a vast number of very minor "infamous crimes" such as: "shipment of alcoholic beverages to an unlicensed person," "willful

failure to provide tax information," "false statements" or "knowing misstatements" on applications for any number of state benefit programs, "misrepresentation of tobacco leaf weight," "misrepresentation by refrigerator contractors," being "an accessory after the fact to a felony," "sodomy," "intentionally removing/defacing/obliterating serial number," and so forth.

7. Information about disenfranchised misdemeanants can be found in Alec Ewald, "A 'Crazy-Quilt' of Tiny Pieces: State and Local Administration of American Criminal Disenfranchisement Law," report prepared for the Sentencing Project, July 2005. As Ewald notes, such practices make the term "felon disenfranchisement" sometimes inaccurate, as nonfelony offenders can suffer loss of voting rights in some places.

8. See Christopher Uggen, Jeff Manza, and Melissa Thompson, "Citizenship, Democracy, and the Civic Reintegration of Criminal Offenders," *The Annals of the American Academy of Political and Social Science* (forthcoming).

9. In his 2004 State of the Union address, President George W. Bush included a surprising new spending proposal to help inmates returning to their communities upon release from prison, dubbed the Prisoner Re-Entry Initiative. Bush proposed to spend $300 million over four years to help returning inmates find stable jobs and housing. In explaining the logic of this initiative, Bush noted that "if [ex-prisoners] can't find work, or a home, or help, they are much more likely to commit crime and return to prison."

## *1. Foundations*

1. "Ideas of the Year," *New York Times Sunday Magazine*, December 14, 2003, 70.

2. To cite just one example of the one-sided nature of the debate here, it is striking that there are at this writing at least two dozen law review articles analyzing felon disenfranchisement in recent years. All but one have uniformly rejected the constitutionality of felon disenfranchisement. For the exception, see Roger Clegg, "Who Should Vote?" *Texas Review of Law and Politics* 6 (2001): 159–78. Indeed, the consensus in the world of legal scholarship is so strong that one scholar has even asserted that "there are so many constitutional arguments against the disenfranchisement of felons that one can only wonder at the survival of the practice." See George Fletcher, "Disenfranchisement as Punishment: Reflections on the Raical Uses of Infamia," *UCLA Law Review* 46 (1999): 1895–1907, quotation at 1903. The most sophisticated philosophical defense of disenfranchisement is offered by Canadian political theorist Christopher Manfredi in "Judicial Review and Criminal Disenfranchisement

in the United States and Canada," *Review of Politics* 60 (1998): 277–305. A thorough overview of the defenses of disenfranchisement can be found in Alec Ewald, " 'Civil Death': The Ideological Paradox of Criminal Disenfranchisement Law in the United States," *University of Wisconsin Law Review* 2002 (2002): 1045–1137.

3. *Washington v. State*, 75 Ala. 582, 585 (1884).

4. See *Congressional Record*, vol. 148, 107th Cong., 2nd sess., Debate on Equal Protection of Voting Rights Act of 2001, February 14, 2002, S797-S809, S802.

5. See Todd Graziano and Roger Clegg's remarks before a Congressional panel considering legislation that would have restored the voting rights of ex-offenders: House Committee of the Judiciary, *Civic Participation and Rehabilitation Act of 1999: Hearings before the Subcommittee on the Constitution*, 106th Cong., 1st sess., October 21, 1999, at 44 and 17, respectively; for the McConnell quotation, see his remarks on the floor debate in the U.S. Senate over ex-felon disenfranchisement, *Congressional Record*, vol. 148, 107th Cong., 2nd sess., February 14, 2002, S802. The underlying logic of this position is explored in more detail in Alec Ewald, "An 'Agenda for Demolition': The Fallacy and the Danger of the 'Subversive Voting' Argument for Felony Disenfranchisement," *Columbia Human Rights Law Review* 36 (2004): 109–43.

6. See Alexander Keyssar, *The Right to Vote* (New York: Basic Books, 2000), 127–61, for overviews of the antifraud initiatives undertaken in this period.

7. The possibility of inmates banding together in a context where they are allowed to vote could influence the outcome of a local election, but that problem would mitigated by simply having inmates register and vote from their last address before entering prison (as is currently done in both Maine and Vermont).

8. See *Congressional Record*, vol. 148, 107th Cong., 2nd sess., February 14, 2002, S803.

9. John Lott and James Glassman, "The Felon Vote," *New York Post* online edition, available at: www.nypost.com, March 10, 2005; "Felons to Vote?" *Hannity and Colmes*, Fox News Network, transcript, March 4, 2005; see also "Felons and Democratic Politicking," editorial, *Washington Times*, March 8, 2005, A18. George Will, "Give Ballots to Felons?" *Newsweek*, March 14, 2005, 64.

10. 380 U.S. 89, 94 (internal citations omitted).

11. For further discussion, see Ewald, "An 'Agenda for Demolition.' "

12. Jeb Bush, "Comment," *Sarasota Herald-Tribune*, January 11, 2001.

13. We discuss these empirical details in much more detail in chapter 3. It is important to note that the proportion of *incarcerated* offenders who have been convicted of violent offenses is much higher, because such offenders typically

receive longer prison sentences than nonviolent offenders. But since all felons are typically subject to disenfranchisement, not just violent offenders, such statistics are of limited significance.

14. See Mary Fainsod Katzenstein and Katherine Davison Rubin, "How Different? A Comparison of the Movement Challenging Ex-felon Disenfranchisement with Suffrage Politics of an Earlier Time," unpublished paper presented at the annual meeting of the American Political Science Association, Boston, August 2002.

15. In chapter 2, we consider this point in more detail, analyzing both the important role of racial factors in the crucial post–Civil War era and the contemporary residues they have left.

16. In presenting this genealogical reconstruction of felon disenfranchisement, we have benefited significantly from the outstanding recent work of two political scientists who have written on aspects of the philosophical and historical foundations of felon disenfranchisement: Ewald, " 'Civil Death' "; and Katherine Pettus, *Felony Disenfranchisement in America* (New York: LFB Scholarly Publishing, 2005). Readers interested in broader and more sophisticated expositions of these points should consult those works.

17. Francisco O. Ramirez, Yasemin Soysal, and Suzanne Shanahan, "The Changing Logic of Political Citizenship: Cross-National Acquisition of Women's Suffrage Rights, 1890 to 1990," *American Sociological Review* 62 (1997): 735–45. For an excellent short overview of the current wave of democratization in comparative and historical perspective, see John Markoff, *Waves of Democracy* (Newbury Park, Calif.: Sage, 1996).

18. These were primarily countries aligned with the Soviet Union or China, including all of eastern Europe, and a large number of countries in Asia and Africa. In addition, longstanding noncommunist dictatorships in many other countries, in Latin America, Asia, and Africa, also dotted the globe.

19. See for example the work of "critical" theorists of public opinion such as Jurgen Habermas, Pierre Bourdieu, and their American counterparts. See Jurgen Habermas, *The Structural Transformation of the Public Sphere: An Inquiry into a Category of Bourgeois Society* (Cambridge: MIT Press, 1989 [orig. 1962]); Pierre Bourdieu, "Public Opinion Does Not Exist," in *Communication and Class Struggle*, ed. A. Matelart and S. Siegelaub, vol. 1 (New York: International General, 1979), 124–30; Susan Herbst, *Numbered Voices* (Chicago: University of Chicago Press, 1993); Benjamin Ginzburg, *The Captive Public* (New York: Basic Books, 1986). The innovative work on "deliberative" polling by James Fishkin has demonstrated a related point: when citizens are given the opportunity to extensively deliberate, they will frequently come to different policy and political conclusions than their "passive" starting point would have sug-

gested; see Fishkin, *The Voice of the People* (New Haven: Yale University Press, 1995).

20. For an engaging examination of some of these emerging models of democratic participation at the grassroots in different parts of the world, see Archon Fung and Erik Olin Wright, eds., *Deepening Democracy: Institutional Innovations in Empowered Participatory Governance* (London: Verso, 2003).

21. The authoritative comparative-historical survey is developed by Dietrich Rueschemeyer, Evelyn Huber Stephens, and John Stephens, *Capitalist Development and Democracy* (Chicago: University of Chicago Press, 1994), while Robert Dahl's indispensable *On Democracy* (New Haven: Yale University Press, 1998) provides an exceptional one–volume introduction.

22. See Jeffrey Goodwin, *No Other Way Out* (New York: Cambridge University Press, 2001).

23. Sidney Verba and his colleagues note that "casting a ballot is, by far, the most common act of citizenship in any democracy." See Sidney Verba, Kay Lehman Schlozman, and Henry E. Brady, *Voice and Equality* (Cambridge: Harvard University Press, 1995), 23. For the classic statement about the centrality of the right to vote as a marker of citizenship in the United States, see Judith Shklar, *American Citizenship* (Cambridge: Harvard University Press, 1991). On the importance of voting as expression of identity, see Alexander Schussler, *The Logic of Expressive Choice* (Princeton: Princeton University Press, 2000).

24. In spite of the commonly voiced claim in the world of social movement activism that elections are not the key sources of political change, a long line of research clearly documents the policy consequences of election outcomes. See G. Bingham Powell, *Elections as Instruments of Democracy* (New Haven: Yale University Press, 2000); Robert S. Erikson, Michael MacKuen, and James A. Stimson, *The Macro Polity* (New York: Cambridge University Press, 2002), chap. 7.

25. For discussions of deliberation in the electoral context, see Fishkin, *The Voice of the People*.

26. The most elegant introduction to the problem, and one that guides our discussion here, is Dahl, *On Democracy*. For the origins of the term "democracy," see also David Held, *Models of Democracy* (Stanford: Stanford University Press, 1988), chaps. 1–4.

27. On the Greeks, see Moses I. Finley, *Politics in the Ancient World* (New York: Cambridge University Press, 1983); Walter Agard, *What Democracy Meant to the Greeks* (Madison: University of Wisconsin Press, 1965); Held, *Models of Democracy*, chap. 1. One of the unique contributions of Rome was an attempt to extend the right to participate to citizens far beyond Rome; but in practice, travel to Rome from any distance was exceptionally difficult, and thus de facto

exclusion continued. On Roman democracy, see F. E. Adcock, *Roman Political Ideas and Practice* (Ann Arbor: University of Michigan Press, 1959).

28. England was the first country to establish a durable national forum for representation that was (nominally at first) independent from the monarchy. As Parliament evolved from its founding in the late thirteenth century to its expanded powers after the seventeenth-century revolution, it provided the model for a national alternative to the authoritarian rule of the monarch. English institutions in turn exerted a powerful influence on the Founding Fathers in America and the early course of the French revolution of 1789. In the United States, it was not until the original Articles of Confederation were ditched in favor of a stronger national government in the Constitution of 1789 that national political institutions took hold in America. In other countries, the nationalization of political institutions would occur at different times.

29. The classical work on civil society is Jurgen Habermas, *The Rise and Fall of the Bourgeois Public Sphere* (Cambridge: MIT Press, 1989 [orig. 1962]). See also Jean Cohen and Andrew Arato, *Civil Society* (Cambridge: MIT Press, 1992).

30. Rueschemeyer et al., *Capitalist Development.* For an elegant overview of some of the critics of the expansion of voting rights, see Albert O. Hirschman, *The Rhetoric of Reaction* (Cambridge: Harvard University Press, 1991), 86–110.

31. See Markoff, *Waves of Democracy.*

32. This point is documented most forcefully by Richard Valelly, *The Two Reconstructions: The Struggle for Black Enfranchisement* (Chicago: University of Chicago Press, 2004); see also J. Morgan Kousser, *Colorblind Injustice: Minority Voting Rights and the Undoing of the Second Reconstruction* (Chapel Hill, N.C.: University of North Carolina Press, 1999), chap. 1.

33. See Keyssar, *The Right to Vote,* 12. For an extended mediation on the visions of democracy embedded in the Constitution, see Robert Dahl, *How Democratic Is the American Constitution?* (New Haven: Yale University Press, 2003).

34. Interestingly, the states are not required to limit the ballot to citizens. Indeed, noncitizen voting was very common through much of the nineteenth century and in some states well into the twentieth. See Jamin Raskin, "Legal Aliens, Local Citizens: The Historical, Constitutional and Theoretical Meanings of Alien Suffrage," *University of Pennsylvania Law Review* 141 (1993): 1428–69.

35. Pettus, *Felony Disenfranchisement,* 61.

36. 377 U.S. 533 (1964) 533, 561. The phrase "fundamental right" as applied to voting was used by the Court as early as 1886 (*Yick Wo v. Hopkins,* 118 U.S. 356, 370) and can be found in numerous cases since then. See Ewald, " 'Civil Death,' " 1067, n. 86, who identified seven cases employing that language.

37. *Carrington v. Rash*, 380 U.S. 89 (1965).

38. *Harper v. Virginia State Board of Elections*, 383 U.S. 663 (1966).

39. *Dunn v. Blumstein*, 405 U.S. 330 (1972).

40. For overviews, see Howard Itzkowitz and Lauren Oldak, "Restoring the Ex-Offender's Right to Vote: Background and Development," *American Criminal Law Review* 11 (1973): 721–70; Pettus, *Felony Disenfranchisement*; Ewald, " 'Civil Death.' "

41. Our discussion in this paragraph and the next owes much to Pettus, *Felony Disenfranchisement*.

42. Itzkowitz and Oldak, "Restoring the Ex-Offender's Right to Vote," 722.

43. See Note, "Civil Death Statutes—Medieval Fiction in a Modern World," *Harvard Law Review* 50 (1936–37): 968–77, 969–70. The author identifies New York as the first state to adopt a civil death statute, in 1799, although several states adopted provisional bills of attainder during the Revolutionary War.

44. See William Blackstone, *Commentaries on the Laws of England* (Boston: Beacon Press, 1962), esp. bk. 4, chap. 1.

45. Quoted in Courtland Bishop, *History of Elections in the American Colonies* (New York: Columbia College Press, 1893), 53. This paragraph draws upon materials unearthed by Ewald, " 'Civic Death,' " 1061–62.

46. Ewald, " 'Civil Death,' " 1062.

47. Ironically, some of the early colonists had been released from English prisons, as for example the founders of the state of Georgia. See Nora Demleitner, "Preventing Internal Exile: The Need for Restrictions on Collateral Sentencing Consequences," *Stanford Law and Policy Review* 11 (1999): 153–70, at 153.

48. For example, the first constitutions of Kentucky, Ohio, and Virginia granted their state legislatures the power to disenfranchise for some offenses. See Note, "Civil Death Statutes," for further details.

49. This section draws upon the very useful overview and reconstruction developed by Zdravko Planinc, "Should Imprisoned Criminals Have a Constitutional Right to Vote?" *Canadian Journal of Law and Society* 2 (1987): 153–64; and Pettus, *Felony Disenfranchisement*.

50. Planinc, "Should Imprisoned Criminals Have a Constitutional Right to Vote," 160.

51. Baron de Montesquieu, *The Spirit of the Laws*, trans. Thomas Nugent (New York: Hafner, 1949), 22, 2, p. 184 (cited in Planinc, "Should Imprisoned Criminals Have a Constitutional Right to Vote," 162).

52. Ewald, " 'Civil Death.' " Ewald's interpretation defines our reading in this paragraph.

53. John Locke, *Second Treatise of Government,* ed. C. B. MacPherson (Indian-apolis: Hackett, 1980), 67.

54. Jean Jacques Rousseau, *On the Social Contract,* trans. R. D. and J. R. Masters (New York: St. Martin's Press, 1978), 65.

55. T. H. Marshall, "Citizenship and Social Class," in *The Citizenship Debates,* ed. Gershon Shafir (Minneapolis: University of Minnesota Press, 1998), 93–111.

56. While most important for its influence on penological practice, and its rejec-tion of the harshest versions of medieval justice, Beccaria, *On Crimes and Punishments,* trans. Henry Paolucci (Indianapolis: Bobbs-Merrill, 1963), 23, nonetheless endorsed the exclusion of criminals from the polity on the grounds that criminal offenders "who [do] not obey the laws, that is, the conditions under which men agree to support and defend one another, must be excluded from society" (quoted in Planinc, "Should Imprisoned Criminals Have a Con-stitutional Right to Vote," 157).

57. See Zebulon R. Brockway, "The Ideal of a True Prison System for a State," in *Transactions of the National Congress on Penitentiary and Reformatory Dis-cipline, 1870,* ed. E. C. Wines (Albany: Weed, Parsons, 1871). The quoted text is from *New York State Reformatory Report* of 1877, referenced in David J. Rothman, *Conscience and Convenience* (Boston: Little, Brown, 1980), 33. See also Norval Morris and David J. Rothman, *The Oxford History of the Prison: The Practice of Punishment in Western Society* (New York: Oxford University Press, 1995).

58. To be sure, there were always exceptions to the rehabilitative ideal in correc-tional practice. Michel Foucault's influential book *Discipline and Punish* (New York: Vintage, 1977) develops a counternarrative, in which rehabilitation is merely another form of control of socially constructed "deviants." Moreover, the persistence of biological accounts of criminal behavior leaves room for redrawing the line between citizen and offender. Nevertheless, the trajectory of modern penology has been away from notions of biological determinism and toward various models of rehabilitation.

59. Ewald, " 'Civil Death.' " Ewald builds from and applies the work of Rogers Smith on the multiple sources of civic ideals in American history. See Rogers M. Smith, *Civic Ideals* (New Haven: Yale University Press, 1997). Smith dis-cusses the extension of the franchise in the nineteenth century quite exten-sively, especially in relation to race, but not in the specific case of felon dis-enfranchisement.

60. One rare exception can be found in the work of Manfredi, "Judicial Review and Criminal Disenfranchisement," 297. Manfredi argues that a liberal defense of felon disenfranchisement remains viable insofar as such laws (1) assume

citizens are good until proved otherwise; and (2) are universally applied. Both of these assumptions are dubious in the context of the American case, as we will show in the rest of the book.

61. Sarah B. Gordon, *The Mormon Question: Polygamy and Constitutional Conflict in Nineteenth-Century America* (Chapel Hill: University of North Carolina Press, 2002); Winston Bowman, "Life after Civil Death: Felony and Mormon Disenfranchisement in the U.S. West, 1880–1890," unpublished manuscript.

62. *Murphy v. Ramsey,* 114 U.S. 15 (1885); *Davis v. Beason,* 133 U.S. 333 (1890).

63. We do not have a good history of the legal campaign, but a sense of it can be seen in law review articles and notes from that time. See for example Gary L. Reback, "Disenfranchisement of Ex-felons: A Reassessment," *Stanford Law Review* 25 (1973): 845–64; Itzkowitz and Oldak, "Restoring the Ex-Offender's Right to Vote"; Note, "The Equal Protection Clause as a Limitation on the States' Power to Disenfranchise Those Convicted of a Crime," *Rutgers Law Review* 21 (1966–67): 297–321.

64. 380 F.2d 445, 451–52 (2d Cir. 1967) (citations omitted). For further discussion of *Green,* see Ewald, "An 'Agenda for Demolition,' " 117–18.

65. See, for example, *Carrington v. Rash,* 380 U.S. 89 (1965).

66. *Richardson v. Ramirez,* 418 U.S. 24 (1974).

67. California abolished its policy of disenfranchising former felons shortly after the *Ramirez* decision in a statewide referendum. A good overview of the background to the *Ramirez* case can be found in Manfredi, "Judicial Review and Criminal Disenfranchisement," 280.

68. *Ramirez v. Brown,* 507 P.2d 1345 (1973). At the time the Court agreed to hear *Ramirez,* it had already denied certiorari in an equal protection case from North Carolina. See *Fincher v. Scott,* 352 F. Supp 117 (1973), *aff'd* 411 U.S. 961 (1973).

69. Emphasis added.

70. For quoted passages, see *Ramirez,* 418 U.S. at 45, 48, 53–55, 55.

71. *Ramirez,* 418 U.S. at 55.

72. *Ramirez,* 418 U.S. at 76, n. 24.

73. See, for example, the widely cited early evaluation of the verdict in David L. Shapiro, "Mr. Justice Rehnquist: A Preliminary View," *Harvard Law Review* 90 (1976): 293–376. Shapiro argued that "there is not a word in the Fourteenth Amendment suggesting that the exemptions in Section 2's formula are in any way a barrier to the judicial application of section 1 in voting rights cases, whether or not they involve the rights of ex-convicts" (p. 303). Laurence Tribe sharply criticized the *Ramirez* verdict for failing to apply strict scrutiny on grounds that there were no compelling state interests to justify the exclusion.

Tribe, *American Constitutional Law* (Mineola, N.Y.: Foundation Press, 1978). For further discussion of this inconsistency, see Ewald, " 'Civil Death,' " 1066–72.

74. In a challenge to New York's laws disenfranchising nonincarcerated felons, a federal appellate court ruled that application of the VRA to overturn the state's law could not be relevant because "the legitimacy of felon disenfranchisement is affirmed in the text of the Fourteenth Amendment itself." See *Baker v. Pataki*, 85 F.3d 919, 929 (2d Cir. 1996) (*en banc*). See Gabriel J. Chin, "Reconstruction, Felon Disenfranchisement, and the Right to Vote: Did the Fifteenth Amendment Repeal the Second Section of the Fourteenth Amendment?" *Georgetown Law Journal* 92 (2004): 259–316, at 316, for other examples. Intriguingly, Chin also notes that several courts have held that the literal wording of the Fourteenth Amendment precludes applying the Voting Rights Act to reconsidering felon disenfranchisement (unless the VRA itself is unconstitutional), but in doing so those federal courts invoking the Fourteenth Amendment are invoking a repealed amendment.

75. John R. Cosgrove, "Four New Arguments against the Constitutionality of Felony Disenfranchisement," *Thomas Jefferson Law Review* 26 (2004): 157–202.

76. *Muntaqim v. Coombe*, 366 F.3d 102, 115 (2d Cir. 2004), *cert. denied* 125 S.Ct. 480 (2004); *Farrakhan v. Washington*, 338 F.3d 1009 (9th Cir. 2003), *reh'g denied by* 359 F.3d 1116 (9th Cir. 2004), *cert. denied sub nom. Locke v. Farrakhan*, 125 S. Ct. 477 (2004).

77. This irony is pointed out by Fletcher, "Disenfranchisement as Punishment," 1900.

78. Eric Foner, *Reconstruction* (New York: Harper and Row, 1988), 251–61; Xi Wang, "Black Suffrage and the Redefinition of American Freedom, 1860–70," *Cardozo Law Review* 17 (1996): 2153–2223.

79. See Itzkowitz and Oldak, "Restoring the Ex-Offender's Right to Vote," 746–47.

80. Chin, "Reconstruction, Felon Disenfranchisement, and the Right to Vote."

81. See also Pamela S. Karlan, "Unduly Partial: The Supreme Court and the Fourteenth Amendment in Bush v. Gore," *Florida State University Law Review* 29 (2001): 591, n. 26; Horace Edgar Flack, *The Adoption of the Fourteenth Amendment* (Buffalo: W. S. Hein, 2003 [orig. 1908]), 98; and Arthur E. Bonfield, "The Right to Vote and Judicial Enforcement of Section 2 of the Fourteenth Amendment," *Cornell Law Quarterly* 48 (1960): 108–37. At least one legal scholar has proposed to bend the stick in the other direction, arguing that section 2's remedy could be applied by Congress to punish the state of Florida for disenfranchising such a large group of ex-offenders. See Kate Shaw,

"Invoking the Penalty: How Florida's Disenfranchisement Law Violates the Constitutional Requirement of Population Equality in Congressional Representation, and What to Do about It," *Northwestern University Law Review* 100 (forthcoming).

82. Chin, "Reconstruction, Felon Disenfranchisement, and the Right to Vote," 269.

83. *Slaughter House Cases*, 83 U.S. 36 (1873).

84. *Hunter v. Underwood*, 471 U.S. 222 (1985).

85. *Hunter*, 471 U.S. at 233.

86. See for example Andrew L. Shapiro, "Challenging Criminal Disenfranchisement Under the Voting Rights Act: A New Strategy," *Yale Law Journal* 103 (1993): 537–66; Alice Harvey, "Ex-felon Disenfranchisement and Its Influence on the Black Vote: The Need for a Second Look," *University of Pennsylvania Law Review* 142 (1994): 1145–89; Virginia E. Hench, "The Death of Voting Rights: The Legal Disenfranchisement of Minority Voters," *Case Western Law Review* 48 (summer 1998): 727–98.

87. See, e.g., *Woodruff v. Wyoming*, 49 Fed. Appx. 199, 201 (10th Cir. 2002); *Cotton v. Fordice*, 157 F.3d 388, 391 (5th Cir. 1998); *Baker v. Pataki*, 85 F.3d 919, 924 (2d Cir. 1996); *Wesley v. Collins*, 791 F.2d 1255, 1257 (6th Cir. 1986); *Johnson v. Bush*, 214 F. Supp. 2d 1333, 1335 (S.D. Fla. 2002); *Johnson v. Governor of Florida*, 353 F.3d 1287, 1308 (11th Cir. 2003), vacated *en banc* by 377 F.3d 1163 (11th Cir. 2004); *Jones v. Edgar*, 3 F. Supp. 2d 979, 980 (C.D. Ill. 1998). For a challenge under the First Amendment, see *Johnson*, 214 F. Supp. 2d at 1338. For claims under the "cruel and unusual punishment" ban of the Eighth Amendment, see *Woodruff*, 49 Fed. Appx. at 201; *Farrakhan v. Locke*, 987 F. Supp. 1304, 1314 (E.D. Wash. 1997); *McLaughlin v. City of Canton*, 947 F. Supp. 954, 961 (S.D. Miss. 1995). For a challenge under the Twenty-fourth Amendment, see *Johnson*, 214 F. Supp. 2d at 1342, where the plaintiff likens the restoration process to a poll tax, and *Howard v. Gilmore* 205 F.3d 1333 (4th Cir. 2000).

88. In recent years, the Court has twice reversed earlier decisions, on the basis, in part, of changing empirical circumstances. See, for example, *Roper v. Simmons*, 125 S.Ct. 1183 (2005), which overruled *Stanford v. Kentucky*, 492 U.S. 361 (1989) on the constitutionality of sentencing juvenile offenders to death; and *Lawrence v. Texas*, 539 U.S. 558 (2003) (overruling *Bowers v. Hardwick*, 478 U.S. 186 (1986) on the constitutionality of sodomy laws).

89. A recent *amici curiae* brief signed by 20 prominent criminologists in *NAACP v. Harvey* also explores these issues. See Brief for *Amici Curiae* at 9–33, *NAACP v. Harvey*, no. A-6881–03T5 (N.J. Super. Ct. App. Div. filed Dec. 15, 2004). Our discussion in this section is also informed by the work of Andrew von

Hirsh and Martin Wasik, "Civil Disqualifications Attending Conviction: A Suggested Conceptual Framework," *Cambridge Law Journal* 56 (1997): 599–624.

90. See Andrew Von Hirsch, *Doing Justice: The Choice of Punishments* (New York: Hill and Wang, 1976).

91. Gresham M. Sykes identifies deprivation of liberty, deprivation of goods and services, deprivation of heterosexual relations, deprivation of autonomy, and deprivation of security as "pains of imprisonment" in *The Society of Captives: A Study of a Maximum Security Prison* (Princeton: Princeton University Press, 1958).

92. See J. Cohen, "The Incapacitation Effect of Imprisonment: A Critical Review of the Literature," in *Deterrence and Incapacitation: Estimating the Effects of Criminal Sanctions on Crime Rates: Report of the National Research Council Panel on Research on Deterrent and Incapacitative Effects*, ed. Alfred Blumstein, J. Cohen, and Daniel Nagin (Washington, D.C.: National Academy of Sciences, 1987), 187–243.

93. Perhaps the most influential of these critiques came in Robert Martinson's famous "Martinson Report": Martinson, "What Works? Questions and Answers about Prison Reform," *Public Interest* 35 (1974): 22–54.

94. See Francis T. Cullen, "The Twelve People Who Saved Rehabilitation: How the Science of Criminology Made a Difference," *Criminology* 43 (2005): 1–42; Ann Chih Lin, *Reform in the Making: The Implementation of Social Policy in Prison* (Princeton: Princeton University Press, 2000).

95. See chapter 8 for details of the Florida restoration procedure.

96. See Jeremy Travis, "Invisible Punishment: An Instrument of Social Exclusion," in *Invisible Punishment: The Collateral Consequences of Mass Imprisonment*, ed. Marc Mauer and Meda Chesney-Lind (New York: New Press, 2002), 15–36.

97. See chapter 3 for details and documentation.

98. The most comprehensive available source is Brandon Rottinghaus, *Incarceration and Enfranchisement: International Practices, Impact, and Recommendations for Reform* (Washington, D.C.: International Foundation for Election Systems, 2003). For other sources, see Alec Ewald, "Of Constitutions, Politics, and Punishment: Criminal Disenfranchisement Law in Comparative Context," paper presented at the annual meeting of the American Political Science Association, Boston, August 29–September 1, 2002; Jamie Fellner and Marc Mauer, *Losing the Vote: The Impact of Felony Disenfranchisement Laws in the United States* (Washington, D.C.: Sentencing Project, 1998); Joe Levinson, *Barred from Voting* (London: Prison Reform Trust, 2001).

99. Nora Demleitner, "Continuing Payment on One's Debt to Society: The

German Model of Felon Disenfranchisement as an Alternative," *Minnesota Law Review* 874 (2000): 759.

## 2. The Racial Origins of Felon Disenfranchisement

1. *Reports of the Proceedings and Debates of the New York Constitutional Convention of 1821* (Albany: E. and E. Hosford, 1821; reprint, New York: Da Capo Press, 1970), 191, quoted in Christopher Malone, " 'The Mind of Blacks Are Not Competent to Vote': Racial Voting Restrictions in New York," unpublished manuscript, Pace University, 2003, 19.
2. The adopted property qualification requirement in 1825 disenfranchised all but 298 of New York's black population of 29,701. See Philip Klinkner and Rogers M. Smith, *The Unsteady March: The Rise and Decline of Racial Equality in America* (Chicago: University of Chicago Press, 1999), 35.
3. *Ratliff v Beale*, 74 Miss. 247, 266–67 (1896) (emphasis added).
4. Warren Wise, "House Doesn't Kill Bill to Delay Felons Voting," Charleston (S.C.) *Post and Courier,* February 16, 2001, A3.
5. For other examples, see Christopher Uggen, Jeff Manza, and Angela Behrens, "Felony Voting Rights and the Disenfranchisement of African Americans," *Souls* 5, 3 (fall 2003): 48–57.
6. For example, see George Fletcher, "Disenfranchisement as Punishment: Reflections on the Racial Uses of *Infamia*," *UCLA Law Review* 46 (August 1999): 1895–1908; Alice Harvey, "Ex-felon Disenfranchisement and Its Influence on the Black Vote: The Need for a Second Look," *University of Pennsylvania Law Review* 142 (January 1994): 1145–89; Virginia E. Hench, "The Death of Voting Rights: The Legal Disenfranchisement of Minority Voters," *Case Western Law Review* 48 (summer 1998): 727–98; Andrew L. Shapiro, "Challenging Criminal Disenfranchisement under the Voting Rights Act: A New Strategy," *Yale Law Journal* 103 (November 1993): 537–66; Pamela Karlan, "Conviction and Doubts: Retribution, Representation, and the Debate over Felon Disenfranchisement," *Stanford Law Review* 56 (2004): 1147–70. Our first attempt to unpack this history was developed in Angela Behrens, Christopher Uggen, and Jeff Manza, "Ballot Manipulation and the 'Menace of Negro Domination': Racial Threat and Felon Disenfranchisement in the United States, 1850–2002," *American Journal of Sociology* 109 (November 2003): 559–605.
7. Marc Mauer, "Felon Disenfranchisement: A Policy Whose Time Has Passed?" *Human Rights* 31 (winter 2004): 16–17.
8. Other commentators have noted the lack of systematic research about the

historical origins of felon disenfranchisement. See, e.g., Alex Keyssar, "The Right to Vote and Election 2000," in *The Unfinished Election of 2000*, ed. Jack Rakove (New York: Basic Books, 2001), 86; Alec C. Ewald, " 'Civil Death': The Ideological Paradox of Criminal Disenfranchisement Law in the United States," *University of Wisconsin Law Review* 2002 (2002), 1065.

9. This list is by no means intended to be exhaustive: in particular, there are much broader arguments about the *cultural* impact of race and racial antagonism in American history and law. For example, see Nicola Beisel, *Imperiled Innocents: Anthony Comstock and Family Reproduction in Victorian America* (Princeton: Princeton University Press, 1997); Matthew Frye Jacobson, *Whiteness of a Different Color: European Immigrants and the Alchemy of Race* (Cambridge: Harvard University Press, 1998); Michael Rogin, "The Two Declarations of Independence," in *Race and Representation: Affirmative Action*, ed. Robert Post and Michael Rogin (New York: Zone Books, 1998), 73–98.

10. For analyses of the role of race in the construction of American political institutions, see, e.g., Jill Quadagno, *The Color of Welfare* (New York: Oxford University Press, 1994), esp. chap. 8; and Michael Goldfield, *The Color of Politics* (New York: New Press, 1997); on the Constitution, William Wiecek, *Sources of Antislavery Constitutionalism in America, 1760–1848* (Ithaca, N.Y.: Cornell University Press, 1977).

11. See Richard M. Valelly, *The Two Reconstructions* (Chicago: University of Chicago Press, 2004), chaps. 2–5; Paul Frymer, *Uneasy Alliances: Race and Party Competition in America* (Princeton: Princeton University Press, 1998), esp. chap. 3.

12. For broader overviews contrasting a number of "populist" movements on the left and the tensions around race, see especially Michael Kazin, *The Populist Persuasion* (New York: Basic Books, 1995); and from the perspective of civil rights activism, Klinkner and Smith, *The Unsteady March*. On the Knights of Labor, see Kim Voss, *The Making of American Exceptionalism* (Ithaca, N.Y.: Cornell University Press, 1994); on the populist movement, see Lawrence Goodwyn, *The Populist Moment* (New York: Oxford University Press, 1978); for discussions of race and New Deal–era social movements, see e.g. Dona C. Hamilton and Charles V. Hamilton, *The Dual Agenda* (New York: Columbia University Press, 1997); Robert C. Lieberman, *Shifting the Color Line: Race and the American Welfare State* (Cambridge: Harvard University Press, 1998); Goldfield, *The Color of Politics*, chap. 6; and Michael K. Brown, *Race, Money, and the American Welfare State* (Ithaca, N.Y.: Cornell University Press, 1999).

13. For an overview of these issues, and reference to the relevant literatures, see Jeff Manza, "The Political Sociology of the New Deal," *Annual Review of Sociology* 26 (2000): 297–322.

14. For overviews, see especially Quadagno, *The Color of Welfare*; Klinkner and Smith, *The Unsteady March*; and Brown, *Race, Money, and the American Welfare State*.

15. See, e.g., Margaret Weir, Ann S. Orloff, and Theda Skocpol, *The Politics of Social Policy in the United States* (Princeton: Princeton University Press, 1988); for the comparative evidence, see Duane Swank, *Global Capital, Political Institutions, and Policy Change in Developed Welfare States* (New York: Cambridge University Press, 2002); and Evelyn Huber Stephens and John Stephens, *Development and Crisis of the Welfare State: Parties and Policies in Global Markets* (Chicago: University of Chicago Press, 2001). For an overview of the historical sociology on race and the American welfare state, see Manza, "Race and the Underdevelopment of the American Welfare State."

16. See, e.g., Donald Kinder and Lynn Sanders, *Divided by Color: Racial Politics and Democratic Ideals* (Chicago: University of Chicago Press, 1996); Jennifer Hochschild, *Facing up to the American Dream: Race, Class, and the Soul of the Nation* (Princeton: Princeton University Press, 1995); Martin Gilens, *Why Americans Hate Welfare: Race, Media, and the Politics of Antipoverty Policy* (Chicago: University of Chicago Press, 1999); David Sears, Jim Sidanius, and Lawrence Bobo, eds., *Racialized Politics: The Debate about Racism in America* (Chicago: University of Chicago Press, 2000).

17. Roosevelt quoted in Klinkner and Smith, *The Unsteady March*, 337.

18. Felton quoted in Joel Williamson, *The Crucible of Race: Black-White Relations in the American South since Emancipation* (New York: Oxford University Press, 1984), 128. For other examples, see Forest Wood, *Black Scare: The Racist Response to Emancipation and Reconstruction* (Berkeley: University of California Press, 1968); and Tali Mendelberg, *The Race Card: Campaign Strategy, Implicit Messages, and the Norm of Equality* (Princeton: Princeton University Press, 2001), chap. 2.

19. The literature on "whiteness" provides a valuable lens into the larger patterns of group-based stereotypes in this period. Large immigrant groups from Europe were frequently not allowed to be "white" for decades after their arrival, and they faced high levels of group-based discrimination and negative stereotyping. For examples of this genre, see especially Jacobson, *Whiteness of a Different Color*; Noel Ignatiev, *How the Irish Became White* (New York: Routledge, 1995).

20. Gina Lombroso-Ferrero, *Criminal Man, According to the Classifications of Cesare Lombroso* (Montclair, N.J.: Patterson Smith, 1972).

21. Clifford Shaw and Henry D. McKay, *Juvenile Delinquency and Urban Areas* (Chicago: University of Chicago, 1942).

22. A classical example of "race–neutral" discourse is reflected in the shift from

explicit racial arguments to more abstract claims about the sanctity of "state's rights." For discussion, see Lawrence D. Bobo and Ryan A. Smith, "From Jim Crow Racism to Laissez-Faire Racism: The Transformation of Racial Attitudes," in *Beyond Pluralism: The Conception of Groups and Groups Identities in America,* ed. Wendy R. Katkin, Ned Landsman, and Andrea Tyree (Urbana: University of Illinois Press, 1998); Gilens, *Why Americans Hate Welfare*; Kinder and Sanders, *Divided by Color*; Mendelberg, *The Race Card*; Quadagno, *The Color of Welfare.*

23. See Lawrence D. Bobo, James R. Kluegel, and Ryan A. Smith, "Laissez Faire Racism: The Crystallization of a 'Kinder, Gentler' Anti-Black Ideology," in *Racial Attitudes in the 1990s: Continuity and Change*, ed. Steven A. Tuch and Jack K. Martin (Westport, Conn.: Praeger, 1997), 15–44; Kinder and Sanders, *Divided by Color*; Mendelberg, *The Race Card.*

24. For overviews of the importance of the South and some of these political dynamics, see especially David James, "The Transformation of the Southern Racial State: Class and Race Determinants of Local-State Structures," *American Sociological Review* 53 (1988): 191–208; Richard Bensel, *Sectionalism and American Political Development* (Madison: University of Wisconsin Press, 1984); Lee Alston and Joseph Ferrie, *Southern Partneralism and the American Welfare State: Economics, Politics and Institutions in the South, 1865–1965* (New York: Cambridge University Press, 1999); G. William Domhoff, *State Autonomy or Class Dominance?* (New York: de Gruyter, 1996); and Lieberman, *Shifting the Color Line.*

25. The outstanding work on this topic is that of Alston and Ferrie, *Southern Paternalism and the American Welfare State.*

26. See Earl Black and Merle Black, *The Vital South* (Cambridge: Harvard University Press, 1992).

27. Appendix table A2.1 provides a full listing of changes in state laws.

28. Suffrage restrictions on free African Americans and women were largely unaffected by this wave of democracy. Indeed, as we note later in the chapter, the right to vote was increasingly compromised in this period for African Americans.

29. See Keyssar, *The Right to Vote*, chap. 2 and tables A.1, A.2, and A.5, for a detailed account of state restrictions on suffrage during the late eighteenth century. See also Richard F. Bensel, *The American Ballot Box in the Mid–Nineteenth Century* (New York: Cambridge University Press, 2004).

30. Keyssar, *The Right to Vote*, chap. 2.

31. Keyssar, *The Right to Vote*, 29 and table A.2.

32. Keyssar, *The Right to Vote*, table A.3. The three states that retained a property requirement were Rhode Island, New York, and South Carolina. As Keyssar

notes, Rhode Island did not enforce its requirement against native-born citizens, New York's requirement did not apply to whites, and in South Carolina, a resident could vote notwithstanding the property requirement if he had been a resident for six months and paid a tax within the preceding year.

33. The states were Delaware, Louisiana, Maine, Massachusetts, New Hampshire, New Jersey, Rhode Island, South Carolina, and Virginia. For a discussion of the exclusion of paupers from the franchise, see Keyssar, *The Right to Vote*, 134–36, table A.6.

34. Keyssar, *The Right to Vote*, 142, table A.13.

35. For overviews, see, e.g., Malone, "Racial Voting Restrictions in New York," 19; Keyssar, *The Right to Vote*, 54–59, table A.5; Chilton Williamson, *American Suffrage: From Property to Democracy, 1760–1860* (Princeton: Princeton University Press, 1960), 235, 278; Judith Shklar, *American Citizenship* (Cambridge: Harvard University Press, 1991), 51–52.

36. Ward Elliott, *The Rise of Guardian Democracy* (Chicago: University of Chicago Press, 1974), 43.

37. Keyssar, *The Right to Vote*, table A.10.

38. See, e.g., Keyssar, *The Right to Vote*, tables A.10 and A.11, for a list of state provisions concerning taxpaying and property requirements.

39. Keyssar estimates that in 1855 the states allowing African Americans to vote contained only 4 percent of the free black population. See Keyssar, *The Right to Vote*, 55.

40. See Keyssar, *The Right to Vote*, 306. As we noted in chapter 1, before 1880 few states had developed a legal distinction between felony offenses and "crimes at common law." This meant that only common–law offenses (murder, rape, assault, burglary) constituted disenfranchising offenses. For a good history of this issue, see John Cosgrove, "Four New Arguments against the Constitutionality of Felony Disenfranchisement," *Thomas Jefferson Law Review* 26 (2004): 157–202.

41. Shapiro, "Challenging Criminal Disenfranchisement," 541, quoting Francis Butler Simkins, *Pitchfork Ben Tillman* (Columbia, S.C.: University of South Carolina Press, 1944), 297.

42. See Bensel, *The American Ballot Box in the Mid–Nineteenth Century*, 29 (noting that "if a man was not personally known by those attending the polls, there was no way to determine whether he had been disqualified by criminal conviction. As a result, very few voters were challenged on the ground that they were convicted felons").

43. The Fourteenth Amendment says, in relevant part: "All persons born or naturalized in the United States and subject to the jurisdiction thereof, are citizens

of the United States and of the State wherein they reside. No State shall make or enforce any law which shall abridge the privileges or immunities of citizens of the United States; nor shall any State deprive any person of life, liberty, or property, without due process of law; nor deny to any person within its jurisdiction the equal protection of the laws. . . . When the right to vote at any election for the choice of electors . . . is denied to any of the male inhabitants of such State, being twenty-one years of age, and citizens of the United States, or in any way abridged, except for participation in rebellion, or other crime, the basis of representation therein shall be reduced in the proportion which the number of such male citizens shall bear to the whole number of male citizens twenty-one years of age in such State."

44. *Scott v. Sandford*, 60 U.S. 393 (1857).

45. See especially the important work of J. Morgan Kousser, *The Shaping of Southern Politics: Suffrage Restriction and the Establishment of the One-Party South, 1880–1910* (New Haven: Yale University Press, 1974); see also Michael Perman, *Struggle for Mastery: Disenfranchisement in the South, 1888–1908* (Chapel Hill: University of North Carolina Press, 2001); Kent Redding, *Making Race, Making Power: North Carolina's Road to Disenfranchisement* (Urbana: University of Illinois Press, 2003).

46. A 1959 report by the United States Commission on Civil Rights indicates that in the South, only one-quarter of the African American voting-age population was registered to vote, whereas close to 60 percent of the white voting-age population was registered. U.S. Commission on Civil Rights, *Report of the United States Commission on Civil Rights* (Washington, D.C.: U.S. Government Printing Office, 1959), 40–41.

47. The main purpose of the VRA was to enforce the Fifteenth Amendment. See, e.g., *South Carolina v. Katzenbach*, 383 U.S. 301, 308 (1966) (noting that "the Voting Rights Act was designed by Congress to banish the blight of racial discrimination in voting, which has infected the electoral process in parts of our country for nearly a century").

The VRA was further amended in 1982 in an effort to eliminate continuing electoral practices that had a negative impact on racial minorities attempting to vote. Reports tracking the effect of the VRA had not been promising and indicated that election officials continued to use a range of tactics to prevent racial minorities from voting. See, e.g., U.S. Commission on Civil Rights, *The Voting Rights Act: Ten Years After* (Washington, D.C.: U.S. Government Printing Office, 1975), 98–104; U.S. Commission on Civil Rights, *The Voting Rights Act: Unfulfilled Goals* (Washington, D.C.: U.S. Government Printing Office, 1981), 28. The 1982 amendment changed the standard for evaluating claims of racial discrimination. The amendments eliminated the onerous requirement of proving discriminatory intent and instead changed to a "totality of the circumstances" standard.

48. Keyssar, *The Right to Vote,* chap. 5, provides a detailed account of these measures, which are frequently overlooked in assessments of the progress of universal suffrage in the United States.

49. Jamin Raskin, "Legal Aliens, Local Citizens: The Historical, Constitutional and Theoretical Meanings of Alien Suffrage," *University of Pennsylvania Law Review* 141 (1993): 1391–1471; see also Keyssar, *The Right to Vote,* table A.12.

50. Lawrence Friedman, *Crime and Punishment in American History* (New York: Basic Books, 1993).

51. U.S. Department of Commerce, Bureau of the Census, *Census of the United States* (Washington, D.C.: Government Printing Office, 1853, 1872). Alabama's nonwhite population increased by only 3 percent between 1850 and 1870.

52. *Washington v. Alabama,* 75 Ala. 582, 585 (1884).

53. Quoted in Malcolm C. McMillan, *Constitutional Development in Alabama, 1798–1901* (Chapel Hill: University of North Carolina Press, 1955), 275. The disenfranchising provisions from the 1901 convention held until the 1985 Supreme Court ruling in *Hunter v. Underwood,* 471 U.S. 222 [1985], which found explicit racial intent in the state's law. See chapter 1 for a discussion of the *Underwood* case. Many southern states held disenfranchising conventions during this period, and the issue of race was ever present. See Paul Lewinson, *Race, Class, and Party: A History of Negro Suffrage and White Politics in the South* (1932), 82–84; Perman, *The Struggle for Mastery,* esp. 28–30, 70–90 (Mississippi), 135–45 (Louisiana), and 91–116 (South Carolina).

54. *Hunter v. Underwood,* 471 U.S. 222 (1985).

55. See Keyssar, *The Right to Vote,* chap. 8 ("The Quiet Years").

56. Hubert M. Blalock, *Toward a Theory of Minority-Group Relations* (New York: Wiley, 1967); Herbert Blumer, "Race Prejudice as a Sense of Group Position," *Pacific Sociological Review* 1 (1958): 3–7; Edna Bonacich, "A Theory of Ethnic Antagonism: The Split Labor Market," *American Sociological Review* 37 (1972): 547–59.

57. Blumer, "Race Prejudice as a Sense of Group Position," 4.

58. See, e.g., Mark A. Fossett and Jill K. Kiecolt, "The Relative Size of Minority Populations and White Racial Attitudes," *Social Science Quarterly* 70 (December 1989): 820–35; Michael W. Giles and Arthur S. Evans, "External Threat, Perceived Threat, and Group Identity," *Social Science Quarterly* 66 (1995): 50–66; Lincoln Quillian, "Group Threat and Regional Change in Attitudes toward African Americans," *American Journal of Sociology* 102 (1996): 816–60;

Marylee C. Taylor, "How White Attitudes Vary with the Racial Composition of Local Populations: Numbers Count," *American Sociological Review* 63 (1998): 512–35.

59. An additional, and more general, problem with models of economic threat is that they may overgeneralize from the economic to the political and cultural. Theories of *symbolic racism* or *racial resentment*, for example, suggest that racial antagonism toward blacks among white Americans are deeply held and not simply reducible to economic conflict. Although these attitudes may remain latent, they can be triggered by events such as the invocation of the name Willie Horton by George Bush in the 1988 presidential campaign. On symbolic racism, see David O. Sears, "Symbolic Racism," in *Eliminating Racism: Profiles in Controversy*, ed. P. A. Katz and D. A. Taylor (New York: Plenum, 1988); David O. Sears and Carolyn L. Funk, "The Role of Self-Interest in Social and Political Attitudes," in *Advances in Experimental Social Psychology*, ed. Mark Zanna (Orlando, Fl.: Academic Press, 1991), 1–91. On racial resentment, see Kinder and Sanders, *Divided by Color*. On triggering the emergence of latent attitudes, see Mendelberg, *The Race Card*.

60. Lincoln Quillian and Devah Pager, "Black Neighbors, Higher Crime? The Role of Racial Stereotypes in Evaluations of Neighborhood Crime," *American Journal of Sociology* 107 (2001): 717–67.

61. Taylor, "How White Attitudes Vary with the Racial Composition of Local Populations."

62. Michael W. Giles and Melanie A. Buckner, "David Duke and Black Threat: An Old Hypothesis Revisited," *Journal of Politics* 55 (August 1993): 702–13.

63. See Karen Heimer, Thomas Stucky, and Joseph B. Lang, "Economic Competition, Racial Threat, and Rates of Imprisonment," paper presented at the annual meeting of the American Society of Criminology, Toronto, November 1999; Martha A. Myers, *Race, Labor, and Punishment in the New South* (Columbus: Ohio State University Press, 1998).

64. Note that most states also disenfranchise felons out of prison on early release (parole) or felony probationers. However, we do not have data for the entire period in question permitting us to include those groups of felons as well.

65. For the period from 1850 to 1990, we take data from Steven Ruggles and Matthew Sobek, *Integrated Public Use Microdata Series, ver. 2.0* (Minneapolis: Historical Census Projects, University of Minnesota, 1997).

66. Geoffrey H. Moore, ed., *Business Cycle Indicators* (Princeton: Princeton University Press, 1961), 670–71; National Bureau of Economic Research, *Business Cycle Expansions and Contractions* (New York: National Bureau of Economic Research, 2003).

67. Susan Olzak, "The Political Context of Competition: Lynching and Urban

Racial Violence, 1882–1914," *Social Forces* 69 (December 1990): 395–421; Susan Olzak and Suzanne Shanahan, "Racial Policy and Racial Conflict in the Urban United States, 1869–1924," *Social Forces* 82 (December 2003): 481–577.

68. Martha A. Myers, "Black Threat and Incarceration in Postbellum Georgia," *Social Forces* 69 (December 1990): 373–93; Myers, *Race, Labor, and Punishment.*

69. We used U.S. census and Census Bureau "institutional population" and "group quarters" subject reports to calculate this percentage between 1850 and 1990. Because data on the race of prisoners were unavailable between 1900 and 1920, we interpolated estimates for these years based on data from 1890 and historical correctional statistics from 1926–30. U.S. Department of Justice, *Race of Prisoners Admitted to State and Federal Institutions, 1926–1986* (Washington, D.C.: Government Printing Office, 1991).

70. U.S. Department of Justice, *Correction Populations in the United States* (Washington, D.C.: Government Printing Office, 2000).

71. Keyssar, *The Right to Vote*, 162. Southern states have historically adopted more restrictive laws limiting both voting rights and general civil rights of felons. See Keyssar, *The Right to Vote*, 89. We use Census Bureau categories to represent region, coding Northeast, Midwest, South, and West as separate indicator variables.

72. The state electorate sometimes makes the final decision on a law, as was the case with the recent referenda in Utah (1998) and Massachusetts (2000) where each voted to disenfranchise inmates.

73. See, e.g., Frymer, *Uneasy Alliances*; Vallely, *The Two Reconstructions*; Frances Fox Piven, "Structural Constraints and Political Development: The Case of the American Democratic Party," in *Labor Parties in Postindustrial Societies*, ed. Frances Piven (New York: Oxford University Press, 1992), 235–64. For the later period, see especially Edward G. Carmines and James A. Stimson, *Issue Evolution: Race and the Transformation of American Politics* (Princeton: Princeton University Press, 1989); and Robert Huckfeldt and Carol W. Kohfeld, *Race and the Decline of Class in American Politics* (Urbana: University of Illinois Press, 1989).

74. Perhaps surprisingly, we found no statistically significant interactions between political partisanship and time or region. This is likely due to the low statistical power to detect such effects in an analysis of state legal change.

75. Our political data are taken from Council of State Governments, *The Book of the States* (Lexington, Ky.: Council of State Governments, 1937–87); U.S. Bureau of the Census, *Statistical Abstract* (Washington, D.C.: Government Printing Office, 1980–2001); Inter-University Consortium for Political and Social Research, *Candidate Name and Constituency Totals, 1788–1990* (Ann Arbor: Inter-University Consortium for Political and Social Research, 1995).

76. In addition to using the U.S. census, we also draw data from U.S. Department of Justice, Bureau of Justice Statistics, *Historical Corrections Statistics in the United States, 1850–1984* (Washington, D.C.: Government Printing Office, 1987).

77. We use decennial-level state data, but each decade does not include 50 states because we excluded states from our data set until the decade of official statehood, regardless of a state's status as a recognized territory preceding statehood. In 1850, for example, the United States had only 31 states.

78. Some states that disenfranchised ex-felons changed their clemency eligibility criteria or processes, but these administrative changes generally affected few ex-felons and were not considered new laws in this analysis. We also did not consider a state to have a felon disenfranchisement law if its law disenfranchised only for conviction of a few narrowly defined crimes, such as treason or violation of election laws. We considered a state to have a felon disenfranchisement law when its law disenfranchised for felony convictions in general.

79. Although we estimated all models with both a linear time trend and separate dummy variables for each decade, a likelihood ratio test established that the set of time indicators representing time with the dummy variables improves the fit of the models. We therefore report tables using the more conservative dummy variable specification.

80. Since Blalock hypothesized a curvilinear relationship between minority group size and discrimination under some conditions, we also fit models with both linear and quadratic terms. See Blalock, *Toward a Theory of Minority-Group Relations*, 148–49. Although the squared term is not statistically distinguishable from zero in these models, a positive linear effect and negative second-order effect are consistent with the idea that the odds of disenfranchisement may diminish as the percentage of nonwhite prisoners reaches very high levels.

81. These trends are consistent with other models of legal diffusion. See, e.g., Lauren B. Edelman, "Legal Environments and Organizational Governance: The Expansion of Due Process in the American Workplace," *American Journal of Sociology* 95 (May 1990): 1401–40.

82. The Depression and World War II eras had no restrictive changes and are coded as part of the immediately preceding interval (e.g., the 1930s are considered within the 1910–49 period). See Paul Allison, *Survival Analysis Using the SAS System: A Practical Guide* (Cary, N.C.: SAS Institute, 1995), 226.

83. We used several models to estimate the effects of Democratic partisanship. Appendix table A2.4 models Democratic control as a single variable because interactions between region and partisanship (and more complex interactions among region, partisanship, and time) were not statistically significant.

84. See Behrens et al., "Ballot Manipulation and the 'Menace of Negro Domination,' " 587, table 6.

85. See, e.g., Eric Foner, *Reconstruction: America's Unfinished Revolution, 1863–1877* (New York: Harper and Row, 1988); Keyssar, *The Right to Vote*; Kousser, *The Shaping of Southern Politics*.

86. Because there are relatively few events to predict, we are limited to two-period models.

87. See Hench, "The Death of Voting Rights," 730.


## 3. The Disenfranchised Population

1. Voting rights are typically tied to felony convictions but not misdemeanors. Distinctions within these broad categories (e.g., between capital felonies and other felonies or between gross misdemeanors, petty misdemeanors, and violations) generally have little bearing on the right to vote.

2. Frederick Pollock and Frederic William Maitland trace the origins of the term "felon" to France. See Pollock and Maitland, *The History of English Law before the Time of Edward I,* 2nd ed. (Cambridge, England: Cambridge University Press, 1899), 462.

3. The technical details and actual practices of some state laws are confusing, even to state and local election officials. In unpublished research, Alec Ewald has found evidence that a number of states disenfranchise misdemeanants as well as felons. See his "A 'Crazy-Quilt' of Tiny Pieces: State and Local Administration of American Criminal Disenfranchisement Law," report prepared for the Sentencing Project, July 2005.

4. U.S. Department of Justice, *Felony Sentences in State Courts in 2002* (Washington, D.C.: Government Printing Office, 2004).

5. See U.S. Department of Justice, *Prisoners in the United States* (Washington, D.C.: Government Printing Office, 1980–2003).

6. See U.S. Department of Justice, *Probation and Parole in the United States* (Washington, D.C.: Government Printing Office, 1981–2004).

7. See U.S. Department of Justice, *Prevalence of Imprisonment in the U.S. Population, 1974–2001* (Washington, D.C.: Government Printing Office).

8. See Becky Pettit and Bruce Western, "Mass Imprisonment and the Life Course: Race and Class Inequality in U.S. Incarceration," *American Sociological Review* 69 (2004): 151–69.

9. See *Reentry Trends in the United States* (Washington, D.C.: U.S. Department of Justice).

10. For the estimates from the Sentencing Project, see Jamie Fellner and Marc Mauer, *Losing the Vote: The Impact of Felony Disenfranchisement Laws in the United States* (Washington, D.C.: Sentencing Project, 1998).

Demographers have developed techniques for estimating populations where an analyst can make an educated guess about factors such as mortality. Such life-table techniques provide the foundation for a rigorous—if imperfect—estimate of the size of the disenfranchised population. We therefore used life-table methods to produce a more rigorous estimate.

11. For our investigation, see Christopher Uggen and Jeff Manza, "Democratic Contraction? The Political Consequences of Felon Disenfranchisement in the United States," *American Sociological Review* 67 (2002): 777–803. A recent (April 2005) Google search turned up over 300 references to the 4.7 million figure.

12. See Patricia Allard and Marc Mauer, *Regaining the Vote: An Assessment of Activity Relating to Felon Disenfranchisement Laws* (Washington, D.C.: Sentencing Project, 1999); Velmer S. Burton, Francis T. Cullen, and Lawrence F. Travis III, "The Collateral Consequences of a Felony Conviction: A National Study of State Statutes," *Federal Probation* 51 (1986): 52–60; Fellner and Mauer, *Losing the Vote*; Marc Mauer, *Intended and Unintended Consequences: State Racial Disparities in Imprisonment* (Washington, D.C.: Sentencing Project, 1997). Kathleen M. Olivares, Velmer S. Burton, and Francis T. Cullen, "The Collateral Consequences of a Felony Conviction: A National Study of State Legal Codes Ten Years Later," *Federal Probation* 60 (1996): 10–17; U.S. Department of Justice Office of the Pardon Attorney, *Civil Disabilities of Convicted Felons: A State-by-State Survey* (Washington, D.C.: U.S. Government Printing Office, 1996).

13. The data on felons under supervision come from Justice Department publications, such as the *Correctional Populations in the United States* series.

14. See U.S. Department of Justice, *Probation and Parole in the United States, 2003* (Washington, D.C.: U.S. Government Printing Office, 2004).

15. Connecticut, Rhode Island, Vermont, Delaware, Alaska, and Hawaii combine their prison and jail systems. In such cases, we classify felons serving greater than one year as prisoners and felons with shorter sentences as jail inmates (taking 10 percent of the latter group to represent convicted felony jail inmates). For five states that do not distinguish felony and nonfelony probationers, we estimate that 50 percent of probationers are felons (a more conservative figure than the 52 percent national average). See U.S. Department of Justice, *Probation and Parole in the United States, 2000* (Washington, D.C.: U.S. Government Printing Office, 2001). Convicted felons who serve their sentences in jail represent a smaller but potentially important group not con-

sidered in prior estimates. As noted earlier, 28 percent of felony convictions today result in jail sentences. We therefore include a conservative estimate of the number of convicted felons in jail—10 percent of the total jail population.

16. See Fellner and Mauer, *Losing the Vote*; Mauer, *Intended and Unintended Consequences*.

17. Because these numbers are important and widely cited, we need to explain carefully how we derive them. Our data sources included a wide range of reports and data generated by the U.S. Department of Justice (USDOJ) that track both federal and state criminal population trends. The most important of these are the annual *Sourcebook of Criminal Justice Statistics* and *Correctional Populations in the United States* series, *Probation and Parole in the United States*, and *Prison and Jail Inmates at Midyear*. See Thomas P. Bonczar and Allen J. Beck, *Lifetime Likelihood of Going to State or Federal Prison*, Bureau of Justice Statistics special report (Washington, D.C.: Government Printing Office, 1997). For early years, we also referenced *National Prisoner Statistics*, and *Race of Prisoners Admitted to State and Federal Institutions, 1926–1986* (all of these are USDOJ publications). We determined the median age of released prisoners based on annual data from the National Corrections Reporting Program. We used recidivism data based on large-scale national samples of prison releasees and probationers to establish the number reincarcerated. See Peter B. Hoffman and Barbara Stone-Meierhoefer, "Reporting Recidivism Rates: The Criterion and Follow-up Issues," *Journal of Criminal Justice* 8 (1980): 53–60; Allen J. Beck and Bernard E. Shipley, *Recidivism of Prisoners Released in 1983*, U.S. Department of Justice Statistics, (Washington, D.C.: U.S. Government Printing Office). We then compiled demographic life tables for the period 1948–2004 to determine the number of released felons lost to recidivism (and therefore already included in our annual head counts) and to mortality each year. Each cohort of disenfranchised releasees is thus successively reduced each year, but joined by a new cohort of releasees. This allows us to compute the number of ex-felons no longer under correctional supervision for states that disenfranchise ex-felons.

18. U.S. Bureau of the Census, *Statistical Abstract of the United States* (Washington, D.C.: Government Printing Office, 1948–2000). Age-specific and year-specific mortality data were obtained from the *Statistical Abstract* series "Expectation of Life and Expected Deaths, by Race, Sex, and Age."

19. It is worth adding that at this writing, Florida (the state with by far the largest disenfranchised felon population) is in the midst of an intense debate over the future of its ex-felon ban. We discuss this debate more extensively in chapter 10.

20. We explain this distinction more clearly in chapter 7; the *voting age population*

(VAP) is everyone living legally in the United States over the age of 18, and is the standard denominator in the calculation of turnout rates. The *voting eligible population* (VEP) excludes legal immigrants, ineligible felons, and other smaller groups who are disenfranchised. See Michael P. McDonald and Samuel L. Popkin, "The Myth of the Vanishing Voter," *American Political Science Review* 95 (2001): 963–74.

21. For further discussion and documentation, see chapter 8.

22. That said, migration is likely to *increase* rather than decrease the disenfranchised population in most of these states. Ten of the 14 states that disenfranchise ex-felons have had net migration gains from 2000 to 2004. See Population Division, U.S. Census Bureau, Table 4: Cumulative Estimates of the Components of Population Change for the United States and States: April 1, 2000 to July 1, 2004 (NST-EST2004–04). According to the U.S. Department of Justice, *Restoring Your Right to Vote* (2000), those convicted in another state must still apply for restoration of voting rights in Alabama, Arizona, Delaware, Florida, Iowa, Kentucky, Maryland, Nebraska, Nevada, Tennessee, Virginia, Washington, and Wyoming. Only in Mississippi are those convicted in other states eligible to vote without receiving restoration from the state of conviction or Mississippi.

23. See Mauer and Fellner, *Losing the Vote*.

24. Senator Allen's remarks can be found in the *Congressional Record*, 107th Cong., 2nd sess., vol. 148, February 14, 2002, S806–07.

25. The underlying presumption behind this line of research is that individual-level factors may not account for the full extent of low turnout in the United States. For example, Americans have as much or more education on average than the citizens of any polity (and more than in earlier periods of American history with higher turnout). Further, their lack of interest in politics, low levels of political efficacy, or apparent apathy toward election outcomes may reflect the party system or the elitist character of political conflicts. See, e.g., Walter Dean Burnham, *The Current Crisis in American Politics* (New York: Oxford University Press, 1982); Richard Vallely, "Vanishing Voters," in *American Society and Politics*, ed. Theda Skocpol and John Campbell (New York: McGraw-Hill, 1995), 194–201; Frances Fox Piven and Richard A. Cloward, *Why Americans Don't Vote* (Boston: Beacon Press, 2002); National Commission on Electoral Reform, *To Ensure Pride and Confidence in the Electoral Process* (Charlottesville, VA.: Miller Center, 2001).

26. This is Ruy Teixeira's conclusion on the basis of an extensive review of previous studies. See Ruy A. Teixeira, *The Disappearing American Voter* (Washington, D.C.: Brookings Institution, 1992), 122.

27. For an overview of the differences in systems of voter registration and an

attempt to use crossnational evidence to estimate the impact of U.S. registration laws, see G. Bingham Powell, "American Voter Turnout in Comparative Perspective," *American Political Science Review* 80 (1986): 17–43.

28. The preamble to the National Voter Registration Act of 1993 says "discriminatory and unfair registration laws and procedures can have a direct and damaging effect on voter participation in elections for Federal office and disproportionately harm voter participation by various groups, including racial minorities." 42 U.S.C. §§ 1973gg(a)(3).

29. For example, the U.S. Supreme Court has held that states must meet a high burden to justify *any* restriction on the fundamental right to vote. The clearest example of this logic is found in cases abolishing poll tax requirements. In *Harper v. Virginia Board of Elections*, the Court held that poll taxes violated the equal protection clause of the Fourteenth Amendment. *Harper v. Virginia Board of Elections*, 383 U.S. 663 (1966). Another example can be seen in the Supreme Court's view of long residency requirements for registration. In *Dunn v. Blumstein*, the Court held that Tennessee's one-year residency requirement constituted an unreasonable restriction on the right to vote. See *Dunn v. Blumstein*, 405 U.S. 330 (1972). In this case, the Court ruled that state interests are limited to those related to a person's qualifications to vote, and that wealth and the ability to pay a poll tax were unrelated to legitimate qualifications. The Court noted that the law was overly broad and did not sufficiently further the state's claimed interests in preventing fraud and ensuring an informed electorate. To be sure, a residency requirement is not inherently unconstitutional, but the permissible length of such a requirement is somewhat ambiguous. The year after the *Dunn* decision, the Court upheld a 50-day residency requirement in *Marsten v. Lewis*, 410 U.S. 679 (1973).

30. Jill E. Simmons, "Beggars Can't Be Voters: Why Washington's Felon Reenfranchisement Law Violates the Equal Protection Clause," *Washington Law Review* 78 (2003): 297–333.

31. Just before the completion of this book, we saw a draft of Alec Ewald's fine report on state administrative practices, "A 'Crazy-Quilt' of Tiny Pieces."

32. Some very helpful online resources have now appeared, such as the website of the National Right to Vote Coalition, (www.righttovote.org) and the Lawyers Committee on Civil Rights' *Fifty-State Report on Re-enfranchisement: A Guide to Restoring Your Right to Vote,* available at: www.lawyerscomm.org. See also American Civil Liberties Union, *Purged! How a Patchwork of Flawed and Inconsistent Voting Systems Could Deprive Millions of the Right to Vote* (New York: American Civil Liberties Union, 2004).

33. State-specific information relating to restoration of voting rights in this section is drawn from the following sources: Marc Mauer and Tushar Kansal, *Barred*

*for Life: Voting Rights Restoration in Permanent Disenfranchisement States* (Washington, D.C.: Sentencing Project, 2005); Nkechi Taifa, *Re-enfranchisement! A Guide for Individual Restoration of Voting Rights in States that Disenfranchise Former Felons* (Washington D.C.: Advancement Project, 2002); and our own archival research.

Alabama: Ala. Code § 15–22–36 (2005); Ala. Code § 15–22–36 (2005); Ala. Code § 17–3–10 (2005); Ala. Code § 36–18–25(f) (2005); *Alabama Board of Pardons and Paroles Rules, Regulations, and Procedures,* available at: www.pardons.state.al.us/rules.html; Alabama Board of Pardons and Paroles, *Frequently Asked Questions,* available at: www.pardons.state.al.us/faq.html.

Arizona: Ariz. Const. art. VII, § 2; Ariz. Rev. Stat. § 13–905 (2005); Ariz. Rev. Stat. § 13–906 (2005) (applications by persons discharged from prison).

Delaware: Del. Const. art. V, § 2 (2005); Del. Const. art. VII, § 1 (2005); Del. Code tit. 11, § 4362 (2005); Del. Code tit.11, § 4362 (2005); Delaware Board of Pardons, *Rules of the Board of Pardons,* available at: www.state.de.us/sos/pardrules.html.

Florida: Fla. Const. art. IV, § 4; Fla. Const. art. IV, § 8; Fla. Stat. ch. 97.041 (2005); Fla. Stat. ch. 940.01 *et seq.* (2005); Fla. Stat. § 944.293 (2005); Florida Parole Commission, *Rules of Executive Clemency* (as revised December 2004), available at: https://fpc.state.fl.us/Clemency.htm; Office of Executive Clemency, *Information and Instructions on Applying for Restoration of Civil Rights,* available at: https://fpc.state.fl.us/PDFs/clemency/instructionsonforrcr.pdf; Abby Goodnough, "Disenfranchised Florida Felons Struggle to Regain Their Rights," *New York Times,* March 28, 2004; Debbie Cenziper and Jason Grotto, "Clemency Proving Elusive for Florida's Ex-Cons," *Miami Herald,* Oct. 31, 2004.

Iowa: Iowa Const. art. II, § 5; Iowa Code § 914.1 et seq (2005); Iowa Admin. Code §§ 205–14.3–14.4 (2005).

Kentucky: Ky. Const. § 145(1) (2005); Ky. Rev. Stat. § 196.045 (2005).

Maryland: Md. Const. art. II, § 4; Md. Code Ann., Election Law § 3–102 (2005).

Mississippi: Miss. Const. art. V, § 124; Miss. Const. art. XII, § 241; Miss. Const. art. XII, § 253; Miss. Code § 23–13–11 (2005); Miss. Code § 47–7–31 (2005); Miss. Code § 99–19–37 (2005).

Nebraska: Neb. Const. art. VI, § 2; Neb. Rev. Stat. § 29–112.01 (2005); Neb. Rev. stat. § 32–313 (2005); L.B 53, 2005 Leg., Reg. Sess. (Neb. 2005).

Nevada: Nev. Const. art. II, § 1 (2005); Nev. Rev. Stat. § 213.155 (2005); Nev. Rev. Stat. § 213.157 (2005).

Tennessee: Tenn. Const. art. IV, § 2 (2005); Tenn. Code 40–20–112 (2005); Tenn. Code 40–29–101 et seq. (2005).

Virginia: Va Const. art. II, § 1; Va Code § 53.1–231.1 (2005); Va Code § 53.1–231.2 (2005).

Washington: Wash. Const. art. VI, § 3 (2005); Wash. Rev. Code § 9.94A.637 (2005); Wash. Rev. Code § 9.94A.760 (2005); Wash. Rev. Code § 9.94A.885 (2005); Wash. Rev. Code § 9.96.010 (2005); Wash. Rev. Code § 9.94A.050 (2005).

Wyoming: Wyo. Const. art. VI, § 6 (2005); Wyo. Stat. § 6–10–106 (2005); Wyo. Stat. § 7–13–105 (2005); Wyo. Stat. § 7–13–803 (2005); Wyo. Stat. § 7–13–804 (2005).

34. See Mauer and Kansal, *Barred for Life: Voting Rights Restoration in Permanent Disenfranchisement States.*

35. In recent years, there have been growing demands that state departments of corrections aid ex-felons in navigating the restoration process, or at least notify state voting officials of persons who become eligible to regain their voting rights.

36. Among the offenses requiring such an evaluation are convictions for an act causing death, a sexual offense, kidnapping, arson, first- or second-degree burglary, robbery, offenses related to children and incompetents, cruelty to animals, abusing a corpse, unlawful use of explosives, child abuse, distribution of a controlled substance to a minor, and an attempt to commit any of these offenses. Del. Code tit. 11 § 4362 (2005).

37. Iowa Code §. 914.3 (2005).

38. Abby Goodnough, "Disenfranchised Florida Felons Struggle to Regain Their Rights," *New York Times,* March 28, 2004, 1.

39. Prior to Governor Tom Vilsack's issuance of a blanket clemency on July 4, 2005, Iowa required an explanation for either decision.

40. We obtained figures on state releases from supervision from USDOJ Bureau of Justice Statistics sources, including *Prisoners and Jail Inmates at Midyear, Probation and Parole in the United States,* and *Sourcebook of Criminal Justice Statistics.* Unlike our estimates of the total disenfranchised population, the estimate of felons released during the period is not reduced for recidivism or mortality.

41. See especially the ACLU report, *Purged,* for these details.

42. "Felon Voting Laws Confused, Ignored," staff report, *Seattle Times,* May 22, 2005, 1.

43. Goodnough, "Disenfranchised Florida Felons Struggle to Regain Their Rights."

44. The following discussion contains materials from a publicly available expert witness report that we prepared that examined how some of the procedures outlined earlier operate in Florida and discussed the influence of race and class upon this process, as well as various secondary sources.

45. Debbie Cenziper and Jason Grotto, "Clemency Proving Elusive," *Miami Herald*, October 31, 2004; Jason Grotto and Debbie Cenziper, "The Long Road to Clemency," *Miami Herald*, November 7, 2004.

46. Stephen Raines, a South Florida parole examiner from 1991 to 1998, quoted in Grotto and Cenzipper, "The Long Road to Clemency."

47. Cenziper and Grotto, "Clemency Proving Elusive."

48. Cenziper and Grotto, "Clemency Proving Elusive."

49. Jason Grotto and Debbie Cenzipper, "Victims Have Say before the Board," *Miami Herald*, November 7, 2004.

50. Cenziper and Grotto, "Clemency Proving Elusive."

51. Mauer and Kansal, *Barred for Life*, 10.

52. Debbie Cenzipper and Jason Grotto, "Clemency Revisions Restore Rights to Felons," *Miami Herald*, December 10, 2004.

53. Debbie Cenzipper and Jason Grotto, "Ending Ban on Felon Vote Clears Hurdle," *Miami Herald*, April 20, 2005.

54. Gary Kane and Scott Hiaasen, "Clemency Process Unfair to Blacks?" *Palm Beach Post*, December 23, 2001, A1.

55. Our investigation resulted from service as an expert witness in a lawsuit (*Johnson v. Bush*) in the state of Florida over the state's ex-felon disenfranchisement law, originally filed in the federal district court for the Southern District of Florida. See *Johnson v. Bush, 214 F. Supp. 2nd 1331* (S.D. Fla 2002); *Johnson v. Governor of Florida*, 353 F. 3d. 1287 (11th Cir. 2003), *vacated en banc* 377 F. 3d 1163 (11th Cir. 2004). A copy of our full report is publicly available from the original trial court.

56. Scott Hiaasen, "Cabinet Expands Clemency Eligibility," *Palm Beach Post*, June 15, 2001, B7.


4. *The Contemporary Disenfranchisement Regime*

1. See U.S. Department of Justice, *Prison and Jail Inmates at Midyear* (Washington, D.C.: Government Printing Office, 1997–2005).

2. Whether rising rates of incapacitation reduce criminal activity is a hotly debated proposition. See, e.g., Alfred Blumstein and Joel Wallman, eds., *The Crime Drop in America* (New York: Cambridge University Press, 2000), for a good selection of scholarly analyses of the sources of declining crime since the 1990s. There may be some very modest impact of rising incarceration on crime rates, but it is at best a piece of a much larger puzzle.

3. See U.S. Department of Justice, *Felony Sentences in the United States, 1992*

(Washington, D.C.: Government Printing Office, 1996), and U.S. Department of Justice, *Felony Sentences in State Courts, 2002.*

4. See, for example, David Garland, ed., *Mass Incarceration: Social Causes and Consequences* (Newbury Park, Calif.: Sage, 2001); Mary Pattillo, David Weiman, and Bruce Western, eds., *Imprisoning America: The Social Effects of Mass Incarceration* (New York: Russell Sage Foundation, 2004); Michael Jacobson, *Downsizing Prisons: How to Reduce Crime and End Mass Incarceration* (New York: New York University Press, 2005).

5. Christopher Uggen, Jeff Manza, and Melissa Thompson, "Citizenship, Democracy, and the Civic Reintegration of Criminal Offenders," *The Annals of the American Academy of Political and Social Science* (forthcoming).

6. For excellent comparative research on incarceration, see John Sutton, "Imprisonment and Social Classification in Five Common-Law Democracies, 1955–1985," *American Journal of Sociology* 106 (2000): 350–86; and "The Political Economy of Imprisonment in Affluent Western Democracies, 1960–1990," *American Sociological Review* 69 (2004) 170–89; and Joachim J. Savelsberg, "Knowledge, Domination, and Criminal Punishment," *American Journal of Sociology* 99 (1994): 911–43.

7. See David J. Rothman, *Conscience and Convenience: The Asylum and Its Alternatives in Progressive America* (New York: de Gruyter, 2002).

8. See U.S. Department of Justice, *Truth in Sentencing in State Prisons.*

9. See U.S. Department of Justice, *Time Served in Prison by Federal Offenders, 1986–97* (Washington, D.C.: Government Printing Office, 1999).

10. See Naomi Murakawa, *Punitive Race-to-the-Top: Elections, Race, and the Mandatory Minimum Electoral Staircase,* unpublished manuscript, University of Washington, Department of Political Science, 2005.

11. Pub. L. No. 103-322, 108 Stat. 1796 (September 13, 1994). The misleading name of the measure (Violent Crime Control and Law Enforcement Act of 1994) implies incorrectly that it is solely targeted at violent offenders. For a dissection of sentencing minimums, see Michael Tonry, "Rethinking Unthinkable Punishment Policies in America," *UCLA Law Review* 46 (1999): 1751–92.

12. See U.S. Department of Justice, *Truth in Sentencing in State Prisons* (Washington, D.C.: Government Printing Office, 1999).

13. See U.S. Department of Justice, *Felony Sentences in State Courts, 2002* (Washington, D.C.: Government Printing Office, 2004) and *Sourcebook of Criminal Justice Statistics, 1991,* 544.

14. Jeremy Travis, *Beyond the Prison Gates: The State of Parole in America* (Washington, D.C: Urban Institute, 2002).

15. U.S. Department of Justice, *Cross-National Studies in Crime and Justice*, ed. David P. Farrington, Patrick A. Langan, and Michael Tonry (Washington, D.C.: Government Printing Office, 2004).

16. Note in reading figure 4.6 that the recent increases in conviction rates in Australia give a somewhat misleading portrait of the overall picture.

17. David Garland, *The Culture of Control* (Chicago: University of Chicago Press, 2002).

18. Joachim Savelsberg, "Knowledge, Domination, and Criminal Punishment," *American Journal of Sociology* 99 (1994): 911–43; David Jacobs and Ronald E. Helms, "Toward a Political Model of Incarceration: A Time-Series Examination of Multiple Explanations for Prison Admission Rates," *American Journal of Sociology* 102 (1996): 323–57; Katherine Beckett, *Making Crime Pay: The Politics of Law and Order in the Contemporary United States* (New York: Oxford University Press, 1997).

19. Jacobs and Helms, "Toward a Political Model of Incarceration."

20. Thomas Edsall, *Chain Reaction: The Impact of Race, Rights, and Taxes on American Politics* (New York: Norton, 1991); Donald Sears and Lynn Sanders, *Divided by Race* (Chciago: University of Chicago Press, 1996).

21. Biden in *Congressional Record* 103 (August 24, 1994), p. S12427. This passage is quoted in Alec Ewald, "An 'Agenda for Demolition': The Fallacy and Danger of the 'Subversive Voting' Argument for Felony Disenfranchisement," *Columbia Human Rights Law Review* 36 (2005): 109–43, at 140.

22. Michael Tonry, *Malign Neglect: Race, Crime, and Punishment in America* (New York: Oxford University Press, 1995), chap. 5; Marc Mauer, *Race to Incarcerate* (New York: New Press, 1999), chap. 8.

23. Robert Martinson, "What Works? Questions and Answers about Prison Reform," *Public Interest* 35 (1974): 22–54. James Q. Wilson, *Thinking about Crime* (New York: Basic Books, 1975).

24. Garland, *The Culture of Control.*

25. Savelsberg, "Knowledge, Domination, and Criminal Punishment."

26. Sutton, "Imprisonment and Social Classification in Five Common-Law Democracies, 1955–1985."

27. Generally up to three problems mentioned by respondents are recorded. It is important to note that these items are recoded after the survey into neat categories that do not necessarily correspond to the meaning intended by the respondent.

28. Katherine Beckett, *Making Crime Pay: Law and Order in Contemporary American Politics* (New York: Oxford University Press, 1997); Katherine Beckett and Theodore Sasson, *The Politics of Injustice: Crime and Punishment in America* (Thousand Oaks, Calif.: Pine Forge Press, 2000); and Elaine Sharp, *The*

*Sometime Connection: Public Opinion and Social Policy* (Albany: State University of New York Press, 1999), chap. 2.

29. "Terrorism" as a source of public fear appears to have a similar dynamic. After the events of September 11, 2001, terrorism begins to register as an important problem for a growing number of Americans. Even in this case, however, the percentage of respondents identifying terrorism as the most important problem has fluctuated dramatically, from 22 percent in March 2002 to 10 percent in 2003, to 13 percent in 2004.

30. Robert Entman and Andrew Rojacki, *The Black Image in the White Mind* (Chicago: University of Chicago Press, 2001), chaps. 4–5. An instructive point of comparison is with media depictions of the race of welfare recipients, carefully traced by Martin Gilens in *Why Americans Hate Welfare* (Chicago: University of Chicago Press, 1999), chaps. 5–6.

31. Perhaps the leading work in this area has been that of David Jacobs and his colleagues. Jacobs and Ronald Helms, for example, have highlighted the role of different kinds of race-based political conflicts, partisan politics, and sociodemographic factors. See Jacobs and Helms, "Toward a Political Model of Incarceration"; "Testing Coercive Explanations for Order: The Determinants of Law Enforcement Strength over Time," *Social Forces* 75 (June 1997): 1361–92; and "Collective Outbursts, Politics, and Punitive Resources: Toward a Political Sociology of Spending on Social Control," *Social Forces* 77 (June 1999): 1497–1523.

### 5. Political Attitudes, Voting, and Criminal Behavior

1. The notion of the felony conviction as a "negative credential" is developed in Devah Pager, "The Mark of a Criminal Record," *American Journal of Sociology* 108 (2003): 937–75.

2. A number of major media outlets have recently taken up the question. See for example, Fox Butterfield, "Freed from Prison, but Still Paying a Price," *New York Times,* December 29, 2002, A18. Even political conservatives, not known for their concern about the well-being of ex-offenders, have gotten into the act. See Stephen Greenhouse, "Conservatives' New Cause: Jobs for Ex-Convicts," *New York Times,* December 13, 2002, A29. See also n. 8 to the introduction.

3. For other work on the trajectories of ex-felons, see, e.g., Robert Sampson and John Laub, *Crime in the Making: Pathways and Turning Points through Life* (Cambridge: Harvard University Press, 1993), and *Shared Beginnings, Divergent Lives* (Cambridge: Harvard University Press, 2003); Christopher Uggen,

"Work as a Turning Point in the Life Course of Criminals: A Duration Model of Age, Employment, and Recidivism," *American Sociological Review* 65 (2000): 529–46.

4. Earlier investigations of the social, civic, and political views of criminal offenders would include Erik Olin Wright, *The Politics of Punishment: A Critical Analysis of Prisons in America* (New York: Harper, 1973); Stuart A. Brody, "The Political Prisoner Syndrome: Latest Problem of the American Penal System," *Crime and Delinquency* 20 (1974): 97–106; Milton Burdman, "Ethnic Self-Help Groups in Prison and on Parole," *Crime and Delinquency* 20 (1974): 107–18; Erika S. Fairchild, "Politicization of the Criminal Offender: Prisoner Perceptions on Crime and Politics," *Criminology* 15 (1977): 287–318.

5. See e.g. John Earl Haynes, *Dubious Alliance: The Making of Minnesota's DFL Party* (Minneapolis: University of Minnesota Press, 1984).

6. For comparative information on state incarceration rates, see U.S. Department of Justice, *Sourcebook of Criminal Justice Statistics, 2003* (Washington, D.C.: U.S. Government Printing Office, 2004), 497. For information on racial composition and educational attainment, see U.S. Bureau of the Census, *Statistical Abstract of the United States: 2003* (Washington, D.C.: U.S. Government Printing Office, 2004), 25, 155.

7. For discussion of Jesse Ventura's campaign and time in office see Tom Hauser, *Inside the Ropes with Jesse Ventura* (Minneapolis: University of Minnesota Press, 2002), and Jesse Ventura, *I Ain't Got Time to Bleed: Reworking the Body Politic from the Bottom Up* (New York: Penguin, 2000).

8. The classical work is that of the "Michigan School"; see especially Angus Campbell, Philip E. Converse, Warren E. Miller, and Donald Stokes, *The American Voter* (New York: Wiley, 1960); and Converse's famous treatment of the ideological inconsistency of most Americans in "The Nature of Belief Systems in the Mass Public," in *Ideology and Discontent*, ed. David Apter (New York: Free Press, 1964), 206–61.

9. The argument that higher levels of education and the increasing availability of information about politics and the news are increasing citizens' knowledge and political capacities was made most forcefully by Norman H. Nie, Sidney Verba, and John R. Petrocik, *The Changing American Voter*, 2nd ed. (Cambridge: Harvard University Press, 1979); and Ronald Inglehart, *Culture Shift in Advanced Industrial Society* (Princeton: Princeton University Press, 1990), esp. chap. 10. Critiques of the "we're-getting-politically-smarter" idea can be found in Michael X. Delli Carpini and Scott Keeter, *What Americans Know about Politics and Why It Matters* (New Haven: Yale University Press, 1996); and Eric R.A.N. Smith, *The Unchanging American Voter* (Berkeley: University

of California Press, 1989). Examples of public ignorance are taken from Delli Carpini and Keeter, *What Americans Know about Politics and Why It Matters,* chap. 1. The textbook quotation is from Glynn Carroll, Susan Herbst, Garrett O'Keefe, and Robert Shapiro, *Public Opinion* (Boulder, Colo.: Westview Press, 1999), 251.

10. See Clem Brooks and Simon Cheng, "Declining Government Confidence and Policy Preferences in the U.S.: Devolution, Regime Effects, or Symbolic Change?" *Social Forces* 79 (2001): 1343–75; Joseph S. Nye, Philip D. Zelikow, and David C. King, eds., *Why People Don't Trust Government* (Cambridge: Harvard University Press 1997); and Marc J. Hetherington, *Why Trust Matters: Declining Political Trust and the Demise of American Liberalism* (Princeton: Princeton University Press, 2004).

11. The most influential statement of the importance of discourse was Jurgen Habermas, *The Structural Transformation of the Public Sphere* (Cambridge: MIT Press, 1989). For more recent varieties of the argument about deliberation, see e.g. James Fishkin, *Democracy and Deliberation* (New Haven: Yale University Press, 1991); Jean Bethke Elshtain, *Democracy on Trial* (New York: Basic Books, 1995); Amy Guttman and Dennis Thompson, *Democracy and Disagreement* (Cambridge: Harvard University Press, 1996); cf. Michael Schudson, "Why Conversation Is Not the Soul of Democracy," *Critical Studies in Mass Communication* 14 (1997): 297–309.

12. Nina Eliasoph, *Avoiding Politics* (New York: Cambridge University Press, 1998).

13. On the current status of rehabilitation programs, see Ann Chih Lin, *Reform in the Making: The Implementation of Social Policy in Prisons* (Princeton: Princeton University Press, 1999). On the opportunities for intellectual growth in prison, see Kathryn Edin, Timothy Nelson, and Rechelle Paranal, "Fatherhood and Incarceration as Potential Turning Points in the Criminal Careers of Unskilled Men," in *The Impact of Incarceration on Families and Communities,* ed. Mary Patillo, David Weiman, and Bruce Western (New York: Russell Sage, 2003), 46–75; see also Shadd Maruna, *Making Good: How Ex-Convicts Reform and Rebuild Their Lives* (Washington, D.C.: American Psychological Association, 2001), "Going Straight: Desistance from Crime and Self-Narratives of Reform," *Narrative Study of Lives* 5 (1997): 59–97, and "Desistance and Development: The Psychosocial Process of 'Going Straight,' " in *Emerging Issues in British Criminology,* ed. M. Brogden (Belfast: British Society of Criminology, 1999).

14. See *The Autobiography of Malcolm X*, assisted by Alex Haley (New York: Grove Press, 1965), 180, 182 (quotations); Sanyika Shakur, *Monster: The Autobiography*

*of an L.A. Gang Member* (New York: Viking Penguin, 1994), 341 (quotation); and Jack Henry Abbott, *In the Belly of the Beast: Letters from Prison* (New York: Vintage, 1981).

15. On the development of new identities while in prison, see Maruna, *Making Good*; and our own discussion in Christopher Uggen, Jeff Manza, and Angela Behrens, "Stigma, Role Transition, and the Civic Reintegration of Convicted Felons," in *After Crime and Punishment: Ex-Offender Reintegration and Desistance from Crime*, ed. Shadd Maruna and Russ Immarigeon (Albany: State University of New York Press, 2004), 261–93; Lin, *Reform in the Making*, 144–51; John Irwin, *The Felon* (Englewood Cliffs, N.J.: Prentice-Hall, 1970).

16. On prison riots as a form of collective action, see especially Bert Useem and Peter Kimball, *States of Siege: U.S. Prison Riots, 1971–86* (New York: Oxford University Press, 1991), and Jack Goldstone and Bert Useem, "Prison Riots as Microrevolutions: An Extension of State-Centered Theories of Revolution," *American Journal of Sociology* 104 (1999): 985–1029. The rise and decline of prisoners' rights movements is traced in James B. Jacobs, "The Prisoners' Rights Movement and Its Impact, 1960–80," *Crime and Justice* 2 (1980): 429–70; and Christopher Smith, "Black Muslims and the Development of Prisoners' Rights," *Journal of Black Studies* 24 (1993): 131–46.

17. See Zachary R. Dowdy, "Prisoners Forming Mass. PAC," *Boston Globe,* August 2, 1997, Metro/Region sec., A1; Regina Montague, "Ballot Question Would Not Ban Vote by Inmates, Critics Say Wording Erroneous, Rights Would Be Limited," *Boston Globe,* October 2, 2000, Metro/Region sec., B1.

18. As Todd Clear and colleagues point out, much of the research on prisons and religion has been narrowly focused on recidivism effects. Religion appears to have more immediate benefits to inmates in promoting safety, self-esteem, and combating their "devaluation." See Todd R. Clear, Patricia L. Hardyman, Bruce Stout, Karol Lucken, and Harry R. Dammer, "The Value of Religion in Prison: An Inmate Perspective," *Journal of Contemporary Criminal Justice* 16 (2000): 53–74.

19. For details about the YDS study, see Jeylan T. Mortimer, *Working and Growing Up in America* (Cambridge: Harvard University Press, 2003)

20. A substantial majority of crimes that lead to arrests and felony convictions are committed in urban areas. See for example U.S. Department of Justice, *Sourcebook of Criminal Justice Statistics, 2002* (Washington, D.C.: U.S. Government Printing Office, 2003), 373–74.

21. To place these figures in context, we present some comparative information about the national inmate population in the next chapter. See also U.S. Department of Justice, *Survey of Inmates in State and Federal Correctional Facil-*

*ities, 1997,* computer file (Ann Arbor: Inter-University Consortium for Political and Social Research, 2000).

22. In addition to the material presented hereafter, see also Lucia Benaquisto and Peter J. Freed, "The Myth of Inmate Lawlessness: The Perceived Contradiction Between Self and Other in Inmates' Support for Criminal Justice Sanctioning Norms," *Law and Society Review* 30 (1996): 481–511.

23. See for example Gabriel Almond and Sidney Verba, *The Civic Culture* (Boston: Little, Brown, 1963); and Sidney Verba, Kay L. Scholzman, and Henry E. Brady, *Voice and Equality* (Cambridge: Harvard University Press, 1995).

24. The importance of networks in shaping voting behavior was first in the work of Paul Lazarsfeld, Bernard Berelson, and Helen Gaudet, *The People's Choice* (New York: Columbia University Press, 1948), and Bernard Berelson, Paul Lazarsfeld, and William McPhee, *Voting* (Chicago: University of Chicago Press, 1954). For more recent treatment, see Robert Huckfeldt and John Sprague, *Citizens, Politics, and Social Communication* (New York: Cambridge University Press, 1995); and Verba et al., *Voice and Equality*.

25. It is likely that at least part of this turnout gap is due to the legal disenfranchisement of arrestees due to ongoing criminal sanctions. In Minnesota, those convicted of felonies may not vote until after they have completed probation or parole supervision, in addition to any prison sentence. Unfortunately, we lack data indicating whether an individual was under correctional supervision at the time of the election.

26. Since better educated and more affluent citizens are more likely to report voting, and criminal offenders have levels of income and education significantly below those of nonoffenders, some of the differences between the two groups may reflect sociodemographic differences (see chapter 7).

27. Sampson and Laub, *Crime in the Making*; Uggen, "Work as a Turning Point in the Life Course of Criminals."

28. On adult role transition, see Frank Furstenberg, Jr., Sheela Kennedy, Vonnie G. McCloyd, Ruben G. Rumbaut, and Richard A. Settersten, Jr., "Becoming an Adult: The Changing Nature of Early Adulthood," *Contexts* 3 (2004): 33–41; Michael J. Shanahan, "Pathways to Adulthood in Changing Societies: Variability and Mechanisms in Life Course Perspective," *Annual Review of Sociology* 26 (2000): 667–92.

29. Maruna, *Making Good: How Ex-Convicts Reform and Rebuild Their Lives*; Neal Shover, *Great Pretenders: Pursuits and Careers of Persistent Thieves* (Boulder, Colo.: Westview Press, 1996).

30. Sampson and Laub, *Crime in the Making*.

31. Maruna, *Making Good*, 88. On work, see Robert Sampson and John Laub,

"Crime and Deviance Over the Life Course: The Salience of Adult Social Bonds," *American Sociological Review* 55 (1990): 609–27; Uggen, "Work as a Turning Point." For family, see John Laub, Daniel Nagin, and Robert Sampson, "Trajectories of Change in Criminal Offending: Good Marriages and the Desistance Process," *American Sociological Review* 63 (1998): 225–38.

32. Christopher Uggen, Jeff Manza, and Melissa Thompson, "Citizenship, Democracy, and the Civic Reintegration of Criminal Offenders," *The Annals of the American Academy of Political and Social Science* (forthcoming in 2006).

33. It is possible, in fact, that work and family roles may even be subsumed within a much more general master role as a "law-abiding adult citizen."

34. T. H. Marshall, *Citizenship and Social Class* (Cambridge, England: Cambridge University Press, 1950).

35. See, e.g., Christopher Uggen and Michael Massoglia, "Desistance from Crime and Deviance as a Turning Point in the Life Course," in *Handbook of the Life Course*, ed. Jeylan T. Mortimer and Michael Shanahan (New York: Plenum, 2002); Christopher Uggen and Sara Wakefield, "Young Adults Reentering the Community from the Criminal Justice System: Challenges to Adulthood," in *On Your Own without a Net: The Transition to Adulthood for Vulnerable Populations*, ed. D. Wayne Osgood, E. Michael Foster, Constance Flanagan, and Gretchen R. Ruth (Chicago: University of Chicago Press, 2005); U.S. Department of Justice, *Survey of State Prison Inmates, 1991* (Washington, D.C.: Government Printing Office, 1993); U.S. Department of Justice, *Survey of Inmates in State and Federal Correctional Facilities, 1997*.

36. Maruna, *Making Good*, 97.

37. Kathryn Edin, Timothy Nelson, and Rechelle Parnal, "Fatherhood and Incarceration as Potential Turning Points in the Criminal Careers of Unskilled Men," in *Imprisoning America: The Social Effects of Mass Incarceration*, ed. Mary Pattillo, David Weiman, and Bruce Western (New York: Russell Sage, 2003), 46–75.

38. David A. Snow and Leon Anderson, "Identity Work among the Homeless: The Verbal Construction and Avowal of Personal Identities," *American Journal of Sociology* 92 (1987): 1336–71.

39. Social psychologists have long suggested that people generally seek to create and maintain stable and coherent identities. See Michael Schwartz and Sheldon Stryker, *Deviance, Selves and Others* (Washington, D.C.: American Sociological Association, 1970), 15. Albert K. Cohen described this process as becoming "hooked" on a role in *Deviance and Control* (Englewood Cliffs, N.J.: Prentice-Hall, 1966), 101; Peggy C. Giordano, Stephen A. Cernkovich, and Jennifer L. Rudolph use the term "hooks for change" in a somewhat different

sense in their "Gender, Crime, and Desistance: Toward a Theory of Cognitive Transformation," *American Journal of Sociology* (2002): 990–1064.

40. We develop a social-psychological model of this process in Uggen, Manza, and Behrens, "Stigma, Role Transition, and the Civic Reintegration of Convicted Felons," in *After Crime and Punishment.* Some of the fundamental assumptions of this model are that people seek stable and coherent identities, that these identities are motivational and can impel behavior, and that identities are fixed or stabilized by role commitments. Although identity shifts may appear to occur rapidly among convicted persons, role commitments and the relative salience of these identities will only change gradually after sustained social interaction. See Schwartz and Stryker, "Deviance, Selves and Others."

41. Some of the rights and opportunities potentially affected by a felony conviction include immigration status, marital dissolution, military service, occupation, parental rights, privacy, public housing, public office, and public assistance. Gabriel J. Chin, "Race, the War on Drugs, and the Collateral Consequences of Criminal Conviction," *Journal of Gender, Race, and Justice* 6 (2002): 253–75; Walter Matthews Grant, John LeCournu, John Andrews Pickens, Dean Hill Rivkin, and C. Roger Vinson, "The Collateral Consequences of a Criminal Conviction," *Vanderbilt Law Review* (1970): 929–1241; Brian C. Kalt, "The Exclusion of Felons from Jury Service," *American University Law Review* 53 (2003): 65–189; Marc Mauer and Meda Chesney-Lind, eds., *Invisible Punishment: The Collateral Consequences of Mass Imprisonment* (New York: New Press, 2002); Office of the Pardon Attorney, *Federal Statutes Imposing Collateral Consequences upon Conviction* (Washington, D.C.: United States Department of Justice, 2000); Kathleen M. Olivares, Velmer S. Burton, Jr., and Francis T. Cullen, "The Collateral Consequences of a Felony Conviction: A National Study of State Legal Codes Ten Years Later," *Federal Probation* 60 (1997): 10–17; Andrea Steinacker, "The Prisoner's Campaign: Felony Disenfranchisement Laws and the Right to Hold Public Office," *Brigham Young University Law Review* (2003): 801–28.

42. Jeremy Travis, "Invisible Punishment: An Instrument of Social Exclusion," in *Invisible Punishment: The Collateral Consequences of Mass Imprisonment,* ed. Mauer and Chesney-Lind, 15–36.

43. For recent collections of essays on these collateral consequences, see Mauer and Chesney-Lind, *Invisible Punishment*; Christopher Mele and Teresa A. Miller, eds., *Civil Penalties, Social Consequences* (New York: Routledge, 2005); and *Journal of Contemporary Criminal Justice* 21 (February 2005), special issue, "Collateral Consequences of Criminal Sanctions."

44. For studies of the wide range of social settings, including families, in which a felony conviction introduces informal barriers to reintegration, see Mary

Pattillo, Bruce Western, and David Weiman, eds., *Incarceration and Families* (New York: Russell Sage, 2003).

45. Judith Shklar, *American Citizenship* (Cambridge: Harvard University Press, 1991), pt. 1.

46. John Stuart Mill, *Essays on Politics and Society: Collected Works*, ed. J. M. Robson (London: Routledge, 1977); Carol Pateman, *Participation and Democratic Theory* (New York: Cambridge University Press, 1970); Benjamin Barber, *Strong Democracy* (Berkeley: University of California Press, 1984).

47. See Mill, *Essays on Politics and Society;* Alexis de Tocqueville, *Democracy in America*, trans. G. Lawrence (Garden City, N.Y.: Doubleday, 1969; orig. pub. 1835).

48. Gabriel Almond and Sidney Verba, *The Civic Culture: Political Attitudes and Democracy in Five Countries* (Princeton: Princeton University Press, 1963); Lester Milbraith and M. L. Goel, *Political Participation,* 2nd ed. (Chicago: Rand McNally, 1977); and W. Kent Jennings and Richard Niemi, *Generations and Politics* (Princeton: Princeton University Press, 1981). For further discussion of this point, see M. Margaret Conway, *Political Participation in the United States*, 3rd ed. (Washington, D.C.: Congressional Quarterly Press, 2000), 185–86.

49. On expressive voting, see Adam Winkler, "Expressive Voting," *New York University Law Review* 68 (1993): 330–88; Alexander Schuessler, *A Logic of Expressive Choice* (Princeton: Princeton University Press, 2000); and Dennis F. Thompson, *Just Elections* (Chicago: University of Chicago Press, 2001), chap. 1. On the communitarian arguments about the benefits of participation, see Alasdair McIntyre, *After Virtue: A Study in Moral Theory* (Notre Dame, Ind.: University of Notre Dame Press, 1981); Michael Sandel, *Liberalism and the Limits of Justice* (New York: Cambridge University Press, 1982); Sanford Levinson, *Constitutional Faith* (Princeton: Princeton University Press, 1988); and Frank Michelman, "Conceptions of Democracy in American Constitutional Argument: Voting Rights," *Florida Law Review* 41 (1989): 443–90.

50. Winkler, "Expressive Voting," 331.

51. Pateman, *Participation and Democratic Theory*, 14.

52. Barber, *Strong Democracy;* Jurgen Habermas, *The Structural Transformation of the Public Sphere: An Inquiry into a Category of Bourgeois Society* (Cambridge: MIT Press, 1989); Susan Herbst, *Politics at the Margins: Historical Studies of Political Expression outside the Mainstream* (New York: Cambridge University Press, 1994); Nina Eliasoph, *Avoiding Politics: How Americans Produce Apathy in Everyday Life* (New York: Cambridge University Press, 1998).

53. Doug McAdam, *Freedom Summer* (New York: Oxford University Press, 1988).

54. There are longitudinal studies such as the National Longitudinal Study of Youth or the Panel Study of Income Dynamics that include some information about criminal background, but these surveys do not include information about political participation. The handful of election panel studies, such as the panels associated with the American National Election Study, do not include any information about criminal history.

55. Jeylan T. Mortimer, *Working and Growing Up in America* (Cambridge: Harvard University Press, 2003).

56. While this approach cannot firmly establish political participation as a cause of desistance from crime, it allows us to rule out some of the most compelling alternative reasons for the correlation.

57. U.S. Bureau of the Census, *Reported Voting and Registration, BY Sex and Age, for States: November 1996* (Washington, D.C.: U.S. Government Printing Office, 1998), available at: www.census.gov/population/socdemo/voting/96cps/tab4B.txt. A number of methodological issues are raised by reliance on self-reported turnout. Some nonvoting survey respondents claim to have voted, although overreporting rates tend to be higher among better educated and more privileged groups with much lower levels of criminal activity. See Robert Bernstein, Anita Chadha, and Robert Montjoy, "Overreporting Voting: Why It Happens and Why It Matters," *Public Opinion Quarterly* 65 (2001): 22–44, esp. 41.

58. As in other longitudinal surveys, race and family income are associated with sample attrition in the YDS. In supplementary analysis, however, we found no evidence that estimates reported here are biased by sample selectivity or attrition. For example, the magnitude and direction of the voting effects appear to be consistent across income and racial groups, although the estimated standard errors are larger, and fewer of the relationships are statistically significant in the subgroup analyses. More complete information about YDS sample attrition can be found in Mortimer, *Working and Growing Up in America*, 36, and further details about the crime measures are reported in Christopher Uggen and Jennifer Janikula, "Volunteer Work and Arrest in the Transition to Adulthood," *Social Forces* 78 (1999): 331–62, at 337.

59. See e.g. David Huizinga and Delbert S. Elliott, "Reassessing the Reliability and Validity of Self-Report Delinquency Measures," *Journal of Quantitative Criminology* 2 (1986): 293–327, at 323.

60. U.S. Bureau of the Census, *Statistical Abstract of the United States: 2002* (Washington D.C.: Government Printing Office, 2003), 253; U.S. Department of Justice, *Sourcebook of Criminal Justice Statistics 2002* (Washington D.C.: Government Printing Office, 2003), 354–56.

61. Christopher Uggen and Jeff Manza, "Democratic Contraction? The Political

Consequences of Felon Disenfranchisement in the United States," *American Sociological Review* 67 (2002): 791; U.S. Department of Justice, *Survey of Inmates in State and Federal Correctional Facilities, 1997.*

62. For details, see Christopher Uggen and Jeff Manza, "Voting and Subsequent Crime and Arrest: Evidence from a Community Sample," *Columbia Human Rights Law Review* 35 (2004): 193–215.

63. When the crime items are examined individually, or added in a summative scale and analyzed using ordinary least squares regression, we find similar results: a large bivariate relationship is partially mediated by indicators of socioeconomic status (mainly education) and prior official and self-reported criminal behavior. Regardless of the particular crime outcome we examined, the voting effect is consistently negative in direction, but does not consistently reach standard levels of statistical significance in the final models that include all of the relevant statistical controls.

## 6. Disenfranchisement and Civic Reintegration

1. The use of in-depth interviews to explore political attitudes has a long history. See especially the classical work of Robert Lane, *Political Ideology* (New York: Free Press, 1962); and more recently, William Gamson, *Talking Politics* (New York: Cambridge University Press, 1992). For historically informed critiques of the limitations of survey research to measure individual opinions, see Susan Herbst, *Numbered Voices: How Opinion Polling Has Shaped American Politics* (Chicago: University of Chicago Press, 1993); and Taeku Lee, *Mobilizing Public Opinion: Black Insurgency and Racial Attitudes in the Civil Rights Era* (Chicago: University of Chicago Press, 2002), esp. chap. 3.

2. To be sure, there is clear evidence of a growing political gender gap in the United States; for a broad overview, see Jeff Manza and Clem Brooks, *Social Cleavages and Political Change*, chap. 5. Surely there are important policy and partisan differences between men and women offenders; but our focus does not center on such differences.

3. Minn. §253B.02 Subd. 18b–18c.

4. See Jonathan Casper, *American Criminal Justice: The Defendant's Perspective* (Englewood Cliffs, N.J.: Prentice-Hall, 1972); Lucia Benaquisto and Peter J. Freed, "The Myth of Inmate Lawlessness: The Perceived Contradiction between Self and Other in Inmates' Support for Criminal Justice Sanctioning Norms," *Law and Society Review* 30 (1996): 481–511.

5. See Martin Wattenberg, *The Rise of Candidate-Centered Politics* (Cambridge: Harvard University Press, 1991).

6. It is also important to keep in mind the point we made at the beginning of this chapter about the major (but perhaps temporary) impact the governorship of political independent Jesse Ventura had on our respondents at the time we spoke to them.

7. In response to specific questions about party affiliations, those who classified themselves as "independents" often mentioned independent political parties, whereas those who were unfamiliar with political parties responded with "I don't know." Many respondents referred to themselves as independent thinkers but still indicated a preference for either the Republican or (more typically) the Democratic Party. For analysis of the complexities of political "independence" in American politics, see Bruce Keith et al., *The Myth of the Independent Voter* (Berkeley: University of California Press, 1991).

8. These findings are broadly similar to the results of surveys comparing African Americans and whites' views about the criminal justice system. See, e.g., Devon Johnson, "Punitive Attitudes on Crime: Economic Insecurity, Racial Prejudice, or Both?" *Sociological Focus* 34 (2001): 33–54.

9. Unlike most job-seekers, felons often lack the "weak ties" that most people rely upon for jobs. See Mark S. Granovetter, "The Strength of Weak Ties," *American Journal of Sociology* 78 (1973): 1360–80; Harry Holzer, Steven Raphael, and Michael Stoll, "Will Employers Hire Former Offenders?" in *Imprisoning America: The Social Effects of Mass Incarceration*, ed. Mary Pattillo, David Weiman, and Bruce Western (New York: Russell Sage, 2003); Devah Pager, "The Mark of a Criminal Record" (Ph.D. diss., University of Wisconsin–Madison, 2002); Christopher Uggen, "Ex-Offenders and the Conformist Alternative: A Job Quality Model of Work and Crime," *Social Problems* 46 (1999): 127–51.

10. Philippe Bourgois, *In Search of Respect: Selling Crack in El Barrio* (New York: Cambridge University Press, 1995); John Hagan, "The Social Embeddedness of Crime and Unemployment," *Criminology* 31 (1993): 465–91; Mercer L. Sullivan, *Getting Paid: Youth Crime and Work in the Inner City* (Ithaca, N.Y.: Cornell University Press, 1989).

11. Cf. Kathryn Edin, Laura Lein, and Timothy Nelson, "Taking Care of Business: The Economic Survival Strategies of Low-Income Non-custodial Fathers," in *The Low Wage Labor Market*, ed. Frank Munger (New York: Russell Sage Foundation, 2001).

12. Amnesty International, *"Not Part of My Sentence": Violations of the Human Rights of Women in Custody* (New York: Amnesty International, 1999); Sandra Enos, *Mothering from the Inside: Parenting in a Women's Prison* (Albany: State University of New York Press, 2001); Kathryn Gabel and Denise Johnston, eds., *Children of Incarcerated Parents* (San Francisco: Jossey-Bass, 1995); John

Hagan and Ronit Dinovitzer, "Collateral Consequences of Imprisonment for Children, Communities, and Prisoners," *Crime and Justice* 26 (2000): 121–62; Barbara E. Smith and Sharon Goretsky Elstein, *Children on Hold: Improving the Response to Children Whose Parents Are Arrested and Incarcerated* (Washington, D.C.: ABA Center on Children and the Law, 1994); U.S. Department of Justice, Bureau of Justice Statistics, *Incarcerated Parents and Their Children* (Washington, D.C.: Government Printing Office, 2000).

13. We report interview findings on work and family reintegration in Christopher Uggen, Jeff Manza, and Angela Behrens, "Stigma, Role Transition, and the Civic Reintegration of Convicted Felons," in *After Crime and Punishment: Ex-Offender Reintegration and Desistance from Crime*, ed. Shadd Maruna and Russ Immarigeon (Portland: Willan Publishing, 2004), 261–93.

14. This paradox, popularized by Anthony Downs's classic 1957 work *An Economic Theory of Democracy* (New York: Harper, 1957), has bedeviled rational choice theories of politics; for some examples of the recent debates, see John H. Aldrich, "Rational Choice and Turnout," *American Journal of Political Science* 37 (1993): 246–78; Donald P. Green and Ian Shapiro, *Pathologies of Rational Choice* (New Haven: Yale University Press, 1994), 47–71.

15. See Kathryn Edin, Timothy J. Nelson, and Rechelle Paranal, "Fatherhood and Incarceration as Potential Turning Points," in Pattillo, Weiman, and Western, *Imprisoning America*, 46–75.

16. See, e.g., Gordon Bazemore, "Restorative Justice and Earned Redemption: Communities, Victims, and Offender Reintegration," *American Behavioral Scientist* 41 (1998): 768–813.

17. Harrison M. Trice and Paul M. Roman, "Delabeling, Relabeling, and Alcoholics Anonymous," *Social Problems* 17 (1970): 538–46.


*7. The Impact of Disenfranchisement on Political Participation*

1. These studies have generally tried to get at the consequences of felon disenfranchisement for turnout rates by estimating the average impact across the states, looking in particular to see if states with higher levels of turnout have lower rates of participation. For an example, see Thomas J. Miles, "Felon Disenfranchisement and Voter Turnout," *Journal of Legal Studies* 33 (January 2004): 85–129; and Paul Hirschfield, "Losing the Prize: Assessing the Impact of Felon Disenfranchisement Laws on Black Male Voting Participation," unpublished paper presented at the annual meeting of the Law and Society Association, Chicago, June 1999.

2. Alexander Keyssar, *The Right to Vote: The Contested History of Democracy in*

*the United States* (New York: Basic Books, 2000), 308. See also Christian R. Grose and Antoine Yoshinaka, "Electoral Institutions and Voter Participation: The Effect of Felon Disenfranchisement Laws on Voter Turnout in the U.S. Southern States, 1984–2000," unpublished paper presented at the annual meeting of the American Political Science Association, Boston, September 2002.

3. Two recent elections stand out for having had slightly higher turnout: the 1992 presidential election, the first campaign of the two campaigns by Texas billionaire H. Ross Perot, achieved a 55 percent turnout rate, sandwiched between a 50.1 percent turnout rate in 1988 and a 49.8 percent turnout in 1996; and the 2002 midterm congressional election had a turnout of 39.4 percent, up from only 32.9 percent in 1998.

4. International Institute for Democracy and Electoral Assistance, *Voter Turnout from 1945 to 1997: A Global Report* (Stockholm: International Institute for Democracy and Electoral Assistance, 1997).

5. For a recent survey of these debates, see Jeff Manza, Clem Brooks, and Michael Sauder, "Money, Participation, and Votes: Social Cleavages and Electoral Politics," in *Handbook of Political Sociology*, ed. Thomas Janoski, Margaret Schwartz, Robert Alford, and Alexander Hicks (New York: Cambridge University Press, 2005), 201–26.

6. It is important to note that lower turnout rates have been shown to be associated with *larger* gaps in turnout rates among higher and lower participation groups. In countries with very high participation rates (turnout rates of 80 percent or more are common in many European democracies, for example), nonvoters tend to be spread more evenly across the entire population. Some of the differences between groups in turnout rates are explained by the fact that better educated or more affluent voters, in particular, are more likely to incorrectly report having voted to pollsters or survey researchers. See Robert Bernstein, Anita Chadha, and Robert Montjoy, "Overreporting Voting: Why It Happens and Why It Matters," *Public Opinion Quarterly* 65 (spring 2001): 22–44. Nonetheless, we would expect to find a relatively greater gap between voting rates among felons and nonfelons than in many other democracies with more universal rates of political participation.

7. Harold F. Gosnell, *Getting out the Vote: An Experiment in the Stimulation of Voting* (Chicago: University of Chicago Press, 1927), 98.

8. Sidney Verba, Kay Lehman Schlozman, and Henry E. Brady, *Voice and Equality* (Cambridge: Harvard University Press, 1995); Raymond Wolfinger and Steven Rosenstone, *Who Votes?* (New Haven: Yale University Press, 1980), chap. 2; and Ruy Teixiera, *The Disappearing American Voter* (Washington D.C.: Brookings Institute, 1992).

9. See especially Margaret Conway, *Political Participation* (Washington, D.C.: Congressional Quarterly Press, 2000) for a summary of these factors. For an overview of some of the massive turnout literatures and the sources of group-based differences, see Arend Lijphart, "Unequal Participation: Democracy's Unresolved Dilemma," *American Political Science Review* 91 (1997): 1–14.

10. U.S. Department of Justice, *Survey of State Prison Inmates, 1991* (Washington, D.C.: Government Printing Office, 1993); U.S. Department of Justice, *Survey of Inmates of State Correctional Facilities* Series, *1974–1997* (Washington D.C.: U.S. Bureau of the Census, 2000).

11. U.S. Bureau of the Census, *Statistical Abstract of the United States* (Washington, D.C.: Government Printing Office, 2000), 157.

12. U.S. Department of Justice, *Trends in State Parole, 1990–2000* (Washington, D.C.: Government Printing Office, 2001).

13. For fuller description of our methods and results, see our earlier article "Democratic Contraction? The Political Consequences of Felon Disenfranchisement in the United States," *American Sociological Review* 67 (2002): 777–803.

14. The most important work on the life-courses of criminal offenders is that of John H. Laub and Robert J. Sampson, *Shared Beginnings, Divergent Lives: Delinquent Boys to Age Seventy* (Cambridge: Harvard University Press, 2003), and *Crime in the Making: Pathways and Turning Points through Life* (Cambridge: Harvard University Press, 1993). Following a group of delinquent and nondelinquent boys from childhood to age 70, Laub and Sampson establish that almost all criminal offenders eventually desist from crime. Moreover, a great number go on to build relatively stable work and family lives.

15. The most forceful presentation of this argument—perhaps too strong—can be found in Michael R. Gottfredson and Travis Hirschi, *A General Theory of Crime* (Stanford: Stanford University Press, 1990).

16. Uggen and Manza, "Democratic Contraction," 791.

17. These figures are not adjusted for respondents' overreporting of their actual rate of participation, but since we are not concerned here with the absolute size of the vote (as we are in trying to estimate national turnout rates) we can safely disregard the differences. Note also that overall turnout in Minnesota in the 2000 election was 69 percent, suggesting that overreporting in the YDS is comparable to that of the CPS.

18. More details about the YDS analysis are presented in Uggen and Manza, "Democratic Contraction."

19. See for example Robert Putnam's widely discussed work on declining social capital in the United States, which identifies declining voter turnout as a key empirical example. *Bowling Alone* (New York: Simon and Shuster, 2000), chap. 2.

20. Richard Brody identified this as a key analytical puzzle in "The Puzzle of Non-Participation," in *The New American Political System*, ed. Anthony King (Washington D.C.: American Enterprise Institute, 1978), 291–99.

21. Michael P. McDonald and Samuel Popkin, "The Myth of the Vanishing Voter," *American Political Science Review* 95 (2001): 963–74. An updated time-series is available from the authors at: http://elections.gmu.edu/Voter_Turnout_2004.htm.

22. The work of Bruce Western and Katherine Beckett on the effects of incarceration on unemployment rates highlights this issue nicely, and indeed has significantly influenced our discussion here. They consider the possibility that low unemployment rates in the United States are artificially being pushed down by high incarceration rates. They estimate a gross accounting impact, but then reduce this by taking into account below–average expected employment rates for the incarcerated population. See their article "How Unregulated Is the U.S. Labor Market? The Penal System as a Labor Market Institution," *American Journal of Sociology* 104 (1999): 1030–60.

23. Miles, "Felon Disenfranchisement and Voter Turnout," quotations at 85 and 118.

24. For example, race and gender categories may not provide comparison groups that would identify the causal effect of disenfranchisement laws. Miles also limited his analysis to ex-felon disenfranchisement rather than felon voting restrictions more generally, and it assumed stability in the restrictions and their impact over a long period. In addition, several states were excluded from the analysis because of insufficient data.

25. For intriguing evidence of this possibility, see Ernest Drucker and Ricardo Berreras, "Studies of Voting Behavior and Felony Disenfranchisement among Individuals in the Criminal Justice System in New York, Connecticut, and Ohio," unpublished manuscript, Montefiore Medical Center, September 2005.

## 8. A Threat to Democracy?

1. The speech can be found in the *Congressional Record*, 107th Cong., 2nd sess., vol. 148, U.S. Senate (debate on Equal Protection of Voting Rights Act of 2001), February 14, 2002, S802 (quotation). The reference to jailhouse blocs parallels Judge Henry Friendly's famous remark about the dangers of Mafiosi electing sheriffs, which we quoted earlier in chapter 1. See *Green v. Board of Elections of the City of New York*, 380 F. 2d 445 (1967).

2. The distinction made by Dennis Thompson between "just elections" and "legitimate elections" is useful here. See Dennis F. Thompson, *Just Elections:*

*Creating a Fair Electoral Process in the United States* (Chicago: University of Chicago Press, 2002). Thompson suggests that "The results of an election may be accepted as legitimate because the procedures are regarded as legitimate, but the procedures may still not be just. Nothing illustrates more vividly the difference between a legitimate and a just election than the reactions of Americans to the controversy over the presidential contest of 2000. Not only did an overwhelming majority accept George Bush as the legitimate president, a substantial majority of those who voted for Al Gore did too. This was so even though a majority of the electorate still preferred Gore" (2).

3. The case for studying institutional practice in relation to democratic theory is made forcefully in Ian Shapiro, *The State of Democratic Theory* (Princeton: Princeton University Press, 2003); see also Robert Dahl, *How Democratic Is the American Constitution?* (New Haven: Yale University Press, 2003); Charles R. Beitz, *Political Equality* (Princeton: Princeton University Press, 1989), chap. 1, and Thompson, *Just Elections*. For a good discussion of the concept of "group" interests as it has developed in electoral law, see Keith Bybee, *Mistaken Identity: The Supreme Court and the Politics of Marginalized Representation* (Princeton: Princeton University Press, 1998); and Heather Gerken, "Understanding the Right to an Undiluted Vote," *Harvard Law Review* 114 (2001): 1663–1743.

4. The literature on the problem of minority group representation is enormous, and beyond the scope of this chapter. For some important treatments, see: Lani Guinier, *Tyranny of the Majority* (New York: Free Press, 1994); Melissa S. Williams, *Voice, Trust and Memory: Marginalized Groups and the Failing of Liberal Representation* (Princeton: Princeton University Press, 1998); and Bybee, *Mistaken Identity;* Pamela S. Karlan, "The Rights to Vote: Some Pessimism About Formalism," *Texas Law Review* 71 (1993): 1705–40; Samuel Issacharoff, "Groups and the Right to Vote," *Emory Law Journal* 44 (1995): 869–909; and Gerken, "Understanding the Right to an Undiluted Vote."

5. For some information about the issue of military ballots, see New York Times, *Thirty-Six Days: The Complete Chronicle of the 2000 Presidential Election Crisis* (New York: Times Books, 2001).

6. David Barstow and Don Van Natta, Jr. "How Bush Took Florida: Mining the Overseas Absentee Vote," *New York Times*, July 15, 2001, A1.

7. There are of course elite models of democracy that rest on a different conceptualization: for example, democratic centralism in Leninist theories of party governance. See chapter 1 for more details and examples.

8. *Trop v. Dulles*, 356 U.S. 86, 92 (1956) (noting that "citizenship is not a license that expires upon misbehavior").

9. Among the key cases were: *Reynolds v. Sims,* 377 U.S. 533 (1964); *Wesberry v. Sanders,* 376 U.S. 1 (1964); and *Baker v. Carr,* 369 U.S. 186 (1962).

10. Stephen Ansolabehere, Alan Gerber, and James Synder, "Equal Votes, Equal Money: Court–Ordered Redistricting and Public Expenditures in the American States," *American Political Science Review* 96 (December 2001): 767–77, esp. 767. This study presents convincing evidence that the "natural experiment" of redrawing the legislative map to create equipopulation districts did result in a significant net transfer of state spending from rural to urban districts. The importance of the *Baker* et al. decisions were well understood at the time; one authoritative casebook suggests that "*Baker* was perhaps the most profoundly destabilizing opinion in the Supreme Court's history." Samuel Issacharoff, Pamela S. Karlan, and Richard H. Pildes, *The Law of Democracy: Legal Structure of the Political Process,* (Westbury, N.Y.: Foundation Press, 1998), 134.

11. *Shaw v. Reno,* 509 U.S. 630 (1993); *Miller v. Johnson,* 515 U.S. 90 (1995); *Shaw v. Hunt,* 517 U.S. 899 (1996).

12. *Easley v. Cromartie,* 532 U.S. 234 (2001).

13. See, e.g., *Davis v. Bandemer,* 478 U.S. 109 (1986); *Baker v. Carr,* 369 U.S. 186 (1962); *Colgrove v. Green,* 328 U.S. 549 (1946).

14. This last comment clearly becomes less obvious as we move further away from national elections and toward local elections in urban areas, where a far greater proportion of the population would be disenfranchised because of a felony conviction, as compared to national or state-level electoral contests. Because we focus in this chapter on the latter types, however, we are less concerned about that possibility.

15. Our test in this comparison is very conservative, at least for the 1960 Kennedy/ Nixon contest, because we are comparing gross disenfranchisement rates between 1960 and 2000. Because the actual 1960 disenfranchisement rate includes a large number of states with ex-felon bans that had repealed them by 1980, the difference between the disenfranchisement rates in the two years are lower. If we held constant the changes in laws (as we did in chapter 3), we would have a much larger difference.

16. In applying the counterfactual to the Electoral College for 1960, our analysis suggests that Nixon would likely have been victorious in New Mexico (with four electoral votes) but would have lost by more narrow margins in other close states. It is likely that Nixon might have beaten Kennedy in the popular vote but unlikely that he would have won in the Electoral College.

17. Louisiana is the only state that requires a runoff for Senate elections when no candidate receives an outright majority of the votes.

18. Because 2004 election data were not available as we finished this book, we estimate Florida turnout at 30 percent and Democratic preference at 70 percent, figures in line with previous elections.

19. Note, "The Disenfranchisement of Ex-felons: Citizenship, Criminality, and 'the Purity of the Ballot Box,' " *Harvard Law Review* 102 (1989): 1303.

20. Georgia's state constitution disenfranchised "until the granting of pardon" until 1983, when its constitution was amended to restore voting rights upon "completion of this sentence."

21. Of the 32 U.S. Senate elections in 1978, for example, the incumbent party retained the seat through at least 1990 in 29 cases (91 percent), through at least 1996 in 27 cases (84 percent), and through at least 2002 in 23 cases (72 percent). To be certain, advantages of incumbency are significantly lower in Senate than in House elections. On this and other aspects of Senate elections, see especially Alan I. Abramowitz and Jeffrey A. Segal, *Senate Elections* (Ann Arbor: University of Michigan Press, 1992), esp. chap. 3.

22. For a trenchant overview of the political transformation of the South in Congressional elections, see Ira Katznelson, "Reversing Southern Republicanism," in *The New Majority: Toward a Popular Progressive Politics*, ed. Stanley B. Greenberg and Theda Skocpol (New Haven: Yale University Press, 1997), 238; see also Earl Black and Merle Black, *Politics and Society in the South* (Cambridge: Harvard University Press, 1987).

23. E.g., Gregory Palast, "Florida's 'Disappeared Voters': Disenfranchised by the GOP," *Nation*, February 5, 2001, 20. Mary Ellen Klas, Debbie Cenziper, and Erika Bolstad, "State Drops Felon-Voter List," *Miami Herald*, July 11, 2004, 1A; "Thousands of Eligible Voters on Florida Purge List," National Public Radio broadcast, July 2, 2004. Brennan Center for Justice, "Legal Groups Notify Florida Secretary of State that 'Potential Felon' Purge List Violates State and Federal Law," press release, July 8, 2004. For a scholarly analysis, see Guy Stuart, "Databases, Felons, and Voting: Bias and Partisanship of the Florida Felons List in the 2000 Election," *Political Science Quarterly* 119 (2004): 453–75.

24. See e.g. Lisa Arthur, Geoff Dougherty, and William Yardley, "452 Felons Cast Votes Illegally in Broward," *Miami Herald*, January 23, 2002; David Kidwell, Phil Long, and Geoff Dougherty, "Hundreds of Felons Cast Votes Illegally," *Miami Herald*, December 1, 2000; Jessica McBride and Linda Spice, "Felons Turn Up on City's List of November 7 Voters: Spot Check Shows at Least Two Appear Ineligible for Ballots," *Milwaukee Journal-Sentinal*, November 29, 2000; "Special Report: Felons Vote Too—But It's a Crime," *Miami Herald*, February 15, 1998. Seattle Times staff, "Toss out Felon Vote: Gregoire Still Wins," *Seattle Times*, May 22, 2005.

25. Jessica McBride, "Felon Voting Numbers Surprise Officials," *Milwaukee Journal-Sentinel,* January 12, 2001; Joni James, Jamie Thompson, and Saundra Amrhein, "GOP: Florida Felons Already Voting," *St. Petersburg Times,* October 29, 2004.

26. We will never know for certain whether the true illegal felon votes were sufficient to throw the 2004 Washington governor's race to Democrat Christine Gregoire, but that was in an extraordinary close (129–vote margin) election.

27. Janine DeFao, "Many Felons Surprised They Get to Vote," *San Francisco Chronicle,* October 6, 2004, B3.

28. Alec Ewald, "A 'Crazy-Quilt' of Tiny Pieces: State and Local Administration of American Criminal Disenfranchisement Law," report prepared for the Sentencing Project, June 2005. See also Ernest Drucker and Ricardo Berreras, "Studies of Voting Behavior and Felony Disenfranchisement among Individuals in the Criminal Justice System in New York, Connecticut, and Ohio," unpublished manuscript, Montefiore Medical Center, September 2005.

29. See U.S. Department of Justice, *Prison and Jail Inmates at Midyear 2003* (Washington, D.C.: Government Printing Office, 2004), 8.

30. See Eric Lotke and Peter Wagner, "Prisoners of the Census: Electoral and Financial Consequences of Counting Prisoners Where They Go, Not Where They Come From," *Pace Law Review* 4 (2004): 587–607.

31. Rose Heyer and Peter Wagner, *Too Big to Ignore: How Counting People in Prisons Distorted Census 2000* (New York: Prison Policy Intiative, 2004).

32. Beitz, *Political Equality,* 5.

33. By embracing a law-and-order agenda in the 1990s, Democrats attempted to neutralize crime as a partisan political issue. Research decomposing the unique contribution of crime policy to individual vote choice to determine whether the votes gained by such strategies outweigh the votes lost with the disenfranchisement of potential Democratic voters is still lacking. We should note, however, that returning the right to vote to those people convicted of a felony is not necessarily inconsistent with a crime control agenda. One may advocate extending the franchise on public safety and reintegration grounds, arguing that those who become stakeholders in their communities will have lower rates of recidivism. We take up such questions in chapters 9 and 10.

34. We should note that in many local races, especially in mostly black urban districts, the partisan impact of felon disenfranchisement might be diminished because Republican candidates are already uncompetitive in these districts.

1. For our own previous effort, from which this chapter draws, see Jeff Manza, Clem Brooks, and Christopher Uggen, "Public Attitudes Toward Felon Disenfranchisement Laws in the United States," *Public Opinion Quarterly* 68 (summer 2004): 276–87. See also Brian Pinaire and Milton Heumann, "Barred from the Vote: Public Attitudes toward Felon Disenfranchisement of Felons," *Fordham Urban Law Journal* 30 (2003): 1519–50.
2. John DiIulio, "Are Voters Fools? Crime, Public Opinion, and Representative Democracy," *Corrections Management Quarterly* 1 (1997): 1–5, quotation at 2.
3. Elaine B. Sharp, *The Sometime Connection: Public Opinion and Public Policy* (Albany: State University of New York Press, 1999), chap. 2.
4. Katherine Beckett, *Making Crime Pay* (New York: Oxford University Press, 1997), and "Political Preoccupation with Crime Leads, Not Follows, Public Opinion," in *Penal Reform in Overcrowded Times*, ed. Michael Tonry (New York: Oxford University Press, 2001), 40–45.
5. William J. Bowers, Margaret Vandiver, and Patricia H. Dugan, "A New Look at Public Opinion on Capital Punishment: What Citizens and Legislators Prefer," *American Journal of Criminal Law* 22 (1994): 77–150; Frances T. Cullen, Bonnie S. Fisher, and Brandon K. Applegate, "Public Opinion about Punishment and Corrections," *Crime and Justice: A Review of Research* 27 (2000): 10–25. The Cullen et al. survey of public opinion data on crime has heavily shaped our interpretation in this paragraph.
6. Peter Rossi and Richard H. Berk, *Just Punishments: Federal Guidelines and Public Views Compared* (New York: de Gruyter, 1997).
7. See the review of the relevant survey-based literature in Cullen et al., "Public Opinion about Punishment and Corrections," 47–57.
8. See, e.g., James Davis, "Communism, Conformity, Cohorts, and Categories: American Tolerance in 1954 and 1972–1973," *American Journal of Sociology* 81 (1975): 491–513; Tom W. Smith, "Liberal and Conservative Trends in the United States since World War II," *Public Opinion Quarterly* 54 (1990): 479–507; Robert Erikson and Kent Tedin, *American Public Opinion,* 5th ed. (Boston: Allyn and Bacon, 1995). The broader political significance of these opinion trends is discussed in Clem Brooks, "Civil Rights Liberalism and the Suppression of a Republican Political Realignment in the United States, 1972 to 1996," *American Sociological Review* 65 (2000): 483–505.
9. See Clyde Nunn, Harry Crockett, Jr., and Allen Williams, Jr., *Tolerance for Nonconformity: A National Survey of Americans' Changing Commitment to Civil Liberties* (San Francisco: Jossey-Bass, 1978); Benjamin Page and Robert Sha-

piro, *The Rational Public: Fifty Years of Trends in Americans' Policy Preference.* (Chicago: University of Chicago Press, 1992); Thomas C. Wilson, "Trends in Tolerance toward Rightist and Leftist Groups, 1976–1988: Effects of Attitude Change and Cohort Succession," *Public Opinion Quarterly* 58 (1994): 539–56.

10. See Howard Schumann, Charlotte Stech, Lawrence Bobo, and Maria Kryson, *Racial Attitudes in America,* 2nd ed. (Cambridge: Harvard University Press, 1997).

11. See Myra Marx Ferree, "A Woman for President? Changing Responses: 1958–1972," *Public Opinion Quarterly* 38 (1974): 390–99; Arland Thornton and Deborah Freedman, "Changes in the Sex Role Attitudes of Women, 1962–1977: Evidence from a Panel Study," *American Sociological Review* 44 (1979): 831–42; Karen Mason and Yu-Hsia Lu, "Attitudes toward Women's Familial Roles: Changes in the United States, 1977–1985," *Gender and Society* 2 (1988): 9–57.

12. See especially Shmuel Lock, *Crime, Public Opinion, and Civil Liberties* (Westport, Conn.: Praeger, 1998), chap. 3.

13. See, e.g., Greg Shaw, Robert Y. Shapiro, Shmuel Lock, and Lawrence R. Jacobs, "The Polls: Crime, the Police, and Civil Liberties," *Public Opinion Quarterly* 62 (1998): 405–26.

14. Our survey items were fielded in Harris Interactive's regular monthly omnibus telephone survey. Care was taken to ensure that question-order effects were minimized.

15. First states, then counties, then minor civil divisions were selected, with probability of selection proportionate to the U.S. Census Bureau estimates of the population. A telephone number was dialed at least four times before a new telephone number was generated for that area. Once a residential contact was established, the interviewer used the "youngest adult male/oldest adult female" procedure for selecting a respondent in the household for the interview. At least one additional call-back was made to convert refusals into completed interviews, and the interviews were conducted using a computer–assisted telephone interviewing (CATI) system.

16. The response rate quoted here (39 percent) is based on the standard Harris Interactive calculation. The calculation is not, however, a simple one. Determining what number belongs in the denominator in an age of multiple household phone lines, modem lines, fax lines, and so on is complicated. A more technical presentation of the response rate calculation is presented in Manza et al., "Public Attitudes towards Felon Disenfranchisment," 277. There we estimated the response rate at between 29 percent and 38 percent, using the American Association of Public Opinion Research standard. However calculated, this response rate is typical of telephone surveys these days, partially

reflecting the explosion of call screening, cell phones (which are off-limits to survey researchers), and phone numbers used for modems, fax machines, and other business purposes.

17. Converse's thesis about nonattitudes was based on an NES panel in the late 1950s that found that most respondents did not maintain ideologically consistent responses to repeated survey questions when asked at different points in time. See "The Nature of Belief Systems in Mass Publics," in *Ideology and Discontent*, ed. David Apter (New York: Free Press, 1964), 206–64.

18. G. William Domhoff, *Who Rules America?* 4th ed. (Boston: McGraw Hill, 2001); See also Pierre Bourdieu, "Public Opinion Does Not Exist," in A. Matelart and S. Siegelaub, eds., *Communication and Class Struggle*, vol. 1 (New York: International General, 1979), 124–30; Susan Herbst, *Numbered Voices: How Public Opinion Has Shaped American Politics* (Chicago: University of Chicago Press, 1993).

19. John Zaller, *The Nature and Origins of Mass Opinion* (New York: Cambridge University Press, 1992); John Zaller and Stanley Feldman, "A Simple Theory of the Survey Response: Answering Questions versus Revealing Preferences," *American Journal of Political Science* 36 (1992): 579–616.

20. Zaller's "receive-accept-sample" model of individual respondents' processing of political information and responding to survey questions assumes a dominant role for elites in framing the issues and providing the range of choices in the minds of citizens/survey respondents. This aspect of his argument cuts against a strong interpretation of the independent causal role of opinion in the sense that it is elites who do the framing of issues. See Robert Y. Shapiro, "Public Opinion, Elites, and Democracy," *Critical Review* 12 (1998): 501–28; Taeku Lee, *Mobilizing Public Opinion: Black Insurgency and Racial Attitudes in the Civil Rights Era* (Chicago: University of Chicago Press, 2002).

21. See e.g. John A. Ferejohn and James H. Kuklinski, eds., *Information and Democratic Processes* (Urbana: University of Illinois Press, 1990); Dennis Chong, *Rational Lives: Norms and Values in Politics and Society* (Chicago: University of Chicago Press, 1999); Arthur Lupia, Mathew D. McCubbins, and Samuel L. Popkin, eds., *Elements of Reason: Cognition, Choice, and the Bounds of Rationality*, (New York: Cambridge University Press, 2000). While the cognitive models provide an elegant and hopeful view of poorly informed citizenry, they do not necessarily exhaust the problem suggested by the Converse thesis. Low information, even when heuristic shortcuts are available, may distort citizens' expressed policy preferences in significant ways, and better informed citizens are also equipped with the tools to resist elite influences.

22. Page and Shapiro, *The Rational Public*.

23. See e.g. Paul Sniderman and Douglas Grob, "Innovations in Experimental

Design in Attitude Surveys," *Annual Review of Sociology* 22 (1996): 377–99; Donald Kinder, "Communication and Opinion," *Annual Review of Political Science* 1 (1998):167–87; and William Gamson, *Talking Politics* (New York: Cambridge University Press, 1992).

24. The *t*-score for comparing these two proportions is-1.35, under the critical 1.96 value for rejecting the null hypothesis ($\alpha_{.05}$, 2-tailed test).

25. We emphasize that these four items all refer to *ex*-felons (i.e., individuals who have served their entire prison sentence); the earlier results suggest low levels of public support for currently-incarcerated individuals, and this second set of items thus enables us to probe further how variability in the details of ex-felons' criminal convictions affect individual attitudes.

26. Sarah J. Brown, "Public Attitudes towards the Treatment of Sex Offenders," *Legal and Criminological Psychology* 4 (1999): 239–52; Philip Jenkins, *Moral Panic: Changing Concepts of the Child Molester in Modern America* (New Haven: Yale University Press, 1998).

27. In 2001, there were an estimated 386,112 offenders in state sex offender registries, representing 6 percent of the 6.6 million persons under correctional supervision. U.S. Department of Justice, *Sourcebook of Criminal Justice Statistics* (Washington, D.C.: Government Printing Office, 2001); U.S. Department of Justice, *Press Release: U.S. Correctional Population Reaches 6.6 Million* (Washington, D.C.: Government Printing Office, 2002). In 1994, approximately 234,000 offenders convicted of rape or sexual assault were under correctional supervision, with about 60 percent serving sentences in the community. U.S. Department of Justice, *Sex Offenses and Sex Offenders* (Washington, D.C.: Government Printing Office, 1997).

28. See, for example, Paul Burstein, Shawn Bauldry, and Paul Froese, "Public Opinion and Congressional Support for Policy Change," paper presented at the annual meeting of the American Political Science Association, San Francisco, September 2001.

*10. Unlocking the Vote*

1. Alec Ewald, *Punishing at the Polls: The Case against Disenfranchising Citizens with Felony Convictions* (New York: Demos Foundation, 2003), 34. See also Alex Keyssar, *The Right to Vote* (New York: Basic Books, 2000).

2. The executive order immediately reinstated voting rights for all current ex-felons (98,000 by our estimate in chapter 3) and will automatically restore rights for people released from supervision from now on. The state Department of Corrections will forward a list of names to the governor's office on

a monthly basis. Nevertheless, Govenor Vilsack's successor could sign another executive order overturning the first, which would apply to future ex-felons but not those who have just regained their rights. We thank Marc Mauer for clarifying these details.

3. In the interests of full disclosure, we should note that we received a grant from the Open Society Institute to support part of the research reported in this book.

4. See the Right to Vote website, at www.righttovote.org.

5. Mauer is the author of a widely cited work on the incarceration boom, *Race to Incarcerate* (New York: New Press, 1999), and coeditor, with Meda Chesney-Lind, of *Invisible Punishment: The Collateral Consequences of Mass Imprisonment* (New York: New Press, 2002).

6. In social network theory, the Sentencing Project (and Marc Mauer) would be classified as a hub of the network. A network diagram of the movement and its participants would look something like a hub and spokes, with the Sentencing Project in the key center position.

7. The Sentencing Project website (www.sentencingproject.org/) and the national Right to Vote website (www.righttovote.org/) provide further details and information.

8. For discussion of the role of partisan politics in legislative debates over felon disenfranchisement, see Jason Belmont Conn, "The Partisan Politics of Ex-felon Disenfranchisement Laws" (undergraduate honors thesis, Department of Government, Cornell University, 2003).

9. For a survey of some campaigns, see Steven Kalogeras, *Jail-Based Voter Registration Campaigns* (Washington, D.C.: Sentencing Project, 2003).

10. See, e.g., Sherri Williams, "Many Felons Surprised to Learn They Can Vote," *Columbus Dispatch*, October 3, 2004.

11. These states are Alabama, California, Florida, Georgia, Illinois, Mississippi, Montana, New Hampshire, New Jersey, New York, North Carolina, Pennsylvania, Tennessee, Texas, Virginia, Washington, and Wyoming. See Angela Behrens, "Voting—Not Quite a Fundamental Right? A Look at Legal and Legislative Challenges to Felon Disenfranchisement Laws," *Minnesota Law Review* 89 (November 2004): 231–75, 250.

12. Among the successful challenges to felon disenfranchisement laws have been *Hunter v. Underwood*, 471 U.S. 222, 233 (1985) (which ruled disenfranchisement unconstitutional if based on an intent to discriminate racially); *Farrakhan v. Washington*, 338 F.3d 1009 (9th Cir. 2003); *McLaughlin*, 947 F. Supp. at 973 (which held that disenfranchisement for a misdemeanor violates equal protection); *Stephens v. Yeomans*, 327 F. Supp. 1182, 1188 (D.N.J. 1970) (holding

New Jersey's law violated equal protection); and *Mixon v. Commonwealth*, 759 A.2d 442, 451–52 (Pa. Commw. Ct. 2000) (precluding Pennsylvania from disenfranchising beyond sentence only those who were not registered to vote prior to incarceration), *aff'd mem.* 783 A.2d 763 (Pa. 2001). For further discussion, see Behrens, "Voting—Not Quite a Fundamental Right?"

13. The VRA is codified at 42 U.S.C. § 1973. As amended, it reads:

> (a) No voting qualification or prerequisite to voting or standard, practice, or procedure shall be imposed or applied . . . in a manner which results in a denial or abridgement of the right of any citizen of the United States to vote on account of race or color. . . . (b) A violation of subsection (a) of this section is established if, based on the totality of circumstances, it is shown that the political processes leading to nomination or election in the State or political subdivision are not equally open to participation by members of a class of citizens protected by subsection (a) of this section in that its members have less opportunity than other members of the electorate to participate in the political process and to elect representatives of their choice.

42 U.S.C. § 1973 (2000) (emphasis added). Prior to the 1982 amendments, the VRA required proof of a discriminatory intent, rather than effect, to show a violation of the Act. See, e.g., *City of Mobile v. Bolden*, 446 U.S. 55 (1980).

14. *Wesley v. Collins*, 605 F. Supp. 802 (1985), at 1261–62. For a useful discussion of *Wesley*, see Alice Harvey, "Ex-felon Disenfranchisement and Its Influence on the Black Vote: The Need for a Second Look," *University of Pennsylvania Law Review* 142 (1994): 1145–89.

15. *Farrakhan*, at 1011. The court concluded that "Plaintiffs presented statistical evidence of the [racial] disparities in arrest, bail and pre-trial release rates, charging decisions, and sentencing outcomes in certain aspects of Washington's criminal justice system."

16. *Farrakhan*, 2000 U.S. Dist. LEXIS 22212, at 9–10, 14. The court noted that "at most, [evidence of discrimination in the criminal justice system] establishes a flaw with the criminal justice system, not with the disenfranchisement provision."

17. *Farrakhan*, 338 F.3d at 1011–12 (citing *Thornburg v. Gingles*, 478 U.S. 30, 47 [1986]). The Ninth Circuit's standard holds promise, and a panel of the Eleventh Circuit recently agreed, but that decision was reversed by the entire court. See *Johnson v. Governor of Florida*, 353 F.3d 1287 (11th Cir. 2003), *vacated en banc* by 377 F.3d 1163 (11th Cir. 2004). In applying the Act, the district court

had looked to *Wesley* and agreed that "there must be a nexus between the discriminatory exclusion of blacks . . . and the disenfranchisement of felons." *Johnson v. Bush*, 214 F. Supp. 2d 1331, 1341 (S.D. Fla. 2002) *aff'd in part, rev'd in part sub nom. Johnson v. Governor of Florida*, 353 F.3d 1287, 1308 (11th Cir. 2003), *vacated en banc* by 377 F.3d 1163 (11th Cir. 2004). The Eleventh Circuit panel held that the court erred by failing to consider how felon disenfranchisement laws interacted with social and historical circumstances. *Johnson*, 353 F.3d at 1305. The full court reversed. *Johnson v. Bush*, no. 02–14469, 2005 U.S. App. LEXIS 5945 (11th Cir. Apr. 12, 2005). The *Johnson* case is examined in a documentary film by Laurel Greenberg, *Trouble in Paradise* (Magic Couch Pictures, 2003).

18. See Florida Rules of Executive Clemency, as revised December 9, 2004. For a critical dissection of a similar practice in the state of Washington, see Jill Simmons, "Beggars Can't Be Voters: Why Washington's Felon Disenfranchisement Law Violates the Equal Protection Clause," *Washington Law Review* 78 (2003): 297–333.

19. The Help America Vote Act requires that the states "coordinate the computerized list with State agency records on felony status," for purposes of determining who to remove. 42 U.S.C. 15483 (a)(2)(a).

20. *Cutter v. Wilkinson*, 544 U.S. 00 (2005).

21. *Hudson v. Palmer*, 468 U.S. 517, 547 (1984).

22. See Pam Belluck, "When the Voting Bloc Lives inside a Cellblock," *New York Times,* November 1, 2004.

23. See Debra Parkes, "Ballot Boxes behind Bars: Toward the Repeal of Prisoner Disenfranchisement Laws," *Temple Political and Civil Rights Law Review* 13 (2003): 71–110.

24. Our discussion of these cases in this paragraph is indebted to Alec Ewald. See his "An 'Agenda for Demolition': The Fallacy and the Danger of the 'Subversive Voting' Argument for Felony Disenfranchisement," *Columbia Human Rights Law Review* 36 (2004): 109–43, at 134–39.

25. Quoted in Ewald, "An 'Agenda for Demolition,' " 134.

26. *Suave v. Canada* 3 S.C.R. 519 [2002], cited in Ewald, "An 'Agenda for Demolition,' " 137.

27. *August v. Electoral Commission,* 1999 (8) SA at 23. This is quoted in Ewald, "An 'Agenda for Demolition,' " 135.

28. *Minister of Home Affairs v. Nicro* CCt 03/04 (2004), available at: http://sentencingproject.org/pdfs/southafrica-decision.pdf.

*Appendix*

1. Our description of the Youth Development Study is adapted from Jeylan T. Mortimer, *Working and Growing Up in America* (Cambridge: Harvard University Press, 2003).

2. For the general statistical issues, see especially Paul W. Holland, "Statistics and Causal Inference," *Journal of the American Statistical Association* 81 (December 1986): 945–70. For applications to research in sociology, see Michael Sobel, "Causal Inference in the Social and Behavioral Sciences," in *Handbook of Statistical Modeling for the Social and Behavioral Sciences*, ed. Gerhard Arminger, Clifford C. Clogg, and Michael E. Sobel (New York: Plenum Press, 1995), 1–38; Christopher Winship and Michael Sobel, "Causal Inference in Sociological Studies," unpublished manuscript, Department of Sociology, Harvard University, 2001.

3. See e.g. Western and Beckett, "How Unregulated Is the U.S. Labor Market"; Richard B. Freeman, "Crime and the Labor Market," in *Crime*, ed. James Q. Wilson and Joan Petersilia (San Francisco: ICS Press, 1996), chap. 8.

4. The argument that the incarceration boom has had beneficial economic effects on certain industries and regions is developed in various accounts; see e.g. Joseph T. Hallinan, *Going up the River: Travels in a Prison Nation* (New York: Random House, 2001); Sasha Abramsky, *Hard Time Blues: How Politics Built a Prison Nation* (New York: Thomas Dunn Books, 2002); and Christian Parenti, *Lockdown America* (New York: Verso, 1999).

5. This is not to say that the campaign strategies the major parties have employed since the mid-1970s have been optimal vote-getting strategies; only that having adopted those strategies for what appeared to be sound reasons, there would have been little reason to think that a fundamentally different strategy would have been adopted for an enlarged electorate.

6. Our approach is distinct from the use of matching techniques used in some biomedical research, in which matching pairs of individuals based on some underlying attribute and assigning them to test or control groups provides the basis for examining a treatment effect. For an overview of matching with sociological examples, see Herbert L. Smith, "Matching with Multiple Controls to Estimate Treatment Effects in Observational Research," *Sociological Methodology* 27 (1997): 325–53.

7. The use of proxy respondents to report on the voting behavior of others in the household is a potentially greater threat to validity. However, Census Bureau verification tests show that proxy and self-reports were in agreement about 99 percent of the time in 1984 and 98 percent of the time in 1992. U.S.

Bureau of the Census, *Voting and Registration in the Election of 1992* (Washington, D.C.: U.S. Government Printing Office, 1996).

8. Brian D. Silver, Barbara A. Anderson, and Paul Abramson, "Who Overreports Voting?" *American Political Science Review* 80 (1986): 612–34; Bernstein, Chadha, and Montjoy, "Overreporting Voting."

9. Logistic regression models are employed when the dependent variable, as here, is dichotomous (voted/did not vote). In this case, the logistic transformation is the natural logarithm of the odds of voting. Unlike linear probability models, logistic regression models do not assume linearity, and the expected probabilities of the logistic transformation are constrained to fall within the appropriate range between 0 and 1. The resulting estimates thus overcome problems associated with conventional linear probability regression models for dichotomous dependent variables.

10. See chapter 5 for a description of our data and information about the characteristics of the disenfranchised felon population.

11. The other major, repeated cross-sectional survey, the General Social Survey (GSS), also contains items measuring social group memberships and vote choice in presidential elections. The GSS, however, also has significant limitations for our research. First, the GSS surveys respondents months or years after the election; second, the GSS lacks the economic items we use to measure aspects of class-related interests; third, the GSS has employed a split-ballot design that sharply restricts the sample size in multivariate analysis; and most important, the GSS does not cover the critical period of time prior to 1968. Private polling organizations such as Gallup, Harris Interactive, CBS/New York Times, and others have conducted ongoing surveys of voters and exit polls that could also be drawn upon in this study. The Gallup poll in particular goes back to the 1930s. These surveys, however, do not include the entire battery of sociodemographic items required to measure social group memberships.

12. For an overview of the history of the NES in the institutional context of Michigan survey research, see Jean M. Converse, *Survey Research in the United States: Roots and Emergence 1890–1960* (Berkeley: University of California Press, 1987), 340–78.

13. On this issue, see e.g. Warren E. Miller and J. Merrill Shanks, *The New American Voter* (Cambridge: Harvard University Press, 1996); and Clem Brooks, Jeff Manza, and Catherine Bolzendahl, "Voting Behavior and Political Sociology: Theories, Debates, and Future Directions," *Research in Political Sociology* 12 (2003): 137–73.

14. The larger theoretical issues raised by these restrictions get to the question of what a purely "sociological" model of political behavior can tell us about how

individuals vote. We believe that such a model is useful, but not without limits. See Jeff Manza and Clem Brooks, *Social Cleavages and Political Change: Voter Alignments and U.S. Party Coalitions, 1950s–1990s* (New York: Oxford University Press, 1999); and Brooks et al., "Voting Behavior and Political Sociology."

15. To estimate the hypothetical felon vote in the 1992 and 1996 presidential elections, in which H. Ross Perot received a significant share of the total votes cast, the dependent variable was coded as a contrast between Democratic (Bill Clinton) voters versus Republican (George Bush or Bob Dole) or Perot voters.

16. See Christopher Uggen and Jeff Manza, "Democratic Contraction? The Political Consequences of Felon Disenfranchisement in the United States," *American Sociological Review* 67 (2002): 777–803.

17. S.B. 204, 2001 45th Leg., 1st Sess. (N.M. 2001).

18. Timothy Canova, personal communication to authors, May 11, 2001. We thank Professor Canova for supplying us with these details.

19. Donovan Kabalka, "Felons Might Be Able to Vote Again," *Albuquerque Tribune,* June 29, 2001, A2 (quoting John Dendahl).

20. Conn. Stat. § 9–46 (2005). People still serving their sentences in prison and on parole remain disenfranchised. The Connecticut campaign is described by one of its leaders, former secretary of state and current president of Demos Miles Rappoport, in "Restoring the Vote," *American Prospect,* August 13, 2001, available at: www.demos-usa.org/pubs/Restoring.pdf; see also Darrell McMiller, *The Right to Vote: The Campaign to Restore Voting Rights of Persons Convicted to Felony and Sentenced to Probation in Connecticut* (Hartford, Conn.: DemocracyWorks, 2004), available at: www.sentencingproject.org/pdfs/dw-rtv-ct.pdf.

21. Md. Code Election Law § 3–102 (2005).

22. Nev. Rev. Stat. § 213.155 (2005); Nev. Rev. Stat. § 213.157 (2005).

23. Wy. Stat. § 7–13–105 (2005); Wy. stat. § 7–13–804 (2005).

24. Ala. Code § 15–22–36 (2005); Ala. Code § 17–3–10 (2005).

25. See, e.g., Marc Mauer and Tushar Kansal, *Barred for Life: Voting Rights Restoration in Permanent Disenfranchisement States* (Washington, D.C.: Sentencing Project, 2005).

26. See Unicameral Update Online, March 8–11, 2005, available at: www.unicam.state.ne.us/update/stories/2005/government/lb53v.htm.

# Index

misdemeanor, disenfranchisement of
misdemeanants, 9
Mississippi, 42
Mondale, Walter, 182
Montesquieu, Baron de, 25
Morman disenfranchisement cases, 28–9

NAACP, 224
National Election Study (NES), 118, 190,
273–4
National Opinion Research Center
(NORC), 110
National Right to Vote, 224
Netherlands, 103–5
New Deal, 45–6
New Mexico 286–7
New York City, 54
*New York Post*, 14
*New York Times*, 11
New Zealand, 38, 108
Nineteenth Amendment, 21
Nixon, Richard, 5, 105, 193, 207

Open Society Institute, 223

Page, Benjamin, 212
Pager, Devah, 61
parole, 9
Pateman, Carol, 129
penological theory
classical, 26, 47
deterrence, 35–6
incapacitation, 36
modern theories of, 35–7, 105–8
rehabilitation, 36–7
retribution, 35
Pettit, Becky, 71
Pettus, Catherine, 21
Philadelphia, 54
Piven, Frances Fox, 291n.4
Plymouth, 24
political participation, 83–4, 117–8, 165–80,
269–72
state variation in turnout rates, 168
theories of turnout, 167–8
trends in turnout, 176–8

politics of criminal justice, 105–12
Popkin, Samuel, 177
Populism, 45
prisons
inmates released from, 9
Norfolk Prison Colony, 117
San Quentin, 117
public opinion, 7, 46–8, 108–10, 205–19
civil rights liberalism, 209–11
elite framing of, 105–8, 207–8
fear of crime, 7
non-attitudes regarding felon
disenfranchisement, 211–3
support for felon disenfranchisement,
211–9
support of punitive policies, 206–8
survey experiments, 213–9

Quillian, Lincoln, 61

Rabin, Yitzhak, 232
race
American political institutions, 44–6
attitudes, racial, 46–8
Jim Crow system, 48
politics of, 9–10
racial threat, theories of, 60–2, 64–5
Radical Republicans, 45
Reagan, Ronald, 5, 107, 182
Reconstruction, 43, 45, 55
growth of felon disenfranchisement
following, 55–8
(second) Reconstruction (1960s), 222–5
reenfranchisement of felons and ex-felons,
221–33
changes in state laws, 222–5
contemporary legal challenges, 225–7
ex-felons, 229–30
informational campaigns, 225
inmates, 231–2
national campaign, 223–5
non-incarcerated felons, 230–1
proposed policy changes, 227–33
rehabilitation, 36–7
Rehnquist, William, 30, 115, 299n.73
Reid, Harry, 181